AQUINAS *the* AUGUSTINIAN

AQUINAS
the
AUGUSTINIAN

EDITED BY

Michael Dauphinais, Barry David,
& Matthew Levering

The Catholic University of America Press
Washington, D.C.

LIBRARY OF CONGRESS CATALOGING-IN-PUBLICATION DATA

Aquinas the Augustinian / edited by Michael Dauphinais, Barry David,
and Matthew Levering.
p. cm.
Proceedings of a conference held in Feb. 2005 at Ave Maria University.
Includes bibliographical references and index.
ISBN-13: 978-0-8132-1492-4 (pbk. : alk. paper)
ISBN-10: 0-8132-1492-0 (pbk. : alk. paper)
1. Thomas, Aquinas, Saint, 1225?-1274—Congresses.   2. Augustine,
Saint, Bishop of Hippo—Congresses.   I. Dauphinais, Michael,
1973– . II. David, Barry, 1961– . II. Levering, Matthew Webb,
1971– .
B765.T54A687 2007
230´.2092—DC22
2006026346

TO MATTHEW L. LAMB,

distinguished colleague, mentor, friend,

on the occasion of his seventieth birthday

Contents

Acknowledgments

This book had its origins in a conference sponsored by the Aquinas Center for Theological Renewal at Ave Maria University in February 2005. We wish to thank first all those people who were involved with the conference, especially Mercedes Cox, who so superbly assisted us in organizing it. The first class of graduate students in theology at Ave Maria University provided the backbone of labor during the conference, and we are particularly appreciative of their help. Louise Mitchell, currently completing her doctoral studies in moral theology, deserves special thanks for her editorial labors over the manuscript. The provost of Ave Maria University, Joseph Fessio, S.J., has given enthusiastic support to our efforts, and his presence has proven a great source of encouragement. Our colleagues at Ave Maria University also deserve thanks, in particular those in the theology, philosophy, and classics departments. For their encouragement of our work, we owe deepest gratitude to our families, above all our wonderful wives, Nancy Dauphinais, Christiane David, and Joy Levering.

Our debt to the book's contributors is an enormous one, since their labors have made the book what it is. It is fitting to observe that one of those contributors played a unique role. Fr. Matthew Lamb not only founded the graduate program in theology at Ave Maria University in fall 2004, but also suggested the original idea for the conference and made it possible through his seemingly limitless generosity. His friendship and wisdom have sustained and enriched our lives in exceptional ways. We are thus privileged to dedicate this book, which testifies to his sapiential theological vision, to Matthew L. Lamb in celebration of his seventieth birthday. It represents our admiration and love for him as a magnificent theologian, teacher, counselor, and friend.

Introduction

Partly in response to neo-Thomistic criticisms of Augustine, the relationship between Augustine's thought and Thomas Aquinas's received a central place in the French Dominican Marie-Dominique Chenu's research on Aquinas. Thomas Aquinas inherits from Augustine a theological and philosophical patrimony, says Chenu, "outside of which it is impossible to conceive a Saint Thomas."[1] During the thirteenth century, he notes, "the works of Augustine were being more assiduously read in the original form," and Augustine's major writings formed the basis of the new university libraries.[2] He recognizes that Augustine's influence on Aquinas is deeper for some theological topics than for others,[3] and also that the framework of scholastic logic shapes the Augustine who appears in Aquinas's works.[4] In particular, as we would expect, Aquinas's Augustinianism is informed by Aristotle's and Dionysius's thought: as Chenu observes, "In just the first twelve questions of the *Summa Theologi-*

1. M.-D. Chenu, O.P., *Toward Understanding Saint Thomas,* trans. A.-M. Landry, O.P., and D. Hughes, O.P. (Chicago: Henry Regnery, 1963 [1950]), 54.

2. Ibid., 54–55. See A. Wilmart, "La tradition des grands ouvrages de S. Augustin," *Studi Agostiniani* 2 (1931): 267–315. Chenu (134, n. 10) also cites G. von Hertling's survey of 250 quotations from Augustine (200 from the *Summa theologiae*) in von Hertling, "Augustinuszitate bei Thomas von Aquin," *Sitzungberichte der Bayerischen Akademie der Wissenschaften* (1914): 535–602. See more recently the study by Leo Elders, S.V.D., "Les citations de saint Augustin dans la *Somme Théologique* de saint Thomas d'Aquin," *Doctor communis* 40 (1987): 115–67.

3. Chenu speaks of Aquinas's "Dionysian sense of God's transcendency, his Augustinian outlook on the primacy of beatitude, his Cyrillian theandricism, the realism of grace he took from the Greeks, his well-balanced Christology inspired by Damascene" (*Understanding Saint Thomas,* 151).

4. As Chenu says, "Thought is decanted and a scientific quality is achieved, but to the detriment of the spiritual and even literary *aura* that expanded their immediate signification. It is with this in mind and putting all of one's acumen, and respect as well, to the task that one should read anew those *Disputed Questions* that are so Augustinian in their substance: the *De mente (De ver.,* q. 10), the *De magistro* (q. 11), the *De superiori et inferiori ratione* (q. 15). It is not just a question of precise but inadequate formulations given to a thought still remaining primitive in its very richness—as some scholastics, not without disdain for Augustine, sometimes appear to assert. It is, without doubt, a question of a mental attitude that has built up its own methods of analyzing reality" (Ibid., 173–74).

ae, Saint Thomas refers to other authors 160 times: Aristotle 55 times, Augustine 44, Dionysius 25, the Latin Fathers 23, the Greek Fathers 4, and secular authors 9."[5] This diversity of sources does not take away, however, from the fact that Aquinas is "genuinely reared in Augustine" and remains Augustine's "faithful disciple, both in theological doctrine and in the quality of his spirituality."[6]

More recent scholars have similarly remarked upon the importance of Augustine for Aquinas. Jean-Pierre Torrell's volumes on questions 1–59 of the *tertia pars* of the *Summa theologiae* consistently contain more references to Augustine than to any other thinker, ancient, patristic, or medieval.[7] Torrell shows that Aquinas's "'theology of the mysteries' of the life of Jesus" in *Summa theologiae* III, qq. 27–59 flows preeminently from Ambrose and Augustine, although with roots also in the early Fathers.[8] In his historical study of Aquinas's life and work, Torrell takes issue particularly with the textbook division of thirteenth-century scholasticism into Augustinians and Aristotelians, with Aquinas belonging strictly to the latter. As Torrell points out at the outset of his study,

This view is so well anchored in many minds that it has become a veritable historical commonplace. Meanwhile, over the last fifty years the work of several intellectual historians for this period shows without a shadow of a doubt that Augustinianism quietly made use of Arab and Jewish sources, and its own practitioners studied Aristotle. By contrast, their adversaries, Thomas Aquinas at their head, considered themselves legitimate heirs of Saint Augustine as well. To render justice to these actors—and we will have many occasions to repeat this point—the history requires a much more nuanced approach than the summary schemes allow us to suppose.[9]

Even with regard to such representative debates as substantial form, Torrell argues, the issue cannot be properly grasped by rigidly separating medieval Au-

---

5. Ibid., 127. After Augustine, the most frequently cited theological "authority" in Aquinas's works is Dionysius at 1,702 times.

6. Ibid. With regard to Aquinas's careful attention to the meaning intended by his sources, Chenu comments later in the volume, "Aristotle and Augustine really live anew in Thomas Aquinas, but it is Thomas Aquinas who, via Aristotle and Augustine, adheres to timeless truth" (155).

7. See Jean-Pierre Torrell, O.P., *Le Christ en ses mystères: La vie et l'oeuvre de Jésus selon saint Thomas d'Aquin,* 2 vols. (Paris: Desclée, 1999), as well as the text and appendices to *Summa theologiae* III, qq. 1–26 found in Torrell, ed., *Saint Thomas d'Aquin: Le Verbe incarné,* 3 vols. (Paris: Cerf, 2002).

8. Jean-Pierre Torrell, O.P., *Saint Thomas Aquinas,* vol. 1: *The Person and His Work,* trans. Robert Royal (Washington, DC: The Catholic University of America Press, 1996), 264.

9. Ibid., 39. Torrell refers the reader to earlier studies, most importantly F. Van Steenberghen's *Aristotle in the West: The Origins of Latin Aristotelianism,* trans. Leonard Johnston (Louvain, 1955).

gustinianism and Aristotelianism. As he states, "Today it is widely recognized that the partisans of the plurality of forms claimed themselves to be in the school of Aristotle; as to Thomas, he could have placed himself in an authentic line of descent from Augustine."[10] On other important theological topics, too, Torrell depicts Aquinas as an Augustinian. For instance, on Trinitarian indwelling and the *imago Dei,* Torrell holds—following the work of D. Juvenal Merriell—that Aquinas's thought developed over the course of his career due to his deeper reading of Augustine.[11] Similarly, regarding the Paschal mystery, Torrell names Augustine and Anselm as Aquinas's two key sources.[12] Recounting Aquinas's theological exegesis of John 10, with its Christological and ecclesiological themes, Torrell observes that "[t]here are thus several memories of Augustine that come spontaneously to Friar Thomas's mind, but he is so imbued with Augustine that these traces transform his own usual style," elevating his rhetoric.[13] Certainly Augustine's influence upon Aquinas's theology has always been evident. Yet in Torrell's considered view, due to the later conflicts between Augustinians and Aristotelians, "only in our time have the riches of the scriptural commentaries been rediscovered, along with Thomas's great debt to Saint Augustine."[14]

---

10. Torrell, *Saint Thomas Aquinas,* vol. 1, 187. As is well known, some "Augustinian" theologians fought the introduction into theology of Aristotelian ideas. For how this played out between Franciscans and Dominicans in Aquinas's canonization process, see ibid., 308.

11. Jean-Pierre Torrell, O.P., *Saint Thomas Aquinas,* vol. 2: *Spiritual Master,* trans. Robert Royal (Washington, DC: The Catholic University of America Press, 2003), 85; cf. 90–91, 95. See D. Juvenal Merriell, *To the Image of the Trinity: A Study in the Development of Aquinas' Teaching* (Toronto: Pontifical Institute of Mediaeval Studies, 1990).

12. Torrell, *Saint Thomas Aquinas,* vol. 2, 106; cf. 120.

13. Ibid., 124. See also Matthew Levering's essay in this volume.

14. Ibid., 3. Torrell describes "the Thomistic school" as continuing "a tradition begun by Saint Augustine and Saint Anselm" (4). He remarks, "In the same vein as Saint Augustine and Saint Anselm, Saint Thomas's thought maintains that theology's origin is its relationship to faith, and that it would not even exist without constant dependence on faith" (5). He is well aware, of course, that Aquinas's speculative organization of theological teaching differs from Augustine's. On *sacra doctrina,* says Torrell, "Thomas takes a stance unique among his contemporaries. Peter Lombard, following Saint Augustine, saw the material of theology in the opposition between the letter of Scripture and the reality it signified *(res* and *signa);* Hugh of Saint Victor situated the material of theology in the work of the redemption; and the Franciscans, among them Saint Bonaventure, saw it as rather in Christ and the Church. Thomas concedes that theology speaks about all these things, but he refuses to see in them the subject of theology properly understood. These varied points of view only *describe* reality; he himself wished to *explain* that reality, something far more ambitious. But that is precisely what he proposes in making God himself the subject of this particular science. His disciples were not mistaken about this; since the first generation of Thomas's students, they have made it one of their special themes" (9–10). See also Romanus Cessario, O.P., "Toward Understanding Aquinas' Theological Method: The

Contemporary Thomistic moral theologians and philosophers are not least among those responsible for this "rediscovery," if such it can be called. Alasdair MacIntyre proposes that the key to Aquinas's thought resides in his training under Albert the Great. MacIntyre identifies Aquinas as the student of Albert who, more than any other of Albert's students, managed to hold together what Albert himself sought to integrate:

Himself an Augustinian theologian, he [Albert] took unusual care to separate out this work of commentary and exposition from any declaration of his own views. So that although Albertus rejected a variety of Aristotelian doctrines in his theology and quarreled with Aristotle's observations of rational phenomena on the basis of his own scientific investigations, he did not allow these critical stances to undermine the presentation of Aristotle and of Aristotelianism in his and its own terms. It thus became possible for his pupils to understand the Aristotelian standpoint from within in a thoroughgoing way, in a way and to a degree that no other teacher who was not himself an Averroist made possible. Yet at the same time Albertus as a theologian taught, and indeed reformed and revived, what was distinctively Augustinian, including what was Platonic in Augustine, assimilating to that theology only that in Aristotle which the Augustinian framework permitted. So that his pupils also could come to know Augustinianism from within. Most notable among those pupils in the Dominican *studium generale* at Cologne from 1248 to 1252, was Aquinas. Albertus's other notable pupils, insofar as they became philosophers as well as theologians, developed themes out of his Augustinian theology, often enough Platonic themes. They learned part of what Albertus had to teach, but only part. Only Aquinas seems to have immersed himself in both the Aristotelianism and the Augustinianism so as to make a central problem, not only of his intellectual enquiries, but of his existence, that of how what he took, or at least was to come to take, to be the truth in each could be reconciled with that of the other.[15]

For MacIntyre, Aquinas's lifelong project consisted in integrating, in *sacra doctrina,* the Augustinian and Aristotelian inheritances. In the same vein, Servais Pinckaers has emphasized how Aquinas's ethics, whose Aristotelian elements are evident, flows out of the Augustinian tradition in which beatitude plays the central role. Like Chenu aware of the earlier tendency to downgrade Augustine in favor of Aquinas, Pinckaers affirms the integrity and value of

Early Twelfth-Century Experience," in *Studies in Thomistic Theology,* ed. Paul Lockey (Houston, TX: Center for Thomistic Studies, 1995), 17–89.

15. Alasdair MacIntyre, *Three Rival Versions of Moral Enquiry: Encyclopedia, Genealogy, and Tradition* (Notre Dame, IN: University of Notre Dame Press, 1990), 115. See also Simon Tugwell's splendid introductions to Albert and Aquinas in *Albert & Thomas: Selected Writings,* ed. Simon Tugwell, O.P. (New York: Paulist Press, 1988). The one on Albert is particularly valuable.

Augustine's theology and denies that Augustine's thought can be contained "within Thomistic categories, at least not those of the modern textbooks."[16] But Pinckaers numbers Aquinas among Augustine's disciples and remarks, "We cannot emphasize too strongly the importance of St. Augustine for Latin theology."[17]

Many other contemporary Thomistic scholars have reflected fruitfully upon Aquinas's indebtedness to Augustine's thought. For example, drawing upon the research of Henri Bouillard, Joseph Wawrykow suggests that Aquinas's theology of merit and predestination was enriched during the course of his career by reading Augustine's late works on grace, lost to earlier medieval theologians and which Aquinas appears to have located while at the papal court in the 1260s.[18] Pierre-Yves Maillard interprets Aquinas's account of the saints' vision of God, as presented in Aquinas's *Commentary on the Gospel of John*, in terms of its Augustinian sources.[19] Simon Gaine engages Augustine's view on heavenly impeccability and freedom in setting forth Aquinas's position, which draws heavily from Augustine and contrasts with the views of Scotus, Ockham, and Suárez.[20] Timothy L. Smith compares Augustine and Aquinas's Trinitarian theology, arguing that Aquinas's approach belongs to the Augustinian tradition but is greatly altered by the interposition of Abelardian theological method.[21] Thomas Ryan shows how deeply Augustine's commentary on the Psalms influenced Aquinas's own: as Ryan notes, Augustine "helps make sense of obscure words (RPS 4.3); he elucidates ancient religious practices (49.6); he contributes to discussions of signs and signification (49.7); he provides material for the *sed contra* (cf. 36.18) and responses to scholastic-type questions (cf. 21.9), all this in addition to assistance in negotiating theological concerns such as God (33.10), Christ (21.1), creation (32.8), catechumens

---

16. Servais Pinckaers, O.P., *The Sources of Christian Ethics,* trans. from the 3rd ed. by Mary Thomas Noble, O.P. (Washington, DC: The Catholic University of America Press, 1995), 212.

17. Ibid., 210, 213.

18. See Joseph P. Wawrykow, *God's Grace and Human Action: "Merit" in the Theology of Thomas Aquinas* (Notre Dame, IN: University of Notre Dame Press, 1995), 266–76. Wawrykow holds that Aquinas goes beyond Augustine's teaching in certain significant ways. See also Michal Paluch, O.P., *La profondeur de l'amour divin: Évolution de la doctrine de la prédestination dans l'oeuvre de saint Thomas d'Aquin* (Paris: Vrin, 2004), which engages Augustine's influence throughout.

19. Pierre-Yves Maillard, *La vision de dieu chez Thomas d'Aquin: Une lecture de l'In Ioannem à la lumière de ses sources augustiniennes* (Paris: Vrin, 2001).

20. Simon Francis Gaine, O.P., *Will There Be Free Will in Heaven?: Freedom, Impeccability and Beatitude* (New York: T. & T. Clark, 2003).

21. Timothy L. Smith, *Thomas Aquinas' Trinitarian Theology: A Study in Theological Method* (Washington, DC: The Catholic University of America Press, 2003), 109–37.

(41.1), love and fear (37.10), and the like."[22] Numerous other scholars could be cited, but these will suffice to indicate the general emphasis.

Even if Augustine's influence on Aquinas is profound and undeniable, however, significant historical, philosophical, and theological problems remain when reading together the two theologians' works. First, perhaps, is the problem of assessing what books of Augustine (as opposed to the standard extracts found in the collections of "sentences") were read more fully by Aquinas and when he read them. Second, an emphasis on Augustine's influence risks distorting Aquinas's use of "authorities," as if Augustine's influence were equally great on every topic, or as if Aquinas were not profoundly influenced as well by Scripture, Aristotle, the Greek Fathers, and so forth. Third, it might seem that the present volume will inevitably minimize the differences between Augustine's and Aquinas's thought, even for those who do not agree with the stronger disjunctions proposed by, for instance, Etienne Gilson and Charles Boyer, S.J.[23] Furthermore, in the contemporary academy, historical study of Augustine necessarily takes place separately from historical study of Aquinas; those who study Aquinas may know less about Augustine than Aquinas did, or at least be less influenced by Augustine's thought. In short, there is still some mistrust when the attempt is made, as it is in the present volume, to read Aquinas in light of Augustine, and to read Augustine with later Thomistic approaches in mind.

Perhaps this situation explains the lacuna in Thomistic studies that this volume hopes to assist in rectifying. While, as we have seen, there has been much work over the past century that recognizes Augustine's influence upon Aquinas and Aquinas's role in transmitting Augustinian thought, there have been no book-length studies of this relationship. It hardly needs mentioning that the present volume cannot aim at anything approaching exhaustiveness or comprehensiveness. Even so, it can make a start toward understanding more systematically the relationship of Augustine and Aquinas, and toward understanding what that relationship means for those who today, in a much different context, seek to retrieve their insights. The importance of reading Aquinas with Augustine in mind has been confirmed by the works of the scholars cit-

---

22. Thomas F. Ryan, *Thomas Aquinas as Reader of the Psalms* (Notre Dame, IN: University of Notre Dame Press, 2000), 41.

23. See Etienne Gilson's presentation of Augustine as an "essentialist" in *God and Philosophy* (New Haven, CT: Yale University Press, 1941); Charles Boyer, S.J., *L'idée de verité dans la philosophie de saint Augustin,* 2nd ed. (Paris: Beauchesne, 1940).

ed above, who demonstrate how much richer contemporary appropriation of
Aquinas's thought becomes when its Augustinian roots are identified and exploited. Certainly our understanding of Augustine's thought, too, is enriched
by reflection upon the continuities and discontinuities between his thought
and that of one of his greatest medieval interpreters, Thomas Aquinas.

In order to indicate the variety of perspectives from which the essays in
this volume contribute to our knowledge of the relationship of Augustine and
Aquinas and to future paths for historical and speculative work, it will be useful to offer a brief sketch of each of the eleven essays. The volume opens with
three studies on Trinitarian theology. Gilles Emery's essay raises the question
of the degree to which Aquinas's purposes in his Trinitarian theology accord
with Augustine's. As Emery notes, some scholars argue that Augustine offers
a sapiential spiritual exercise or *exercitatio mentis,* whereas Aquinas appears
simply to offer high-level dialectics or logical clarification. In response, Emery first devotes substantial analysis to Augustine's Trinitarian theology, and in
particular the relationship of faith and reason and the function of the investigation of the *imago Dei.* Emery then turns to Aquinas's Trinitarian theology
and, with equal care, traces its purposes. By rendering more manifest to our
minds the truth of the Catholic doctrine of the Trinity, Aquinas seeks to offer a spiritual exercise and to assist in the "spiritual comfort" of believers. Emery shows that in the movement of Trinitarian theology as envisioned by both
Augustine and Aquinas, readers possessed of faith are prompted to be conformed to spiritual realities; and, by grasping "something of the truth," they
gain insight into the Trinitarian heresies and the more difficult scriptural passages. Such exercise requires not only knowledge of the divine Truth, but love
as well. Thus despite the differences between the two theologians as regards
the *ordo disciplinae* and some specific points of doctrine, both theologians en-
vision Trinitarian theology as a spiritual exercise, a purification of the believing mind.

Bruce D. Marshall probes how Augustine and Aquinas deal with a difficult issue in Trinitarian theology, namely whether the divine essence generates
the essence. As Marshall points out, well before Aquinas wrote, Lateran Council IV definitively answered no. Aquinas, however, is faced with the possibility
that Augustine had treated the same problem and answered yes. At stake is the
theological problem of "essentialism," in which the essence in effect substi-
tutes for the divine Persons. Some recent theologians have accused Augustine
of precisely such essentialism as regards the Trinity. If Aquinas corrects Augus-

tine on whether the divine essence generates, should Aquinas also be counted among those who critique Augustine's Trinitarian theology as essentialist (and thus fundamentally flawed)? As a first step, Marshall turns to Augustine's *De Trinitate* and finds that he does not in fact fall into the apparent confusion, which actually comes from Lombard's *Sentences*. In this regard Marshall raises questions about D. Juvenal Merriell's contention that Aquinas thoroughly read the *De Trinitate* itself. As a second step, Marshall suggests that Aquinas is not so much concerned to get Augustine right, as to make manifest the truth about whether the divine essence generates. Marshall here explores the concept of "relation" as employed in Augustine's and Aquinas's Trinitarian theologies. The key question, he suggests, is whether the divine Person, understood through the concept of "relation," can be said to be identical with the divine essence. Throughout Marshall emphasizes that no account of Aquinas as an "Augustinian" should plaster over their differences.

Harm Goris takes up the theological and philosophical meanings of *"verbum"* (word) in Augustine and Aquinas. He identifies how Aquinas's mature position arises from questions present in Augustine's account of *"verbum"* and answers these questions in a distinctive fashion. Goris argues, not surprisingly, that it is Aquinas's growing familiarity with Aristotle's account of human knowing that distinguishes Aquinas from Augustine. While pushing beyond Augustine by means of categories taken over from Aristotle, however, Aquinas achieves a position that powerfully substantiates Augustine's central claims in his theology of the divine Word. Goris provides a careful reading of Aquinas's cognitive theory, with attention to Aquinas's account of the divine ideas and divine simplicity, as progressively developed in the *Commentary on the Sentences,* the *De veritate,* and the *Summa contra gentiles.* In the process of showing how Aquinas gradually integrates insights from Aristotle and Augustine into a synthesis, Goris also helpfully sets forth evidence against the standard views regarding the dating of Aquinas's *Roman Commentary* (on Book I of the *Sentences*).

John M. Rist turns our attention to Aquinas's metaphysics, and in particular to the way in which Aquinas, in contrast to other commentators (Jewish and Muslim), succeeded in integrating Aristotelian philosophy with a tradition of faith. He treats three metaphysical issues regarding which Aquinas seeks to integrate Augustinian and Aristotelian insights (while differentiating between the historical Aristotle and Aristotle as received through the commentators of late antiquity): the distinction between *esse* and *essentia;* the question of human freedom after the Fall; and the soul-body relationship. On the first issue, Rist's erudition in late Platonism leads him to disagree with Etienne Gilson's positioning of Augustine as an "essentialist." Rist shows that Augustine, under the influence of Victorinus and in accord with other patristic thinkers, analyzes God's power in a way that enables him to attain the insights, in a different language, that Aquinas articulates through his Aristotelian use of act/potency. On the second issue, Rist takes as his starting point Robert Pasnau's much-criticized recent book *Thomas Aquinas on Human Nature* and argues that Aquinas falls into a difficulty as regards human freedom because Aquinas, guided by the need to respond to Aristotle's insights, conceives freedom from a perspective that asks what freedom was prior to the Fall and that addresses freedom's metaphysical as well as moral range. In contrast, Augustine's analysis of human freedom occurs largely within the moral context delimited by the Fall. Rist concludes that Aquinas's attempted integration does not take seriously enough original sin. On the third point, Rist reviews Augustine's account of the soul-body relationship and compares it to Aquinas's Aristotelian hylomorphism. He focuses on how the two thinkers understand male-female sexual difference in light of the doctrine of the *imago Dei*. Aquinas, Rist thinks, follows the wrong parts of Aristotle in agreeing with Augustine. Had Aquinas teased out more fully the implications of hylomorphism, he could have avoided the claim that women are inferior to men. Thus Rist argues that to speak of Aquinas as an "Augustinian" means to recognize that at times Aquinas enriches Augustine's positions, at times neglects them, and at times worsens them.

John P. O'Callaghan probes Aquinas's understanding of the *imago Dei*. While O'Callaghan does not disagree with D. Juvenal Merriell's exposition of the theological development that occurs in Aquinas's position, O'Callaghan suggests that more attention needs to be paid to the impact of Aristotelian philosophical insights upon Aquinas's appropriation of Augustine's *imago Dei*. O'Callaghan first sketches Augustine's position in the *De Trinitate*. Secondly, he compares Aquinas's account of the *imago Dei* in the *De veritate* and the *Summa theologiae*. The treatment in the *De veritate*, O'Callaghan shows, is deeply Augustinian, although he also finds an Aristotelian reliance on the distinction between "powers" and "essence" as well as the Aristotelian distinction between knowing "that something is" and knowing "what it is." In the *De veritate*, Aquinas differentiates "mind" as a "general power" from memory, intellect, and will as "particular powers." In contrast, the treatment in the

Summa theologiae, while remaining significantly in continuity with the Augustinianism of the *De veritate,* turns from "mind" to "soul," and uses "mind" now as a synonym for "intellect," one of the soul's powers (which do not constitute the soul's essence or detract from its unity). As would be expected, this shift changes Aquinas's account of the *imago Dei.* In the first place, Aquinas cannot account for the soul's imaging of the divine unity in terms of the soul's powers, but now does so in terms of genus and specific difference (rationality) understood hylomorphically. Similarly, the soul's imaging of the divine Trinity flows from the Aristotelian use of genus and specific difference, since human animal life is "according to reason": the image of the Trinity belongs to the soul according to its acts. In short, Aquinas's Augustinianism is tempered and altered by his Aristotelianism.

Mark Johnson explores Augustine and Aquinas on original sin. As Johnson points out, Peter Lombard's discussion of the transmission of original sin is filled with texts from Augustine, whereas Aquinas's treatment of this topic in *Summa theologiae* I-II, q. 81, a. 1 hardly employs Augustine at all. Augustine engages original sin in the context of his controversies with the Donatists and Pelagians. Here theological exegesis of Romans 5:12, with its claim that all have sinned in Adam and its corresponding difficulty as regards how this might be so, plays a key role. Whereas Augustine leaves the question of the transmission of original sin somewhat unsettled, Lombard, working both with Augustine's texts and with texts attributed to Augustine, shifts the attention from the soul to the body as the source for the transmission of original sin. Investigating Aquinas's response to the problem posed by Augustine and Lombard, Johnson shows that Aquinas changed his view. The *Commentary on the Sentences* follows Lombard's emphasis on the body as the source; whereas in the *prima secundae* of the *Summa theologiae,* he recognizes more clearly that bodily fault cannot be punishable. In the *Summa* Aquinas therefore seeks to develop a position that goes beyond earlier ones, including Augustine's, by arguing that an individual human being is to the whole "body" of human beings as an individual member (e.g., a hand) of a particular body is to the soul. Adam moves all other human beings by the motion of generation. Given the analogy, all who come from Adam receive the disorder intrinsic to Adam's fallen nature. Here Aquinas is an "Augustinian" insofar as he responds to the dilemma posed by Augustine and mediated by Lombard.

Guy Mansini engages the issue of grace and free will through the lens of John 15:5, "Without me you can do nothing." Mansini first explores Augustine's reading of the passage, which Augustine takes to affirm the necessity of the grace of Christ for good works. Augustine's interpretation of this passage is found not only in his commentary but also, and earlier, throughout his anti-Pelagian works. Having explored these texts and thus the breadth of Augustine's rejection of good works without the grace of Christ, Mansini examines Aquinas's reading. Aquinas's *Catena Aurea* includes a text from Augustine on John 15:5, but Aquinas's commentary on John 15:5 does not directly cite Augustine. Even so, Aquinas follows Augustine in reading John 15:5 against the Pelagians and in many other particulars. Aquinas also reads the passage metaphysically and in an explicitly Trinitarian context, however. Specifically he argues that no human action can occur without God (as the creative source of all created act) acting in us, and that God the Father does nothing without God the Son. Aquinas thereby draws out the order of grace in a way that accords with and deepens Augustine's emphasis on grace in his commentary. Mansini concludes by pointing out that this order of grace and receptivity is further extended by John Paul II and Joseph Ratzinger/Benedict XVI in their remarks on John 15:5, which emphasize that the apostles (and their successors) can do nothing without Christ. In this way Mansini shows how continuity and development mark a tradition of interpretation, in which new thinkers articulate what is indeed present, though not explicit, in their predecessors—in Aquinas, in Augustine, in the evangelist John, in Jesus Christ.

Michael S. Sherwin begins with the twelfth-century theological crisis regarding Augustine's interpretation of charity, a crisis that emerged out of the question of the extent to which charity is connected with desire (and thus with seeking God for oneself as well as for God's own sake). Certainly God does not "desire" his creatures, since he is perfection itself, lacking nothing. If charity were connected to desire, then it would seem that God could not love us from charity. Sherwin examines Augustine's definition of charity in terms of the contrast between *"uti"* and *"frui"* in his *De doctrina christiana,* the work that stirred the medieval controversy. Following Robert Wielockx, he then explores the positions of the major figures in the twelfth-century interpretive debate, and connects this debate with the twentieth-century controversy generated by Anders Nygren's strict separation of *eros* from *agape.* Returning to Augustine's work in the context of Augustine's engagement with and critique of the Neoplatonists, Sherwin sets forth in some detail the central elements of Augustine's approach. He then argues that Aquinas, facing the same question that had plagued the twelfth-century thinkers (although probably without having read their writings), takes up Augustine's insights within an Aristotelian conceptual framework that emphasizes friendship and locates *eros* within the theology of hope. Once again it is Aquinas the Aristotelian who comes to the aid of Aquinas the Augustinian.

Matthew Levering compares Augustine's and Aquinas's theological exegesis of John 10:1–18, Jesus' depiction of himself as the good shepherd of the flock of believers. In order to highlight what is distinctive about Augustine's and Aquinas's readings, he reads them in light of the interpretations of John 10:1–18 offered by the contemporary biblical exegetes Francis J. Moloney and Ben Witherington III (Catholic and evangelical Protestant, respectively). Both Moloney and Witherington use historical-critical insights into the original context of John 10 to speak to contemporary theological, and specifically ecclesiological, concerns—although both authors are careful to avoid asking theological or philosophical questions that do not have clear answers in the text or its historical context. In contrast, Augustine and Aquinas read Christ's discourse as aimed not only at his original audience but also at all who hear in the Church, and thus they do not consider it "anachronistic" to interpret the discourse in terms of the Church's practices and doctrines (as well as with reference to heresies). Similarly, they are willing to adduce parallel passages from throughout Scripture as well as to interject philosophical precisions. Levering argues that this approach, which amplifies the material continuities between Augustine's and Aquinas's exegesis of the passage, reflects a "participatory" theology of history in which the gospels participate in earlier and later temporal realities from within the Mystical Body of Christ, in which time is ordered to eternity. Levering proposes in conclusion that Aquinas's use of Augustine's exegetical insights offers a model for contemporary integration of the patristic-medieval tradition with historical-critical insights, with benefits for our understanding of ecclesial authority.

Wayne J. Hankey explores Aquinas's engagement with Augustine in teaching about the Eucharist. As Hankey skillfully shows, appreciating this engagement requires understanding the complex mediation of sources to the medieval thinkers. First, Aquinas receives from the canonist Gratian, or from Peter Lombard quoting Gratian, the text of Augustine's that Aquinas interprets in his Eucharistic teaching. Second, Gratian received this text not directly from one of Augustine's manuscripts, but from a *florilegium* titled the *Sentences of Prosper*. Third, the text in fact was falsely attributed to Augustine, having been written instead by the eleventh-century theologian Lanfranc of Bec, mentor of Anselm, during Lanfranc's famous debate with Berengar of Tours. Fourth, both Bonaventure and Aquinas took up this text, and while Bonaventure is generally appreciated as the more "Augustinian" of the two, he arrives at a conclusion that opposes the true teaching of Augustine. At issue in the interpretation of the text is the relationship of the sacramental, heavenly, and earthly/historical bodies of Christ. Lanfranc's text, Aquinas (and Bonaventure) recognized, conflicted with "other" texts from Augustine on this point. Investigating Aquinas's solution, Hankey points out that its central insight takes its cue from Dionysius the pseudo-Areopagite. Thus it is by means of an alternative Platonism (Dionysius's Iamblichan strand), as well as by means of Aristotle, that Aquinas is able to move from Lanfranc's misleading text to the position truly held by Augustine.

Matthew L. Lamb explores Augustine's and Aquinas's eschatology. He shows that a key continuity between the two thinkers consists in their sapiential approach, that is to say their interpretation of reality in terms of its *telos* as ordered by God and revealed in Christ, divine wisdom incarnate. Lamb observes this approach first in Augustine's *Confessions,* books 5–7, where Augustine records his conversion, through faith in Christ the Word incarnate, to an awareness of personal identity as a sharing in the infinite presence and truth of the divine Persons. Created realities can be viewed in their proper perspective only when one views them from this revealed divine perspective. Following Pierre Manent, Lamb shows that the opposite approach is adopted by modern thinkers such as Rousseau, who imagine that personal fulfillment comes through narrowing one's perspective to the individual ego and its temporal-spatial manifestations. This narrowed perspective is applied to the Bible's teachings by Spinoza, who limits biblical interpretation to research into the Bible's discrete parts disjoined from any whole and from any appeal to a truth outside direct empirical perception. Having contrasted Augustine's sapiential perspective with the approaches of Rousseau and Spinoza, Lamb explores Aquinas's appropriation and development of Augustine's eschatology. He focuses upon how a sapiential eschatology avoids false dualisms between soul and body, between historical and eschatological fulfillment, and between divine power and divine wisdom. As Lamb shows, the consummation of the whole Body of Christ, which embraces the whole of creation including each and every instance of human suffering, sublimely overcomes any such dualism and manifests the participation of all things in the infinite humility and wisdom of the triune God, a wisdom operative in drawing all things to their fulfillment.

In short, this volume aids in understanding the kinds of debt owed by St. Thomas Aquinas to St. Augustine. Any overly facile application of the term "Augustinian" to a theology whose roots are as philosophically and theologically diverse as Aquinas's must be rejected. We might say rather that Aquinas is an "Augustinian" in the sense that, like all of Augustine's greatest interpreters, he engages with and elaborates upon Augustine's insights in a manner that challenges us to think afresh about the realities known and loved by Augustine.

AQUINAS *the* AUGUSTINIAN

Trinitarian Theology as Spiritual Exercise in Augustine and Aquinas

Gilles Emery, O.P.

(English translation by John Baptist Ku, O.P.)

St. Thomas presents his speculative Trinitarian doctrine as an extension or personal development of the teaching of the Fathers and of St. Augustine in particular. Thus, for example, when he introduces his teaching on Trinitarian relations, St. Thomas explains that he is going to unfold it "by following the statements of the holy [Fathers]";[1] and when he shows the plurality of the persons, he announces that he is going to do it "especially in accordance with the way by which Augustine manifested it,"[2] in other words, by means of the analogy of the word and of love. In Thomas's Trinitarian theology, recourse to "similitudes" drawn from creatures (the use of the notion of substance and relation, the observation of Trinitarian vestiges, the exploitation of anthropological analogies) is presented expressly as a reflection extending the path traced out by Augustine in his *De Trinitate*.[3]

But is St. Thomas faithful to the spirit that motivated the inquiry of the

---

1. *De potentia*, q. 8, a. 1: "Qualiter sit, sequendo sanctorum dicta, investigari oportet." The references on particular points of doctrine are numerous; see for instance ibid., q. 10, a. 2: "doctores nostri."

2. Ibid., q. 9, a. 5: "Ad manifestationem ergo aliqualem huius quaestionis, et praecipue secundum quod Augustinus eam manifestat." Let us recall that in this context, the doctrine of the Word and Love makes it possible to show the unity of persons and their distinction by relations.

3. See, for example, *Super Boetium de Trinitate*, q. 2, a. 3: "Sicut Augustinus in libro *De Trinitate* utitur multis similitudinibus ex doctrinis philosophicis sumptis ad manifestandum Trinitatem."

bishop of Hippo? Does he grasp St. Augustine's objective, and does he respect it? Numerous studies call into question the authenticity of St. Thomas's Augustinian heritage. And it is not rare that the spiritual inquiry of St. Augustine is juxtaposed over against the speculative exposition of the Trinitarian faith of Aquinas. Thus, according to Basil Studer, St. Thomas was trying to explain the mystery of the divine processions by means of analogies drawn from the interior life of man, while St. Augustine was, instead, aiming at a spiritual exercise *(exercitatio mentis)*.[4] While St. Augustine was proposing a sapiential contemplation, St. Thomas "limited himself in his questions on the Trinity (I, qq. 27–32) to a purely intellectual dialectic."[5] Certain authors, juxtaposing the spiritual objective of St. Augustine to the speculative thought of St. Thomas, reproach the latter for having weakened the Augustinian sense of Trinitarian paradox by seeking to represent the mystery with a conceptual objectification.[6] Even the finest experts on St. Thomas sometimes allow themselves to be led to such juxtapositions: "living dialectic of union with God" in St. Augustine, doctrine "more purely intellectual" in St. Thomas.[7] It is certain that writing eight and a half centuries after St. Augustine and in profoundly different circumstances, St. Thomas did not limit himself to repeating his master. But does his objective differ radically from Augustine's? This is the question that I propose to consider here in examining these two authors' explanations of the objective or intention of their Trinitarian theology.

A. St. Augustine: *Exercitatio mentis*

1. Scripture and Reason

The purpose of St. Augustine's *De Trinitate* is "to account for the Trinity being the one and only and true God."[8] St. Augustine seeks in particular to show

---

4. Basil Studer, "La teologia trinitaria in Agostino d'Ippona," in *Mysterium caritatis, Studien zur Exegese und zur Trinitätslehre in der Alten Kirche* (Rome: Pontificio Ateneo S. Anselmo, 1999), 308–9.

5. Fulbert Cayré, "Théologie, sagesse et contemplation dans le *De Trinitate*," in *Œuvres de saint Augustin*, vol. 16, *La Trinité (books viii–xv)*, trans. P. Agaësse and J. Moingt (Paris: Desclée de Brouwer, 1955), 639.

6. See the critique of Michel Corbin, *La Trinité ou l'excès de Dieu* (Paris: Cerf, 1997), 21–86. To the Thomistic objective, which in his opinion seeks the "control" of human understanding over the Trinity, the author juxtaposes a "patristic proposition" which deliberately rejects every reference to the thought of St. Thomas.

7. Hyacinthe Dondaine, in Saint Thomas d'Aquin, *Somme théologique, La Trinité*, vol. 1 (Paris: Cerf, 1997), 7.

8. *De Trinitate*, I, 2, 4: "reddere rationem, quod Trinitas sit unus et solus et verus Deus." Our

the unity, equality, and inseparability of the Father, Son, and Holy Spirit.[9] To give account of this *(reddere rationem),* his inquiry includes two sections: the first part shows the unity of the three persons "by the authority of the Holy Scriptures"; the second proposes to manifest the dogma of the Church (the teaching of Scripture) by speculation.[10] St. Augustine submits his whole reflection to a double criterion: Holy Scripture and, at another level (under the guidance of Scripture), reason.[11] This distinction, which is not a separation, is founded on the very action of God who is the source of Scripture, and who is also the source of the creatures that offer the similitudes from which human understanding can be lifted toward God. Thus, if one searches for the substance of God "either through his Scriptures [*per Scripturam*] or his creatures [*per creaturam*]," it is because "both are offered us for our observation and scrutiny in order that in them, He may be sought, He may be loved, who inspired the one and created the other."[12] The explanations given at the beginning of book XV are very clear: "Whether [the nature of God] is Trinity, we ought to demonstrate, not merely to believers by the authority of divine Scripture but also to the ones who understand, if we can, by some reason."[13] That is why, having spelled out the teaching of Scripture (which suffices for faith), Augustine responds to "those who demand the reason concerning such things," "by making use of the creatures which God has made . . . , especially through

---

translation is taken, with some modifications, from St. Augustine, *The Trinity,* ed. John E. Rotelle, trans. Edmund Hill, O.P. (New York: New City Press, 1996). For the Latin text and its numbering, I have followed the edition of the Bibliothèque Augustinienne (Paris: Desclée de Brouwer, 1955) and the edition by W. J. Mountain: Sancti Aurelii Augustini, *De Trinitate libri XV,* 2 vols. (Turnhout: Brepols, 1968).

9. *De Trinitate,* XV, 3, 5. This does not mean that Augustine starts with unity in order to consider the three Persons subsequently. Unity is rather what St. Augustine seeks to show by considering the teaching of revelation concerning the Father, the Son, and the Spirit (ibid.); see the numerous texts pointed out by Marie-François Berrouard in Saint Augustin, *Homélies sur l'évangile de saint Jean XXXIV–XLIII* (Paris: Institut d'Etudes Augustiniennes, 1988), 278. Cf. Berrouard, "La Trinité est le seul Dieu," in Saint Augustin, *Homélies sur l'évangile de saint Jean CIV–CXXIV* (Paris: Institut d'Etudes Augustiniennes, 2003), 475–78; see also Berrouard, "La Trinité qui est Dieu," in *Augustin, le message de la foi,* ed. Goulven Madec (Paris: Desclée de Brouwer, 1987), 99–117.

10. *De Trinitate,* I, 2, 4; cf. ibid., XV, 3, 5. For the complex structure of the *De Trinitate,* see Edmund Hill, introduction, in Saint Augustine, *The Trinity,* 21–27.

11. *De Trinitate,* III, prooemium, 2. This reference to Scripture and reason is recalled in numerous reprises; see, for example, *De Trinitate,* IV, 6, 10; XV, 20, 39.

12. Ibid., II, prooemium; cf. XV, 20, 39.

13. Ibid., XV, 1, 1: "Quae utrum sit Trinitas, non solum credentibus, divinae Scripturae auctoritate; verum etiam intelligentibus, aliqua, si possumus, ratione jam demonstrare debemus." Cf. ibid., XV, 27, 49: "videatur mente quod tenetur fide."

that rational or intellectual creature which was made to the image of God."[14]

The purpose of reason is formulated thus: to give account of that which one holds by faith, for the sake of understanding. The study of the Trinitarian mystery therefore entails two *modes:* having spelled out the Trinitarian faith according to Scripture and the Tradition of the Church (books I–VII), Augustine treats this *same* Trinitarian faith "in a more inward manner" *(modo interiore)* in order to grasp to some extent, by means of images, what the faith confesses (books VIII–XV).[15] Augustine's main purpose is to show the conformity of Catholic faith with the teaching of Holy Scriptures.

This purpose implies a very clear priority of faith with respect to the inquiry of reason, formulated in numerous reprises: "we must believe before we can understand."[16] The order of inquiry thus consists in a path which takes its direction from biblical faith: "Let us first adhere through faith, that there may be that which may be quickened by understanding."[17] Understanding is the reward of faith.[18] St. Augustine's objective therefore eschews all rationalism. The analysis of the image of God takes place precisely in order to aid the believer in grasping, to some extent, what he holds by faith. The question posed by Augustine in the study of the image of God is not "How are we going to believe?" but "If there is some way in which we can see by our understanding what we believe, what might this way be?"[19] This purpose is strictly that of faith's understanding: "I desired to see with my understanding that which I believed."[20] The inquiry of understanding flows from the act of faith. Faith unleashes intellectual inquiry, judges it, nourishes it, makes it fruitful, and completes it.

---

14. Ibid., XV, 20, 49: "Admonuimus eos qui rationem de rebus talibus poscunt, ut invisibilia ejus per ea quae facta sunt, sicut possent, intellecta conspicerent, et maxime per rationalem vel intellectualem creaturam quae facta est ad imaginem Dei."

15. Ibid., VIII, 1, 1. In the summary given at the beginning of book XV, Augustine states clearly that it was in book VIII that he began "to raise the intention of the mind . . . in order to understand." Ibid., XV, 6, 10. Book VIII can also be considered as a transition between books I–VII and books IX–XV.

16. Ibid., VIII, 5, 8.

17. *Tractatus in Iohannis Evangelium,* XXVII, 7: "Prius haereamus per fidem, ut sit quod vivificetur per intellectum." Ibid., XXIX, 6: "Intellectus enim est merces fidei. Ergo noli quaerere intelligere ut credas, sed crede ut intelligas." Cf. also ibid., XXXIX, 3; *Sermo 122,* 1; etc. The references to the Latin text of St. Augustine's *Homilies on St. John* are taken from Sancti Aurelii Augustini, *In Iohannis Evangelium Tractatus CXXIV,* ed. Radbodus Willems (Turnhout: Brepols, 1954).

18. *Tractatus in Iohannis Evangelium,* XXIX, 6: "Intellectus enim merces est fidei." Cf. ibid., XLVIII, 1.

19. *De Trinitate,* XV, 6, 9: "Sed si aliquo modo per intelligentiam possumus videre quod credimus, quis iste erit modus?"

20. Ibid., XV, 28, 51: "desideravi intellectu videre quod credidi."

2. The Similitude of the Image of God

The Augustinian usage of similitudes in order to manifest the Trinitarian mystery has given rise to an immense philosophical and theological body of literature. I do not intend to take up this vast debate here but only to outline a few hints provided by Augustine himself. One must note first that the study of the image of God does not occupy first place in St. Augustine's thought. First place goes rather to *the unity of action* of the Father, the Son, and the Holy Spirit, that is, to their common operation. Augustine's understanding of the inseparability of Father, Son, and Holy Spirit implies a solid teaching on *God's simplicity* (the Triune God is non-composite), *immutability* (the divine Persons are not submitted to change), and *incomprehensibility* (the Triune God is beyond human understanding). The analysis of the image of God occurs in a second step in order to manifest to our understanding how we can conceive this common action of the three Persons, within the frame of God's simplicity, immutability, and incomprehensibility.

Beginning with book VIII, having shown according to Scripture and the Tradition of the Church that the Trinity is the only one God, Augustine sets out to give a rational account of it (this reflection has already been prepared in the preceding books),[21] in particular "through charity": "Here at last our minds began to perceive in some fashion the Trinity, like lover and what is loved and love."[22] Having reached this point, Augustine pursues his reflection *(disputatio)* in book IX, by turning to the image of God *(ad imaginem Dei quod est homo secundum mentem)* in considering the triad of *mens, notitia* (by which *mens* knows itself), and *amor* (by which it loves itself and its knowledge), in order to manifest their essential unity and equality. Aware of the difficulty of his explanation, Augustine pursues his exposition in book X with the examination of a "clearer" *(evidentius)* trinity of *mens:* memory, understanding, and will *(memoria, intelligentia, voluntas)*. At this point, still aware of the difficulty of his plan, Augustine digresses from his discussion of the mind as an image of the Trinity in order to find a trinity in the perception of corporeal things, in which the distinction will appear more clearly to readers (albeit the expression of unity is weaker here). Thus book XI considers

---

21. See the summary given in ibid., XV, 3, 5: "ratione etiam reddita intelligentibus."

22. Ibid.: "Et per charitatem . . . per quam coepit utcumque etiam Trinitas intelligentibus apparere, sicut sunt amans, et quod amatur, et amor." Cf. ibid., VIII, 8, 12: "Imo vero vides Trinitatem, si charitatem vides."

the "trinity of the exterior man."[23] From there, Augustine takes up again the inquiry into the interior man, in a movement of development that goes from the exterior to the interior *(introrsus tendere)*. Distinguishing "science" (which concerns temporal realities) and wisdom (the contemplation of eternal realities), book XII offers a sort of transition which shows that not every Trinitarian similitude is an "image of God." Following this movement of interior ascension *(introrsum ascendere)*, book XIII presents an exercise of the purification of the heart through faith that leads to wisdom. On this basis, book XIV returns to the image of God in the soul (that of book X), by showing that the image is in the soul when this soul is turned toward God, by virtue of the *reformatio* which procures true wisdom for the soul. Finally, book XV offers a paradoxical crowning of the whole of this inquiry. On one hand, Augustine rises from the trinity of man to that of God, by showing the unity and distinction of the divine Persons (the Son as Word and the Holy Spirit as Charity). On the other hand, he ends his work with a confession of ignorance; it is impossible to grasp the Trinitarian mystery, the Trinity cannot be explained: "We say many things and do not attain (Sir 43:27)."[24] The inquiry of understanding *(disputatio)* therefore gives way to prayer *(precatio)*.[25]

Readers of Augustine will notice without effort that his approach is complex—carried away by detours, repetitions, and digressions. Each solution only seems to make the problem bounce back. It must be added that the analysis of *mens,* in a Trinitarian context, does not constitute an inquiry of a purely philosophical order. It is guided, nourished, and completed by faith. It is in reflecting the light that comes to it from God that the *mens* becomes somehow enlightening, that is, by reflection. Augustine's inquiry shows that the soul discovers its Trinitarian structure by analyzing the conditions of its faith in God (that is the sense of book VIII). If the mystery of God the Trinity can somehow be enlightened by the image of God, it is because it throws its own light upon this image. The mystery of God the Trinity is not enlightened from outside; rather, it is the source of the light.[26] That is why the analysis of the relationship of the soul to itself does not suffice: "The trinity of the mind

---

23. Book XI considers two "trinities" successively: the trinity of perception (the body which is seen, the form which is impressed from it, and the intention of the will which couples the two together) and the trinity of memory (the image of the body which is in the memory, the form derived from it when the thinking attention turns to it, and the intention of the will joining the two together).

24. Ibid., XV, 28, 51.   25. Ibid.

26. Cf. ibid., XV, 23–24, 44.

is not really the image of God because the mind remembers and understands and understands and loves itself, but because it is also able to remember and understand and love Him by whom it was made."[27] The soul is the image of God because it is called to see God.[28] This intellectual inquiry is not separated from an affective approach; rather, it is enlivened by a love which leads the mind toward an effort to understand ("We are carried away by love to track down the truth"),[29] and it is accomplished in love ("Let me love you").[30] Augustine thus requires of his readers or listeners not only attention but also devotion.[31] He recalls constantly that the Trinitarian image must be grasped according to a contemplative wisdom, with love. The more one loves God, the more one sees him.[32] Let us yet add that the analysis of *mens* is not first of all "psychological" in the modern sense of the term but rather ontological: in turning toward God, whose image it is, the soul attains what it is, its proper nature.[33]

3. The Function of the Similitude of Image

The analysis of the image of God in man emerges as the fulfillment of the program that St. Augustine had traced out at Cassiciacum, shortly after his conversion: "God and the soul, that is what I desire to know.—Nothing more?—Nothing whatever."[34] In the *De Trinitate,* an aspect of this vast program that reunites the study of God and the study of man in a continual back-and-forth appears in the foreground. The analysis of this image intends to reveal to the mind "something" of the mystery of God the Trinity. This "something" is, before all else, the substantial unity and equality of the Father, the Son, and the Holy Spirit in their distinction. The similitudes and traditional comparisons borrowed from the material world (the sun, a ray, the root, the branch, the fruit, etc.) that one finds among numerous Fathers before St. Augustine (Hippolytus, Tertullian, etc.) occur infrequently in St. Augustine. Clearly, he wanted better than that! The created similitudes that he retains, in particular that of the image of God, are adduced in order to aid in grasping the *unity of action* of the divine Trinity, the *inseparability*

---

27. Ibid., XIV, 12, 15. Augustine insists often on this aspect which, like many others, will be repeated by St. Thomas: *De veritate,* q. 10, a. 7; *Summa theologiae* (hereafter *ST)* I, q. 93, a. 8.

28. *De Trinitate,* XIV, 8, 11.   29. Ibid., I, 5, 8.

30. Ibid., XV, 28, 51.

31. See, for example, *Sermo,* 52, 15 (*PL* 38, 359).   32. *De Trinitate,* VIII, 8, 12–9, 13.

33. Cf. Etienne Gilson, *Introduction à l'étude de saint Augustin* (Paris: Vrin, 1943), 294.

34. *Soliloquia,* I, 2, 7: "Deum et animam scire cupio.—Nihil de plus?—Nihil omnino." Cf. E. Hendrickx, in Saint Augustin, *La Trinité,* vol. 1 (Paris: Desclée de Brouwer, 1955), 9–10.

of the Three,[35] their *mutual immanence*[36] and *equality,*[37] *their unity of essence or substance,*[38] in a distinction which *excludes confusion.*[39] The similitudes aim in particular at giving some idea of the relations of origin. Through these, St. Augustine wants to manifest to the mind what constitutes the object itself of his treatise: the Trinity is only one God, God is Trinity.

The distinction between the *generation of the Son* and the *procession of the Holy Spirit,* which the image of God (in particular the similitude of the word and charity) attempts to manifest, also occupies a central place in St. Augustine's inquiry. Far from being marginal, this question (the Holy Spirit is not generated) appears from the very beginning of the *De Trinitate.*[40] Augustine judges it to be "extremely difficult" *(difficillimum).*[41] This question is born of the Pneumatomachi controversy and aims to manifest the full divinity of the Holy Spirit by giving account of his distinction with respect to the Son. The similitude of love or the will makes it possible to show, in some way, how we can grasp that the Holy Spirit is not generated (he is not the Son): love is not generated.[42] It is proper to the will not to be produced as an "offspring" *(proles)* from a "parent" *(parens)* but rather to unite *(copulare)* the one generating and the one generated.[43]

Thus the study of this image is designed to suggest the unity and distinction in God the Trinity, to give believers some grasp of understanding, to glimpse by reason what they hold by faith. Such an objective is addressed to believers. However, in one passage of the *De Trinitate,* St. Augustine seems to suggest that he is addressing an audience broader than just believing Catholics. In book XV, when he tries to show that the procession of the Holy Spirit is distinguished from the generation of the Son, having observed that this concerns an extremely difficult question, he writes out an excerpt of a sermon for the benefit of the less sophisticated minds, stating, "I have transcribed these words from that sermon into the present book, but there I was speaking

35. See, for example, *De Trinitate,* IX, 4, 6.

36. See, for example, ibid., IX, 5, 8; 10, 15.

37. See, for example, ibid., IX, 4, 4; 11, 16; X, 11, 18.

38. See, for example, ibid., IX, 4, 4–7; 5, 8; 12, 18; X, 11, 18; XI, 3, 6–7; XV, 3, 5; etc.

39. See, for example, ibid., IX, 4, 7–5, 8; 12, 17; cf. ibid., VIII, 4, 6.

40. Ibid., I, 5, 8; II, 3, 5. The question is taken up again in full measure in book XV (XV, 25, 45; 26, 47; 27, 48; 27, 50).

41. Ibid., XV, 27, 48.

42. Ibid., IX, 12, 17–18.

43. Ibid., XIV, 6, 8; 7, 10; 10, 13; XV, 27, 50. Cf. also ibid., XI, 7, 12; 8, 15–9, 16; 11, 18.

to the faithful, not to unbelievers."[44] This observation seems to indicate that St. Augustine had the ambition of being read by unbelievers or by heretical Christians in order to show that the mystery of the Trinity is not unreasonable since the human mind offers an image of it. One can discern that he has not ruled out leading them to the faith at the same time that he advances the faithful already cultivated in understanding this faith. Besides, this is the way Augustine conceives "knowledge of the faith."[45]

This function of the image is well expressed in the *Contra sermonem Arianorum*. There St. Augustine explains first that the Trinity is not three gods but only one God: the Father acts inseparably with the Son and the Holy Spirit in one single operation. Then he adds that there is in man "something similar" *(simile quiddam),* even though in no way comparable to God the Trinity, something where one can, in a certain way, grasp the *unity of action* that the Catholic faith recognizes in God the Trinity: it is the image of God which consists of memory, understanding, and will. Recalling once more the dissimilarity between the created image and God the Trinity, St. Augustine concludes by explaining that he wanted to employ the image of the creature: "so that they [the Arian heretics], if they can do it, might understand that what we say about the Father, the Son, and the Holy Spirit *is not absurd,* namely that they accomplish their works inseparably."[46]

Recourse to the similitude of this image thus aims at a double end (at least). On one hand, it seeks to nourish the *understanding of the faith* for Christians who can grasp such explanations. On the other hand, it makes it possible to manifest the *plausibility of the faith* to unbelievers: the Trinitarian faith does not appear impossible to reason, it is not absurd. This second point is certainly not central in the *De Trinitate*. Heretical teachings are often mentioned, but St. Augustine wants to lead his inquiry "in the peace of the

---

44. Ibid., XV, 27, 48: "Haec de illo sermone in hunc librum transtuli, sed fidelibus, non infidelibus loquens."

45. Cf. ibid., XIV, 1, 3: "It is one thing merely to know what a man must believe in order to gain the happy life which is nothing if it is not eternal, but another thing to know how this may help the godly and be defended against the godless, which the Apostle seems to call by the proper name of knowledge [*scientia*]."

46. *Contra sermonem Arianorum* 16, 9 (*PL* 42, 695–696): "Sed ideo tantum hoc commemorandum putavi, ut etiam de ipsa creatura aliquid adhiberem; *unde isti, si possunt, intellegant quam non sit absurdum quod de Patre et Filio et Spiritu Sancto dicimus, inseparabilia fieri ab omnibus opera,* non solum ad omnes, verum etiam ad singulos pertinentia." Cf. *Corpus Scriptorum Ecclesiasticorum Latinorum,* vol. 92, ed. Max Josef Suda (Vienna: Verlag der Österreichischen Akademie der Wissenschaften, 2000), 78.

Catholic faith, with peaceful study."[47] This aspect is often developed in other works. He explains, for example, in connection with the heretics, in his *Homilies on St. John:*

For inasmuch as they have not understood how the divinity of Christ is set forth to our acceptance, they have concluded according to their will: and by not discerning aright, they have brought in most troublesome questions [*quaestiones molestissimas*] upon Catholic believers; and the hearts of believers began to be disturbed and to waver [*exagitari et fluctuare*]. Then immediately it became a necessity for spiritual men who had not only read in the Gospel anything respecting the divinity of our Lord Jesus Christ but had also understood it [*etiam intellexerant*], to . . . fight in most open conflict for the divinity of Christ against false and deceitful teachers; lest, while they were silent, others might perish.[48]

The problem posed by the heretics is not only voluntary (refusal of the faith) but also intellectual. In the *De Trinitate,* Augustine explains, for instance, that Eunomius of Cyzicus (radical Arianism) *could not grasp* and *did not want to believe,*[49] since his heresy was tied to a difficulty of an intellectual order. Thus to defend the faith against heresies, one must have an *understanding* of this faith. Such a task is demanded of spiritual men in order to protect the faith of those who are weaker and to show the plausibility of the Catholic faith to those who do not share it.

4. Knowing "a Little Bit"

St. Augustine constantly recalls that the mystery of God is incomprehensible. The famous formulas of his sermons are well known: "If you have grasped, it is not God; if you were able to understand, then you have understood something else in God's place."[50] The *De Trinitate* is no exception. God the Trinity cannot be "understood,"[51] he cannot be spoken (he is ineffable),[52]

---

47. *De Trinitate,* II, 9, 16: "in pace catholica pacifico studio requiramus."

48. *Tractatus in Iohannis Evangelium,* XXXVI, 6. Here it is a matter of the unity of substance of Christ with his Father.

49. *De Trinitate,* XV, 20, 38: "Qui cum non potuisset intelligere, nec credere voluisset."

50. *Sermo,* 52, 6, 16 (*PL* 38, 360): "Si cepisti, non est Deus: si comprehendere potuisti, aliud pro Deo comprehendisti" (here Augustine makes this affirmation before presenting the image of God in man). Cf. *Sermo,* 117, 3, 5 (*PL* 38, 663), in connection with the divine Word: "Et Deus erat Verbum. De Deo loquimur, quid mirum si non comprehendis? Si enim comprehendis, non est Deus. Sit pia confessio ignorantiae magis quam temeraria professio scientiae."

51. See, for example, *De Trinitate,* XV, 7, 13.

52. See, for example, ibid., VII, 4, 7; XV, 23, 43.

he cannot be explained,[53] his mystery is not "grasped,"[54] we do not know him.[55] In this domain more than in any other, one must exclude all presumption *(praesumptio).*[56]

When St. Augustine evokes the light that the study of the image of God can offer and when he treats of our human knowledge of the mystery, he speaks of a very limited knowledge: knowing "inasmuch as we can" *(quantum possumus),*[57] "as far as human weakness is able,"[58] "after our limited manner,"[59] "as much as God the Trinity allows,"[60] "in some way."[61] Among the words which Augustine uses to qualify the knowledge that we can have of the Trinitarian mystery, in particular, to signify the imperfection of the knowledge offered by an image, one of the most characteristic is the adverb *"utcumque"* (in whatever manner, in some fashion, to some extent).[62] This vocabulary will be abundantly repeated by St. Thomas. Speculative reflection does not give comprehension of God the Trinity, but it makes it possible to *insinuate* his mystery *(insinuare:* to make manifest, often with the meaning of inserting by indirect or subtle means, teaching in a skillful way, giving an idea of something).[63] This indirect knowledge of the Trinity through similitudes and this image, which insinuates in some way the mystery of God the Trinity for our understanding, constitutes a knowledge "through a mirror in an enigma" *(per*

---

53. See, for example, ibid., XV, 27, 50. Cf. *Sermo,* 52, 9, 21 (*PL* 38, 363–364): "Non possum dicere, non possum explicare."

54. *De Trinitate,* XV, 27, 49: "non capitur"; cf. ibid., VIII, 1, 2: "non potest intueri."

55. See, for example, ibid., VIII, 5, 8.

56. See, for example, ibid., II, 1, prooemium; X, 1, 1.

57. See, for example, ibid., I, 2, 4; cf. ibid., VIII, 5, 8: "quantum datur."

58. See, for example, ibid., II, 1, prooemium: "pro captu infirmitatis humanae"; ibid., VII, 4, 9; IX, 1, 1; 2, 2; XIII, 20, 26; XV, 1, 1; 20, 39.

59. See, for example, ibid., III, 11, 21: "pro modulo nostro"; ibid., XIII, 20, 26: "pro nostro modulo"; etc.

60. See, for example, ibid., VIII, 2, 3.

61. See, for example, ibid., XV, 6, 9: "aliquo modo"; XV, 9, 16: "quomodocumque"; XV, 21, 40: "quantulumcumque." Cf. ibid., XV, 21, 40; 22, 44; etc.

62. See, for example, ibid., IX, 1, 1; 12, 17 ("in mente humana utcumque investigare conamur"); 7, 11; XV, 3, 5 ("cernebamus utcumque"); 11, 20 ("hominis verbum, per cujus similitudinem sicut in aenigmate videatur utcumque Dei Verbum"); 14, 24 ("verbum nostrum . . . utcumque simile est . . . , utcumque illi simile"); 24, 44; 27, 49 ("per intelligentiam utcumque cernandam"); etc. This vocabulary occurs as well in other works of St. Augustine. See, for example, *Contra Faustum,* 22, 14: "Eligit doctrina sapientiae per quaslibet corporeas imagines et similitudines utcumque cogitanda insinuare divina."

63. See, for example, *De Trinitate,* XI, 5, 9 ("personam Spiritus insinuare"); 7, 11; XIV, 6, 8; XV, 17, 27; 27, 50 ("nativitatis et processionis insinuari distantiam"). Cf. ibid., VI, 10, 11 ("insinuare propria"); cf. ibid., II, 11, 20; VII, 3, 5; VIII, 4, 7; XI, 1, 1.

speculum in aenigmate), according to the words of St. Paul (1 Cor 13:12 Vulgate).[64]

In every case (and not only at the end of book XV of the *De Trinitate*), Augustine emphasizes the radical *dissimilitude* of this created image with respect to the uncreated Trinity. In the resemblance, one must also see the great dissimilarity.[65] Therefore it is never a matter of "comparing" the creature with God.[66] Augustine takes care to note in detail the dissimilarities of the image with respect to God the Trinity.[67] He rules out the possibility of identifying the Father with one's memory, the Son with one's understanding, and the Spirit with one's love.[68] The image allows a glimpse of the relations and the unity of the Trinity by analogy but without identification of one element of this image with a certain divine Person (the same goes for St. Thomas). These elements of criticism are integrated into the knowledge that we can have of God: "For it is not a small part of knowledge . . . to able to know what He is not [*quid non sit*]."[69]

5. Exercitatio

The use of Trinitarian similitudes, in their function of understanding the faith (and of the defense of the faith against errors), is presented in St. Augustine as an "exercise of the mind." This theme belongs to the pedagogical *(paideia)* culture of antiquity. It is present in many philosophical currents (Stoicism and Epicureanism, Neoplatonism) which conceive philosophy as a "spiritual exercise."[70] In spite of obvious differences, the elevation of the spirit proposed by St. Augustine presents certain likenesses to the spiritual exercises required by Plotinus to lift oneself up to a grasp of the One.[71] For Augustine, the musical, literary, and philosophical disciplines have as their end to lift the

---

64. See, for example, ibid., XIII, 20, 26; XIV, 17, 23; XV, 8, 14; 9, 15–16; 11, 20; 20, 39; 22, 44; etc.

65. See, for example, ibid., XV, 20, 39: "magnam dissimilitudinem"; 23, 43: "magna disparitas."

66. *Sermo,* 52, 19 (*PL* 38, 362): "dissimilem rem dico. Nemo dicat: Ecce quod comparavit Deo." *Contra sermonem Arianorum,* 16 (*PL* 42, 695): "Est in homine simile quiddam, quamvis nequaquam illius Trinitatis, quae Deus est, comparandum." Cf. *Corpus Scriptorum Ecclesiasticorum Latinorum,* vol. 92, 76.

67. See, for example, *De Trinitate,* XV, 13, 22–16, 26; 22, 42–23, 43. Cf. *De civitate Dei,* XI, 26.

68. *De Trinitate,* XV, 7, 12; cf. ibid., XV, 17, 28.

69. Ibid., VIII, 2, 3; cf. *De ordine,* II, 16, 44: "De summo illo Deo, qui scitur melius nesciendo."

70. See Pierre Hadot's basic study *Exercices spirituels et philosophie antique* (Paris: Etudes Augustiniennes, 1981); Hadot, *Qu'est-ce que la philosophie antique?* (Paris: Gallimard, 1995), 276–333: "Les exercices spirituels."

71. Concerning Plotinus, see Pierre Hadot's explanations in Plotin, *Traité 9* (VI, 9), trans. Pierre Hadot (Paris: Cerf, 1994), 45 and 139–42.

spirit from corporeal things toward incorporeal realities; they "prepare" the soul for the contemplation of eternal truth. In his *De quantitate animae,* for example, Augustine explains that the study of the liberal arts not only supplies reason with arguments but also "exercises the spirit to render it capable of perceiving subtler realities" *(nam et exercet animum ad subtiliora cernenda):* such study prevents the spirit from being dazzled by their light and slipping back into darkness, finding itself incapable of contemplating them face to face.[72] Henri-Irénée Marrou has demonstrated the central place this exercise has in the thought and practice of St. Augustine. Before being able to contemplate the truth, the soul must become accustomed to its light through a preparatory training, a sort of spiritual gymnastics. The *exercitatio* introduces the soul to the climate of supra-sensible realities and causes it to blossom there little by little. This aspect is omnipresent in St. Augustine: to be able to contemplate the truth, the soul needs an *exercitatio,* a conditioning of the spirit which renders it capable of looking at the light.[73]

So one discovers that the interminable detours, repetitions, and digressions of the *De Trinitate* are on purpose and are part of Augustine's deliberate intention:[74] to exercise the spirit of his reader, to lead it to the ascension toward God the Trinity by sharpening the tip of his soul *(acies mentis).* This objective is recalled each time Augustine glances retrospectively at the preceding books.[75] It is formulated very clearly, for instance, at the beginning of book XV: "We wanted to train the reader [*exercere lectorem*] in the things that were made, so that he might know Him by whom they were made."[76] In this Christian setting, the spiritual exercise takes on a specific aspect.[77] It is performed on the foundation of revelation, through divine grace, in the adherence of faith to the Triune God.

St. Augustine recalls constantly that God cannot be measured by visible

---

72. *De quantitate animae,* 15, 25 (*PL* 32, 1049).

73. Henri-Irénée Marrou, *Saint Augustin et la fin de la culture antique* (Paris: De Boccard, 1983), 299–327: "Exercitatio animi." This *exercitatio* is a training that disposes the believer's mind to the contemplation of God's truth. One finds a great number of references here to the works of Augustine as well as enlightening explanations. See also Basil Studer, *Augustins De Trinitate. Eine Einführung* (Paderborn: Schöningh, 2005), 59–84.

74. Marrou, *Saint Augustin,* 319–20. On the Augustinian concept of Trinitarian theology as a spiritual exercise, see Basil Studer, *Mysterium caritatis,* 291–310 (the author is wrong, however, in opposing St. Thomas to St. Augustine on this point, cf. 308–9).

75. In particular, *De Trinitate,* XIII, 20, 26; XV, 1, 1; 3, 5; 6, 10. Cf. ibid., XV, 27, 49.

76. Ibid., XV, 1, 1.

77. On this theme of "exercitatio" in Fathers of the Church, see Basil Studer, *Schola Christiana, Die Theologie zwischen Nizäa (325) und Chalzedon (451)* (Paderborn: Schöningh, 1998), 16–19.

and mortal things. Therefore in order to grasp God to some extent, man needs a "purification of spirit,"[78] both intellectual and moral, because only purified spirits *(purgatissimae mentes)* can glimpse God.[79] The source of this purification that renders the human spirit capable of contemplating eternal realities is *faith*[80] and the charity that faith enlivens.[81] Along with faith, Augustine also notes the purificatory role of prayer (purification of desire), virtuous action, and abstention from sin which is necessary in order to grasp the mystery of God.[82]

Augustine emphasizes in particular that in order to glimpse God, the spirit must purify itself of corporeal representations and "phantasmata."[83] The spirit must not stop at created images but must rise to what the created realities "insinuate."[84] This is precisely the usefulness of the study of creatures and the goal of the exercise. The *exercitatio* proposed by Augustine is an *ascension (ascendere, erigere mentis intentionem, superius)* toward God from the image that is inferior and unequal to him,[85] and it is at the same time a gradual movement *toward the interior (introrsus tendere).*[86] From these corporeal realities and sensible perceptions, Augustine invites his reader to turn toward the spiritual nature of man, toward the soul itself and its grasp of incorporeal realities, in a manner ever more interior *(modo interiore),* in order to rise toward the divine Trinity.[87] The exercise of the spirit is "a gradual ascension toward the interior,"[88] in other words, an *elevation* from inferior realities toward superior realities and a *penetration* from exterior realities toward interior realities.[89] One enters, and one rises in a gradual manner by degrees *(gradatim).*[90] Such is the way characteristic of Augustine: "pull back into yourself [*in teipsum redi*]. . . , and transcend yourself."[91]

---

78. *De Trinitate,* I, 1, 3; IV, 18, 24.   79. Ibid., I, 2, 4.

80. Ibid., IV, 18, 24; 19, 25; XV, 24, 44.

81. Ibid., VIII, 4, 6: "nisi per fidem [Deus] diligatur, non poterit cor mundari."

82. Ibid., IV, 21, 31.   83. Ibid., VII, 6, 11–12.

84. Ibid., VIII, 4, 7.

85. Ibid., VIII, 10, 14; X, 12, 19 (conclusion of book X); XI, 7, 11; XV, 6, 10.

86. Ibid., XI, 11, 18.   87. Ibid., VIII, 1, 1; XI, 1, 1; XIII, 20, 26.

88. Ibid., XII, 8, 13: "Ascendentibus itaque introrsus quibusdam gradibus." On the gradual *(gradatim)* aspect, see also ibid., XIII, 20, 26 (conclusion of book XIII); cf. ibid., XV, 2, 3.

89. Ibid., XIV, 3, 5: "Nempe ab inferioribus ad superiora ascendentes, vel ab exterioribus ad interiora ingredientes." This is the way of books XI to XIV: exterior man, trinity of perception and memory; interior man, knowledge of temporal realities, then wisdom and contemplation of eternal realities.

90. The gradation of beings created by God is detailed elsewhere, for example in *De civitate Dei,* XI, 16: living creatures, sensate, intellectual, immortal.

91. *De vera religione,* XXXIX, 72; cf. *De civitate Dei,* XI, 28 (about the image of God): "ad nos-

The pedagogical intention of this exercise is manifest: by considering the image inferior to God, knowledge starts with what is "more familiar" *(familiarius)* and easier *(facilius)* for us, in order to direct *utcumque* the spirit's gaze toward what is above us and more difficult to grasp.[92] This movement is not linear; rather Augustine works a constant back-and-forth meant to render the spirit's tip gradually "better exercised" *(exercitatius)* in order to grasp the Trinitarian mystery.[93]

This *exercitatio* concerns not only the similitude of the image. It is applied, in a more general manner, to the reading of Holy Scripture concerning God the Trinity and Christ. Augustine notes, for example, that by showing us that the Holy Spirit is the Spirit common to the Father and the Son, Scripture suggests *(insinuat)* to us the Charity by which the Father and the Son love each other mutually: "In order to exercise us [*ut nos exerceret sermo divinitus*], the divine Word has caused us to inquire with greater zeal not into those things that lie openly at hand but into those that are to be searched out in the depths, and brought to light from the depths."[94] Augustine often proposes the same method of *exercitatio,* of purification and elevation of spirit, in his homilies and in his reading of Scripture.[95] With his clear words, Christ has nourished the small and the great; with his more difficult words, he has "exercised" the spirit of those who are capable of it, in order to raise their understanding toward the contemplation of truth.[96]

Augustine clearly rejects all esotericism: Scripture gives everyone the necessary nourishment. Nevertheless he calls "spiritual" Christians to exercise in order to understand the words of Christ more profoundly, in order to receive not only "milk" but also the "solid food" of doctrine (cf. 1 Cor 3:1–3). Believers thus progress in understanding their faith.[97] This progress fulfills the very will of God who calls men to see Him: God does not want us to be nour-

---

metipsos reversi surgamus ad illum"; *Tractatus in Iohannis Evangelium,* XX, 11: "transcende et corpus, et sape animum; transcende et animum, et sape Deum."

92. *De Trinitate,* IX, 2, 1; 12, 17 (love is not generated); XI, 1, 1 (study of the exterior man); 7, 11; XIII, 20, 26 (conclusion of book XIII); XV, 6, 10. Cf. *Sermo,* 52, 5, 15.

93. See, for example, *De Trinitate,* IX, 12, 17; XV, 3, 5; cf. XI, 7, 11.

94. Ibid., XV, 17, 27.

95. See, for example, *Tractatus in Iohannis Evangelium* XVIII, 11.

96. See, for example, ibid., 1.

97. See the numerous texts of St. Augustine indicated by Marie-François Berrouard in Saint Augustin, *Homélies sur l'évangile de saint Jean LXXX–CIII* (Paris: Institut d'Etudes Augustiniennes, 1998), 470–74. The author notes that the qualifier "carnal" in Augustine designates not only practical behavior but also a defect in the inquiry of faith's understanding (473).

ished by milk only, rather He wants us to be able to take solid food also, by understanding.[98] This is an exigency inherent in faith, the characteristic of an "adult" faith which strives to know. And for this reason, God has permitted heresies.[99] An understanding of the faith protects believers from the false doctrines of the heretics. In fact, those who have a weak and "unexercised" spirit *(inexercitata mente)* are supported by the "milk of the faith," but they risk being seduced by the corporeal images of God which the heretics propose. But other believers, accustomed to solid food, have understanding as well, thanks to their "exercised" soul, and they are better able to resist heretical doctrines.[100] In a word, God permits heresies for the exercise *(exercitatio)* and strengthening *(probatio)* of believers in their faith.[101] The Augustinian objective of *exercitatio* thus constitutes the soul of his Trinitarian meditation, carried by the desire to rise toward God with a pure heart, to see God:

"We see now through a mirror in an enigma, but then it will be face to face" (1 Cor 13:12). So, what we have been trying to do is somehow to see Him by Whom we were made by means of this image which we ourselves are, as through a mirror. . . . "Looking at the glory of the Lord in a mirror, we are being transformed into the same image from glory to glory as by the Spirit of the Lord" (2 Cor 3:18). . . . So, we are being changed from form to form and are passing from a blurred form to a clear one. But even the blurred one is the image of God, and if image then of course glory, in which men were created surpassing the other animals. . . . From the glory of faith to the glory by which we shall be like Him, because "we shall see Him as He is" (1 Jn 3:2).[102]

In summary, the *exercitatio* refers to the reading of Scripture and to the understanding of the faith, and is tied directly to three principal themes. The first is the *common action* of the three Persons. Orthodox Trinitarian faith appears especially in the affirmation of the inseparable operation of the Trinity.[103] The analysis of the image of God serves to show how we can grasp the inseparable activity of the Father, the Son, and the Holy Spirit, that is, the

---

98. See the explanations and numerous texts of Augustine indicated by Marie-François Berrouard, in Saint Augustin, *Homélies sur l'évangile de saint Jean XLIV–LIV* (Paris: Institut d'Etudes Augustiniennes, 1989), 454–59.

99. *Tractatus in Iohannis Evangelium*, XXXVI, 6. See the texts indicated by Marie-François Berrouard, in Saint Augustin, *Homélies sur l'évangile de saint Jean XXXIV–XLIII*, 465–67.

100. *Tractatus in Iohannis Evangelium*, XCVIII, 4.

101. St. Augustine, *Sermo Morin Guelferbytanus* 33, in *Patrologiae cursus completus, Series Latina, Supplementum*, vol. 2/2, ed. Adalbert Hamman (Paris: Garnier Frères, 1960), 650–51.

102. *De Trinitate* XV, 8, 14.

103. Cf. ibid., I, 5, 8. This theme is omnipresent in Augustine's Trinitarian thought.

unity without confusion of the Trinity. The second theme is that of the *simplicity, immateriality,* and *incomprehensibility* of the divine Trinity. Attributing to the divine Trinity what belongs to creatures but not to God would constitute a "sacrilegious error."[104] Third, the exercise is tied directly to a process of moral and intellectual *purification* of the mind which is indispensable to grasping the truth of God. In every case, *exercitatio* is based on faith.

B. St. Thomas Aquinas: Ad fidelium exercitium et solatium

1. Speculative Trinitarian Theology: Understanding the Faith

In the explanations that follow, the expression "speculative theology" will designate the doctrine, ordered conceptually, by which the theologian seeks to manifest the faith (in other words, to *render it more manifest*) to the understanding of believers, by proposing "reasons." The meaning of such reasons and the task of speculative theology are very well expressed in a celebrated *Quodlibet* in which Thomas explains that, if the master or professor is content to rest his case on "authorities" (the texts which are authoritative within theology), his audience will doubtless know what is true and what is false, but they will not have any idea what the truth proposed to them means:

So it is necessary to rest one's case on reasons which seek out the roots of the truth and which enable people to see how what one proposes is true [*oportet rationibus inniti investigantibus veritatis radicem, et facientibus scire quo modo sit verum quod dicitur*]. Unless one does this, if the master's response is based purely on authorities, the listener will know that things are so, but he will have achieved neither knowledge nor understanding and will go away with an empty head.[105]

---

104. Ibid., IX, 1, 1.

105. *Quodlibet,* IV, q. 9, a. 3. See J.-P. Torrell, "Le savoir théologique chez S. Thomas," *Revue Thomiste* 96 (1996): 355–96. My references to St. Thomas's works are taken from the following editions: *Scriptum super libros Sententiarum,* lib. I–II, 2 vols., ed. Pierre Mandonnet (Paris: Lethielleux, 1929); lib. III–IV, ed. Marie-Fabien Moos, 2 vols. (Paris: Lethielleux, 1933 and 1947); lib. IV, dist. 23–50, ed. Parmensis, vol. 7 (Parma: P. Fiaccadori, 1857), 872–1355; *Summa theologiae: cura et studio Instituti Studiorum Medievalium Ottaviensis,* 5 vols. (Ottawa: Harpell, 1941–1945); *Liber de veritate catholicae fidei contra errores infidelium seu Summa contra Gentiles,* ed. P. Marc, C. Pera, and P. Caramello, 3 vols. (Turin/Rome: Marietti, 1961–1967); *Quaestiones Disputatae de Potentia,* ed. P. Bazzi et al. (Turin/Rome: Marietti, 1965); *Lectura in Ioannem,* ed. R. Cai (Turin/Rome: Marietti, 1952); *Super Evangelium S. Matthaei lectura,* ed. R. Cai (Turin/Rome: Marietti, 1951); *Super Epistolas S. Pauli lectura,* ed. R. Cai, 2 vols. (Turin/Rome: Marietti, 1953); *Catena aurea in quatuor Evangelia,* ed. A. Guarienti, 2 vols. (Turin/Rome: Marietti, 1953); *In librum beati Dionysii de divinis nominibus expositio,* ed. C. Pera (Turin/Rome: Marietti, 1950); *Quaestiones disputatae de veritate,* ed. Antoine Dondaine, Leonine ed., tomus 22, 3 vols. (Rome: Editori di San Tommaso, 1975–1976); *Super Boetium de Trinitate,* ed. Pierre-M.

The objective here is an understanding of the faith: it is not a matter of proving the faith but of grasping to some extent what one believes, in other words,
to help believers to enter into a better understanding of what they believe by
showing *how (quo modo)* what the faith proposes is true.[106] Let us add that
this objective does not belong exclusively to synthetic works like the *Summa
theologiae;* one finds it in St. Thomas's biblical commentaries as well. Since
the end of a Thomistic reading of Scripture is to manifest the truth of revelation to the minds of believers, speculative doctrine fully takes part in biblical
exegesis.[107]

St. Thomas's Trinitarian theology is characterized by a very clear rejection
of all rationalism. St. Thomas rules out, with great determination, those "necessary reasons" by which theologians of his time attempted to show the necessity of the Trinity for the believer exercising reason.[108] In the domain of truths
belonging exclusively to the faith, the speculative reasons advanced by theologians do not have demonstrative force, rather they are "approximations," "ad-
aptations," or "probable arguments" *(rationes verisimiles, verisimilitudines).*[109]
St. Thomas explains that the reasons advanced in Trinitarian theology (procession by mode of intellect and will, analogy of the Word and Love) are "fitting arguments" seeking to show the coherence and intelligibility of the faith,
and also to eschew errors contrary to the faith.[110] When St. Thomas discloses

---

J. Gils, Leonine ed., tomus 50 (Rome: Commissio Leonina–Éditions du Cerf, 1992), 73–171; *Quaestiones de Quolibet,* ed. René-Antoine Gauthier, Leonine ed., tomus 25, 2 vols. (Rome: Commissio
Leonina–Éditions du Cerf, 1996); *De rationibus fidei,* ed. Hyacinthe Dondaine, Leonine ed., tomus
40 B (Rome: Ad Sanctae Sabinae, 1968).

106. *Quodlibet,* IV, q. 9, a. 3: "Ad instruendum auditores ut inducantur ad intellectum veritatis
quam credunt."

107. See my *Trinity in Aquinas* (Ypsilanti, MI: Sapientia Press, 2003), ch. 7, "Biblical Exegesis and
the Speculative Doctrine of the Trinity in St. Thomas Aquinas's Commentary on Saint John," 271–319.
The terms "contemplative" and "speculative" mean practically the same thing and designate the same
reality (*speculativus* is used more often in the treatises that are inspired by Aristotelianism, whereas the
word *contemplativus* appears more frequently in the treatises drawing on Christian sources); cf. Servais Pinckaers, "Recherche de la signification véritable du terme spéculatif," *Nouvelle revue théologique*
81 (1959): 673–95.

108. See my *La théologie trinitaire de saint Thomas d'Aquin* (Paris: Cerf, 2004), 34–48. For a shorter
account, see my *Trinity in Aquinas,* 23–25.

109. I *Scriptum super libros Sententiarum,* dist. 3, q. 1, a. 4, ad 3 *(adaptationes quaedam); Summa
contra gentiles* (hereafter *SCG*) I, chs. 8–9.

110. *ST* I, q. 32, a. 1, ad 2: "Inducitur ratio quae non sufficienter probat radicem, sed quae radi-
ci iam positae ostendat congruere consequentes effectus; . . . non tamen ratio haec est sufficienter
probans. . . . Secundo modo se habet ratio quae inducitur ad manifestationem Trinitatis: quia scilicet,
Trinitate posita, congruunt huiusmodi rationes."

the intelligibility of the faith through "likely arguments," he shows—without *demonstrating* the faith—that the arguments of the heretics (Arianism, Sabellianism) and the arguments of those who reject the Trinity do not have the force of necessity: he does this by indicating a different approach which establishes an alternative. This is the function of the "comparisons" *(similitudines, verisimilitudines)* or of "likely reasons" *(rationes verisimiles),* that is, the analogies which allow one to give an account of faith in three divine Persons—chiefly, the Augustinian analogy of the Word and Love. We will return to this topic further on. For the moment, let us keep in mind that in the domain of Trinitarian faith, some assertions are drawn from the principles of the faith, that is from Holy Scripture, while others constitute fitting arguments, "persuasions or probable arguments which show that *what the faith proposes is not impossible.*"[111] We encounter here the explanations of St. Augustine.[112]

2. The Incomprehensibility of the Trinity and the Insufficiency of Reasons

St. Thomas constantly rules out the idea that the mystery of God can be "understood" *(comprehendere)* by a created intellect: no creature can know God in all his profundity as far as he is knowable.[113] If a created intellect were to "comprehend" God, this would signify that God does not exceed the limits of the created intellect:[114] this is "impossible," adds St. Thomas, in terms that directly evoke St. Augustine.[115] The mystery of the Father and of the Son remains incomprehensible for us.[116] The generation of the Word is incomprehensible, as is the mode of this generation,[117] so is the procession of the Holy Spirit.[118] As for the distinction of the generation of the Word from the procession of the Spirit, which occupies a central place in St. Thomas's Trinitarian reflection as in that of St. Augustine, it also remains incomprehensible: St. Thomas says this with the words of St. Augustine, handed on by Peter Lom-

---

111. *ST* II-II, q. 1, a. 5, ad 2, emphasis added: "Rationes quae inducuntur ad probandum ea quae sunt fidei non sunt demonstrativae, sed persuasiones quaedam manifestantes non esse impossibile quod in fide proponitur."

112. See note 46 above, "quam non sit absurdum."

113. *ST* I, q. 12, a. 7.   114. *SCG* III, ch. 55 (no. 232).

115. See note 50 above.

116. *In Ioannem,* 1:18 (no. 218); 10:15 (no. 1414); etc.

117. Ibid., 1:1 (no. 31); *SCG* IV, ch. 13 (no. 3495); *In Matthaeum,* 1:1 (no. 15): "Quia etsi aliquo modo dicimus Filium genitum, modum tamen quo gignitur, nec homo, nec angelus potest comprehendere."

118. I *Scriptum super libros Sententiarum,* dist. 13, div. text.

bard.[119] Even the works of the Trinity (the vestige and image of the Trinity) which lead us to a certain knowledge of the mystery remain incomprehensible for us.[120] The result of this is that every approach to the mystery of the Trinity will have to be carried out with humility, with neither the intention nor the pretension of comprehending *(modeste et reverenter absque comprehendi praesumptione)*.[121] The theological inquiry of understanding God the Trinity must therefore rule out every "presumption" *(praesumptio)*.[122] St. Thomas explains this approach of the believer in St. Augustine's terms: "To reach God in some way with the mind is a great happiness; but to comprehend him is impossible."[123]

In addition, Thomas constantly recalls the "deficiencies" of all our human representations of God. Since God is incomprehensible and transcendent, He cannot be represented by any adequate similitude.[124]

> The realities of the faith are proposed to the understanding of believers not in themselves but through certain words which *do not suffice* to express them and through certain similitudes which *do not suffice* to represent them; that is why it is said that one knows them *through a mirror in an enigma*.[125]

The reasons adduced by the theologian, like the similitudes which Scripture uses to signify the Trinitarian mystery, will be deficient because no creature can adequately represent the transcendent perfection of God. Following Augustine, Thomas adds that the image of God *(imago Dei)* does not escape this deficiency: *"similitudo Trinitatis relucens in anima est omnino imperfecta et deficiens."*[126] Therefore there is no *"ratio sufficiens"*—not even the image of the

---

119. Ibid.; cf. Peter Lombard, *Sententiae in IV libris distinctae,* vol. I/2 (Grottaferrata: Editiones Collegii S. Bonaventurae, 1971), book I, dist. 13, ch. 3; Augustine, *Contra Maximinum* II, ch. 14, no. 1 (*PL* 42, 770).

120. I *Scriptum super libros Sententiarum,* dist. 3, q. 2, a. 1, arg. 1 and ad 1.

121. *De potentia,* q. 9, a. 5; cf. *SCG* IV, ch. 1 (no. 3348); *Super Boetium de Trinitate,* q. 2, a. 1.

122. *Super Boetium de Trinitate,* q. 2, a. 1. Thomas notes three forms of presumption: pretending to comprehend, placing reason before faith (wanting to know in order to believe), and wanting to surpass the limited mode of human knowledge.

123. *In Ioannem,* 1:5 (no. 102); St. Augustine, *Sermo,* 117, 3, 5 (*PL* 38, 663). Cf. St. Thomas, *ST* I, q. 12, a. 7; I-II, q. 4, a. 3, arg. 1; *De potentia,* q. 7, a. 1, arg. 2.

124. *ST* I-II, q. 102, a. 4, ad 6.

125. III *Scriptum super libros Sententiarum,* dist. 24, q. 1, a. 2, qla 3, sol.

126. Ibid., I, dist. 3, q. 1, a. 4, ad 2; cf. *ST* I, q. 56, a. 3: "Nulla similitudo creata est sufficiens ad repraesentandum divinam essentiam. Unde magis ista cognitio tenet se cum speculari." See, for example, specification of the differences between the divine Word and a created word in *De rationibus fidei* (ch. 3), where one encounters Augustine's explanations.

Trinity—for disclosing the Trinitarian faith.[127] St. Thomas explains this with the greatest clarity: "Of the unity of the divine essence and the distinction of the divine Persons, one finds no sufficient similitude in created things."[128] The similitudes are fitting only *secundum aliquid,* by a sort of "conjecture," in the measure to which they participate in God, in a deficient manner.[129] The intimate mystery of God remains hidden.[130] It follows that our knowledge of God, in faith, is a knowledge *per speculum,* a knowledge through a mirror in an enigma (1 Cor 13:12), which St. Thomas explains with the words of St. Augustine.[131]

Again following Augustine, Thomas often uses the adverb *"utcumque"* to signify the limits of our knowledge of the mystery of God the Trinity: *"utcumque mente capere"* (to grasp as much as the mind can), *"utcumque concipere"* (to conceive in some fashion), or *"utcumque accipi"* (to understand as well as possible).[132] The term *"utcumque"* appears often in the context of the knowledge of God, to avoid all presumption of perfect knowledge and to indicate the function of analogies.[133] In the *Summa contra gentiles,* the entire doctrine of the Word is found between these expressions, in a sort of inclusion.[134]

3. Knowing How God the Trinity Is Not

Along with Augustine and Pseudo-Dionysius, St. Thomas maintains that one can know neither what God is *(quid)* nor how God is *(quomodo):* one can

127. *ST* I, q. 32, a. 1, ad 2; I *Scriptum super libros Sententiarum,* dist. 10, q. 1, a. 1; *De potentia,* q. 8, a. 1, ad 12. Cf. *SCG* I, ch. 3 (no. 18); *De potentia,* q. 8, a. 1: "ad plenum ad hoc ratio pervenire non possit."

128. *Super Dionysium de divinis nominibus,* prooemium: "Ea de Deo tradidit quae ad unitatem divinae essentiae et distinctionem personarum pertinent. Cuius unitatis et distinctionis sufficiens similitudo in rebus creatis non invenitur."

129. Ibid.

130. *In I Ad Cor.,* 12:13 (nos. 800–801).

131. *ST* I, q. 12, a. 2, sed contra; St. Augustine, *De Trinitate,* XV, 9, 16.

132. *SCG* IV, ch. 1 (no. 3348); ch. 11 (no. 3468); and ch. 13 (no. 3496); see also ch. 19 (no. 3557). These formulae refer to the incomprehensibility of the mystery and are linked with the plan to defend the faith against errors. For the direct influence of St. Augustine *(De Trinitate* and *Sermons on John),* see St. Thomas's *Catena in Matthaeum,* 3:17 (Marietti ed., vol. 1, 55) or the *Catena in Ioannem,* 14:26 (vol. 2, 524). Cf. note 62 above.

133. See, for example, *SCG* II, ch. 2 (no. 859); III, ch. 49 (no. 2270); and III, ch. 113 (no. 2873); IV, ch. 21 (no. 3575).

134. *SCG* IV, ch. 11 (no. 3468): "His consideratis, utcumque concipere possumus qualiter sit divina generatio accipienda"; and IV, ch. 13 (no. 3496): "Haec ergo sunt quae de generatione divina, et de virtute Unigeniti Filii Dei, ex Sacris Scripturis edocti, utcumque concipere possumus."

grasp only that God is *(quia est)*, what God is not *(quid non est)*, and how he is not *(quomodo non est)*. These explanations, laid out from the very beginning of the *Summa*,[135] are at the heart of his doctrine of analogy and the divine names.[136] They apply not only to the natural knowledge of God but also to the knowledge of God through revelation. Revelation lifts our mind to the knowledge of realities unknown to natural reason, but the *mode* of our knowledge remains the same: we know God "through a mirror" by means of creatures.[137] St. Thomas explains this in particular when he treats of the generation of the Son or the "speaking" of the Word:

It is not permitted to scrutinize the mysteries on high with the intention of comprehending them. This appears in what St. Ambrose writes: "One can know *that* he [the Son] is born, but one must not question *how* he is born." Because to question the mode of his birth is to seek to know what his birth is: now, on the subject of divine realities, we can know *that* they are but not *what* they are.[138]

Although natural reason is able to succeed in proving that God is intellect, it is not able to discover adequately his mode of understanding. Just as we are able to know *that* God is but not *what* He is, even so we are able to know *that* God understands but not *how* He understands. Now to understand by conceiving a Word belongs to the mode of understanding: wherefore reason cannot prove this adequately, but it can form a kind of conjecture by comparison with what takes place in us.[139]

An understanding of the faith can grasp neither what *(quid sit)* the Word in God is nor how *(quomodo)* the Father generates his Word. It can only form a certain conception by "conjecture" from a study of a created word, through a mirror (analogy). To know "what the Word is not" or "how he is not" does not constitute a total ignorance: it definitely concerns a certain knowledge, albeit "confused," founded on the affirmation that there is a Word in God ac-

---

135. *ST* I, q. 2, prol.   136. Cf. *ST* I, q. 12, a. 12–13.

137. *Super Boetium de Trinitate*, q. 6, a. 3; cf. *ST* I, q. 12, a. 13, ad 1.

138. *Super Boetium de Trinitate*, q. 2, a. 1, ad 4, emphasis added: "Non licet hoc modo scrutari superna misteria, ut ad eorum compreensionem intentio habeatur; quod patet ex hoc quod sequitur 'Licet scire quod natus sit, non licet discutere quomodo natus sit': ille enim modum nativitatis discutit, qui querit scire quid sit illa nativitas, cum de divinis possimus scire quia sunt, non quid sunt."

139. *De potentia*, q. 8, a. 1, ad 12: "Licet ratio naturalis possit pervenire ad ostendendum quod Deus sit intellectus, modum tamen intelligendi non potest invenire sufficienter. Sicut enim de Deo scire possumus quod est, sed non quid est; ita de Deo scire possumus quod intelligit, sed non quo modo intelligit. Habere autem conceptionem verbi in intelligendo, pertinet ad modum intelligendi: unde ratio haec sufficienter probare non potest; sed ex eo quod est in nobis aliqualiter per simile coniecturare." The term *"conjecturare"* is an echo of St. Augustine, *De Trinitate*, XV, 17, 28 (*"conjectare"*); 21, 40 (*"conjicere"*).

cording to the teaching of the faith.[140] We encounter here the explanations of Augustine: "The analogy from our intellect does not establish anything about God conclusively because it is not in the same sense that we speak of intellect in God and in us. And that is why Augustine says that it is by faith that one arrives at knowledge but not vice versa."[141] Thus Thomas refers explicitly to Augustine in order to mark out the limits of the study of the image of God in Trinitarian theology and to signify the order of knowledge of the mystery: it is faith that seeks understanding, and not understanding that precedes faith. Placing reason before faith would be a sin: the sin of presumption.[142] These explanations raise a question: what can be the value of a speculative research that makes use of "reasons," and what is the point of the discussion?

4. Manifesting the Truth, and Eschewing Errors

It is in exposing his doctrine of relation, person, the Word, and Love that St. Thomas explains the meaning of the analogies that the theologian examines in order to manifest the Trinitarian faith. One of the best explanations is found in the study of *personal plurality* in God:

The plurality of persons in God belongs to those realities that are held by faith and that natural human reason can neither investigate nor grasp in an adequate manner; but one hopes to grasp it in Heaven, since God will be seen in his essence, when faith will have given way to vision. However, the holy Fathers have been obliged to treat it in a manner developed because of objections raised by those who have contradicted the faith in this matter and in others that pertain also to the faith; they have done it, however, in a modest manner and with respect, without pretending to comprehend. And such a search is not useless, since by it our spirit is elevated to get some glimpse of the truth that suffices for excluding the errors [*nec talis inquisitio est inutilis, cum per eam elevetur animus ad aliquid veritatis capiendum quod sufficiat ad excludendos errores*]. This is why St. Hilary explains: "Believing in this," namely the plurality of persons in God, "set out, advance, persevere. And though I may know that you will not attain the end, still I shall praise you for your progress. He who pursues the infinite with reverent devotion, even though he never attains it, will profit from advancing forward."[143]

---

140. Cf. *De potentia,* q. 7, a. 5. Cf. *ST* I, q. 13, a. 10, sed contra; *Super Boetium de Trinitate,* q. 6, a. 3: "De Deo et de aliis substantiis immaterialibus non possemus scire an est nisi sciremus quoquo modo de eis quid est sub quadam confusione."

141. *ST* I, q. 32, a. 1, ad 2. See note 17 above.

142. *Super Boetium de Trinitate,* q. 2, a. 1.

143. *De potentia,* q. 9, a. 5; St. Hilary of Poitiers, *De Trinitate,* II, 10, in *Sources Chrétiennes,* 443, 294.

These explanations summarize the purpose of speculative knowledge of the mystery of the Trinity. This is the plan which St. Thomas puts to work in all of his writings: Trinitarian theology is directed toward a *contemplative* end which will also supply Christians with ways to *defend their faith*. The manifestation of truth and the criticism of errors constitute two aspects of one theological enterprise. To avoid errors, it is not enough to adduce scriptural texts; one must show the conformity of the Catholic faith and Scripture, and one must again respond to the arguments which are opposed to the Church's faith. For its part, the truth will not be fully disclosed until we have refuted the errors opposing it. The elaboration of a speculative reflection on the Trinity, using analogies and philosophical resources, has therefore a twofold purpose: the contemplation of revealed truth, which, in turn, enables one to defend the faith against errors. The goal of Trinitarian theology is to show that faith in the Trinity is reasonably conceivable (we can reasonably contemplate the Trinity in faith) and that, therefore, arguments against Trinitarian faith cannot stand: it is not a matter of proving the faith but of showing the intelligibility of the faith by using "plausible" or "likely reasons." By giving believers some grasp of the mystery, these "reasons" show that arguments against Trinitarian faith can be answered, and they provide believers with a foretaste of the truth which they hope to contemplate in the beatific vision. It must be clear that the contemplation of the truth is neither limited nor subordinated to the exclusion of errors. Rather, contemplation of the truth *for itself* is the very end (the primary end) of speculative theology, but such a theological purpose involves the critical discussion of errors.

St. Thomas adduces these same explanations when he presents the Trinitarian *relations*.[144] He repeats them when he explains the use of the word "person" in Trinitarian theology.[145] He brings them up again when he proposes his doctrine of immanent *processions*.[146] And he reiterates the same explanations when he seeks to show the *distinction* of the generation of the Son from the procession of the Holy Spirit: in order to avoid the error of Arius, "the holy Fathers had to show that *it is not impossible* for someone to proceed from the Father and yet be consubstantial with Him, inasmuch as he receives from

---

144. *De potentia,* q. 8, a. 1: "Relinquitur ergo quod oportet dicere, relationes in Deo quasdam res esse: quod qualiter sit, sequendo sanctorum dicta, investigari oportet, licet ad plenum ad hoc ratio pervenire non possit."

145. *ST* I, q. 29, a. 3, ad 1; *De potentia,* q. 9, a. 4. Cf. St. Augustine, *De Trinitate,* VII, 4, 9.

146. *ST* I, q. 27, a. 1.

Him the same nature the Father has."[147] And since the semi-Arian Pneumatomachi could not accept that the divine nature was communicated otherwise than by generation (origin of the Son),

it was therefore necessary for our doctors [*doctores nostri*] to show that the divine nature can be communicated by a twofold procession, one being generation or birth [*generatio vel nativitas*] and the other not: *and this is the same as to seek the distinction between the divine processions.*[148]

It is precisely in order to find an answer to this question that St. Thomas, following St. Augustine, moves to the consideration of the image of the Trinity in the human soul: love does not come forth from our mind by being generated or begotten like the Word, but it proceeds in another way.[149] In St. Thomas, as in St. Augustine, the doctrine of the Holy Spirit as Love thus intends to manifest the origin and property of the Holy Spirit in order to account for the Church's faith in his divinity and in his personal distinction from the Son.

Along with Augustine, Thomas notes that heresies are partly connected with a thesis in the speculative order. He explains with Augustine, for instance, that the Arians did not want to believe that the Son possesses the same divinity as the Father, and *they could not understand it,* their position being motivated not only by a deliberate refusal but also by an intellectual difficulty.[150] To respond to heresies, therefore, one must manifest the plausibility of the orthodox faith by showing that it does not propose anything impossible: such is the goal of the "reasons" drawn from the analogy of intellect and love. They constitute a contemplation offering to believers the means to defend their faith.

We have already noted above that as far as the Trinity is concerned, Thomas dismisses necessary reasons invoked by other theologians. He does not look to prove the faith but rather to show its intelligibility with speculative reasons, the plausibility of which human thought can recognize (that is, reasons of fittingness). Since the principles of human reason come from God,

147. *De potentia,* q. 10, a. 2: "Ad cuius erroris destructionem necessarium fuit sanctis patribus manifestare quod non est impossibile esse aliquid procedens a Deo Patre quod sit ei coessentiale, in quantum accipit ab eo eamdem naturam quam Pater habet."

148. Ibid.: "Et hoc est quaerere processionum distinctionem in divinis."

149. Cf. St. Augustine, *De Trinitate,* IX, 12, 17–18.

150. *SCG* IV, ch. 6 (no. 3387): "Non enim intelligere poterant, nec credere volebant, quod aliqui duo, secundum personam distincti, habeant unam essentiam et naturam." See note 49 above.

they cannot be contrary to the faith that is given by God. For this reason arguments opposed to Trinitarian faith "do not have demonstrative force but are either probable reasons [*rationes probabiles*] or sophisms [*rationes sophisticae*]."[151] Actually, in some cases, one can refute arguments against Trinitarian faith by establishing that they are erroneous: then it is a matter of sophisms. But in other cases, one cannot establish directly the intrinsic falsity of the argument: "Realities pertaining to faith cannot be proved demonstratively; likewise, the falsity of certain statements contrary to faith cannot be demonstrated, but one can show that they are not necessary."[152]

In this last case, one can merely show that the arguments contrary to the faith are only "probable reasons," that is, arguments which, in spite of a certain plausibility from the viewpoint of the philosophical reason, do not necessarily stand. And, in order to show this in a comprehensive manner, one must establish an alternative by proposing other "reasons": it is here, as we have already noted, that the Trinitarian analogies come into play. Faith, which surpasses human reason, fulfills our mind without doing it any violence. In these explanations, we will observe the three modes of reasoning indicated by St. Thomas: demonstrative, probable, and sophistic arguments. The distinction among these three types of reasoning comes from the first lines of Aristotle's *Topics*,[153] which provide a common element of scholastic logic.[154] Although "probable reasons" receive a different sense in St. Thomas than in the "dialectical syllogism" of Aristotle, it is easy to notice that St. Thomas uses Aristotelian logical categories in order to clarify his plan as a theologian: the Aristotelian categories are put to use in service of the Augustinian project of understanding the faith.

5. The Exercise and the Consolation of Believers

The purpose of St. Thomas's Trinitarian theology is what he expresses, in a more general manner, concerning truths that the faith alone can make known to us and that one cannot demonstrate with reasons:

---

151. *SCG* I, ch. 7 (no. 47).

152. *Super Boetium de Trinitate,* q. 2, a. 3: "Sicut enim ea quae sunt fidei non possunt demonstrative probari, ita quaedam contraria eis non possunt demonstrative ostendi esse falsa, sed potest ostendi ea non esse necessaria."

153. Aristotle, *Topics* I, 1 (100a 25–101a 4). I thank Prof. Luca Tuninetti, who pointed this out to me.

154. See, for example, the division of syllogisms in William of Sherwood, *Introductiones in Logicam* IV, ed. Hartmut Brands and Christoph Kann (Hamburg: Felix Meiner Verlag, 1995), 78: "syllogismus

In order to manifest this kind of truth, one must provide likely, probable reasons [*rationes aliquae verisimiles*] for the exercise and encouragement of the faithful [*ad fidelium quidem exercitium et solatium*], and not in order to convince opponents; for the insufficiency of these reasons would rather confirm them in their error if they thought that we adhered to the faith for such weak reasons.[155]

St. Thomas expresses here the task of speculative theology concerning the mystery of the Trinity and of Christ: it is a matter of manifesting *(manifestare)*, in other words, *rendering more manifest to our minds,* the truth of the faith. The means is equally clear: these are probable or plausible reasons, and not demonstrations. The addressees are also identified: it concerns believers *(fideles)*. And the end of such an undertaking is expressed by the words *exercitium* and *solatium*. It is not easy to translate *solatium* (or *solacium*) with a single term. This word can mean: relief in sorrow or misfortune, solace, comfort, support, (domestic) help, service, consolation, compensation, or even entertainment.[156] In St. Thomas's Latin Bible, the word *"solatium"* translates the Greek term *"paraklèsis"* (exhortation, appeal, address, summons, encouragement, intercession, consolation).[157] In the natural domain, St. Thomas associates it in particular with the security procured through the possession of temporal goods or financial aid[158] but also with the support that spouses or friends give each other[159] or even the enjoyment that entertainment and the theater provide (the *solatium* that the virtue of *eutrapelia* procures).[160] In the domain of grace, he links it in particular to the virtue of hope (hope procures *solatium*),[161] peace and contemplation,[162] in other words, to "spiritual consolation."[163] The study of the holy books is a special source of *solatium* by procur-

---

alius est demonstrativus, alius dialecticus, alius sophisticus. . . . Dialecticus vero est ex probabilibus, faciens opinionem."

155. *SCG* I, ch. 9 (no. 54).

156. See, for instance, St. Thomas, *In Ad Gal.,* 1:1 (no. 8); IV *Scriptum super libros Sententiarum,* dist. 48, q. 2, a. 1; *ST* I, q. 51, a. 1, arg. 1.

157. See for instance 1 Mc 12:9 or Heb 6:18. Cf. St. Thomas, *In Ad Rom.,* 1:2 (no. 27) and 7:22 (no. 585).

158. IV *Scriptum super libros Sententiarum,* dist. 49, q. 4, a. 1, sed contra 2 and ad 3; *Contra impugnantes,* ch. 6, no. 6, ad 17 (Leonine ed., vol. 41 A, 104).

159. *In Isaiam,* 3:17 and 3:25 (Leonine ed., vol. 28, pp. 29 and 31).

160. *ST* II-II, q. 168, a. 2; ibid., a. 3, ad 3.

161. See *SCG* III, ch. 153 (no. 3252); *De veritate,* q. 17, a. 2, arg. 8; *In Ad Hebr.,* 6:18 (no. 324).

162. See for instance *In Isaiam,* 7:14 and 48:22 (Leonine ed., vol. 28, 59, and 200).

163. *In Ad Rom.,* 15:5 (no. 1149): "Deus autem patientiae, scilicet dator, Ps. LXX, v. 5: tu es patientia mea, et solatii, idest qui spiritualem consolationem largitur." On the tight link between *solatium*

ing "a remedy against tribulations."[164] At the beginning of his *Contra impugn-antes*, he notes that the adversaries of mendicant religious life want to deprive mendicants of *spiritualia solatia* by refusing them the right to study and to teach, "so that they can neither resist adversaries nor find the consolation of the Spirit in the Scriptures: that is the trick of the Philistines."[165] This last passage suggests well the meaning that one must give to the word *solatium* in the *Summa contra gentiles* I, ch. 9: the search for "reasons" in order to manifest the faith procures for believers support, remedy, defense, and spiritual consolation by giving them a grasp of the intelligibility of their faith and showing them that this faith resists the objections (heresies and rational arguments) that are posed to it.

As to the word "exercise" *(exercitium),* it indicates the nature and purpose of the theologian's study. St. Thomas often applies this theme of exercise *(exercitatio* and *exercitium)* to study and teaching sustained by perseverance, training, and frequent practice.[166] The study and teaching of wisdom are counted among the "spiritual exercises" *(spiritualia exercitia)* that lead one to know God and to love him.[167] This exercise is comparable to a "school."[168] In the formula "spiritual exercise," the adjective "spiritual" carries a religious sense (seeking knowledge of God in faith)[169] without losing, for all that, its anthropological significance *(spiritual* as distinguished from *manual* or *corporeal).*[170]

---

and *consolatio*, see also *Contra impugnantes*, prol. (Leonine ed., vol. 41 A, 52); *In Isaiam*, 1:7 and 6:8 (Leonine ed., vol. 28, 12, and 51); *In Ad Hebr.*, 13:22 (no. 772).

164. *In II Ad Tim.*, 4:13 (no. 158).

165. *Contra impugnantes*, prol. (Leonine ed., vol. 41/A, 52): "eis subtrahere nituntur spiritualia so-latia, corporalia onera imponentes. Primo enim eis pro posse studium et doctrinam auferre conantur, ut sic adversariis resistere non possint nec in Scripturis consolationem Spiritus invenire. Et haec est as-tutia Philistinorum, I Reg. 13:19."

166. Cf. *ST* III, q. 86, a. 5, ad 3; *De veritate*, q. 24, a. 10; III *Scriptum super libros Sententiarum*, dist. 37, q. 1, a. 5, qla 1, arg. 2.

167. *SCG* III, ch. 132 (no. 3047): "studium sapientiae, et doctrina, et alia huiusmodi spiritualia ex-ercitia." Cf. *ST* II-II, q. 122, a. 4, ad 3.

168. St. Thomas explains this in connection with religious life, which he considers an exercise for coming to the perfection of charity: "exercitium sive schola perfectionis." *Quodlibet* IV, q. 12, a. 1, ad 7; cf. ad 9. Cf. *ST* II-II, q. 186, a. 3: "exercitium et disciplina."

169. The expression "spiritual exercise" is applied to study and teaching, to the religious state, and to activities proper to this state (*ST* II-II, q. 189, a. 1; *Contra impugnantes*, ch. 5, ad 8; Leonine ed., vol. 41 A, 92) and, more generally, to the practice of virtue (*In Eph.*, 3:14 [no. 166]; *ST* III, q. 69, a. 3). Voluntary poverty constitutes an "exercise" as well (*ST* II-II, q. 186, a. 3, ad 4).

170. Cf., for example, *Contra impugnantes*, ch. 5, no. 3 (Leonine ed., vol. 41 A, 89–90): the works of piety (among which Aquinas counts the study of Holy Scriptures, teaching, and preaching) are distinguished from *"corporalis exercitatio," "corporale exercitium,"* and *"labor manuum"*; cf. ibid., ad 8:

In various contexts, the theme of exercise is especially tied to difficulties, tribulations, and adversities: difficulties and tribulations are the occasion of an
exercitium or *exercitatio* which makes it possible to overcome them. Thus, for
instance, Providence uses demons, evildoers, troubles in this life, dangers, and
tribulations in general for the *exercitatio* of just men, that is, to make them
stronger.[171]

As far as doctrine is concerned, St. Thomas presents exercise as an "elevation" of the spirit that takes place according to a progression. This elevation
starts with the "easiest" things in order to reach the "most difficult" things:[172]
it begins in the senses, with sensible representations and the imagination, in
order to reach intelligible realities.[173] The exercise consists in passing from corporeal realities to spiritual realities, from light things to those which are more
arduous, from a simple teaching to a more subtle teaching, from faith to a
spiritual understanding of the faith.[174] The theme of exercise also implies (as
with Augustine) an order of disciplines of knowledge, which prepares minds
so that they become capable of grasping realities that transcend the senses and
the imagination.[175] Three aspects of this exercise of wisdom merit mention on
this topic.

a. Errors and Heresies   In the context of the quest for an understanding of the
faith, the theme of exercise appears, first of all, tightly linked to the challenge
posed by heresies. "After the divine truth was manifested, certain errors arose
on account of the weakness of human minds. But these errors have exercised
[*exercuerunt*] the understanding of believers to search out and grasp the divine truths more attentively [*diligentius*]."[176] The most complete explanations
are found in a *reportatio* on the first letter to the Corinthians, in connection

---

the *"exercitia spiritualia"* are distinguished from the *"opera manualia"* (92); cf. *In I Ad Tim.*, 4:8 (nos.
153–162). For the nuances of the vocabulary of "spirituality," see Jean-Pierre Torrell, *"Spiritualitas* chez
saint Thomas d'Aquin," *Revue des sciences philosophiques et théologiques* 73 (1989): 575–84.

171. See, for example, *ST* I, q. 64, a. 4; q. 109, a. 4, ad 1 (demons); q. 114, a. 1, arg. 3 and ad 3; *ST* I-
II, q. 87, a. 7; *In Matthaeum*, 13:29 (no. 1149); *Catena in Lucam*, 8:23 (Marietti ed., vol. 2, 114–115); IV
Scriptum super libros Sententiarum, dist. 46, q. 1, a. 2, qla 3, ad 3 and ad 4. References to these themes
are numerous.

172. *ST* II-II, q. 189, a. 1, ad 4: "a facilioribus ad difficiliora."

173. See, for example, *ST* I, q. 1, a. 9, ad 2.

174. Cf. *In Ad Hebr.*, 5:14 (nos. 269–274).

175. *Sententia libri Ethicorum*, VI, 7 (Leonine ed., vol. 47/2, 358–359): logic, mathematics, natural
philosophy, ethics, then the study of wisdom and divine realities.

176. *SCG* IV, ch. 55 (no. 3939).

with St. Paul's words: *"nam oportet haereses esse"* (1 Cor 11:19).[177] Following St. Augustine, St. Thomas explains that heresies take on a double utility *(utilitas)*. First, because of heresies "the holy doctors were more exercised [*magis exercitati*] in order to bring the truth of the faith to light, and their minds were rendered more subtle [*subtiliata*]."[178] "After the heresies, the saints spoke more prudently *(cautius)* of the things of the faith, as Augustine on the subject of grace after the Pelagians and as Pope Leo on the subject of the Incarnation after Nestorius and Eutyches."[179] The second benefit of heresies is to manifest the constancy of the faithful in the faith *(constantia fidei)* by making those who resist these heresies stronger and more proven *(probati)*.[180] The same goes for philosophical errors: these errors are the occasion of an exercise *(exercitium)* that gives rise to a clearer *(limpidius)* grasp of the truth; regarding those who have spoken of the truth superficially, although we do not accept their opinion, they provide us the occasion of an exercise *(exercitium)* of inquiry into the truth.[181] The same explanations are applied again to events. By exercising his disciples in grasping the parables according to their spiritual sense, Christ leads them to understand that the events *(res gestae)* of the First Covenant are figures *(figurae)* of the New Covenant.[182] This teaching comes in particular from St. Augustine.[183] It makes it possible to clarify the meaning of ex-

177. This text was published among the *Reportationes ineditae Leoninae* in the edition of the works of St. Thomas serving as a basis for the *Index Thomisticus: S. Thomae Aquinatis, Opera omnia,* vol. 6 (Stuttgart/Bad Cannstatt: Frommann/Holzboog, 1980), 367. This text is from the manuscript Padova, Bibliotheca Antoniana 333. Undoubtedly one will have to await the Leonine edition of the commentary on St. Paul to obtain more details concerning the double recension of the commentary on 1 Corinthians.

178. *Super I Corinthios,* 11, 19: "Una est quia sancti doctores ex hoc sunt magis exercitati ad veritatem fidei elucidandam, et eorum ingenia magis subtiliata."

179. Ibid. On this same theme, with the example of St. Augustine, see *Contra errores Graecorum,* prol. (Leonine ed., vol. 40 A, 71).

180. Ibid. The other commentary given by the Marietti edition (no. 628) indicates St. Thomas's Augustinian sources: *Enchiridion* and *De civitate Dei.* St. Thomas, citing Augustine, notes a double utility of heresies here as well: "ad maiorem declarationem veritatis" and "ad manifestandam infirmitatem fidei in his qui recte credunt."

181. *Super libri Metaphysicae,* II, lect. 1 (Marietti ed., nos. 287–288): "Inquantum priores errantes circa veritatem posterioribus exercitii occasionem dederunt, ut diligenti discussione habita, veritas limpidius appareret. . . . Etiam illis, qui superficialiter locuti sunt ad veritatem investigandam, licet eorum opiniones non sequamur, quia etiam aliquid conferunt nobis. Praestiterunt enim nobis quoddam exercitium circa inquisitionem veritatis."

182. *In Matthaeum,* 13:52 (no. 1206). Here St. Thomas distinguishes the crowds, to which Jesus spoke in parables, and the disciples, "exercised" *(exercitati)* to grasp this teaching in its spiritual sense.

183. Ibid. See the Augustinian texts cited in the *Catena in Matthaeum* 13:52 (Marietti ed., vol. 1, 224).

ercitium in the *Summa contra gentiles* I, ch. 9: the "reasons" adduced by the theologian in order to manifest the faith do not prove the faith but exercise the mind of the believer to better grasp the truth of the faith with prudence and precision, by giving him the occasion to confirm the faith. And thanks to studious men capable of refuting errors, those who possess a simpler faith are confirmed in the faith.[184]

b. The Obscurities and Figurative Language of the Scriptures   This theme of exercise appears as well, in a great number of reprises, in connection with the difficulties, "obscurities," and figurative language of the Holy Scriptures. This obscure language is useful for two tightly linked reasons: 1) for the exercise of studious men *(ad exercitium studiosorum);* and 2) to protect revelation from the derision of unbelievers *(contra irrisiones infidelium).*[185] The divine truth is sometimes given in a "hidden" manner so that unbelievers "might not make a mockery of it and so that the simpler believers will not be led into error."[186] As to the exercise invoked for the first reason, it concerns "studious" men, that is, readers formed by the doctrinal and spiritual reading of Scripture: this exercise consists in an "elevation of the mind" which leads from created similitudes and obscure expressions to the grasp of intelligible spiritual realities.[187] Here we are very close to the Augustinian *exercitatio.* The Augustinian inspiration appears explicitly in the Commentary on St. John 10:6 where St. Thomas takes up St. Augustine's explanation concerning the words of Christ: "He gives what is plain for food; what is obscure for exercise."[188] The ignorance re-

---

184. *ST* II-II, q. 10, a. 7.

185. *ST* I, q. 1, a. 9, ad 2; cf. I *Scriptum super libros Sententiarum,* dist. 34, q. 3, a. 2. See Vincent Serverat, "*L'irrisio fidei.* Encore sur Raymond Lulle et Thomas d'Aquin," *Revue Thomiste* 90 (1990): 436–48.

186. I *Scriptum super libros Sententiarum,* dist. 34, q. 3, a. 1.

187. *ST* I, q. 1, a. 9, ad 2: "Ut mentes quibus fit revelatio, non permittat in similitudinibus permanere, sed elevet eas ad cognitionem intelligibilium." *ST* II-II, q. 1, a. 9, ad 1: "longum studium atque exercitium." This exercise is required in order to be capable of teaching. *In I Ad Tim.,* 4:13 (no. 171). Cf. *Super Dionysium de divinis nominibus* I, lect. 2 (Marietti ed., no. 65): "In Scripturis exprimuntur nobis intelligibilia per sensibilia, et supersubstantialia per existentia, et incorporalia per corporalia, et simplicia per composita et diversa."

188. St. Augustine, *Tractatus in evangelium Iohannis,* 45, 6: "Pascit enim manifestis, exercet obscuris." See the indication of other texts of St. Augustine on the same theme in Saint Augustin, *Homélies sur l'Évangile de saint Jean XLIV–LIV,* 54. St. Thomas cites this text of St. Augustine in his *Catena in Ioannem,* 10:6 (Marietti ed., vol. 2, 472); in his *Commentary on St. John,* he comments on this passage, clarifying that plain food is given to the crowds of believers and that exercise is addressed to the disciples: "Pascit Dominus manifestis, scilicet fideles turbas, exercet obscuris, scilicet discipulos." *In Ioannem,* 10:6 (no. 1379).

vived by the "proverbs" (figures, parables) of Christ "was useful for the good and the just who tried to grasp them, as an exercise, for giving praise to God; for although they do not understand, they believe and praise the Lord and his wisdom which is so far above them."[189] Other authors are invoked as well to explain this pedagogy of revelation. In his Catena in Lucam, for example, St. Thomas reports the explanations of Theophylactus: Christ speaks first of all by means of "similitudes" in order to attract the attention of his listeners *(ut attentiores faceret auditores)* and to exercise them *(exercitare),* and also so that those who are unworthy *(indigni)* will not be able to grasp the spiritual sense of the obscure words.[190] "The secrets of the faith should not be exposed to unbelievers."[191] Here again St. Thomas invokes a defense of the faith.[192]

c. The Wise and the Simple   As with St. Augustine, the theme of exercise brings to bear a distinction between the "wise" and the "simple" or the "small." By "wise," one must understand believers experienced in reading the Scriptures and in understanding the faith. As to the "simple" or "small," these are believers "still only slightly initiated in the perfect doctrine of the faith."[193] Against all elitism, Thomas explains that the same reality of faith must be handed on to the wise and the small, without any difference; nevertheless, the mode of this handing on is not identical. Drawing on St. Augustine, he explains that when one proposes the realities of the faith to the small *(parvuli)*, it is not fitting to treat the realities in their difficulties or to explore them to the very bottom.[194] This applies especially to the "mystery of the Trinity" and to the "sacrament of the Incarnation," subjects about which St. Paul hands on "very difficult" *(valde difficilia)* and arduous *(ardua)* teachings.[195] The example often developed by St. Thomas is that of the birth of the Word:

189. St. Thomas, *In Ioannem,* 10:6 (no. 1380): "Utilis et bonis et justis ad exercitium in Dei laudem quaerentibus: nam dum ea non intelligunt, credunt, glorificant Dominum, et eius sapientiam supra se existentem." Exercise produces a conscience more alive in the faith for the praise of God.

190. *Catena in Lucam,* 8:4 (Marietti ed., vol. 2, 110).

191. *De rationibus fidei,* ch. 8.

192. *Super Boetium de Trinitate,* q. 2, a. 4. Cf. Augustine, *De doctrina christiana* IV, ch. 9 (*PL* 34, 99).

193. *In I Ad Cor.,* 3:1 (no. 124): "tamquam parvulis in Christo, id est, parum adhuc introductis in perfectam doctrinam fidei, quae spiritualibus debetur."

194. *In Ad Hebr.,* 5:13 (no. 270): "Eadem enim utrisque proponenda sunt, sed parvulis proponenda sunt, sed non exponenda nec pertractanda: quia intellectus eorum magis deficeret, quam elevaretur."

195. Ibid.

It is easy enough to know by simple faith [*per simplicem fidem est satis facile*] that the "Word became flesh" [Jn 1:14], because this can come into the imagination and in a certain manner into the senses. But to know the "Word that was in the beginning with God" [Jn 1:1] surpasses all the senses and can only be grasped by reason and with numerous difficulties—the greatest difficulties.[196]

Thus there is an order of teaching *(ordo doctrinae)* which corresponds to spiritual progress in the faith: it is the order by which one passes from "easier" things to "more difficult" things.[197] In this way, the believer must first be nourished by "milk" in order to be able to obtain solid food later:[198] one must first receive the nourishment of the "Word made flesh" in order to be able to grow and become capable of receiving the teaching concerning "the Word that was in the beginning with God."[199] The heretics committed the error of modifying this order, in yielding to the presumption of obtaining solid food before the opportune time.[200] Now, spiritual doctrine ("solid food")[201] must be given to each according to his ability and disposition.[202] The realities of the faith must therefore be handed on in a simple manner to the simple and "in a subtler manner for subtler men."[203]

One more clarification must be added. As far as knowledge of the faith is concerned, the "spiritual doctrine" proposed to the *maiores* is not a pure matter of understanding, rather it demands as well a right affectivity and inclination toward God. Under this aspect, sacred doctrine is distinguished from other domains of knowledge. In other sciences, intellectual perfection suffices. But the "doctrine of Sacred Scripture" requires a double perfection, intellectual and affective. It communicates realities which not only are the object of speculation *(speculanda)* but also must be received in charity *(approbanda*

---

196. Ibid. (no. 271). See also *Contra doctrinam retrahentium,* ch. 7 (Leonine ed., vol. 41 C, 50); *ST* II-II, q. 189, a. 1, arg. 4.

197. *ST* II-II, q. 189, a. 1, ad 4: "de ordine doctrinae, prout transeundum est a facilioribus ad difficiliora."

198. "Milk," in the symbolic sense, signifies the "doctrine of the simple" *(simplicium doctrina): In Isaiam,* 60:16 (Leonine ed., vol. 28, 237).

199. *ST* II-II, q. 189, a. 1, ad 4; cf. arg. 4. This interpretation is taken from the *Gloss;* cf. Peter Lombard *(PL* 191, 1172). On this subject, one notes a pedagogical priority of the economy (the Word made flesh) with respect to theology (the eternal Word with his Father). See also *Contra doctrinam retrahentium,* ch. 7 (Leonine ed., vol. 41 C, 50).

200. Ibid.   201. Cf. *In I Ad Cor.,* 3:2 (nos. 125–130)

202. *In Ioannem,* 4:32 (no. 635).

203. *In Matthaeum,* 25:15 (no. 2039): "Apostolus 1 Cor. 3:2: tamquam parvulis in Christo lac potum dedi vobis, non escam. Ideo magis subtilibus magis subtilia dedit."

per affectum).[204] St. Thomas clarifies: theology is not geometry! Such is the condition of welcome to "solid doctrine": it requires that its addressees be accomplished, both in the intellectual order and in the affective order.[205] Thus conceived, Trinitarian theology demands the practice of *prayer* (as the example of Thomas himself shows) by which the soul is purified, elevated toward the spiritual reality of God, and ordered to God by devotion.[206] There is nothing more foreign to Thomas Aquinas than a rationalist conception of theology. These explanations are summarized in an excerpt from letter 137 of St. Augustine (to Volusian) which St. Thomas cites in the preface of his *Catena in Matthaeum:* Sacred Scripture is accessible to all men *(omnibus accessibilis),* but its deeper mysteries are penetrable to very few *(paucissimis penetrabilis).* It invites all not only "to be fed with the truth which is plain" but also to be exercised by the truth which is concealed *(etiam secreta exerceat veritate):* by these means, wayward minds are corrected, weak minds are nourished, and strong minds are filled with joy.[207]

6. The Image of the Trinity

Thus in Trinitarian theology, the doctrine of image in Thomas has a function similar to that which it has in Augustine. It offers an "exercise" for contemplating the truth, in the manner of a foretaste of the beatific vision, by showing believers an understanding of their faith, making it possible for them to defend the faith against errors. In this context, the study of the Word and Love serves to manifest or "insinuate" the unity and the distinction of the Father, Son, and Holy Spirit, both in their eternal immanence and in the economy of grace.[208]

Like Augustine, Thomas searches out an analogy for grasping to some extent the unity of the divine Trinity, *per speculum,* starting from what is most known to us. Chapter 11 of the fourth book of the *Summa contra gentiles,*

---

204. *In Ad Hebr.,* 5:14 (no. 273). This does not call into question the priority of the speculative dimension of sacred doctrine (cf. *ST* I, q. 1, a. 4). Rather this teaching recalls that the study of sacred doctrine fits into the scheme of the integral organism of the life of faith in the Church.

205. Ibid. (no. 274). Solid food must be handed on to those, who through their training *(consuetudo),* have exercised senses *(exercitatos sensus),* in other words, to the exercised man *(exercitatus)* capable of right judgment.

206. *Super Dionysium de divinis nominibus,* III (Marietti ed., no. 232–233).

207. *Catena in Matthaeum,* praefatio (Marietti ed., vol. 1, 8). St. Augustine, *Epistola* 137, 18 (*PL* 33, 524).

208. This objective is very clear from the very first question of the Trinitarian treatise of the *Summa theologiae (ST* I, q. 27).

where Thomas presents his mature doctrine concerning the Word for the first
time, shows perfectly well the direction of his approach. He uses the criterion
of the *intimacy* of a procession. The believing mind looks for a mode of emanation in which the term that proceeds is interior to its principle (distinction
in unity). Like Augustine, Thomas observes a "gradation" in beings, through
which we progress to discover a procession ever "more interior."[209] In inanimate bodies, a procession takes place in an exterior manner: therefore it will
not be a suitable aid for grasping the Trinitarian mystery. In the first degree
of animate bodies (vegetative, first degree of life), one discovers an emanation that proceeds from the interior: but this procession takes place "toward
the exterior," to the point where the term that proceeds (for example, the fruit
that proceeds from the tree) is completely separated from its principle; furthermore, Thomas observes that the first principle of such an emanation remains exterior. Above this degree, bodies gifted with a sensate soul (animals)
offer an example more suggestive of an interior emanation: this is the analogy of sensible perception which recalls (with important differences) the first
trinity of the exterior man in Augustine: the form of a perceived body is im-
printed in the senses, and from there it proceeds into the imagination and
the memory. But here again, the principle and the term of the procession
are different. Therefore in order to find an example of an intimate procession, one must ascend again to consider the intellect, which constitutes the
"highest degree of life": since it is capable of *reflection,* the intellect (with will
and love, which are linked to it) will be able to suggest the intimacy between
a principle and the term of a procession. But here again Thomas observes a
gradation, by "degrees": in the case of the human intellect, the principle of
knowledge comes from outside, by means of the senses; above man, the angels offer a better example of a knowledge coming "from inside," but their
thought remains different from their being (there is not an identity of substance between the angels' intellectual conception and their being). Therefore
it will be necessary to gradually leave behind the conditions proper to creatures in order to glimpse the conditions of a divine procession in which the
intimacy is a perfect unity of nature. Thus Thomas observes that "the more
elevated the nature, the more intimate to itself what emanates from it [*magis
ei est intimum*]."[210] Beginning with an observation of the world, then, in the

---

209. See note 88 above.
210. *SCG* IV, ch. 11 (no. 3461); cf. no. 3464: "magis ad intima devenitur."

study of the life of the mind and of love, he invites his reader to discover that the more elevated the degree of life, "the more the operation of that life will be contained in intimacy [*magis in intimis continetur*]."[211] The doctrine of the "immanent operation," which constitutes the point of departure of the Trinitarian treatise of the *Summa theologiae*, expresses precisely the *results* of this inquiry in which the mind raises its gaze toward the conditions of superior forms of life up to God himself.[212]

Such is the function of the analogy of the Word and Love.[213] It expresses the result of the inquiry by which Thomas *appropriates and extends Augustine's reflection,* in an original way. He retains the similitude of the Word and Love, because it makes it possible to glimpse, to some extent, the distinction in unity (unity without confusion), in a manner "less foreign" to the spiritual nature of God: "God is not of a fleshly nature, requiring a woman to copulate with to generate offspring, but He is of a spiritual or intellectual nature, indeed beyond every intellectual nature. So generation should be understood *as it applies to an intellectual nature.*" This is the reason why, "even though our own intellect falls far short of the divine intellect," Aquinas turns to the "similitude" of the image of God in the human mind.[214] In a similar context, when Augustine was seeking to show the distinctive property of the Holy Spirit, he explained: "With regard to the Holy Spirit, I pointed out that nothing in this enigma would seem to be like him, except our love or will or charity."[215] Confronted with the same problem, St. Thomas adds: "If the procession of the Word and Love does not suffice for inserting the personal distinction, then there could not be any personal distinction in God."[216] If one doubts that the analogy of the Word and Love suffices to give an idea of personal distinction in the unity of substance, if one rejects this speculative "reason," then one can well *assert* that God is a Trinity, but one cannot *disclose* the truth of Trinitarian

211. *SCG* IV, ch. 11 (no. 3464).

212. *ST* I, q. 27, a. 1: "Secundum actionem quae manet in ipso agente, attenditur processio quaedam ad intra: et hoc maxime patet in intellectu, cuius actio, scilicet intelligere, manet in intelligente." Cf. ad 2: "intima intelligenti"; ad 3: "procedere ut intimum et absque diversitate." See also the enlightening explanations given in the *De potentia,* q. 10, a. 1. And the same applies to love, see *SCG* IV, ch. 19; *ST* I, q. 27, a. 3–5; q. 37.

213. *SCG* IV, ch. 11 and ch. 19. Cf. *ST* I, q. 27, a. 1–5; q. 37, a. 1–2. Cf. my *La théologie trinitaire de saint Thomas d'Aquin,* 217–31, 270–93, 399–424.

214. *De rationibus fidei,* ch. 3, emphasis added.

215. St. Augustine, *De Trinitate,* XV, 21, 41.

216. St. Thomas, *De potentia,* q. 9, a. 9, ad 7: "Si processio verbi et amoris non sufficit ad distinctionem personalem insinuandam, nulla poterit esse personalis distinctio in divinis."

faith, one cannot make the faith *more manifest* to the believer's mind in search of an understanding of the mystery.

Another important point concerning the Thomistic doctrine of image must be added. The analogy of knowledge and love *of the self* must not be opposed to the knowledge and love *of God* by grace. Both aspects come from Augustine. The theme of knowledge and love *of the self* is quite present in the *De Trinitate*,[217] although there it concerns an imperfect image because, in this case, it is not an "immutable" reality that the soul knows and loves.[218] But this theme possesses the advantage of suggesting the *identity of being* because what the soul knows and what the soul loves is the same reality as the soul itself.[219] This makes it possible to give a certain idea of the *consubstantiality* of the Trinity. And this is precisely the aspect that Thomas retains: when he adopts the analogy of the knowledge and love of the self, it is *under the aspect* that makes possible an account of an essential unity (by generating the Son and spirating the Spirit, the Father *communicates his own nature* to them).[220] But for St. Thomas, who follows St. Augustine expressly, the image of God in man resides *primo et principaliter* in the knowledge and love *of God,* that is, in the participation in the knowledge and love that God has of his own mystery.[221] Knowledge and love of the self constitutes a secondary aspect of this image *(secundario), in the measure* that it prepares for and reflects knowledge and love of God Himself, in other words, inasmuch as the mind which knows and loves itself is transported toward God: "not because the mind reflects on itself absolutely so as to come to a halt in itself but so that it can ultimately go on to turn toward God."[222] The sinful man is the image of God in an inferior degree (he remains capable of knowing and loving God), but only the holy man (who knows and loves God according to the image of grace) "rep-

---

217. See, for example, *De Trinitate,* IX, 2, 2; 5, 8; etc.

218. Ibid., IX, 6, 9.

219. See, for example, ibid., IX, 2, 2: "Amans enim et quod amatur, hoc idem est, quando se ipse amat."

220. See, for example, *SCG* IV, ch. 11 (no. 3469); *ST* I, q. 37, a. 1: "When someone knows and loves himself, he is present to himself not simply by an entitative identity but also as the 'object' known in the knower and loved in the lover." Cf. *De rationibus fidei,* ch. 3: "The word of our intellect can be likened to a concept or offspring, especially when the intellect knows itself, and the concept is a likeness of the intellect coming from its intellectual power, just as a son has a likeness to his father, from whose generative power he comes forth."

221. *ST* I, q. 93, a. 8 (with a quotation of the *De Trinitate,* XIV, 12, 15); cf. a. 4; *De veritate,* q. 10, a. 7.

222. *ST* I, q. 93, a. 8.

resents" God the Trinity to some extent, in the measure that God dwells in him.[223] Thomas explains this at greater length in his *De veritate,* with a clear Augustinian accent:

Within the knowledge through which the soul knows itself, there is an *analogous* representation [*secundum analogiam*] of the uncreated Trinity, in that, as the soul knows itself it engenders of itself a word, and love proceeds from both. Thus the Father, in speaking himself, begets his Word from all eternity, and the Holy Spirit proceeds from both. Whereas, in the knowledge through which the soul knows God, the soul itself is *conformed to God* [*Deo conformatur*] in the way that any knowing thing is, in some way, assimilated to the known object.[224]

Just as the economic dimension is present in Thomas as well as in Augustine (the Son is the Word by which the Father speaks himself and all things, the Spirit is the Love by which the Father and the Son love each other and communicate their love to creatures and to the Church),[225] so the eschatological dimension of this image is present in both authors. Commenting on 2 Corinthians 3:18 ("We all who with unveiled faces reflect as in a mirror the glory of the Lord, we are transformed into his likeness, from glory to glory, as by the Lord who is Spirit"), Thomas repeats Augustine's profound views verbatim:

We know the glorious God by the mirror of reason, in which there is an image of God. We behold Him when we rise from a consideration of ourselves to some knowledge of God, and we are transformed. For since all knowledge involves the knower's being assimilated to the thing known, it is necessary that those who see be in some way transformed into God. If they see perfectly, they are perfectly transformed, as the blessed in heaven by the union of fruition: "When he appears we shall be like him" (1 Jn 3:2); but if we see imperfectly, then we are transformed imperfectly, as here by faith: "Now we see in a mirror dimly" (1 Cor 13:12).[226]

The knowledge of God through a mirror of an image takes place when the believer rises *(assurgit)* above himself in order to grasp something of the mystery of God *(cognitio aliqua).* This elevation of faith procures for the believer a conformation to God *(transformatio)* which is a foretaste of the full deifica-

---

223. I *Scriptum super libros Sententiarum,* dist. 1, q. 2, a. 1, ad 4.

224. *De veritate,* q. 10, a. 7: *"secundum analogiam"* is distinguished from *"secundum conformationem,"* the latter being an echo of the Augustinian theme of the mind's *reformatio.*

225. See my *Trinity in Aquinas,* 171–75: the doctrine of the Word and Love is not limited to the "immanent Trinity" but accounts as well for the Trinitarian economy of creation and grace.

226. *In II Ad Cor.,* 3:18 (no. 114). See note 102 above.

tion in the beatific vision. This is the mystery which the theologian seeks to give account of. The study of this image is carried by the same desire of elevation, and it is completed by the same transforming knowledge of faith.

The purpose of Trinitarian theology, for St. Thomas, is therefore at one and the same time ambitious and modest. It is ambitious, for Trinitarian theology sets out to show (that is, to make more manifest to our minds) the unity without confusion of the Persons. And yet this purpose remains modest: it is a matter of studying in order to grasp but a little. Knowledge of the mystery of God given by revelation is compared to a little drop *(parva stilla)*. And this "little drop" of God's mystery is presented to us in Sacred Scripture in the form of similitudes and words that are at times obscure, "in such a way that only studious men can succeed in understanding a little, while others revere these mysteries as hidden, and unbelievers cannot tear them off."[227] Envisaged in this way, Trinitarian theology is a form of study practiced as an exercise and addressed to believers, in order to elevate their minds to the contemplation of God and to make them search for God who is known by faith and loved by charity. St. Thomas expresses this purpose with the words of St. Hilary of Poitiers in his commentary on Boethius's *De Trinitate*, in the *Summa contra gentiles*, and in the disputed questions *De potentia*. Here is the intention and the very nature of speculative Trinitarian theology (with a clear mention of the "exercise" carried out by means of inquiry into "reasons"):

It is useful for the human mind to exercise itself with such reasons, however weak they are [*utile tamen est ut in huiusmodi rationibus, quantumcumque debilibus, se mens humana exerceat*], provided there be not presumptuous attempt to comprehend or demonstrate. For the ability to perceive something of the highest realities, if only with feeble, limited understanding, gives the greatest joy.... In accord with this thought, St. Hilary declares in his book *On the Trinity*, speaking of this sort of truth: in faith, "set out, go forward, persevere. And though I may know that you will not attain the end, still I shall praise you for your progress. He who pursues the infinite with reverent devotion, even though he never attains it, always profits nonetheless from advancing forward. But in penetrating this secret, in plunging into the hidden depth of this birth unlimited (the generation of the one God begotten by the one unbegotten God), beware of presumptu-

227. *SCG* IV, ch. 1 (no. 3345): "Haec etiam pauca quae nobis revelantur, sub quibusdam similitudinibus et obscuritatibus nobis proponuntur: ut ad ea quomodocumque capienda soli studiosi perveniant, alii vero quasi occulta venerentur, et increduli lacerare non possint." This prologue is placed at the beginning of the study of the mystery of the Trinity and of Christ.

ously thinking you have attained a full understanding. Know, rather, that this is incomprehensible."[228]

This exercise is an "elevation of the mind"[229] so as to be made more like God, in an inquiry which tends always "more and more" toward God.[230] We cannot know the essence of God the Trinity, but we can "tend" *(tendere)* toward the mystery above ourselves *(superius)*, through contemplation, in order to know and love him more.[231]

In conclusion, the speculative objective of Thomas Aquinas in Trinitarian theology must not be opposed to the spiritual objective of Augustine. Admittedly there are important differences. Thomas does not present the details of the complex developments of the inquiry as Augustine does; instead he observes another *ordo disciplinae.* Thomas exposes the results of his inquiry *(via expositionis)* rather than the path that led to these results *(via inventionis).* In addition, Thomas's doctrinal resources are many and varied. His Trinitarian theology is intended to be academic. It distinguishes (without separating!) infused wisdom given by God from the wisdom acquired through study. But despite these and other differences, Thomas remains faithful to the spiritual objective of Augustine. He has taken up in his own explanations, in an academic theology, the fundamental intuitions of the bishop of Hippo. Both the nature and purpose of Trinitarian theology in these two doctors are similar in a way that would surprise readers accustomed to a rationalist reading of Thomas: speculative Trinitarian theology constitutes an exercise, an elevation of the believing mind, a training in order to see God, which procures a foretaste of the beatific vision and makes it possible to give an account of the Trinitarian faith.

228. *SCG* I, ch. 8 (nos. 49–50). Cf. *De potentia,* q. 9, a. 5; *Super Boetium de Trinitate,* q. 2, a. 1, ad 7. St. Hilary of Poitiers, *De Trinitate,* II, 10–11 (cf. *Sources Chrétiennes* 443, 294–297). It is a question here of the eternal generation of the Son.

229. *De potentia,* q. 9, a. 5: "Nec talis inquisitio est inutilis, cum per eam elevetur animus ad aliquid veritatis capiendum quod sufficiat ad excludendos errores. Unde Hilarius dicit."

230. *Super Boetium de Trinitate,* q. 2, a. 1, ad 7: "Humana mens semper debet moveri ad cognoscendum de Deo plus et plus secundum modum suum; unde dicit Hilarius."

231. Cf. *Super Dionysium de divinis nominibus* I, lect. 1 (Marietti ed., no. 15).

2

Aquinas the Augustinian?

On the Uses of Augustine in Aquinas's Trinitarian Theology

Bruce D. Marshall

Pia expositio patrum: A Case Study

Deep in the *Summa theologiae*'s questions on the Trinity, St. Thomas Aquinas detects a problem in the Trinitarian theology of St. Augustine. The issue, very extensively discussed in medieval Trinitarian theology from the twelfth century on, is whether the divine essence generates, or is generated—whether the essence itself, and not merely one or another of the divine Persons, can rightly be said to generate or beget anything, or to be generated or begotten by anything. The answer is an emphatic no: "The essence does not generate the essence."[1] Generating and being generated are each characteristics which are proper or unique to a divine Person (to the Father and to the Son, respectively). And, Aquinas says, "those things which are proper to the persons, the characteristics by which they are distinguished from one another, cannot be attributed to the essence" (*ST* I, q. 39, a. 5, c). In defense of this judgment Aquinas offers a semantic argument, the details of which need not concern us here, about modes of signification and the supposition of terms.[2] But in any

---

1. *ST* I, q. 39, a. 5, s.c. I will cite the *Summa theologiae* parenthetically in the text following the Latin text in the Blackfriars edition. Unless otherwise noted, all translations are my own.
2. On the argument itself, see Bruce D. Marshall, "In Search of an Analytic Aquinas: Grammar

case Lateran IV had, some fifty years earlier, already condemned the teaching, which it associated with Joachim of Fiore, that the divine essence generates or is generated.[3] The question that interests Aquinas is not whether it is wrong to hold that the essence generates, but why.

Unhappily, Aquinas observes, no less an authority on the Trinity than St. Augustine apparently held precisely that the essence does generate. In book VII of *De Trinitate,* near the conclusion of an involved discussion of what would later be called Trinitarian appropriations, Augustine says that "the Father and the Son are one wisdom because they are one essence, and taken one by one they are wisdom from wisdom, just as they are essence from essence."[4] This evidently entails what Thomas himself has just denied, that when the Father generates the Son, it happens that the essence generates the essence. Surely the divine essence could not be "from" any essence other than itself, and could not be from anything unless some kind of generation were involved, so Aquinas takes it to be obvious that Augustine's "essentia de essentia" implies the rightly rejected "essentia generat essentiam."

What shall we do when the highest authority among the Fathers in matters pertaining to the Trinity apparently got it wrong? In spite of his standing, Aquinas firmly replies, we do not follow Augustine on this point, lest we repeat his mistake. Instead we correct him. Or perhaps more precisely, we find a way of interpreting him *in optimam partem,* so that whatever their surface meaning, his utterances come out in conformity to a correct view of the matter. When it comes to problems about essence and person in the Trinity, Aquinas points out, "the holy teachers sometimes went beyond what correct speech allows. In such cases we do not repeat what they said, but explain it."[5] What

---

and the Trinity," in *Grammar and Grace,* ed. Robert MacSwain and Jeffrey Stout (London: SCM Press, 2004), 55–74.

3. See especially DH 804 (=*Enchiridion symbolorum definitionum et declarationum de rebus fidei et morum,* ed. Heinrich Denzinger and Peter Hünermann, 40th ed. [Freiburg: Herder, 2005]), and the essays cited in notes 2 above and 20 below.

4. *De Trinitate,* VII, 3. I will cite the *De Trinitate* by book and section number, following the enumeration in *CCL* 50 and 50A, and omitting the intervening chapter numbers. Page and line references are to this edition (here: *CCL* 50, p. 250.22–23).

5. *ST* I, q. 39, a. 5, ad 1: "Ad exprimendam unitatem essentiae et personae sancti doctores aliquando expressius locuti sunt quam proprietas locutionis patiatur. Unde huiusmodi locutiones non sunt extendendae sed exponendae." The practice of putting the best construction on an authoritative text *(authentica scriptura)* applies across the board, and not only to Augustine. Reflecting on the statement "Solus Pater est Deus," for example, Aquinas observes that while it admits of a benign interpretation, nonetheless "non est extendenda talis locutio sed exponenda, sicubi inveniatur in authentica scriptura." *ST* I, q. 31, a. 4, c.

Augustine really meant to say when he let "the essence is from the essence" go through is "the Son, who is the essence . . . is from the Father, who is the essence" (*ST* I, q. 39, a. 5, ad 1). By supplying a concrete term where Augustine used an abstract one, we can bring what he said in line with a right view of what does and does not generate in God, and so uphold his high standing as an authority on Trinitarian questions, as on all matters theological.

Essentialism?

Though the problem so far discussed may seem technical, even arcane, it has to do with perhaps the most basic of all theological questions about the Trinity. How do we understand the Father, the Son, and the Holy Spirit to be in truth one God? How, in other words, do we understand the three to be really distinct from one another, but not really distinct from the one God? For Augustine and Aquinas alike, the three can be one God just in case they not only have, but are, one divine essence. So questions about the precise connection between essence and person, about what Aquinas calls "the unity of essence and person" (*ST* I, q. 39, a. 5, ad 1), are at the heart of the Trinitarian matter.

On just this point, though, recent Trinitarian theology has tended to find Augustine badly wanting. Although he clearly intends to maintain the real distinction of Father, Son, and Spirit together with their unity as the one God (see, among other passages, *De Trinitate,* I, 7; V, 10; VI, 12; VII, 9; IX, 1), in practice his Trinitarian theology lapses into a virtually unmitigated essentialism. Augustine, so this now standard line of objection goes, finds the real distinction of the three from one another a hopeless puzzle and allows it to disappear into the sheer unity and simplicity of the divine essence. His "essentia de essentia," offered precisely as a way of understanding the eternal generation by which the Father and the Son are distinguished from one another (cf. *De Trinitate,* I, 7), seems like a perfect index of this impersonal essentialism. The generation of the Son by the Father is simply a relation of the divine essence to itself. But since there is only one divine essence, any relation of the essence to itself is entirely in our minds, a mere product of thought. It is not a real, but a purely conceptual relation, and supports no real distinction of Son from Father. As a result, so the argument goes, the radical distinctions among the divine Persons on display in the economy of salvation, distinctions which have room for sending and being sent, command and obedience, dying and raising from the dead, are reduced by Augustine to mere appearance. The interpersonal drama presented in the economy is not really the triune God's own gift of Himself to the world, but a kind of shadow dance put on by an impersonal monad. This reading of Augustine on the Trinity is now common among systematic theologians.[6]

With this take on Augustine often goes the assumption that the Western Trinitarian tradition is, until the twentieth century, mostly just a series of footnotes to Augustine, an endlessly repetitive millennial project of elaborating and refining his essentialist outlook. It is therefore striking to observe that when he gets even a whiff of essentialism in Augustine, Aquinas is quick to reject it. To be sure, Thomas refuses to believe that Augustine was actually an essentialist. He is too important a theological figure, too high an authority, to have made such a profound blunder. But the fact that Aquinas finds himself

6. The charge of "essentialism" against Augustine is made in a variety of ways and need not use the term. Wolfhart Pannenberg gives a standard version of the claim: "A solution [to 'the problem of the relation between divine unity and plurality'] might be attempted by insisting on the unity of the divine essence *(Wesen)* prior to all Trinitarian differentiation, and by defining this unity in such a way as to rule out any idea of substantial distinction, even at the cost of making the differentiation of the three 'persons' in God an impenetrable secret. Augustine took this path in his work on the Trinity" *(Systematic Theology,* vol. 1, trans. Geoffrey W. Bromily [Grand Rapids, MI: Eerdmans, 1991], 283; translation slightly altered). The problem is then put down, at root, to Augustine's notion of God's simplicity (284). For Karl Rahner the basic problem with "the Augustinian-Western conception of the Trinity" is that "it begins with the one God, the one divine essence as a whole, and only afterwards does it see God as three in persons"; from this stems "a Trinity which is absolutely locked within itself," fatally isolated from the economy of salvation *(The Trinity,* trans. Joseph Donceel, 2nd ed. [New York: Crossroads, 1997], 17–18). In what sense Augustine (as opposed, for example, to the Thomas of the *Summa theologiae*) "begins" with the divine essence rather than the Trinity of persons Rahner does not say, and in any case "beginning" there need not have, and in Aquinas clearly does not have, the consequences that worry Rahner (on this, see Bruce D. Marshall, "The Trinity," in *The Blackwell Companion to Modern Theology,* ed. Gareth Jones [Oxford: Blackwell, 2004], 183–203). Eastern Orthodox theologians regularly make the essentialist charge against Western theology in expansive terms. Of these perhaps the most influential is Vladimir Lossky, though his main target is Aquinas, not Augustine. On this see my essay, *"Ex Occidente Lux?* Aquinas and Eastern Orthodox Theology," *Modern Theology* 20 (2004): 23–50.

Recent opposition to Augustine on the Trinity is not confined to the worry about essentialism. For an especially sweeping repudiation of Augustine's Trinitarian theology, see Colin E. Gunton, "Augustine, the Trinity, and the Theological Crisis of the West," in *The Promise of Trinitarian Theology,* 2nd ed. (Edinburgh: T&T Clark, 2004), 30–55. John C. Cavadini gives a close reading of the *De Trinitate* which shows how implausible is Gunton's suggestion that Augustine aims to know God in a wholly interior way, cut off from both the economy of salvation and human community; see "The Quest for Truth in Augustine's *De Trinitate,*" *Theological Studies* 58 (1997): 429–40; also the essay cited in note 17 below. On some of the historical and theological assumptions which underlie this anti-Augustinian mood, see Michel René Barnes, "Augustine in Contemporary Trinitarian Theology," *Theological Studies* 56 (1995): 237–50.

compelled, at least in this place, explicitly to correct what Augustine said in order to avoid imputing error to him naturally raises a broader question. To what extent does Aquinas really follow Augustine in Trinitarian theology?

Of course Aquinas, like virtually every scholastic writer on the Trinity in the Middle Ages, is more deeply engaged with Augustine than with any other patristic figure. No text of Augustine gets more attention from Thomas than the *De Trinitate,* and very many of the topics and formulas that preoccupy Aquinas and other medieval Trinitarian theologians can be traced to their involvement with this work.[7] They very rarely take explicit issue with Augustine, even in the modest manner to which we have just seen Aquinas resort.

But these surface features of the medieval encounter with Augustine on the Trinity do not by themselves tell us how closely Aquinas, or any other medieval theologian, really follows Augustine on this topic. In order to offer at least a partial answer to this question, we need to see how close the two theologians are on substantive Trinitarian matters. Here I will consider only the issue which is already on the table: Trinitarian essentialism and how properly to avoid it. About this Aquinas suggests, however gently, that he sees the matter more clearly than Augustine. In order to assess the justice of this suggestion, we need first to look at what Aquinas actually knew of Augustine's texts on the Trinity, and how he read them. As it turns out, the question about whether the essence generates provides considerable insight on this score.

Aquinas as Reader of Lombard, and of Augustine

Strikingly, Aquinas's patristic authority for the rejection of "essentia generat" in the passage with which we began is none other than St. Augustine (see *ST* I, q. 39, a. 5, s.c.), who also said, at the beginning of *De Trinitate,* that nothing generates itself.[8] This clearly implies that the one divine essence does not generate itself, no more than anything else brings itself to be. "Essentia generat" is therefore false when used to describe the Father's begetting of the Son; since the Son's generation can involve no numerical multiplication of

---

7. Leo Elders's "Les citations de Saint Augustin dans la *Somme théologique* de saint Thomas d'Aquin" (*Doctor Communis* 40 [1987]: 115–67) is little more than a catalogue of passages from Augustine which show up in the articles of the *Summa theologiae.* But it gives a good idea of the wide range of Augustinian texts upon which Aquinas draws, and of the particular prominence the *De Trinitate* has among them, across a variety of topics besides the Trinity itself.

8. *De Trinitate,* I, 1 (*CCL* 50, 28.35–36): "Nulla enim omnino res est quae se ipsam gignat ut sit."

the divine essence, Augustine's principle rules out any generation of the essence in the begetting of the Son. By correcting Augustine on this Trinitarian question, Aquinas silently suggests, we are really just making Augustine consistent with himself. He allowed *essentia de essentia,* that the essence generates the essence, but he really knew better, as his own arguments show.

Aquinas might also have noticed that Augustine, when he allows *essentia de essentia,* quickly goes on to develop a formulation quite similar to the one Thomas introduces to correct him. Having argued that the Son of God is "wisdom from wisdom" (*De Trinitate,* VII, 3), Augustine then returns to the troubling question of how to interpret 1 Corinthians 1:24: "'Christ is the power and wisdom of God' just because he is from the *Father,* who is power and who is wisdom; thus he himself is power and wisdom, just as he himself is light, from the *Father* who is light."[9] Near the end of the work he is even more explicit. To say that the Word of God is "born of the Father's essence" *(natum est de patris essentia)* is equivalent to saying that he is born "of the Father's knowledge" or "of the Father's wisdom."[10] But a more precise way of putting such things is to say that the Word is born "of the *Father,* who is knowledge," or "of the *Father,* who is wisdom."[11] Augustine does not go on to add explicitly that the Word is born of the Father, "who is the essence," perhaps because it seems too obvious for comment. Having begun by asking how to understand "the Father's essence," of which the Word is born, the implied conclusion is clearly that this should be taken to mean "the Father," of whom the Word is born, "is the essence." Moreover Augustine consistently pairs "sapientia de sapientia" with "essentia de essentia"—as in the passage from *De Trinitate,* VII, 3, which worries Aquinas. He evidently regards the logic of the two as the same.

As we saw at the outset, substituting concrete, and especially personal, terms (like "Son" and "Father") for abstract ones (like "essence") is precisely

---

9. *De Trinitate,* VII, 4 (*CCL* 50, 251.28–252.30), emphasis added : "Et ideo Christus virtus et sapientia dei quia de patre virtute et sapientia etiam ipse virtus et sapientia est sicut lumen de patre lumine." Similarly: "Sapientia ergo filius de sapientia patre sicut lumen de lumine et deus de deo." Ibid. (*CCL* 50, 252.40–41).

10. *De Trinitate,* XV, 22 (*CCL* 50A, 495.48–49). Augustine's use of "de patris essentia" here (cf. XV, 38 [*CCL* 50A, 515.4–5]: "de substantia patris genitum") may descend from "de substantia Patris" in an early Latin version of the creed of 325 (cf. DH 125, which reproduces the text from Hilary of Poitiers, *De Synodis,* 84). The phrase is absent from the creed of 381. Cf. DH 150.

11. *De Trinitate,* XV, 22 (*CCL* 50A, 495.48–50), emphasis added: "Quod est expressius, 'de patre scientia, de patre sapientia.'"

the strategy Aquinas will later use to deal with locutions like "essentia de essentia."[12] Augustine, it appears, needs no *pia expositio* from Aquinas on this point. The bishop of Hippo explains himself clearly, in almost exactly the same terms that Aquinas will one day think it necessary to employ in order to rescue the holy teacher from his own apparent verbal excess.

Why does Aquinas—who can hardly be accused of indifference toward the teaching of Augustine—fail to notice this? One of the chief ways the texts of Augustine reach scholastic theologians in the thirteenth century is by way of Peter Lombard's *Sententiae.* So one might perhaps think that Thomas was largely dependent on Lombard for what he knew of the *De Trinitate,* and simply did not know the passages in which Augustine offers an explanation of "essentia de essentia" almost identical to the one Thomas himself would also work out. Were this the case, then Thomas's reinvention of the wheel at this juncture would actually be a tribute to his fidelity to the mind of Augustine.

In fact, however, the texts we have just cited from Augustine (along with many others) are in Lombard, at just the place where the problem of whether the essence generates comes in for extended treatment.[13] These texts are, moreover, the basis for Lombard's own argument that Augustine does not, despite "essentia de essentia," really attribute generation to the divine essence, since Augustine himself explains that, properly speaking, the Father, not wisdom, power, or the essence, generates. Citing *De Trinitate,* VII, 4 (the Son is power and wisdom "just because he is from the Father, who is power, and who is wisdom"), Lombard comments: "Note that by these words Augustine openly explains in what sense the previous sayings and those like them are to be taken, that is, when he says, 'Substance from substance,' or, 'Sub-

---

12. Aquinas makes a modest distinction between the two cases. "Sapientia de sapientia" is "less improper" than "essentia de essentia," because, as he sees it, "wisdom" is slightly closer to designating a personal act than "essence." But he thinks both cases should still be handled in the same way. In this he agrees with Augustine, and the solution he offers is the one Augustine had already proposed: "the Son, who is the essence and wisdom, is from the Father, who is the essence and wisdom" (*ST* I, q. 39, a. 5, ad 1). Aquinas makes the same kind of distinction when he first treats *essentia generat* in his *Scriptum* on Lombard's *Sentences,* and he offers the same solution, including the suggestion that patristic attributions of generation to wisdom, nature, or essence "non sunt extendendae, sed pie intelligendae"—though without reference to any text of Augustine. *In I Sent.* 5, 1, 2, sol.*(Scriptum super libros Sententiarum,* vol. 1, ed. R. P. Mandonnet [Paris: Lethielleux, 1929]).

13. The passage from *De Trinitate,* VII, 4 (above, note 9) is in *Sent.* I, 5, 1 (8) (*Magistri Petri Lombardi Sententiae in IV libris distinctae,* 3rd ed. [Grottaferrata: Editiones Collegii S. Bonaventurae Ad Claras Aquas, 1971], vol. 1, part 2, 83.14–20), the one from XV, 22 (above, notes 10–11) in *Sent.* I, 5, 2 (4) (*Magistri Petri Lombardi,* 88.17–22). The quotations are virtually exact, with one significant addition in the second case (see below, note 18).

stance generates substance.'"[14] Lombard cannot be faulted for failing to provide Aquinas with sufficient textual resources to see how Augustine actually
understood notions like "essentia de essentia" or for failing to point out what
Augustine evidently meant.[15]

Thomas was, of course, well acquainted with the text of Lombard's *Sentences*. Like most university theologians from the mid-thirteenth century on,
he lectured extensively on it as the last major step in preparation for a university teaching position, and in his case the classroom work yielded a mas-
sive literary product, his *Scriptum* (primarily, in fact, a set of *quaestiones*) on
all four books of the *Sentences*. It is therefore remarkable to observe that in
his own analysis of the issues raised in book I, distinction 5, of the *Sentences*,
where Lombard wrestles in detail with "whether the essence generates" and
cognate questions, Aquinas mentions not even one of the many texts from
Augustine which Lombard introduces on both sides of the issue. None, more
precisely, comes up in the *quaestiones* Aquinas elicits from Lombard's discussion (that is, the five articles which make up *In I Sent.* 5, 1–3).[16]

Some of these Augustinian texts do appear in the *prima pars,* including,
of course, the "essentia de essentia" passage from *De Trinitate,* VII, 3, which
Aquinas thinks is in need of correction. Some scholars have argued that the
presence in the *Summa theologiae* and other mature writings of Aquinas of
texts from Augustine which are absent from the early *Scriptum* must mean
that after the *Scriptum,* Aquinas read firsthand the works of Augustine that he
later cites. This case has been made for the *De Trinitate* in particular, with the
suggestion that through careful study of the original text, Thomas achieved
an unprecedented mastery of Augustine's own position in that work.[17]

---

14. *Sent.* I, 5, 1 (8) (*Magistri Petri Lombardi,* 83.20–23). Similarly, commenting on *De Trinitate,* XV,
22, Lombard observes that "by these words [Augustine] shows that a person must not be said to be
from the essence." *Sent.* I, 5, 2 (4) (*Magistri Petri Lombardi,* 88.15–16).

15. Long dismissed as a mere compiler—not least by Thomists—Lombard is now beginning to get
his due as a theologian in his own right. See Philipp W. Rosemann, *Peter Lombard* (New York: Oxford
University Press, 2004); and Marcia L. Colish, *Peter Lombard,* 2 vols. (Leiden: Brill, 1994).

16. One of the Augustine texts in Lombard does draw explicit attention in Thomas's *expositio textus* on this distinction, and Thomas alludes to several others (see *Scriptum,* vol. 1, 159–62). But none
of these texts has any direct bearing on the debate about whether the essence generates, and Aquinas
brings them up to deal with other questions.

17. See D. Juvenal Merriell, *To the Image of the Trinity: A Study in the Development of Aquinas's
Teaching* (Toronto: Pontifical Institute of Mediaeval Studies, 1990). Merriell traces Thomas's growing
sophistication on the human being as the created image of the triune God to a direct and extensive
study of Augustine's own writings: "Thomas arrived at his fine comprehension of Augustine's *De Trinitate* through a careful study of the text" (243). As a result, Merriell suggests, Aquinas "towers above"

At least with regard to the issues that come up in *Sentences* I, dist. 5, however, there is little evidence of this. Of the two main texts already in Lombard where Augustine explains that it is the Father, not the essence itself, who generates the Son, one (*De Trinitate,* VII, 4) never appears in the *Summa theologiae*'s questions on the Trinity. A fragment of the other (*De Trinitate,* XV, 22) does come up (in *ST* I, q. 41, a. 3, ad 2). But the passage is clearly cited from Lombard, not directly from Augustine. Moreover, Aquinas oddly reverses the language, and with that the intended point, of the Augustinian fragment he cites—the point intended, indeed, by Aquinas himself, as well as by Lombard and, ultimately, by Augustine. This suggests that he is not only quoting Augustine from Lombard, but doing so from somewhat imperfect memory.

In all this one may still perhaps discern that Aquinas recognizes Augustine's own interpretation of *essentia de essentia,* though at best indirectly, while he is on the way to making another point.[18] Either way, the use Thom-

---

previous readers of Augustine (ibid.). "Thomas came to understand how the *De Trinitate* works as a whole and so arrived at a better understanding of Augustine's doctrine than his predecessors" (35).

This claim about Thomas's mastery of the *De Trinitate* depends on Merriell's own reading of Augustine, which takes the whole work to center on Augustine's search for an adequate way of distinguishing the procession of the Holy Spirit from the procession of the Son. "The key question of the *De Trinitate*" thus becomes "why is the procession of love not a kind of generation?" (229), and Augustine's distinction (*De Trinitate,* XV, 50) between the procession of an interior word (which is an image of its source) and of interior love (which is not) becomes at once the answer to this Trinitarian question and the key to Augustine's understanding of the image of God. Especially in the *prima pars* Aquinas offers a developed account of this distinction and its application to the question of the image, so Merriell credits him with seeing what the *De Trinitate* is, as a whole, about. Merriell grants that neither the distinction between the two processions nor its Trinitarian application receives much explicit attention in the *De Trinitate* (34), but remains confident that technical questions of this sort, extensively discussed by Aquinas and other scholastic theologians, must nonetheless lie at the heart of Augustine's work. For a different reading of the aims of the *De Trinitate,* in its own historical context rather than through medieval eyes, see especially John C. Cavadini, "The Structure and Intention of Augustine's *De Trinitate*," *Augustinian Studies* 23 (1992): 103–23.

18. The pertinent lines in Augustine from which Thomas's quotation ultimately stems are as follows: "[Verbum dei] natum est de patris essentia. (Tale est autem ac si dicerem, 'de patris scientia, de patris sapientia'; vel quod est expressius, 'de patre scientia, de patre sapientia'" (*De Trinitate,* XV, 22; *CCL* 50A, 495.48–51; cf. above, notes 10–11). The quotation in Lombard is identical, save for one telling addition: "vel quod est expressius, de Patre essentia, de Patre scientia, de Patre sapientia'" (*Sent.* I, 5, 2 [4] [88.20–22]; cf. above, note 13). The addition of "de Patre essentia" has, according to the *CCL* editor (cf. *CCL* 50A, 495, 583), no support in the manuscript tradition of Augustine's *De Trinitate,* but wherever it originates, it serves the useful purpose of underlining for Lombard the point he wants to make, namely, that when Augustine says the Son is born or begotten "of the essence of the Father," he really means "of the Father, who is the essence." In the *prima pars* the passage now reads: "Augustinus dicit, 'Tale est quod dico de Patre essentia, acsi expressius dicerem, de Patris essentia'" (*ST* I, q. 41, a. 3, ad 2). The attribution of "de Patre essentia" to Augustine no doubt springs from Lombard, who is also quoted here by name. But Aquinas has Augustine saying "When I say 'from the Father, who is

as makes here of this important Augustinian text on *essentia de essentia* is better explained by assuming that Aquinas reread Lombard in preparation for a second course of lectures on the *Sentences*—the so-called "Roman Commentary," abandoned after book I in order to take up the *Summa theologiae*—than by supposing that Aquinas had made a direct study of the relevant sections of *De Trinitate,* XV.[19]

---

the essence' a more precise way of speaking would be 'from the essence of the Father.'" This has the words in Lombard, and Augustine's ultimate point, backwards; it attributes to Augustine the sort of "essentialist" inclination which both the original text and Lombard's use of it aim to avoid. This is especially curious, because in the very process of misquoting Lombard's Augustine here, Thomas apparently attributes to Augustine—as he does not in *ST* I, q. 39, a. 5, ad 1—what he sees as the right view of "de essentia": "the Master in *Sent.* I . . . interprets 'the Son is begotten of the essence of the Father' *(de essentia Patris)* as 'of the Father, who is the essence' *(de Patre essentia)* on account of what Augustine says, 'Tale est . . . .'"

Thomas is, to be sure, worried about a different problem here, although he notes a connection to the earlier discussion of whether the essence generates (cf. *ST* I, q. 41, a. 3, obj. 2). The present problem is what to make of statements like "the Son is begotten from the essence of the Father" *(Filius est genitus de essentia Patris),* as opposed to saying that the Son comes forth "from nothing" *(de nihilo,* cf. I, 41, pro.). This problem leads Aquinas to argue that "genitus de essentia Patris" cannot be handled in an adequate way simply by taking "de essentia Patris" to mean "de Patre essentia," thereby attributing the act of generation to the Father, and not to the essence. While correct as far as it goes, this solution by itself fails to note an important element of truth in "genitus de essentia Patris," namely the (numerical) consubstantiality in God of the begetter and the begotten. This, Aquinas here argues, we can get at by an analysis of the "de" in "genitus de essentia Patris." Cf. *ST* I, q. 41, a. 3, ad 2, in fin.

19. Merriell argues that new quotations from the *De Trinitate* in the *Summa theologiae* and elsewhere must come from Thomas's direct engagement with Augustine, since they reflect a deepened understanding of Augustine's own position. But he never asks whether the quoted texts are in Lombard, the *Glossa ordinaria,* or other medieval compilations known to Thomas, and so might be taken from these later sources. The recently edited "Roman Commentary" gives no evidence that Thomas, on the eve of the *prima pars,* had discovered any Augustinian texts on "utrum essentia generet" which he did not already know from Lombard. On the contrary: in the "Roman Commentary," as in the earlier *Scriptum,* no text of Augustine appears in the discussion of this question, and the pertinent texts from *De Trinitate* VII.4 and XV.22 do not appear anywhere in the work. Rather the "Roman Commentary" explicitly credits Lombard with having seen the issue clearly, while Augustine is the implicit *auctoritas* who needs to be corrected. See Thomas Aquinas, *Lectura romana in primum Sententiarum Petri Lombardi,* ed. Leonard E. Boyle and John F. Boyle (Toronto: Pontifical Institute of Mediaeval Studies, 2006), 5.1.1, ll. 18–22 (126).

Whether the "Roman Commentary" really is the *reportatio* of lectures by Aquinas on *I Sent.* at the Dominican studium in Rome (1265–66) remains disputed. Jean-Pierre Torrell has withdrawn his earlier endorsement of this claim. See his *Saint Thomas Aquinas,* vol. 1: *The Person and His Work,* rev. ed., trans. Robert Royal (Washington, DC: The Catholic University of America Press, 2005), pp. 45–47, and the correction on 412; see also "Lire saint Thomas autrement," Fr. Torrell's introduction to Leonard E. Boyle, *Facing History: A Different Thomas Aquinas* (Louvain-la-neuve: Fédération Internationale des Instituts d'Études Médiévales, 2000), especially xxi–xxiv. In "Aquinas' Roman Commentary on Peter Lombard," *Anuario Filosofico* 39/2 (2006), 477–96, John Boyle defends the claim that the text originates with St. Thomas; see also his "Introduction" to *Lectura romana,* 16.

Why, then, does Aquinas fail to notice that Augustine already agrees with him about how to understand *essentia de essentia?* Not because the textual facts are hidden from view—Lombard provides him with the relevant evidence—but because he reads Augustine in a characteristically scholastic way. Since it stems from the hand of an especially holy teacher on an especially important matter, the *De Trinitate* is surely *authentica scriptura,* an authoritative text. For just this reason, Aquinas, like other scholastic readers of *De Trinitate,* is highly sensitive to language in Augustine that might be cited in support of erroneous, let alone heretical, positions on the Trinity. He is therefore quite concerned to show that apparently dubious passages in a text like the *De Trinitate* can be given an acceptable interpretation, but whether the saint who wrote the text supplied that interpretation himself seems not to be decisive, or even especially important, for our understanding of his authoritative words. Whether Augustine was actually aware of the right way to take *essentia de essentia* does not seem to worry Aquinas very much. What matters is that we can identify a logically and linguistically plausible way to take what he says, and explain the theological sense his words make when we take them that way.

In all this Aquinas, whether he reads Augustine through Lombard or firsthand, evidently finds in the *De Trinitate* not so much a set of solutions to be adopted as a set of problems to be solved. In the process of solving the particular problem of whether essence or person generates in God, Aquinas does Augustine's own view of this matter considerably less than justice. Writing in the wake of the rejection of Trinitarian essentialism at Lateran IV, Aquinas is not chiefly concerned to establish that only a divine Person, and not the divine essence, can generate or be generated. This he regards as basic. So while he ought to have known that Augustine was in fact clear on this point, doing justice to Augustine would not have advanced his main purpose. Like others who come before and after him, he wants compelling reasons why "essentia generat" must be wrong, and whenever the question comes up he devotes most of his attention to finding such reasons. The reasons he finds owe more, as we observed at the outset, to medieval semantic theories than to Augustine or, for that matter, to Lombard.[20]

---

20. On Aquinas's place in the medieval debate over how to argue against "essentia generet," from William of Auxerre to William of Ockham, see my essay "*Utrum essentia generet:* Semantics and Metaphysics in Later Medieval Trinitarian Theology," in *Trinitarian Theology in the Medieval West,* ed. Pekka Kärkkäinen (Helsinki: Luther-Agricola Society, 2007).

Relation, Essence, and Personal Distinction

So far Thomas's suspicion of essentialist outcroppings in Augustine seems, on Thomas's own terms, simply unwarranted. When the question explicitly arises whether essence can do the work of person in God—in particular, whether the essence can do the work of generating the Son and bringing forth the Spirit, without which there would be no distinction of the Persons from one another—Augustine's answer, like Thomas's, is clearly no. But the problem remains of how exactly to account for the distinction of the Persons without sacrificing the unity of essence.

Here the concept of relation plays a pivotal role in Aquinas's Trinitarian theology. "Is it relations that distinguish and constitute the [divine] Persons?" Thomas asks in the *prima pars* (*ST* I, q. 40, pro.), and here he gives an unambiguously affirmative answer (*ST* I, q. 40, a. 2). God is not a monad because there are present *in divinis* mutual and irreducible relations, which suffice to distinguish Father, Son, and Spirit from one another without prejudice to God's unity. This is a contested claim in medieval theology; not everybody agrees with Aquinas's reliance on relation, rather than mode of origin, to account for the real distinction among the Persons of the Trinity.[21] Though

---

21. In the *Scriptum* Aquinas seems not yet to have entirely settled on the idea that opposed relations, rather than different modes of origin, are person-constituting in God. There he allows that a relation of origin, in order to constitute a person, must "involve a specific mode of origin" *(determinetur per specialem modum originis),* and suggests that the Son and the Spirit are distinguished from the Father just by being from the Father in two different ways, namely by generation and by spiration (*In I Sent.* 10, 1, 5, sol.). By the time of the *Summa theologiae* he seems firmly fixed on the idea that opposed relation and mode of origin are two irreconcilable ways of accounting for personal distinction in God, and that the one works, while the other does not: "it is against the very notion of origin that it constitute a hypostasis or person" *(contra rationem originis est quod constituat hypostasim vel personam); ST* I, q. 40, a. 2, c.

This may fairly be called Thomas's standard view, often repeated, but even after the *prima pars* ambiguities can appear. In *Quodlibet* IV, 4, 2, which dates from Thomas's second Parisian regency, he strongly affirms the standard view in the *sed contra,* with reference to Boethius and Anselm. But in the *corpus* of this brief article Thomas argues that while the Son is distinguished from the Father by opposed relation, he is distinguished from the Holy Spirit by possessing the property of characteristic of *filiatio,* which the Spirit does not have: "Filius sua filiatione distinguitur quidem a Patre secundum oppositionem relatiuam filiationis ad paternitatem, sed a Spiritu sancto distinguitur filiatione per hoc quod Spiritus sanctus non habet filiationem quam Filium habet" (Leonine ed., vol. 25/2, 327.40–45). This same view he elsewhere sharply rejects, also at the time of the second Parisian regency. "Si igitur Filius et Spiritus Sanctus sunt personae distinctae procedentes a Patre, oportet quod aliquibus proprietatibus oppositis distinguantur: non autem oppositis secundum affirmationem et negationem aut secundum privationem et habitum, quia sic Filius et Spiritus Sanctus se haberent ad invicem sicut ens et non ens" (*Super Ioannem* 15, 5, no. 2063, ed. Raphael Cai [Turin: Marietti, 1952]; cf. *ST* I, 36, 2.c).

Aquinas's favorite authority on this point is Boethius, it is Augustine who introduces into the Western tradition the idea (which is not entirely original with him) that relation is the conceptual key to understanding the distinctions, utterly basic to Christian faith, between Father, Son, and Spirit.[22] Thomas thus seems to follow Augustine at this crucial juncture.

"Father" and "son," Augustine observes, are relative terms. They retain their relative character when applied to God: "Son and Father are said relatively to one another."[23] When we apply the term "Father" to God we introduce a reference to the Son, and so are speaking of a relation rather than of a substance; the same goes when we apply the term "Son" to God. Thus we have two different ways of speaking about God, two different kinds of categories we can apply to God. "Not everything which is said [of God] is said by way of substance *(secundum substantiam)*. Some things are said with reference to another *(dicitur . . . ad aliquid),* as Father is said with reference to Son, and Son with reference to Father."[24] God, however, is unchangeable, which means on Augustine's account that God can have no accidents or modifications distinct from his substance. The relations we ascribe to God when we apply the terms "Father" and "Son" to him are not, therefore, accidents distinct from his substance. And this slices cleanly to the heart of the Trinitarian matter. "Although to be the Father is one thing and to be the Son another, nevertheless they are not different substances, because these things are not said of them by way of substance, but by way of relation. Yet the relation is not an accident because it is not mutable."[25]

On the medieval development of disparate Trinitarian traditions around these two notions of what distinguishes and constitutes the persons, and on the vigorous opposition, mostly from Franciscans, to Aquinas's view, see Russell L. Friedman, "Divergent Traditions in Later-Medieval Trinitarian Theology: Relations, Emanations, and the Use of Philosophical Psychology, 1250–1325," *Studia Theologica* 53 (1999): 13–25; Friedman, "Gabriel Biel and Later Medieval Trinitarian Theology," in *The Medieval Heritage in Early Modern Metaphysics and Modal Theory, 1400–1700,* ed. Russell L. Friedman and Lauge O. Nielsen (Dordrecht: Kluwer, 2003), 99–120; and Friedman, *In Principio Erat Verbum: Trinitarian Theology, Philosophical Psychology, and the Development of Intellectual Traditions Among Franciscans and Dominicans, 1250–1345* (Leiden: Brill, forthcoming). Michael Schmaus gathers a lot of material on the contrast between relation-oriented and origin-oriented medieval Trinitarian theologies in *Der "Liber propugnatorius" des Thomas Anglicus und die Lehrunterschiede zwischen Thomas von Aquin und Duns Scotus, II Teil: Die trinitarischen Lehrdifferenzen* (Münster: Aschendorff, 1930); see the useful "Rückblick," 650–66.

22. The passage Aquinas likes to cite from Boethius is from *De Trinitate,* 6: "sola relatio multiplicat Trinitatem divinarum personarum." *ST* I, q. 40, a. 2, s.c.; cf. q. 39, a. 1, c.

23. Augustine, *De Trinitate,* VII, 12 (*CCL* 50, 266.139–140).

24. *De Trinitate,* V, 6 (*CCL* 50, 210.2–4).

25. *De Trinitate,* V, 6 (*CCL* 50, 211.19–22): "Quamobrem quamvis diversum sit patrem esse et

For Augustine our understanding of the Trinity, to the extent that we have one, depends on distinguishing consistently between what is said of God by way of substance and what is said by way of relation.[26] Substantial predication gives us some grasp of the unity of the three, and relative predication a grasp of their difference. Terms like "God," "great," "good," "eternal," and "omnipotent" are said substantially of Father, Son, and Spirit.[27] These apply fully to each of the three and to all three together, and apply to each "ad se"—in and of himself, without reference to any of the others. For just this reason such predicates do not introduce any distinction of essence or substance among the three. Thus the characteristic Augustinian formulation: "The Father is God, and the Son is God, and the Holy Spirit is God . . . yet we say that this most excellent Trinity is not three gods but one God."[28] Terms like "Father," "Son," "Word," and "Gift," by contrast, are said relatively.[29] They belong to only one of the three, and not to the others or the whole triad, because they strictly require a reference to another. Such predicates do not at all belong to the one of whom they are said in and of himself, and for just this reason introduce the needed distinctions among the three. Terms which apply uniquely to one of the three, as Augustine puts it, "are in no way said of that one in and of himself, but by mutual reference *(nullo modo ad se ipsa sed ad invicem)* . . . so it is obvious that they are said relatively, and not substantially."[30]

So far so good, it seems, but problems soon set in. Augustine quickly finds reason to doubt that "Father" and "Son" can be wholly relative terms. Relations, after all, do not stand on their own. There is no relation without a sub-

---

filium esse, non est tamen diversa substantia quia hoc non secundum substantiam dicuntur sed secundum relativum, quod tamen relativum non est accidens quia non est mutabile."

26. *De Trinitate*, V, 9 (*CCL* 50, 215.1–4): "Let us first of all hold this, that whatever is said of that most excellent and divine beauty in and of itself is said substantially, while what is said with reference to another is not said substantially, but relatively" *(Quapropter illud praecipue teneamus, quidquid ad se dicitur praestantissima illa et divina sublimitas substantialiter dici; quod autem ad aliquid non substantialiter sed relative).*

27. *De Trinitate*, V, 12 (*CCL* 50, 218.4–5): "trinitas unus deus dicitur magnus, bonus, aeternus, omnipotens."

28. *De Trinitate*, V, 9 (*CCL* 50, 215.7–10): "Quemadmodum enim deus est pater et filius deus est et spiritus sanctus deus est, quod secundum substantiam dici nemo dubitat, non tamen tres deos sed unum deum dicimus eam ipsam praestantissimam trinitatem."

29. *De Trinitate*, V, 12. Cf. *De Trinitate*, VII, 3 (*CCL* 50, 250.26, 30): "The terms ['Father' and 'Son'] exhibit the relationships of each to the other *(his nominibus relativa eorum ostenduntur).* . . . We have already shown that ['Word' and 'Son'] are said relatively." For *De Trinitate*, V, 12 see the next note.

30. *De Trinitate*, V, 12 (*CCL* 50, 218.1–4).

ject which has or possesses the relation. Every relation presupposes a subject to whom it belongs, and it does not seem plausible to say that the subject just *is* the relation. "Master" and "slave," to recall one of Augustine's examples, are relational terms, but the slave is a human being, and not just someone's property, and likewise for the master. In general: "Every being *(essentia)* which is spoken of by way of relation is also something apart from the relation *(excepto relativo).*"[31] Augustine applies this directly to the Trinitarian case. "If the Father is not something in and of himself, nothing at all will be there which can be spoken of with reference to another."[32]

The difficulty is that Augustine had recently insisted on taking "Father" strictly as a relative term, which can in no way be said *ad se.* Now he apparently maintains that it has to be taken *ad se,* and not only *ad aliquid*—indeed it must be taken *ad se* precisely in order to be taken *ad aliquid.* But if this is so, then "Father" has to be taken substantially before it can be taken relatively. The seemingly lucid distinction between substantial and relative terms applied to God thus begins to give way. With that, some suggestions appear which seem hard to reconcile with Augustine's thought that the distinctions among the divine persons are captured by relative predication, and their unity as the one God by substantial predication. On the one hand the person of the Father seems to have some kind of existence as divine substance prior to the relation that distinguishes him from the Son—prior, that is, to being the Father. "The substance of the Father is the Father himself, not insofar as he is the Father, but insofar as he simply is."[33] On the other hand Augustine sometimes seems to violate his own rule that substantial terms cannot be said in a way that introduces reference or relation. Thus the remarks, troubling to his medieval interpreters, with which we began. Although "wisdom," and even more "essence," are supposed to be substantial terms, Augustine nonetheless finds reason to grant that wisdom and even essence in God can be thought of as "from" something ("sapientia de sapientia sicut essentia de essentia," *De Trinitate,* VII, 3). They can, in other words, be said relatively and not just substantially.

To be sure, ideas of this kind come in the midst of Augustine's often-

31. *De Trinitate,* VII, 2 (*CCL* 50, 247.106–107).

32. *De Trinitate,* VII, 2 (*CCL* 50, 247–248.115–117): "Si et pater non est aliquid ad se ipsum, non est omnino qui relative dicatur ad aliquid."

33. *De Trinitate,* VII, 11 (*CCL* 50, 262.20–21): "substantia patris ipse pater est, non quo pater est sed quo est."

repeated insistence on a stringent distinction between substance and relation, and so between what can be said substantially and what can be said relatively. "It is absurd," he remarks, "for substance to be said relatively, since every single thing subsists in and of itself. How much more is this true of God—if it is even worthy for God to be said to subsist?"[34] As Augustine's own hesitations on the point indicate, we have a problem here. If "God" has to be said substantially and "Father" has to be said relatively, then the Father is not God, and God is not the Father. The substance which is God is not relative, and the relation involved in being the Father is not substantial. The same goes for the Son and the Holy Spirit, and the relative terms by which we speak about them.

If we try to deal with this problem by taking "Father," "Son," "Gift," and so forth as substantial terms, then we can say "the Father is God" without difficulty, and likewise the Son and the Spirit. But by doing this we lose the distinctions between them, which only relation introduces; what is said substantially is not said by way of relation. This would be genuine essentialism, or "Sabellianism" in Augustine's lexicon, which he is wholly committed to avoiding (cf. De Trinitate, VII, 9). If we try to deal with the problem by taking "substance," "essence," "wisdom," and the like as relative terms, we retain the real distinctions of Father, Son, and Spirit. But we lose the unity of God. If divine substance can be spoken of only by reference to another divine substance really distinct from it, there are at least two divine substances, and so at least two gods. This Augustine is equally committed to avoiding (cf. De Trinitate, VII, 9). We sense that the idea of relation is crucial to understanding our faith in the Trinity. But as Augustine's searching reflections on the matter make plain, it proves difficult to exploit this idea in a really illuminating way.

When Aquinas takes up the question of divine essence and Trinitarian relations in the Summa theologiae—a problem which had been extensively mooted by medieval theologians well before Thomas turned his hand to it—he immediately observes that Augustine's sharp distinction between the two poses just the sort of problem we have been considering. Citing, on the lips of an objector, Augustine's initial proposal that we take some things said of God relatively, and not substantially (De Trinitate, V, 6), Aquinas notes that this seems to rule out just the position for which he wants to argue (ST I, q. 28, a. 2, obj. 1). It apparently implies that the relations which constitute (as he will

---

34. De Trinitate, VII, 9–10 (CCL 50, 260.148–150): "Absurdum est autem ut substantia relative dicatur; omnis enim res ad se ipsam subsistit. Quanto magis deus si tamen dignum est ut deus dicatur subsistere?"

later insist) the divine Persons, and so the Persons themselves, are not identical with the divine essence, as Aquinas wants to say, but are, in essentialist fashion, "extrinsic" to it, as "Gilbert of Poitiers is said to have held" (*ST* I, q. 28, a. 2, c).

Thomas's solution, to simplify a complicated story, is to think through the implications of the claim that "whatever has accidental existence in created realities has substantial existence when carried over into God" (*ST* I, q. 28, a. 2, c.). This claim, of course, follows closely from Augustine's repeated insistence that in God there are no accidents. It means, though, that relation, while a metaphysical accident in creatures, is not an accident in God, and so must be entirely identical with the divine substance or essence ("idem omnino ei"; *ST* I, q. 28, a. 2, c). Applied to God, "relation" and "essence" do not differ in reality, but only in the conceptual content they have in our understanding: one implies a reference of subject to term, while the other does not.[35] Yet even though relations like fatherhood and sonship in God are not really distinct from the one divine essence, they are really distinct from each other. The specific *ratio* or conceptual content that belongs to our idea of relation in such cases—reference to a uniquely correlative other ("respectus ad suum oppositum")—does carry over into God, but not the real distinction of relation from God's one *esse substantiale*. Thus one of the deeply characteristic claims of Thomas's Trinitarian theology: the relations which constitute the divine Persons are identical with the divine essence, and so with the one God, but they are not identical with each other. The Persons are the essence, but this is no essentialism.

What, though, of Augustine's apparent insistence that what we say of God be taken either substantially or relationally, but not both? Aquinas does not take issue with Augustine at this point, but simply reads what Augustine says as a way of stating his own position. "These words of Augustine," he argues, are not to be taken as denying that a relation like divine fatherhood is actually identical with God's essence (*ST* I, q. 28, a. 2, ad 1). Augustine's words have to do precisely with what is *said* of God, with the irreducible distinction in word and thought between what is predicated substantially and what is predicated relationally.[36] In God, at least, these two different types of predication should

---

35. *ST* I, q. 28, a. 2, c: "Relatio . . . non differt nisi secundum intelligentiae rationem, prout in relatione importatur respectus ad suum oppositum, qui non importatur in nomine essentiae."

36. *ST* I, q. 28, a. 2, ad 1, emphasis added: "Relatio . . . non *praedicatur* secundum modum substantiae, ut existens in eo de quo dicitur, sed ut ad alterum se habens."

not be taken for two different classes of things, some of which subsist or exist substantially and some of which do not. Thus another claim characteristic of Aquinas on the Trinity: in God that which is relative is substantial, and conversely; "*in divinis* relations are subsistent."[37] Augustine seems to have rejected this out of hand ("every single thing subsists in and of itself," and not relatively; *De Trinitate,* VII, 9). Aquinas offers it as an *interpretation* of Augustine, and indeed invokes Augustine's authority, a bit indirectly, in support of this idea (cf. *ST* I, q. 39, a. 1, s.c.).

Aquinas makes the same argument when he responds to objections arising from Augustine's often-noted caution about using the concept "person" in talking about the Trinity. One side of Augustine's concern about this is that "person" seems to be a substantial term, one said *ad se* and not *ad aliquid;* persons, like substances generally, are subjects of relations, but they are not themselves relations. "In the Trinity, when we speak of the person of the Father, we do not speak of anything else than the substance of the Father."[38] If we had to choose between taking "person" as referring to a relation and as referring to something subsistent we would, as before, be stuck. Taking "person" substantially, as Augustine thinks we naturally do, would give us the reality of the one God but would fail to grasp the relations that distinguish Father, Son, and Spirit. Going against the grain and taking it relationally would give us the distinctions among the three, but would fail to grasp them as subsistent realities. Aquinas, however, thinks there is no need to make this choice. In God, even though the term "person" refers to a relation, "it is said *ad se,* and not as a mere reference to another *(dicitur ad se, non ad alterum),* because it signifies the relation not in the manner of a relation, but in the manner of a substance, that is, of a hypostasis" (*ST* I, q. 29, a. 4, ad 1). Here too the objection from Augustine turns out to be a way of making Thomas's own point. "This is what Augustine meant when he said that [person] signifies the essence [Au-

---

37. *ST* I, q. 39, a. 1, ad 1. Similarly *ST* I, q. 29, a. 4, c: "'Divine person' signifies a relation, as subsistent. In other words, it signifies a relation, but signifies it in the manner of a substance, that is, of a hypostasis subsisting in the divine nature" (*Persona igitur divina significat relationem ut subsistentem. Et hoc est significare relationem per modum substantiae quae est hypostasis subsistens in natura divina);* for "hypostasis" here one could say "individual substance," and so "person" (cf. *ST* I, q. 29, a. 1, ad 5). See also *ST* I, q. 30, a. 1, ad 2: "In God, relative properties both subsist and are really distinguished from one another."

38. *De Trinitate,* VII, 11, quoted in *ST* I, q. 29, a. 4, obj. 1 (*CCL* 50, 262.18–20, 22–23): "neque in hac trinitate cum dicimus personam patris aliud dicimus quam substantiam patris. . . . Ad se quippe dicitur persona, non ad filium vel spiritum sanctum." Aquinas also takes up this and several similar texts from *De Trinitate,* VII, in *De potentia,* 9, 4, ad 1–5.

gustine said "substance"], since in God essence is identical with hypostasis."[39]

Surely, though, Aquinas is just covering a mental hiatus with verbal plaster, to borrow a phrase from Austin Farrer. He says that relation and essence are the same in God, but he also admits that we have to think and speak about them differently. Indeed relation, he holds, is not predicated "in the manner of a substance" (*secundum modum substantiae; ST* I, q. 28, a. 2, ad 1), yet to speak of a person in God is precisely to signify or refer to a relation "in the manner of a substance" (*per modum substantiae; ST* I, q. 29, a. 4, c and ad 1).[40] As Aquinas notes in another objection (*ST* I, q. 28, a. 2, obj. 2), Augustine seems to be against him here as well: everything which is rightly said to have a relation is more than just that relation (*De Trinitate*, VII, 2). So how can we make assertions like "relations subsist," when we have to grant that so far as we can understand—so far as we have *rationes* for subsistence and relation—they do not?

This Aquinas handles, as he does a number of cognate questions about the coherence of his Trinitarian theology, by appealing to the limits of our thought and language. We can say why we need to assert that relations subsist in God, but we cannot entirely understand what we mean when we say it. Augustine was right, though perhaps not in quite the way he intended. There *is* more to God than what we can mean by our relative terms, like "Father"

---

39. *ST* I, q. 29, a. 4, ad 1. Augustine also has a more straightforwardly logical worry about speaking of three "persons" in God. This way of speaking obviously holds that being a person is common to the Father, the Son, and the Holy Spirit. But being God is also common to the three. If we can say they are three persons, why can we not with equal justice say they are three gods? (Cf. *De Trinitate*, VII, 8; *CCL* 50, 257.77–81.) This sort of remark is sometimes cited to support an essentialist reading of Augustine, as proof that he has no idea what to make of the real distinction of persons in God. But the point is just the opposite: we should hesitate to apply the concept "person" to the three because, as common to all, it fails to capture their real distinction from one another in an adequate way.

Thomas aims to solve the logical difficulty by arguing that while each person is irreducibly unique—exists (borrowing a concept from Richard of St. Victor) in a way that no one else can share (*persona sit incommunicabilis*)—*having* a unique mode of existence is, of course, common to all persons (*tamen ipse modus existendi incommunicabiliter potest esse pluribus communis; ST* I, q. 30, a. 4, ad 2). "Person," like "essence" but unlike (for example) "fatherhood" is applied in common to the three in God, but unlike "essence" it refers to no reality they actually have in common. As Aquinas characteristically proposes, "person" is conceptually and not really common to the three ("Manifestum est autem quod non est communitas rei, sicut una essentia communis est tribus . . . est commune communitate rationis"; *ST* I, q. 30, a. 4, c.). It gives us the concept of a unique or unshareable way of existing in the divine (or any other rational) nature, rather than locating any unique mode of existence in particular (such as, in God, fatherhood or sonship). Aquinas thus grants Augustine's point that "person" does not itself capture what makes Father, Son, and Spirit each a unique individual, distinct from the others, but only gives us a way of saying *that* each is distinct in a fashion particular to him.

40. Cf. above, notes 36–37.

and "Son." There is "something absolute," which is what we mean when we speak of the divine essence. But when we speak of the essence we are not talking about a reality other than the Father, the Son, and the Holy Spirit; the essence is not "more" than the personal relations in that sense. Rather it is more than what our concepts of the personal relations can contain, just as they are more than our concept of the essence can contain. In God the indivisible essence and the irreducibly distinct Persons are "one and the same reality," but we have no one concept capacious enough for that reality. The one God, Persons and essence, "is not fully expressed by any term, as if it could be completely included under the meaning of such a term."[41]

By making some specific distinctions between the ways we talk about God and the way God is, and then insisting that we stick with both the ways of talk and the distinctions, Aquinas bids to save the Augustinian intuition that relation is basic to any understanding we may have of the Trinity. In just this way he seeks to avoid some of the problems that arise in the way Augustine himself handles the issue—or, as Aquinas sees it, to answer some of the objections suggested by Augustine.[42]

Aquinas the Augustinian?

We have traced, really, just two uses of Augustine by Aquinas in Trinitarian theology: what Aquinas makes of Augustine's apparent suggestion that Father and Son are joined as "essence from essence," and, following from that,

---

41. *ST* I, q. 28, a. 2, ad 2: "Sicut in rebus creatis in illo quod dicitur relative non solum est invenire respectum ad alterum sed etiam aliquid absolutum, ita et in Deo; sed tamen aliter et aliter. Nam id quod invenitur in creatura praeter id quod continetur sub significatione nominis relativi est alia res; in Deo autem non est alia res sed una et eadem, quae non perfecte exprimitur nomine quasi sub significatione talis nominis comprehensa."

42. A good deal of later medieval Trinitarian theology does not, it should be observed, take the same lessons from Augustine that Thomas does. The "Franciscan" tradition (as variously developed by, for example, Henry of Ghent, Duns Scotus, and Peter Auriol) takes up Augustine's suggestion (cf. note 32 above) that substance has an inherent priority over relation, against Aquinas's defense of the idea (also inspired by Augustine) that relations are person-constituting in God. In particular they ask how the Father can be constituted as a person by a relation *(paternitas)* to the Son, since presumably he can only be the subject of the act *(generatio)* by which this relation comes about if he is constituted as a person already—*actus*, after all, *sunt suppositorum*. Or, as Schmaus formulates the problem, "Because the act of generation is the basis of his [person-]constitutive relation, the first person must," on Aquinas's account, "be active before he is constituted, indeed before he exists" (*Der "Liber Propugnatorius,"* 651). Generally unpersuaded by the sort of reply Aquinas gives to this question (in, for example, *De potentia*, 10, 3; *ST* I, q. 40, a. 2, ad 4; and I, q. 40, a. 4), the "Franciscans" face, in turn, the difficulty of accounting for the Father's personal identity and constitution without suggesting (as Augustine

his adaptation of Augustine's idea that relation, and not essence, is the basis of personal distinction in God. There are, of course, countless others. Saying whether, and in what sense, Aquinas is really an Augustinian on the Trinity would require a much more extensive investigation than we have undertaken here. But at least in light of the issues we have had in view, one is struck as much by the differences between the two as by what they have in common.

"Does the essence generate?" is a scholastic question, never explicitly raised by Augustine, though one can discern a negative answer to it in the *De Trinitate*. Yet despite his interest in this question and in Augustine's take on the matter, texts which are telling for Augustine's view are either missing from Aquinas's own account or get slotted to different scholastic questions. This would be even more true, one conjectures, as one moved into areas of the *De Trinitate* more remote from typical scholastic questions. And despite his evident debt to Augustine on the Trinitarian matters we have looked at here, Thomas treats Augustine not only as an authority, but as a problem. Some of the basic objections to his own teaching on essence and relation come from Augustine. Aquinas resolutely handles these problems in his own way, which is not always Augustine's even when he invokes Augustine's authority on their behalf. These two great Catholic teachers both seek the deepest possible *intellectus* of the Church's faith in the Trinity, the later in unmistakable reliance on the earlier. Yet each seeks this understanding in his own distinctive way, and with his own characteristic results.

---

at least once does; cf. note 33 above) that he has some kind of existence, indeed personal existence, prior to being the Father.

3

Theology and Theory of the Word in Aquinas

Understanding Augustine by Innovating Aristotle

Harm Goris

In contemporary discussions, Aquinas's theory of the word plays a role mainly in certain philosophical issues, in particular the semantic and epistemological status of the inner word *(verbum interius)* or concept and the question whether Aquinas represents some form of direct realism or representationalism.[1] Generally, however, little attention is paid to the fact that Aquinas's theory of the word evolved over the course of his career. This neglect can have serious consequences for the interpretation of Aquinas's position.[2]

In this essay, I shall trace the development of Aquinas's reflection on what a word is.[3] I shall not go into the philosophical issue about representationalism, but focus on the theological context within which Aquinas gradually developed his theory of the (inner) word or concept. There were two theological questions, both inherited from Augustine, that motivated him to elaborate this new theory. The first question concerns the doctrine of the Trinity: is

1. Cf., for example, Robert Pasnau, *Theories of Cognition in the Later Middle Ages* (Cambridge: Cambridge University Press, 1997).

2. An exception is Giorgio Pini, "Species, Concept, and Thing: Theories of Signification in the Second Half of the Thirteenth Century," *Medieval Philosophy and Theology* 8 (1999): 21–52.

3. I resume certain elements I discussed in my *Free Creatures of an Eternal God: Thomas Aquinas on God's Infallible Foreknowledge and Irresistible Will* (Louvain: Peeters, 1996), 167–79.

"Word," when said of God, exclusively a personal name? The second question is about the plurality of the divine ideas and its compatibility with divine simplicity. Although the latter has been discussed less extensively by later commentators on Aquinas, the two problems are interconnected in Aquinas's theology. In both cases the confrontation with an Aristotelian doctrine of knowledge inspired Aquinas to develop gradually a new view on the inner word. The new view centers around an innovative elaboration of Aristotle's theory of the cognitive act, which leads to an integration of Aristotelian and Augustinian views on cognition. His innovation in cognitive theory enabled Aquinas to maintain, explain, and substantiate Augustine's theological claims about "Word" and the divine ideas within the framework of an Aristotelian analysis and interpretation of the cognitive act.

I distinguish three subsequent stages in Aquinas's texts that mark the development toward his new cognitive theory: an early stage in the *Commentary on the Sentences,* a middle stage in *De veritate* and the first redaction of *Summa contra gentiles,* book I, chapter 53, and the final stage, represented by the third redaction of *Summa contra gentiles* I, chapter 53, and later texts. In my interpretation of the texts, I shall focus on two things. First, I shall offer a new reading of the texts that represent the second stage, that is, the texts in *De veritate* and the first redaction of *Summa contra gentiles* I, chapter 53. Second, given this new interpretation, it will become clearer that there is a serious problem with the dating of the alleged second redaction of Thomas's *Commentary on the Sentences.*

Before taking a closer look at the three stages of the development of Thomas's theory of the inner word, I shall first introduce in more detail the two theological questions that gave rise to this development.

I. Background

With regard to the question whether "'Word" is exclusively a personal name in God, Augustine had argued that in humans the inner word, or as he calls it "the word of the heart" *(verbum cordis),* always proceeds from, is said by, or is born out of our mind *(mens)* or memory *(memoria).* Therefore, "word" always signifies a real relation of procession and, when predicated of God, does not signify the divine essence, but precisely the Second Person of the Trinity. For Augustine, "Word" is as much a personal name in the Trinity as "Son": "He is Son in the way He is Word, and He is Word in the way He is

Son."[4] This explanation harmonizes, of course, with the wordings of the prologue of the Gospel of John, in which "Word" refers to pre-existent Logos, incarnated in Jesus of Nazareth.

However, the introduction of the Aristotelian doctrine of knowledge in the early thirteenth century challenged Augustine's view and the question came up if, within the context of an Aristotelian epistemology of abstraction, "word" could also have a non-personal, essential meaning or use in Trinitarian theology. Some, including the young Aquinas when writing his commentary on the *Sentences* in the early 1250s, allowed for this possibility, although such an essential meaning does not correspond so nicely with biblical and traditional usage of "word." Apparently, the question was deemed so important that the community of Paris masters in theology took an official stance at a gathering around 1270, at which Thomas was also present, and "solemnly" condemned the opinion that "word" could have a non-personal meaning. But by that time Aquinas had already changed his position and had subscribed to the classical view that "word" can only *(tantum)* be a personal name.[5]

Aquinas's change of view was noticed by commentators as early as the writer(s) of the *Articuli in quibus frater Thomas melius in Summa quam in Scriptis* (ca. 1280), and also by fifteenth-century Thomists like Gerard ter Stege (Gerhardus De Monte Domini) and Peter de Bergomo, and by Cajetan.[6] In 1951 Henri Paissac offered a detailed interpretation of the gradual development of Aquinas's theory of the word in his *Théologie du verbe. Saint Augustin et saint Thomas.*

The second problem, how to reconcile the plurality of divine ideas with God's simplicity, received less attention from Aquinas scholars. Influential Thomists, such as Sertillanges and Etienne Gilson, thought the divine ideas a *Fremdkörper* in Aquinas's theology, incorporated by him only out of respect for the theological authority of St. Augustine—and not for compelling systematic reasons. L.-B. Geiger, on the other hand, held that the doctrine of divine ideas plays a vital role for Thomas in explaining God's intimate

4. Augustine, *De Trinitate,* book VII, ch. 2: "Eo quippe filius quo verbum et eo verbum quo filius."

5. About this gathering of the masters around 1270, see Henri Paissac, *Théologie du verbe. Saint Augustin et saint Thomas* (Paris: Les Editions du Cerf, 1951), 202, n. 1. Also, A. F. von Gunten, "In principio erat verbum. Une évolution de saint Thomas en théologie trinitaire," in *Ordo sapientiae et amoris. Hommage au professeur Jean-Pierre Torrell O.P.,* ed. C.-J. Pinto de Oliveira (Fribourg: Editions Universitaires, 1993), 119–20, n. 2.

6. Paissac, *Théologie du verbe,* 202, n. 1.

knowledge of all things created in combination with divine simplicity. Vivian Boland's extensive study *Ideas in God According to Saint Thomas Aquinas,* published in 1996, shows conclusively, I think, that Geiger is right.[7] In 1963 Geiger also published an article in which he gives a detailed analysis of the three redactions of chapter 53 (on the divine ideas) in the first book of the *Summa contra gentiles.*[8] As will become clear later in this paper, the differences between the first two and the third redaction of this chapter mark the turn toward Thomas's final, mature view on the inner word.

II. First Stage: Commentary on the Sentences

In the *Commentary on the Sentences,* book I, ds. 27, question 2, article 2, qa. 1, we find Aquinas's first attempts to reconcile an Aristotelian epistemology with an Augustinian theology of the Word/word. After having argued in the preceding article (a. 1) that "word" is said properly *(proprie)* in God, Aquinas discusses now the question whether "word" is said personally (*"Utrum verbum dicatur personaliter,"* a. 2) in the Trinity.

However, there is a textual peculiarity about Aquinas's response in this *quaestiuncula.* Leonard Boyle has argued that the text in the Mandonnet edition of book I of the *Commentary on the Sentences* is in fact a second redaction by Thomas, composed in Rome in 1265–1266, while the text of the first redaction is (for the most part) rendered in a footnote in the same edition and dates from the first time Aquinas lectured on the *Sentences* in Paris, around 1252.[9]

The first part of the response is the same in both redactions. Aquinas starts by summarizing and criticizing two opinions. The first one need not concern

7. Vivian Boland, *Ideas in God According to Saint Thomas Aquinas: Sources and Synthesis* (Leiden: Brill Academic Publishers, 1996).

8. L.-B. Geiger, "Les rédactions successives de *Contra gentiles I,* 53 d'après l'autographe," in *Saint Thomas d'Aquin aujourd'hui,* ed. J.Y. Jolif et al. (Paris: 1963), 221–40. The text of the first two, deleted redactions in the autograph is published in volume 13 of the Leonine ed., 20a49–21a51 and in the Busa ed., vol. 2, 163, 006 ADL g1 pg 20a line 49: "Ut igitur intelligi possit quo modo Deus absque sui intellectus compositione multitudinem cognoscat" through g1 pg21a line 51: "ut supra ostendimus." The second redaction starts at g1 pg21a line 5: "Ne autem huiusmodi obstaculo abducamur."

9. Cf. L. Boyle, "Alia lectura fratris Thome," *Mediaeval Studies* 45 (1983): 424–25. The former president of the Leonine Commission, Fr. Bataillon, confirmed to Fr. A. F. von Gunten that there are two redactions of the response in *In I Sent.,* ds. 27, q. 2, a. 2, qa. 1. Fr. Bataillon's rendering of the first redaction is more precise than the one by Mandonnet: cf. von Gunten, "In principio erat verbum," 121, n. 7. Mandonnet's text of the first redaction is in *Scriptum super libros magistri Petri Lombardi,* book I, ed. P. Mandonnet (Paris: 1929), 659–60, n. 3.

us now, but the second one states that "word," when said of God, is always something personal *(personale)* and not something essential *(essentiale)*. This cannot be the case, Aquinas argues, for when we take a closer look at what the inner word or concept *(conceptio intellectus)* is in us humans, we find it can only be either the act of understanding *(operatio intelligendi)* or its formal principle, the *species intellecta*. With *"species intellecta"* Aquinas means here the intelligible species as actually abstracted from the *phantasmata* and purified of material conditions.[10] Aquinas points out that when we apply the term "word" to God—whether in the sense of "act of understanding" or in the sense of *"species intellecta"*—it implies a merely conceptual relation *(relatio rationis tantum)*, not a real relation *(relatio realis)*. After all, in God both the act of knowing and the formal principle by which God knows are, in reality, identical with the divine essence itself because of God's simplicity.[11] If it does not imply a real relation, "word" cannot be a personal name in God. For the distinction of the divine Persons is real and requires a real relation (of origin). Merely conceptual relations do not distinguish one Person from another.

Aquinas himself then sides with a third opinion: "word" can be taken both personally and essentially. For if it implies a real relation, it is a personal name, and if it implies a merely conceptual relation, it is an essential name. However, Aquinas does not specify under what circumstances and for which reasons "word" could actually imply a real relation.[12]

The second redaction of the response does not retract the first one, but adds only a new element. The phrasing of the third—Aquinas's own—opinion now becomes: "word" can be taken both personally and essentially *ex virtute vocabuli*. The added expression *"ex virtute vocabuli"* refers to the inner meaning of a term apart from its actual usage.[13] Thomas admits that one can-

---

10. That *species intellecta* is equivalent to *species intelligibilis* is clear from other passages in the *Commentary on the Sentences: In I Sent.*, ds. 35, q. 1, a. 1, ad 3; *In II Sent.*, ds. 17, q. 2, a. 1; *In III Sent.*, ds. 31, q. 2, a. 4, ad 5. Cf. also J. Chênevert, "Le verbum dans le Commentaire sur les Sentences de saint Thomas d'Aquin," *Sciences Ecclésiastiques. Revue théologique et philosophique* 13 (1960): 191–224 and 359–90, esp. 200, 359–69.

11. Cf. *In I Sent.*, ds. 35, q. 1, a. 1, ad 3.

12. Cf. von Gunten, "In principio," 124: "Il ne donne aucune preuve ni même aucune explication de cette fonction," namely, of "word" implying a real distinction; ibid., 125: "s. Thomas n'avait donné aucune explication pour justifier la seconde hypothèse," that is, of "word" being a personal name.

13. *Virtus vocabuli* is an equivalent of *virtus sermonis* and regards the literal meaning of a term as contrasted with either a figurative meaning or with the *usus loquendi:* see William Courtenay, "Force of Words and Figures of Speech: The Crisis over *Virtus sermonis* in the Fourteenth Century," *Franciscan Studies* 44 (1984): 108–18. Aquinas also uses the expressions "vis suae significationis," "virtus dic-

not explain that "word" is said only personally in God on the basis of its inner meaning, that is, on the basis of a purely conceptual analysis of the term.
But, Aquinas goes on, when we look at how the term "word" is actually used
in Scripture, in the Tradition of the Church—here he has especially Augustine in mind, whom he quotes twice in the *sed contra*—and also in common
language, we see that writers and speakers in fact use "word" as signifying
something that implies a real relation, and, consequently, they use it as a personal name in God. And in the end it is the actual use *(usus)* of a term that
settles the issue. For the meaning of a term is only by convention *(significatio
vocis est ad placitum)*. Therefore, when the majority uses "word" as implying
a real relation, then we have to follow this usage and conclude that "word" is
said personally in God, even if we cannot find a rationale for this in the *ratio*
or conceptual content of the term "word" itself. Aquinas concludes that the
whole question turns out to be just a verbal matter.[14]

Very interesting is a note in the margin of the famous thirteenth-century
Oxford manuscript in Lincoln College, which contains book I of Thomas's
Commentary on the Sentences and which was first described by Hyacinthe Don-
daine. It says:

> The Paris [university] community now holds that "word" is only said personally and that
> also brother Thomas now agrees with this—not that the distinction made here is errone-
> ous but because in general this term is only used personally.[15]

According to Boyle, the "now" *(modo)* refers to the time Aquinas was lectur-
ing for the second time on the *Sentences* (at least on book I), in 1265–1266 at
Rome. The consensus of the Parisian masters, mentioned in the note, that
"word" is exclusively *(tantum)* a personal name, precedes then the "solemn"
condemnation of the "essential name view" in 1270, mentioned above.[16] The
phrase *"non quod distinctio hic posita sit erronea"* also makes clear that there
is no retraction of the arguments which led to the former position, that is,
the one of the first redaction ("word" can be both an essential and a person-

---

tionum," "vis dictionis," "vis verborum," usually as contrasted with a specific ecclesiastical usage. *In I
Sent.,* ds. 10, q. 1, a. 4, ad 1. Cf. also *ST* I, q. 29, a. 4; q. 36, a. 1, ad 1; and a. 2, ad 3.

14. *In I Sent.,* ds. 27, q. 2, a. 2, qa. 1: "Cum enim de rebus constat, frustra in verbis habetur con-
troversia."

15. Boyle, "Alia lectura," 425: "Communitas Parisiensis modo tenet quod uerbum tantum personaliter dicatur, et quod etiam frater Thomas modo in hoc consentit—non quod disctinctio hic posita
sit erronea sed quia communiter non utuntur hoc nomine nisi personaliter."

16. Cf. section I, "Background," of this essay, above.

al name). According to the author of the Lincoln codex, Thomas thinks the original arguments, in particular the interpretation of *conceptio intellectus* as either the act of knowing or as its formal principle, still valid. The only difference, which leads to the new position that "word" is said exclusively personally, is that there is the additional argument of usage, which excludes one of the alternatives left open by the former position. I shall return to the issue of the dating of the so-called second redaction of *In I Sententiarum* later.

We may conclude that both in the first and the alleged second redaction of *In I Sententiarum,* ds. 27, question 2, article 2, qa. 1, Aquinas stays within a traditional, rather basic, Aristotelian framework, identifying the inner word or concept with the act of understanding or with the intelligible species. Within such a framework, he cannot account for the exclusively relational character of the inner word. In fact, it seems, he cannot account at all for the very possibility of a relational interpretation of "word." He merely affirms, but does not explain, that the possibility exists. In the first redaction he allows for both an essential and a personal interpretation of "word." However, in the second redaction he rules out the first interpretation on the basis of an extrinsic reason, namely, the authority of ecclesiastical usage.

In the *Commentary on the Sentences* Thomas also discusses the other theological problem: how can God be said to know a plurality of things without compromising his simplicity? For "knowing" is an immanent act and the objects known seem to have intentional existence in the knower. One gets the impression Thomas does not think it a very pressing problem. He merely distinguishes between a first and a second object of knowledge *(primum* and *secundum intellectum).* The first one is the species, the similitude in the intellect of the extramental thing. This similitude is the formal and specifying principle of the cognitive act. In God there is only one such principle, the divine essence, which is the similitude of all things. The *secundum intellectum* is the real, extramental object. Through the one *primum intellectum* God can know a plurality of extramental things, without thereby excluding his simplicity.[17]

---

17. *In I Sent.,* ds. 35, q. 1, a. 2. Cf. L.-B Geiger, "Les idées divines dans l'œuvre de s. Thomas," in *St. Thomas Aquinas 1274–1974: Commemorative Studies,* vol. 1, ed. A. Maurer (Toronto: Pontifical Institute of Mediaeval Studies, 1974), 189; also Boland, *Ideas in God,* 200–205.

III. Second Stage: *De veritate*

A few years after the first redaction of the *Commentary on the Sentences,* Aquinas resumed the question whether in God "word" can be said essentially or only personally. He does so in *De veritate,* question 4, article 2, written between 1256 and 1257. Again, Thomas remains within the boundaries of traditional Aristotelian teaching, but now he does so in a much more elaborate way. This elaboration, he thinks, can explain why "word" implies by itself (by its inner, proper meaning) a real relation of origin or of procession and is, therefore, a personal name in God.

As in the *Commentary on the Sentences,* the starting point is the human inner word or concept *(conceptio intellectus).* But this time Aquinas no longer identifies the word with the act of understanding or its formal principle, the intelligible species, but instead, he identifies the word with the endterm and effect of the act of understanding, that is, with what is understood (the *intellectum*), whether that is a single concept *("conceptio significabilis per vocem incomplexam")* or a proposition *(conceptio significabilis "per vocem complexam").* However, "what is understood" *(intellectum)* is not the only element in the definition of "concept" or "word of the intellect." There is a second element in the *definiens* of "word": by definition a word is also something that really comes forth from something else *("aliquid realiter progrediens ab altero").* Aquinas underpins this latter claim by arguing that every *intellectum* in the human intellect comes forth from something else. He presents three instances of such an intellectual procession:

Every *intellectum* in us is something that really comes forth from something else; either

1) like the concepts of conclusions come forth from principles; or
2) like concepts of the quiddities of later things come forth from the quiddities of prior things; or at least
3) like an actual concept comes forth from habitual knowledge.[18]

The first two instances of intellectual procession are on a par: both of them regard discursive knowledge.[19] By reasoning we either infer deductively a con-

18. *De veritate,* q. 4, a. 2, sol.: "Omne autem intellectum in nobis est aliquid realiter progrediens ab altero; vel sicut progrediuntur a principiis conceptiones conclusionum, vel sicut conceptiones quidditatum rerum posteriorum a quidditatibus priorum; vel saltem sicut conceptio actualis progreditur ab habituali cognitione."

19. In the *Commentary on the Sentences* there are already some allusions to an interpretation of "word" on the basis of discursive reasoning: *In I Sent.,* ds. 27, q. 2, a. 1, ad 3; and ds. 34, q. 2, ad 2. But

clusion from premises or we find dialectically a definition by adding differences to an indeterminate genus. In both cases there is discursive reasoning, a proceeding from what is known to what is not known.[20] However, what Aquinas does not seem to notice is that founding the intellectual procession of the inner word on discursive reasoning seriously undermines his whole argument.

A first, logical difficulty is that Aquinas leaves undecided the status of what is known first and naturally, that is, the first principles (for example, the principle of non-contradiction) and the primary notions such as "being," "one," etc. These are not discursively known by reasoning from something previously known, but are immediately and intuitively grasped. Therefore they lack the property of "proceeding from something else." This means that these "principles" and "quiddities of prior things," as he calls them in the *De veritate* text, cannot themselves be called "concepts" or "words."[21] Yet Aquinas would not deny, it seems to me, that they are understood *(intellecta)*. So, contrary to what Thomas claims *("Omne autem intellectum in nobis est aliquid realiter progrediens ab altero"),* there seem to be *intellecta* in the human mind that yet do not come forth from something else. I shall return to this later.

A theologically even more serious problem is that discursivity, that is, having to reason from one thing to another, is an imperfect way of knowing. Discursivity is proper to the human rational mind, which unlike the divine or angelic intellect, does not know immediately and in full detail by one intuitive grasp or glance, but has to move from indeterminate or general knowledge to determinate and detailed knowledge. Because it implies an imperfection, discursive knowledge cannot properly, in its literal sense, be predicated of God. God does not have to engage in a process of reasoning in order to attain full knowledge. As Aquinas repeats over and again, it is a basic rule in theological language that words that contain an imperfection in their meaning cannot be said of God *proprie*. If then discursive knowledge cannot be predicated of God literally, but at most metaphorically, then the same must go for "word" if it is necessarily linked to discursive reasoning. But a meta-

---

discursivity does not play a role in the main text that deals with the question of "word" being a personal name in God (*In I Sent.*, ds. 27, q. 2, a. 2, qa. 1).

20. For these two modes of discursive reasoning, see for example, Jan Aertsen, *Nature and Creature: Thomas Aquinas's Way of Thought* (Leiden: 1988), 69–72.

21. Note that in *De veritate*, q. 4, a. 2, Aquinas indeed does not use the expression "concepts" for the first principles and first notions. However, in *De veritate*, q. 11, a. 1, he does call them "concepts," likewise in *Quodl.*, 8, q. 2, a. 2 (probably dating from Advent 1257), and *In De Trinitate*, q. 6, a. 4.

phorical meaning of "word" in God contradicts the whole of Aquinas's intention in this article. At the very beginning of the solution in *De veritate,* question 4, article 2, he states explicitly that creatures may be called God's word insofar as they manifest God, but that this is only a metaphor, while he wants to investigate "word" insofar as it is said *proprie,* literally and not metaphorically, of God. Furthermore, in the preceding article (*De veritate,* q. 4, a. 1) he had already concluded that "word" is said *proprie* in God, and he had stated that "word" does not include discursivity.[22] But, as I have argued, the latter claim is not corroborated in *De veritate,* question 4, article 2.

The very same theological problem is raised by the third alternative Aquinas gives of intellectual procession in the human mind, namely, the proceeding of the actual concept from habitual knowledge. If we take this in the normal Aristotelian sense, that is, the transition from a state of having acquired knowledge but not actually considering it to the actual consideration, then this intellectual procession also implies an imperfection in its very meaning and can at most be said metaphorically of God.[23] Being pure act, God does not have habitual knowledge. A second complicating factor for Aquinas's third example of procession in the human intellect is that for Aristotle and for Aquinas himself the transition from habitual knowledge to actual consideration is a matter of free choice; it happens on command of the will *(per imperium voluntatis).*[24] If this were applied to the procession of the Son from the Father, it would be plain heresy.[25]

We have seen that in the *De veritate* Aquinas argues that when "word" is taken properly *(secundum propriam acceptationem; si proprie accipiatur)* its very meaning *(ratio)* implies a real relation.[26] Although his arguments seem to be inconclusive, as they are based on a discursive mode of knowing, Aquinas's position in the *De veritate* is very different from the one taken in the *Com-*

22. *De veritate,* q. 4, a. 1, ad 1: "Nec hoc requiritur ad rationem verbi quod scilicet actus intellectus, qui terminatur ad verbum interius, fiat cum aliquo discursu."

23. For the transition from having acquired knowledge to actually considering it, cf. *In II De An.,* lc. 11. In the process of acquiring knowledge, there can also be a transition from potential to actual knowledge based on discursivity: ibid., no. 372.

24. Cf. *ST* I, q. 107, a. 1.

25. Cf. *ST* I, q. 41, a. 2.

26. At the very end of the response of *De veritate,* q. 4 a. 2, Thomas also allows for a non-proper, general interpretation ("si accipiatur communiter") of "word" as synonymous with "intellectum" only. Then it can be used as an essential name. Again Aquinas invokes the argument from actual usage, as he had done in the second redaction of the *Commentary on the Sentences.* But unlike in the latter text, the "usage-argument" in *De veritate,* q. 4, a. 2, is not used to decide *pro* the "personal name view," but *contra* the "essential name view."

mentary on the Sentences, both in the first (around 1252) and in the second redaction (around 1265–1266): for as we saw above, both these redactions offer no intrinsic grounds—based on the very meaning of "word"—that "word" is only a personal name. Is it possible that when commenting for the second time on book I of the *Sentences* at Rome in 1265–1266, Thomas had realized that the arguments put forward in *De veritate,* question 4, article 2 (around 1256–1257), were inconclusive? Could that be why he returned to his earliest position, but added the decisive external argument of usage? However, whether this is by itself a plausible explanation or not, I shall argue that it has to be ruled out when we look at how Thomas deals with the other theological problem he inherited from Augustine: the plurality of divine ideas. After discussing Thomas's texts on the divine ideas in the *De veritate,* question 3, article 2, and in *Summa contra gentiles* I, chapter 53, I shall return to the dating of the second redaction of *In I Sententiarum.*

Thomas discusses the plurality of divine ideas also in the *De veritate.* In *De veritate,* question 3, article 2, he introduces a form that is thought-out *(forma excogitata)* by the intellect in act. It is distinguished clearly from the form or species that brings the intellect into act and that is the primary formal principle of the act of understanding *("primum quo intelligitur").*[27] Parallel to what was said about "word" in *De veritate,* question 4, article 2, Thomas describes this thought-out form also as the "endterm" and "effect" of the cognitive act, and specifies it as a quiddity or a proposition. It is something understood *(intellectum),* but at the same time it also functions as a secondary formal principle of the cognitive act *(secundum quo intelligitur),* by which the external thing comes to be known. According to Thomas it is the one divine essence, not as essence but as something understood *(intellecta)* which is the divine

---

27. *De veritate,* q. 3, a. 2: "Modus autem pluralitatis hinc accipi potest. Forma enim in intellectu dupliciter esse potest. Uno modo ita quod sit principium actus intelligendi, sicut forma, quae est intelligentis in quantum est intelligens; et haec est similitudo intellecti in ipso. Alio modo ita quod sit terminus actus intelligendi, sicut artifex intelligendo excogitat formam domus; et cum illa forma sit excogitata per actum intelligendi, et quasi per actum effecta, non potest esse principium actus intelligendi, ut sit primum quo intelligatur; sed magis se habet ut intellectum, quo intelligens aliquid operatur. Nihilominus tamen est forma praedicta secundum quo [read "quo" with the Leonine edition and not "quod" with the Marietti edition] intelligitur: quia per formam excogitatam artifex intelligit quid operandum sit; sicut etiam in intellectu speculativo videmus quod species, qua intellectus informatur ut intelligat actu, est primum quo intelligitur; ex hoc autem quod est effectus in actu, per talem formam operari iam potest formando quidditates rerum et componendo et dividendo; unde ipsa quidditas formata in intellectu, vel etiam compositio et divisio, est quoddam operatum ipsius, per quod tamen intellectus venit in cognitionem rei exterioris; et sic est quasi secundum quo intelligitur."

idea of things. Next, Thomas explains the plurality of ideas by stating that the divine essence qua idea is not understood absolutely, but together with the different "proportions" external things have to the divine essence.[28]

The discussion of the plurality of divine ideas in *De veritate* is more refined than the one in *In I Sententiarum,* ds. 35, question 1, article 2. Apart from the primary formal principle of understanding (the *primum intellectum* in *In I Sent.*) and the external object (the *secundum intellectum* in *In I Sent.*), Thomas now introduces a third element, a form produced by the intellect *(forma excogitata).* But, as Geiger points out, it does not really play an important role in Thomas's solution of the problem of the plurality of ideas, which remains unconvincing anyway.[29] Moreover, and this Geiger does not mention, Aquinas's description of the production of the thought-out form suggests again a process of discursivity. The very expression "to think out" *(excogitare)* and the remarks that the intellect in act works "by forming quiddities and by composing and dividing" seem to imply discursive reasoning. This becomes even more evident when we turn to the next text in which Aquinas deals with the plurality of divine ideas: *Summa contra gentiles,* book I, chapter 53 (first redaction), written shortly after *De veritate,* question 3, article 2. In the *Summa contra gentiles* we find the third and final stage of the development of Aquinas's theory of the word.

IV. Third Stage: *Summa contra gentiles*

The three subsequent redactions in the autograph of *Summa contra gentiles,* book I, chapter 53, show clearly the transition from the second to the third stage in the evolution of Aquinas's theory of the concept. They have been examined by Geiger.[30] The chapter deals with the problem of the plurality of divine ideas: how can a multitude of known things *(intellecta)* exist in the divine mind? The first redaction was probably written at Paris in 1259, about two years after *De veritate,* question 3, article 2. It shows striking similarities with the latter, but it is more elaborated and indicates more clearly the implied discursivity: the thought-out form, which the informed intellect produces and which is the endterm of the cognitive act, is the result of a discursive process: it involves reasoning, gathering, investigating, finding out,

---

28. Ibid.
30. Cf. note 8 above.

29. Geiger, "Les idées divines," 194–97.

and deduction from previous knowledge.[31] Furthermore, as in *De veritate,* question 3, article 2, the thought-out form is described both as "understood" *(intellecta)* and as a formal principle *(quo intelligitur)* by which extramental reality is known.[32] But this time Aquinas is not satisfied with this answer; immediately (says Geiger) upon completing it, he deletes the whole passage and replaces it by a much shorter text (second redaction), which does not mention the thought-out form nor offer any detailed analysis of the cognitive act. Maybe Thomas replaced the former text because he realized that the thought-out form as both a formal principle and an object of knowledge is too ambiguous.[33] But another motive could have been the recognition that the discursivity implied in the production of the thought-out form causes the latter to be (at most) metaphorically and not literally predicable of God.

The third redaction of *Summa contra gentiles,* book I, chapter 53, represents the final stage, in which Aquinas offers his mature view on the concept or inner word—a view that basically will remain unchanged in his later works.[34] This time Aquinas goes beyond the limits of the traditional Aristotelian doctrine of knowledge and elaborates it in an innovative way. Aristotle himself

31. *SCG* I, ch. 53, first redaction (quoted from the Leonine ed., vol. 13, 20b14–22): "Ex hac autem specie intelligibili qua primo intellectus informatur, procedit componendo vel dividendo vel qualitercumque conferendo, ad inveniendum aliquam formam intelligibilem quae dicitur per intellectum formata. Et hoc patet tam in intellectu speculativo quam practico. Intellectus enim speculativus ex aliquibus communibus quae cognoscit per hoc quod est eorum speciebus informatus, definitionem investigat, quandam formam intelligibilem formans quam accepit quasi essentiam definiti." Cf. also the deleted passages in ch. 54 (ibid., 21b52–54): "Haec autem forma est in mente ut per intellectum artificis excogitata, in cuius excogitationem deducitur ex aliqua praecedenti cognitione."

32. Ibid., 20b27–31: "Huiusmodi autem forma se habet primo quidem ut intellecta, secundum quod intelligentis operatio ad eam intelligitur per relationem aliquam terminari; secundo vero ut quo intelligitur, prout per huiusmodi formam excogitatam relatio quaedam similitudinis innascitur intelligenti ad rem exteriorem, quae per huiusmodi formam cognoscitur. Sic igitur respectu secundorum cognitorum [that is, extramental reality] in intelligente duplex intelligibilis forma consideratur, una qua intelligit tantum, ut pote per eam ad intelligendum formata [read "formatus" with Geiger, "Les idées divines," 226, n. 1; or read "formatur"], alia qua intelligit et quae intelligitur simul, utpote per intellectum formata et intellectum rei exteriori conformans."

33. This is suggested by Geiger, "Les rédactions successives," 232; and Luca Tuninetti, *Per se notum* (Leiden: Brill, 1996), 137.

34. In this I differ from Paissac, who considers the discussions in *De veritate* and *SCG* as the second, and the texts in *De potentia* and *ST* as the final stage of the development of Aquinas's theory of the word. Paissac's grouping of texts is mainly based on his specific interpretation of Aquinas's distinction between *relativum secundum esse* and *relativum secundum dici.* That interpretation (and Paissac's notion of a "pure relation") has been criticized in some reviews of his book: cf. the reviews by L.-B. Geiger, *Bulletin thomiste* 8 (1947–1953): 480–83; A. Patfoort, *Bulletin thomiste* 8 (1947–1953): 122–26; F. von Gunten, *Freiburger Zeitschrift für Philosophie und Theologie* 4 (1957): 322–29. However, from their criticisms these reviewers do not draw consequences about Paissac's grouping of texts.

had actually remained content with a theory about the abstraction of the intelligible species and the reception of that species in the potential intellect, and he did not go further than what he called "affections of the soul." But Aquinas now develops Aristotle's view further and adds a new fundamental insight. We can summarize his mature view as follows. According to Aquinas, there is a logical—not chronological—sequence in the human act of understanding:

1) First the agent intellect abstracts the potentially intelligible species from the material conditions it has in the *phantasmata.*
2) Next, the potential intellect receives the abstracted, actually intelligible species, is informed and brought into act by it.
3) Then the intellect in act brings forth an *intentio* or inner word in its act of understanding; it conceives the concept, which is what is understood *(quod intelligitur)*—as it exists intentionally.

The first step (abstraction) is absent from God's mind, because it involves potentiality. But the second (apart from the transition from potentiality to actuality implied by the reception of the species) and third ones can be predicated properly of God. The divine intellect is in act by the divine essence and brings forth an immanent *intentio.* In his self-knowledge, God brings forth a concept, a word, which is identical with the divine essence and, like the divine essence, is the similitude of all external things.[35] The crucial difference in comparison to the accounts in *De veritate* and the first redaction of *Summa contra gentiles,* book I, chapter 53, is that discursive reasoning is no longer required for the procession of the *intentio* or inner word. The *intentio* proceeds immediately from the intellect in act. As endterm of the act of the intellect as such, that is, of immediate intellectual intuition, it docs not involve discursivity. In the background is a clear distinction between the intellect as such *(intellectus)* and reason *(ratio).* The *intentio* may be either a single concept or a proposition, depending on whether it is the endterm of the first or of the sec-

---

35. *SCG* I, ch. 53 (final redaction), no. 3: "Ulterius autem considerandum est quod intellectus, per speciem rei formatus, intelligendo format in seipso quandam intentionem rei intellectae, quae est ratio ipsius, quam significat definitio. Et hoc quidem necessarium est." And no. 5: "Intellectus autem divinus nulla alia specie intelligit quam essentia sua. . . . Sed tamen essentia sua est similitudo omnium rerum, per hoc ergo sequitur quod conceptio intellectus divini, prout seipsum intelligit, quae est verbum ipsius, non solum sit similitudo ipsius Dei intellecti, sed etiam omnium quorum est divina essentia similitudo. Sic ergo per unam speciem intelligibilem, quae est divina essentia, et per unam intentionem intellectam, quae est verbum divinum, multa possunt a Deo intelligi."

ond operation of the intellect, but in both cases it does not necessarily imply the third operation of discursive reasoning, which belongs to reason qua reason.[36] On this new view also, what is known intuitively and non-discursively proceeds from something else, that is, it proceeds from the intellect in act. Hence, also first principles and naturally known notions proceed from the intellect and are truly concepts or inner words. In short, discursivity *(cogitatio)* and the inner word are clearly dissociated.[37] The inner word then is "an act from an act," it does not by itself connote an imperfection or potentiality,[38] and can therefore be predicated of God properly, not just metaphorically.

Both Geiger and R.-A. Gauthier believe that Aquinas's final solution for the problem of the plurality of the divine ideas as expounded in this third redaction of *Summa contra gentiles* I, chapter 53, was in fact discovered by Aquinas earlier and in a different context, namely, in the discussion about the procession of the Word from the Father in *Summa contra gentiles,* book IV, chapter 11. Geiger points out that this long chapter shows the "same movements of ideas and the same vocabulary" as *Summa contra gentiles,* book I, chapter 53, and gives the impression of being "a discovery."[39] In *Summa contra gentiles,* book IV, chapter 11, Aquinas argues that "word" by its very meaning implies a real relation of origin[40]—but he does so without invoking discursive reasoning.

If Aquinas reached his mature view on the inner word when writing *Summa contra gentiles* IV, chapter 11, in which he can account for the relationality of "word" on the basis of the intrinsic meaning *(ratio)* of "word," the dating of the second redaction of *In I Sententiarum,* ds. 27, question 2, article 2, qa. 1 be-

---

36. For the three operations of intellect and reason, cf. *In Periherm.* I, prol. Cf. also *De veritate,* q. 15, a. 1, ad 5: "Sed ratio nostra . . . potest in aliquem actum simplicem, et in aliquem actum compositum vel prout componit praedicatum subiecto, vel prout componit principia in ordine ad conclusionem. Unde eadem potentia in nobis eat quae cognoscit simplices rerum quiditates et quae format propositiones, et quae rationicatur: quorum ultimum proprium est rationis in quantum est ratio; alia duo possunt esse etiam intellectus, in quantum est intellectus."

37. Cf. *In Joh.,* ch. 1, lc. 1: "Et inde est quod in anima nostra est cogitatio, per quam significatur ipse discursus inquisitionis, et verbum, quod est iam formatum secundum perfectam contemplationem veritatis."

38. Cf. *SCG* IV, ch. 14, no. 3.

39. Geiger, "Les rédactions successives," 239–40, n. 1. Cf. also R.-A. Gauthier, *Somme contre les gentils. Introduction* (Paris: Editions Universitaires, 1993), 105.

40. *SCG* IV, ch. 11, no. 13: "Est autem de ratione interioris verbi, quod est intentio intellecta, quod procedat ab intelligente secundum suum intelligere . . . Oportet igitur quod a Deo secundum ipsum suum intelligere procedat verbum ipsius. Comparatur igitur verbum Dei ad Deum intelligentem, cuius est verbum, sicut ad eum a quo est: hoc enim est de ratione verbi."

comes a problem. For Gauthier has argued that the whole of the *Summa contra gentiles* was finished (in its final redaction) in 1264–1265, before Thomas left for Rome in September 1265.[41] But why then would Thomas introduce, about a year later, an extrinsic justification for "word" being a personal name, that is, a justification based on actual usage and not on the intrinsic meaning of "word," in the second redaction of *In I Sententiarum,* ds. 27, question 2, article 2, qa. 1, written in Rome in 1265–1266 according to Leonard Boyle?[42] This, I think, is a serious problem either for the dating of the (final redaction of the) *Summa contra gentiles* or for the dating (if not the whole hypothesis) of the second redaction of the *Commentary on the Sentences,* book I. I do not know of any discussion between Bataillon, Boyle, and Gauthier about the relation between the datings of *Summa contra gentiles* and the second redaction of *In I Sententiarum.* But I am curious what the outcome would have been.

V. Summary

Aquinas's theory and theology of the word show a remarkable development. In my reconstruction of it, the development was motivated by Aquinas's desire to reconcile two theological views, inherited from Augustine, namely, the standpoint that Word is a personal name in God and the doctrine of divine ideas, with an Aristotelian doctrine of knowledge. In the first stage, as found in the *Commentary on the Sentences,* Aquinas remains within an elementary traditional Aristotelian framework and does not succeed in integrating the two Augustinian themes into it. In the second stage, represented by the texts in *De veritate* and the first redaction of *Summa contra gentiles* I, chapter 53, he elaborates the Aristotelian epistemology and focuses on the notion of discursivity in order to account for "word" as personal name and for the plurality of divine ideas. The main theological problem with this view is

41. Gauthier, *Somme contre les gentils,* esp. 105–8. J.-P. Torrell, *Initiation à saint Thomas d'Aquin,* vol. 1, *Sa personne et son œuvre* (Fribourg: Editions Universitaires, 2002), 148–53, adopts Gauthier's view. Gauthier relies heavily on Paissac's grouping of texts for determining the *terminus ante quem* of the *Summa contra gentiles.* I divide the three stages of Aquinas's development differently, but this has no direct bearing on the dating of the *SCG.*

42. Cf. section II of this chapter, "First Stage: *Commentary on the Sentences,*" above. Boyle does point out that a "year or more later . . . he abandoned entirely his *'personaliter-essentialiter'* distinction when he came to compose the *prima pars* of the *Summa theologiae* I, q. 34, a. 1, c.)" (Boyle, "Alia lectura," 425). In this paper I argue that Thomas had already abandoned the distinction at the time of writing the *De veritate* (around 1256–1257). Also in the third redaction of *SCG* I, ch. 53 (1259), the distinction plays no role.

that discursive knowledge cannot be attributed to God properly. The third and final stage, found in the third redaction of *Summa contra gentiles,* book I, chapter 53, in *Summa contra gentiles,* book IV, chapter 11, and later texts, presents Aquinas's mature position. His elaboration of Aristotle's cognitive theory constitutes a radical innovation, going beyond Aristotle himself, by distinguishing sharply between abstraction and formation of the concept (or inner word) and by characterizing this formation as a direct procession from the intellect in act—not as an indirect, mediated process of discursive reasoning. In this way Aquinas reconciles Augustinian theological heritage with an Aristotelian position, to the benefit of both.

However, this reconstruction of Aquinas's development raises a serious problem with regard to the claim of Leonard Boyle that the *textus receptus* of *In I Sententiarum,* ds. 27, question 2, article 2, qa. 1, represents the second redaction of book I of Thomas's *Commentary on the Sentences,* written at Rome in 1265–1266. If Gauthier and Geiger are correct in dating the third redaction of *Summa contra gentiles* I, chapter 53, before Aquinas's departure for Rome, it does not make sense that Thomas would revert to a former position while in fact he had already developed his mature view, which could solve the problem in a more convincing way.

4

Augustine, Aristotelianism, and Aquinas

Three Varieties of Philosophical Adaptation

John M. Rist

Etienne Gilson used to claim, not least in *Being and Some Philosophers*, that Platonists are regularly confused (at best) about the relation between essence and existence: I presume that his attention was primarily directed not at some ancient Platonist, but at Avicenna, who, in distinguishing essence and existence, was induced to argue that existence is an accident of essence.[1] For Plotinus and ancient Neoplatonists, of course, the "essence" of a thing is associated with the degree of its unity as that thing, and that unity, indicating not *that* a thing is but *what* a thing is, is determined by its return to its source. The One itself, however, does not return, nor is it a finite thing.

Augustine thinks in the Platonic tradition, and it may be helpful to see why Gilson's charge should not be brought against him—as indeed against most other ancient Platonists. For Gilson does indeed bring such a charge, at least by misassociation, against Augustine when he writes,

Faithful to the tradition of Plato, St. Augustine thinks less about existence than about being; and since he is convinced that to change is not truly to be, the contingency he

---

1. For a good recent survey of Aquinas's relationship to specific Neoplatonic themes see C. D'Ancona, "Historiographie sur platonisme mediéval: Le cas de saint Thomas," in *Saint Thomas au XXe siècle,* ed. S.-T. Bonino (Paris: Pierre Téqui, 1994), 198–217.

tries to explain is not so much the contingency of *existence,* in the proper sense of the word, as the contingency of *beings* which, even though they are not nothing, still do not have a sufficient reason in themselves for being what they are.[2]

Problems about existence will be one of the topics I want to look at in considering more precisely something of the relationship between Aquinas and Augustine, not least in light of a comment of Alasdair MacIntyre's—on another of my own present themes (that of freedom and the possibility of virtue)—that in Aquinas "the Augustinian understanding of fallen human nature is used to explain the limitations of Aristotle's arguments, just as the detail of Aristotle often corrects Augustine's generalizations."[3] But before proceeding to specific cases, I want to put Aquinas's philosophical situation in the late thirteenth century into a broader cultural context. That should help us understand something of the wider importance of Augustine in Aquinas's philosophical history and hence something of its significance in the fortunes of philosophy itself.

A few years ago—well before 9/11—the novelist Anthony Burgess wrote an article in the *London Times* in which he raised the question of the differing attitudes of orthodox Judaism, Islam, and Catholic Christianity toward philosophy. His main point was that Christianity had succeeded in establishing a modus vivendi with philosophy, while Islam had failed to do so, and he pointed to the comparatively minimal development of philosophy in the Islamic world from the time of al-Ghazzali until Western transplants began to arrive in the nineteenth century. His thesis was that, rightly or wrongly, the dominant cultural figures and forces within Islam judged philosophical inquiry incompatible with right religion and, therefore, secured that it be actively discouraged or emasculated, just as Western secularism and post-Christianity (including the remains of Christianity itself)—the Great Satan in his various sociopolitical guises—are judged incompatible with faith by many Muslims today.

Clearly the picture I have drawn is oversimplified, but there is certainly something in it, and it raises the following question: if it was Aquinas, above all, who achieved a "cohabitation" between Catholic Christianity and philosophy (including what he might think of as bad philosophy), whereas Avicenna and Averroes failed to perform a parallel operation in Islam—and Maimonides (on the Jewish side) may be said to have both failed and succeeded,

---

2. E. Gilson, *The Christian Philosophy of Saint Augustine* (New York: Vintage Books, 1967), 21.
3. A. MacIntyre, *Whose Justice? Which Rationality?* (London: Duckworth, 1988), 205.

though I do not want to push that further in this paper—and if the form of philosophical challenge which they all faced was the same new "Aristotelianism," can we identify some of the reasons for Aquinas's comparative success? For if I am right about him, it was indeed a success which should be identified as one of his major contributions to Western and indeed human culture.

It seems to me that the influence of Augustine in general, and his relationship to Aquinas in particular, provides an approach to significant parts of my question: not that we should think only of Augustine; we should allow Dionysius, Boethius, and many another of his predecessors, both direct and indirect, their due share of the credit. But insofar as everyone in the Catholic Middle Ages was in some sense an Augustinian, one has to recognize the special significance of the bishop of Hippo. In what follows, therefore, I want to discuss, however briefly, three dissimilar instances of how Augustine relates to Aquinas and then attempt a few quick conclusions. The themes I want to talk about, in differing degrees of detail, are: 1) what Aquinas would think of as the distinction between existence and essence and their identity in God; 2) the relationship between Aquinas's semi-Aristotelian account of freedom and Augustine's theories about the fall of man and original sin; and 3) some aspects of the Platonic-Augustinian problem of the relationship between the soul and the body (especially in the case of females) in the context of a Thomistic account of man as created in the image of God. In each of these cases, we shall see Aquinas reacting to his Augustinian heritage—whether consciously or unconsciously—in different ways, but these different ways will help us reach more general conclusions. I shall leave you to make your own decisions as to the degree of philosophical as distinct from cultural success Aquinas has achieved in transforming and adapting what he received, only wishing immediately to draw to your attention the breadth and depth of the specifically Christian tradition of philosophy and theology (not merely of canon law or its equivalent) which Aquinas inherited—as well as some of its limitations and (in that historical phrase) some of its "incomplete successes."

1. Existence

Here I can be comparatively brief on Aquinas, since I believe the basic facts are comparatively well established, but on Augustine, and on the Platonic, Stoic, and Neoplatonic traditions upon which Augustine drew, I shall have to linger a little longer.

First, an important footnote about Aquinas will help us understand why his reconciliation of Aristotle and Augustinianism was somewhat easier than might seem likely, if—in pure historical ignorance—we were simply to read through Aristotle, Avicenna, and Augustine and compare them. Certainly much Thomistic interpretation of Aristotle goes beyond Aristotle. By that I do not mean that if Aristotle had lived in the thirteenth century, he would necessarily have repudiated the thought of Aquinas; what I mean is that if he had been willing to accept the thought of Aquinas, he would have had to abandon some of the ideas he himself proposed in the fourth century B.C., as well as allow that Aquinas had raised new, strictly metaphysical questions which he himself had not considered. (An example of the latter would be that Aristotle's first cause is a first cause of motion; Aquinas's first cause is the cause of the existence of all things.) When I was a student, we were told that many of the differences between Aristotle and Aquinas were caused by the need for Aquinas to bend what he wanted to say so as to make sure his ideas did not come out as counter-Christian (parallel suggestions were made about Maimonides and Averroes). Much of that is just wrong: we now know that an apparently more Thomistic Aristotle, that is, an Aristotle who (for example) is a defender of providence and offers a first principle who is an efficient cause of the universe (not just a final cause) is largely the product not of Abrahamic religion, but of the late-antique Neoplatonic commentators on Aristotle[4]—which brings him much closer to Augustine than his historical original would have wished. Such history, of course, was unknown to Aquinas; what he did know, however, was that there were various versions of Aristotle in circulation, and he set himself to show that of those available—none of which was always the historical Aristotle—some were not only better philosophically, but (a fortiori) more Christian than others.

In a sense all this is a bit irrelevant: there is no reason why Aquinas, as a Christian Aristotelian, should feel any obligation to follow Aristotle slavishly, even had he had the historical knowledge to do so accurately. The more surprising thing about Aquinas (and others in the thirteenth century) is not that they diverged from the historical Aristotle but that they followed him as much as they did, and indeed, on existence, Aquinas hardly followed the historical Aristotle at all.[5]

4. See especially R. Sorabji, ed., *Aristotle Transformed* (Ithaca, NY: Cornell University Press, 1990).

5. *Some* of the comments of C. Fabro are still helpful. "Platonism, Neo-Platonism, and Thomism," *New Scholasticism* 44 (1970): 69–100.

Like all philosophers, Aquinas found his attention drawn to what his predecessors and contemporaries read and what they found puzzling. And along with Aristotle, those read included Avicenna and Averroes, and Aquinas knew that they differed radically over existence, Averroes ridiculing Avicenna's claim that even in God, existence is an accident of essence. But what seems to have interested Aquinas even more than the dispute is the fact that the relation between essence and existence was debated at all. This was not, or at least appeared not to be—I shall pursue this in a moment—a debate with which his early Christian predecessors had been much concerned, but it was clearly an important debate, once begun, for a Christian philosopher. Aquinas's solution, as we know, is that in God existence and essence are one, in that God's necessary existence itself is his essence, while the existence and essence of all else—all, that is, that is created—is possible. So the distinction between creature and Creator can be expressed in terms of possible and necessary existence. This is not a problem in Aristotle precisely because, as I have noted, Aristotle has no concern to explain the existence of things (or God) as such. The Aristotelian world is a given; its nature and its changes, not its existence, are what is to be explained. The reason for this difference between Aristotle and Aquinas is susceptible of a quite simple philosophical explanation, and as we shall see in a moment, the philosophy is borne out by the history of philosophical theology. Of course, since Aquinas takes Aristotle's first principle to be an efficient as well as a final cause (in a Neoplatonizing manner) in refuting both Avicenna and Averroes, he may have supposed that he really was defending Aristotle; in fact he was offering a new defense for what was, by his day, a traditional Christian position.

As I have said, it was one of Gilson's most serious mistakes to claim that Platonists in antiquity as well as later were blind to questions of existence; in part the mistake was due to his tendency to assimilate ancient Platonism to modern idealism. In any case a brief survey of ancient thought and assumption about existence should set the matter out more clearly and bring us down to the position of Augustine.

So far from being blind to existence, most ancient philosophers were puzzled about how one could think about anything else: fictitious subjects, let us say, like chimeras, let alone non-being or nothingness itself. The full name of each Platonic Form is "The existent X itself" *(auto ho estin X)*. In the *Timaeus,* Plato, who had long boldly denied the Parmenidean axiom that what does not exist cannot be spoken of or thought, but who also recognized that, if one wishes to explain what is (and what both is and is not), one must also speak of what is not, suggested that a kind of "bastard reasoning" *(a nothos logismos)* is required to handle non-being. His thinking is clear: if you cannot see or otherwise indicate non-being, what is it that you are speaking about? It might seem—rightly, of course—as though you were referring to something which is no obviously existing object of reference.

Leave Plato aside and turn to Aristotle's *Categories:* here we have ten (or so) ways of speaking about what there is. Aristotle found it very difficult to distinguish true from false statements about non-existent subjects; if something does not exist how can anything "true" (that is, referring to reality) be said of it? So what do you do with the proposition that "Alice in Wonderland is blue"? How do you distinguish it from "Alice in Wonderland is white"? It was not least to remove analogous difficulties, it seems, that the Stoics proposed that before discussing existents in the world in terms of their own category system, we must raise the prior question, "Does X exist or not?"[6] If not, it cannot be categorized (unless we treat it *as if* it exists, and we should be sure that we are making the right judgment on that).

Contrary to some current opinion, there is an existential sense of the ordinary word *einai* (to be) in ancient Greek, but in many Hellenistic quarters, another word *(huparchein)* gradually superseded the more common *einai,* and there eventually followed, especially among philosophers and to meet philosophical needs, a corresponding noun *huparxis,* meaning "existence." But it was probably Philo (for reasons to which we have already alluded) who first (perhaps adopting the Stoic concern to identify whether things exist or not before categorizing what they are) made the move of distinguishing God's existence (we know *that* He exists) from questions about his nature (we do not know *what* He is, that is, his *ousia*).[7] And why then did Philo make this move? Because his God, as distinct from the Greek gods, is somehow omnipotent and because he wanted to distinguish God as some kind of creator from creatures. I say some kind of creator because I do not think that Philo (any more than the earlier Christians) had yet distinguished between the creation of creatures *ex nihilo* and their total dependence on their "Creator."

6. See J. M. Rist, *Stoic Philosophy* (Cambridge: Cambridge University Press, 1969), 153–54.

7. See *Virt.,* 21, and *Post.,* 169, with J. Glucker's comments in "The Origin of ὕπαρξις and ὑπόστασις as Philosophical Terms," in *Hyparxis e hypostasis nel Neoplatonismo,* ed. F. Romano and D. P. Taormina (Firenze: Leo S. Olschki Editore, 1994), 19. The whole volume is essential reading for those who wish to pursue the subject of *huparxis* (and existence) in later antiquity, especially in Neoplatonism.

So we have established that by the Christian era, there was a full awareness among Platonizing philosophers about the importance of existence and no question of its being understood merely as "unity" or "self-identity," and among Jews and Christians, a growing awareness that the old distinction between the One and the many must be explicated as also a distinction between a Creator and a creature. But a key problem remained both for Christians and pagans: how do we name such a first principle? To cut a long story short, Plotinus's view (which Augustine knew) was that the first principle is to be called the One and that it is "beyond *ousia*" (not a particular substance; here the key "source" is Plato, *Republic,* book 6) and that it is beyond *einai* (which in Greek means "beyond finite being"). For the One certainly exists, though it has no specific form (which is why it cannot be directly described) and no specific limits (that is, it is somehow not indefinite but infinite).

Augustine's esteemed predecessor Marius Victorinus (the translator of whatever Plotinus Augustine read) knew that the first principle is to be called the One (so it is *unum, sive unalitas* as well as *ipsum unum* beyond being, *Adv. Arium,* 1.49.11), and that as beyond being, it is a "pre-being" (*proon,* à la Porphyry).[8] He also called it *exsistentia,* the Latin version of "existence itself" (*Adv. Arium,* 3.1.25), which "Candidus" glossed as *ipsum esse et solum esse* (1.2.19).[9] And he was able to use the Latin word *esse* as a mere token—intelligible to the cognoscenti—for the Greek *einai* (finite being), while significantly claiming that it is in virtue of the power *(potentia)* of "existence" that life and happiness are possible. Augustine himself, however, (thinking in Latin rather than in translationese) declined to call God the One and to use any form of the language of "beyond" or pre-being, though, importantly, retaining most of that language's conceptual content. He prefers to call the first principle simply "God" and to refer to Him as the highest or truest (presumably = purest) being, but again as "being itself" (*ipsum esse* rather than *ipsum unum, En Ps.,* 135 (134); *Io Ev.,* 38.8– 9).[10] Of course, he agrees with Victorinus (and with Plotinus, who is some sort of source for both of them) that He exists and that, in a sense, Philo (and

8. Cf. *Ad Cand.,* 2.28; 3.7; 15.2.

9. Porphyrian influence on these matters also reached Aquinas via Boethius's *De hebdomadibus,* but I leave that aside in the present discussion. For the Porphyrian sense of Boethius on "being" and "what is" (and Aquinas's re-reading of Boethius) see P. Hadot, "Interprétation philologique et interprétation philosophique d'une formule de Boèce," *Les Etudes Classiques* 38 (1970): 143–56.

10. Gilson recognizes in the associated phrase (said of God) that "He is what He has" *(quae habet haec et est)* "one of the sources [notice, other than Avicenna and with Boethius added in] for the medieval doctrine of the distinction between essence and existence," *The Christian Philosophy of Saint Augustine,* 353, n. 5 (*De civitate Dei,* 11.10.3).

his many Christian followers) were right in saying that we can agree *that* God exists but it is impossible to determine immediately *what* He is—unless of course God, through Christ, is able to show us something of his true nature.[11] In other words, God exists as such, without further determination readily accessible to us; to be (as Porphyry seems to have put it) is simply his nature[12]— and later on Damascius (if unknown to the mainstream Christian tradition) clarified matters here as elsewhere by often identifying Porphyry's "existence as such" *(to einai monon)* with what we have seen to be the standard term for existence, namely *huparxis.* In this Damascius follows Proclus who, as Carlos Steel put it, used *huparxis* as a technical term to designate divine existence beyond any essence.[13]

So Augustine's position—which clarifies and advances the intent while often discarding the vocabulary of Neoplatonism—is that God exists as the unique Creator *ex nihilo;* the existence of all else is dependent on his will. Since Augustine also followed an ancient Christian tradition (clear since the late second-century bishop Theophilus of Antioch, *Ad Autol.*1.4) that to deny *creatio ex nihilo* (understood as in or with time) would be to undercut the absolute supremacy of God and, indeed, the intelligibility of the concept of God itself, pointing ultimately toward Manichaean dualism,[14] he is able to make the dependence of all else on the first principle clearer and more radical than was possible for Plotinus and the Neoplatonists who wanted to combine total dependence of the many with the notion that since the One has always existed, the others must always have existed too. We shall shortly notice Aquinas's approach to this.

For Augustine, God is the Creator *ex nihilo* of the universe, of which every part is dependent on its Creator. But as I shall emphasize again later, Au-

---

11. For some of this, see *On Psalm 145* (144), 6; *Sermon,* 117.3.5.

12. For something of the Plotinian origins, see K. Corrigan, "Essence and Existence in the *Enneads,*" in *The Cambridge Companion to Plotinus,* ed. L. P. Gerson (Cambridge: Cambridge University Press, 1996), 105–29. P. Hadot should be credited with the first serious account of Porphyrian language about existence, originally in "La métaphysique de Porphyre," in *Porphyre,* ed. H. Dörrie (Geneva: Fondation Hardt, 1966), 125–64. Hadot's attempt, however, to identify Porphyry as the author of a relevant but anonymous commentary on the *Parmenides* is probably to be rejected; see A. Smith, "Porphyrian Studies since 1913," *Aufstieg und Niedergang der römischen Welt* II.38.2 (Berlin: de Gruyter, 1987), 740–41; and M. J. Edwards, "Porphyry and the Intelligible Triad," *Journal of Hellenic Studies* 90 (1990): 14–25.

13. C. Steel, "*Huparxis* chez Proclus," in Romano and Taormina, *Hyparxis e hypostasis,* 100.

14. For Augustine recently see N. J. Torchia, *Creatio ex Nihilo and the Theology of St Augustine: the Anti-Manichaean Treatises and Beyond* (New York: Peter Lang Publishing, 1999); and more broadly G. May, *Schöpfung aus dem Nichts: Die Entstehung der Creatio ex Nihilo* (Berlin/New York: 1999).

gustine, sometimes sadly, knows very little about Aristotle, and some of what he thinks he knows he does not like. He makes no use of anything like the Thomistic language of an "*act* of existing"; nevertheless—and interestingly for comparative purposes—he thinks (as did Victorinus) very particularly of God's power. Hence, if we want to find something in Augustine which does part of the work of the "act-of-existence" language, that is where we must look. God's nature as "being itself" is the power which creates all finite beings from nothing. Perhaps it might be objected to some Neoplatonists that they explain only how the One is some sort of form for what it produces or for what participates in it, not how it imposes that form. But Augustine knows that Plotinus distinguishes two senses of "activity," the activity of a subject as such and the activity of its external effects, a thesis which Aquinas himself deploys (*ST* I, q. 48, a. 5, c.).

So keeping in mind Augustine's position on the total dependence of all on the God whose existence and power of existence is, as we might say, unmitigated, let us turn back to Aquinas confronting Avicenna and Averroes on necessary and possible existence. And let us say that the core of the emphasis on existence (on which Avicenna seems to have misfired) is that only a Creator could be a necessary being—in Augustine's language, has the power to be what he is; all others (though they might exist as possible thoughts) are also only possible existents. At the center of Aquinas's position on necessary being is the Augustinian and Christian doctrine that all of creation depends on God. Where, of course, Aquinas goes further is to combine the essence-existence distinction in Avicenna's version with his inherited, Christian data to produce an argument specifically for the *existence* of God, perhaps indeed the argument of his set which has the greatest rational power. But let us return again to *ex nihilo;* Augustine inherits a view that without it, the concept of God itself is unintelligible; Aquinas, on the other hand, thinks that although God is somehow a creator *ex nihilo,* that does not entail that he must also have created the universe in or with time. That the world has not always existed, he thinks, is given by faith (*ST* I, q. 46, a. 2, s.c.); it cannot be demonstrated, though the philosophical probabilities are in favor of it (*SCG,* II, 38). In this he is arguably closer to the position of Plotinus than to that of Augustine, and it is interesting that the more obviously Augustinian Bonaventure holds a different opinion.

I personally find it hard to understand how one can hold, as Aquinas does, that *creatio ex nihilo* (to be accepted by faith and judged—patristically—as "proper" to God, *ST* I, q. 45, a. 1) does not in itself entail creation with time.[15] There is a modern proposal which is supposed to help with this: Lloyd Gerson has argued that a Plotinian-type dependence of all on a Creator is de facto a *creatio ex nihilo*. I must confess that I see neither the logic of that nor (for that matter) that *creatio-ex-nihilo* language is suitable for Plotinus at all.[16] As for Augustine, perhaps he would have accepted that claims about *both creatio ex nihilo and* the non-eternity of the world are, in philosophy (as understood Thomistically), only probabilistic. But let us move on to simpler things.

2. Virtues and the Fall

In the first part of this paper, I showed Aquinas taking advantage of a new philosophical tradition to express a philosophically technical version of ideas which had been expressed more crudely, but perhaps theologically more challengingly, by Augustine and other patristic writers. In dealing with essence and existence we found Aquinas dealing sympathetically with Aristotelian metaphysical traditions about substances as he understood them mediated through the contrary views of Avicenna and Averroes and on at least one issue, the matter of the eternity of the world, at least seeming to give the Aristotelian picture more credit than Augustine would have allowed. When dealing with the human capacity for moral action and the effects of the fall, we see an area where Aquinas, to the apparent dismay of some of his modern admirers, normally follows Augustine more directly, though I suppose those modern admirers would also want to say that, happily, Aquinas looks, at least at times, a bit more Pelagian.

In the index to Robert Pasnau's recent exactly five-hundred-page book on Aquinas's account of man,[17] there are just two references to grace in the body of the text, and the word "fall" is not indexed. And in those two references, we find an apparent contradiction—or at least an attempt to find some wiggle room in which to slip a slightly less Augustinian (and perhaps more Pelagian) interpretation. In the first passage (discussing *ST* I-II, q. 78, a. 1, c., on the temptations of the passions), we read that Aquinas seems more Augustin-

15. For discussion see N. Kretzmann, *The Metaphysics of Creation* (Oxford: Oxford University Press, 1999), 142–82.

16. L. P. Gerson, *Plotinus* (London/New York: Routledge, 1994), 27 (also citing *ST* I, q. 46, a. 5, s.c.).

17. R. Pasnau, *Thomas Aquinas on Human Nature* (Cambridge: Cambridge University Press, 2002).

ian than Aristotelian. There follows a reference to Augustine's divided will in *Confessions*, book 8, 5.10, but, according to Pasnau, "Aquinas resists the Augustinian suggestion that he never could have overcome his weakness on his own. Augustine, in giving all the credit to God, implies that we are helpless in the face of our weakness. This is quite alien to Aquinas's approach" (252). Pasnau then cites a passage from the *Disputed Questions on Evil* which does not seem to justify the account of "freedom" which he claims is Aquinas's view, and in any case a few pages later, he allows that "by bringing grace into the picture at this point, Aquinas moves in the direction of a more Augustinian account, on which our tendency to act against reason is a part of the human condition that only God can reliably cure" (262; on *ST* II-II, q. 156, a. 3, ad 2). And, Pasnau continues, "Aquinas's broader thinking about grace confirms this perspective. Without grace, human beings inevitably stray from the good. . . . Grace provides us with the infused virtues," etc.

Pasnau's *Thomas Aquinas on Human Nature* is a book full of references, but along with only two references to grace and none to the fall, there is also none to a well-known contemporary philosopher, Alasdair McIntyre, who takes a much less grudging, and much more helpful, view of Aquinas's handling of the role of grace. So far from regretting its appearance as an apparently improper encroachment on human freedom—I find nothing in Pasnau about the important Augustinian distinction between being free and being freed: a fact which, however, may be genuinely informative about Aquinas as well as about Pasnau—MacIntyre rightly notices that it is precisely because of his insistence on grace that Aquinas's ethics breaks with the ethics of Aristotle on important questions: "I also argued earlier that Aquinas does not merely supplement Aristotle, but that he shows Aristotle's account of the teleology of human life to be radically defective."[18]

But although MacIntyre is right in insisting on Aquinas's introduction of a broadly Augustinian account of grace, Pasnau's rather different presentation sheds light on what is certainly a problem for Aquinas and, in a rather different way, for Augustine as well. Let us approach the difficulty via something of what Aquinas says about the notorious problem of the "natural" and more than natural ends at *Summa theologiae* I-II, question 62, article 1:

Our happiness or felicity is twofold. . . . One is proportionate to human nature, and this we can reach through our own resources. The other, a happiness surpassing our nature,

18. MacIntyre, *Whose Justice?* 205, cf. 181.

we can obtain only by the power of God.... To be sent to this supernatural happiness, we have to be divinely endowed with some additional sources of activity; their role is like that of our native capabilities which direct us, not, of course, without God's help, to our connatural end. Such sources of action are called theological virtues.

There is an oddity about this passage which may be illuminated by a text from *De veritate,* 24, a. 14, in which Aquinas observes that man can choose to do non-moral things without grace, but not without God (since a secondary cause is ineffective without God as primary cause). Similarly our present text seems to suggest at the beginning that we can reach our natural end through our own resources, but later a caveat appears: "not, of course without God's help." The idea is glossed elsewhere (for example, *ST* I-II, q. 109, a. 2) as follows, "In the state of corrupt nature, people fall short of what they could do by their nature, so that they are unable to fulfill it by their own powers"; and again

In the state of perfect nature, humanity needs a gratuitous strength added to natural strength for one reason, namely, in order to do and wish supernatural good; but for two reasons in the state of corrupt nature, namely, in order to be healed and furthermore in order to carry out works of supernatural virtue. (*ST* I-II, q. 50, a. 22)

Aquinas's position is now clearer. In the case of moral action—I shall return to "moral" in a moment—Adam before the fall was adequately equipped to reach "natural virtue"; that is, he was free to reach it, it was within his capacity. After the fall, however, we are not so free; we also need, even for natural virtue, to be "healed." The term "healed" is, of course, traditional and Augustinian, but for the sake of clarity—not least to Pasnau—it would have been useful if Aquinas had also said "freed," that is, freed from the effects of original sin, which is *inter alia* what he means.

We can now see *part* of the problem with interpreting Aquinas's account of freedom in general: it is notorious that some think his account is compatibilist, others libertarian; others a combination. I commented on Pasnau's limited references to grace and the absence from his account of the notion of being freed. Now we can see that, in a sense, he is justified. When Aquinas talks about freedom, he is talking about what human nature is—in effect, about the way we were created by God, though we are not now in that condition. And the confusions that arise in our uncertainty over whether we are talking about fallen or unfallen man are compounded by the fact that much of Aquinas's discussion of freedom in questions 82 and 83 of the *prima pars*—the sections primarily treated by Pasnau—is in a broad context: not, that is, whether we are free to act morally, but whether we are free to act in general.[19] But perhaps we need more clarity on the possibly different analyses required, on the one hand, for the proposition "I kick this ball freely," which may introduce metaphysical and "Aristotelian" problems, and, on the other, for "I kick this wretched prisoner freely," which may bring up more "moral" and specifically Augustinian concerns.

Augustine's concern with freedom is almost exclusively (though not entirely) in a "moral" context, embedded in discussion about the nature, effects, and causes of moral evil; Aquinas, in the *Summa,* driven in good measure by his concern with free action in an Aristotelian context of means and ends and of physical determinism, is more general. In questions 82 and 83 of the *Summa theologiae, prima pars,* on the will and its freedom, there is very little about moral freedom, that is, the freedom which is most obviously affected by original sin. We can see this if we look at question 83, article 1. Aquinas begins with a discussion of decision making, and an "Augustinianism" might be expected to follow when he cites St. Paul (Rom 7:15) to the effect that "I do not do the good I will but rather the evil I hate." But whereas Augustine would have been led by this text into reflection on our fallen spiritual state, Aquinas draws the wider conclusion "Man does not have free will" *(liberum arbitrium),* then moves on to Aristotle's *Metaphysics,* and then returns (in article 2) to conclude that we cannot take Paul's meaning to be a denial that we walk and run freely, but that our "free will" needs to be helped by God.

So there are at least two potentially conflicting factors to be recognized in Aquinas's account of freedom and its relationship to Augustine's account of grace; on the one hand, Aquinas's discussions are often set in a wider context than Augustine's debate about moral evil and its cure; on the other, they point (as MacIntyre saw) to a reformed version of Aristotelian "secular" ethics. One must admit, however, that part of the difficulty in explicating Aquinas's account is inherited from Augustine himself: not only in that Aquinas treats Augustine as too systematic a thinker, but by the misleading way in which, by hindsight, Augustine himself encouraged some of his own writings on freedom, especially the *De libero arbitrio,* to be "read."

As I said, Augustine's writings on freedom, though innocent of Thomas's wider Aristotelian context, are embedded in discussion of the origins of mor-

19. Similar ambiguities lurk in the sections on free will in the *Quaestio de veritate,* though here the moral (Augustinian) emphasis is much clearer.

al evil. And as with Aquinas, it is often difficult to determine whether, when Augustine is talking about freedom, he refers to Adam's unfallen state or to our present condition. This difficulty is complicated further by his important thesis that there is a sense in which we are one in Adam, so that in talking about Adam before the fall he is also talking about our original (but, in some sense, also actual) nature. It is true that Augustine tries to extricate himself from ambiguity in that he emphasizes that we are indeed free but only to choose the bad. But there is ambiguity here too, in that while unfallen Adam and we are all free in some sense—we have "free choice"—we are thus "free" in very different ways.

Two final points in summary: first, there is little specific attempt in Aquinas to explicate the ambiguity of the concept of "freedom," such as, that we are now *only* free to choose the bad (though this is touched on in *De veritate*, 24, a. 12); but, second, in trying to refute any Pelagian claim that the *De libero arbitrio* (though not texts composed after 396) offers an account of the will which, in some way, itself looks "Pelagian," Augustine seems to have persuaded himself that he intended in that text to give an account of the "will" other than the account he actually gave.

So how do I close this section? Perhaps first by noting that I see unclarities in the analysis of "freedom" passing from Augustine to Aquinas, and then exacerbated by Aquinas's Aristotelianism (exploited by such as Pasnau) and his easy movement from discussions of moral freedom to questions of freedom to act in a wider sense, but without detailed attention to the relationship between the two topics. Sometimes it at least appears as though one can leave grace and original sin out of straightforward philosophical narratives about freedom while bringing them in as an addendum or correction when the theological going gets tough. This creates difficulties not only in sorting out the relation between moral freedom and freedom to act in general but trivializes the theory of original sin itself.

For that theory is not just a theological dogma. Certainly it is that, but it is also a theological proposal offered in answer to a genuine experiential and empirically observed situation, that identified by Paul (along with a number of earlier pagans) as not being able to do what one knows to be right. For the dogma of original sin is proposed, at least by Augustine, as a response to what he claims are radical and obvious features of human life and the human condition. As I have said elsewhere, in the late nineteenth century the conditions of human life which support the credibility of the dogma of original sin may have seemed remote from the cozy world of North Atlantic liberals. Their contemporary dogmatic successors, however, have no excuse for following their absurdly rosy account of basic human nature as we experience it. When I was a student, I used to say that the only things the Christians had got right were encapsulated in the theory of the fall of man. I conclude this section by agreeing with MacIntyre that Aquinas used Augustine to correct Aristotle's theory of the virtues, but add that he also followed Augustine where he was ambiguous about which human nature was in question, and would perhaps have done well to be more consistently (even blatantly) Augustinian in his treatment of human (incomplete) depravity and the perceived need for us to be not just "healed" but "freed."

3. Souls, Bodies, Females, and the Image of God

We all know that it was a primary concern of the Neoplatonists in antiquity to defend some sort of Platonizing account of the relationship between the soul and the body, primarily against the Stoics, who held that if there is to be any interrelationship between the soul and the body, then the soul must be material, a view attractive to Christians like Tertullian who thought that this Stoic position might assist with an account of bodily resurrection. But Platonists were also under attack from Aristotelians who held that the soul is the form of a living body possessed of organs; indeed Plotinus devoted great efforts to arguing that Aristotle's account of soul-body relations is little more than a glorified, if inglorious, version of the notion of the soul as a harmony of the bodily parts which Aristotle himself (as well as Plato) had specifically rejected. And it seems that Plotinus had persuaded Augustine of the inadequacy of Aristotelian hylomorphism on these grounds. In this connection it should be recalled again that only in late antiquity, when Aristotle had become heavily Neoplatonized, was he of much interest to Christians. Earlier on he was held to be an atheist (that is, a denier of providence like Epicurus) with a dodgy and potentially value-free account of the human soul.

There are basically two accounts (perhaps complementary rather than antithetical) of human nature in Western philosophy: one, which for simplicity I will label "metaphysical" and Aristotelian, the other "moral" and Platonizing. The primary concern of the "metaphysicians" is to explain how we are (or are not) a soul-body unity; the primary concern of the "moralists" is to insist that man is, above all, a moral agent. Augustine is in this latter, Platonizing tradition. But seriously philosophical members of that tradition, while insisting on their own principles, will recognize the need to face the challenge of the "metaphysicians." Hence Augustine quickly grew dissatisfied with saying that we are our souls and simply that we are souls using our bodies. He now preferred to think of us as some kind of "mixture"—a Stoicizing term—and to observe that anyone who thinks he can understand the nature of man without consideration of his body is a fool (*De An. et eius Orig.,* 4.2.3). We are a *persona:* a type of mixture of soul and body which affords a unity which cannot be merely accidental.[20] It seems to have been largely reflection on theological themes such as the Incarnation and the Resurrection of the body (very much part of the *regula fidei* in Christian antiquity) which hastened Augustine's move in this direction.

This is not the place to explain the incomplete success of Augustine's alternative to hylomorphism, but rather to move temporarily to Aquinas, who does have an Aristotelian hylomorphism, properly understood, at his disposal. What I should like to look at, therefore, is the success of such hylomorphism (as deployed by Aquinas) in resolving the philosophical difficulties of another problem area in Augustine (whose treatment of the matter was known to his medieval successor). The matter in question is whether woman was created in God's image.

First some background. In the *Politics,* Aristotle argues against the Platonic view that the virtue of men and women is the same on the ground that bodily differences must reflect and be reflected by significant psychological differences; hence that women are inferior to men in their deliberative capacities, a view which the *De generatione animalium* reinforces by its biological claims that there is a sense in which women are incomplete men (1.737A28). Now Plato's position on the female soul, so far as we can reconstruct it, and as it was reconstructed by later Platonizers in antiquity, is that the souls of women are in fact (at their best) male; hence male virtue is available to them under certain conditions. This sort of position reappears among patristic writers who, more generally, divide into two groups, the larger holding that women are not created in God's image, though they can attain to God's image and likeness by their ways of life, and the others (all Platonizers) who hold that the female soul is originally male (or asexual, understood more or less as male). At least for this latter group, sexual difference is a strictly bodily phe-

20. For my more detailed views see J. M. Rist, *Augustine: Ancient Thought Baptized* (Cambridge: Cambridge University Press, 1994), 92–147.

nomenon—an apparent impossibility in Aristotelian terms. Roughly speaking, however, Augustine belongs to this group.

Now let us turn to the question of the image of God. Obviously for ancient Christians, relevant biblical texts required exegesis if the teaching was to be understood. Among the principal texts were the following:

1) Genesis 1:26–27, dealing with man's creation in God's image and containing the phrase "male and female He created them"—accompanied by Genesis 2:21–24;
2) 1 Corinthians 11:7, man is the image and glory of God, and woman is the glory of man; and
3) Ephesians 4:13, we should arrive at the unity of faith and of knowledge of God, unto a perfect male *(andra),* to the fullness of Christ.[21]

It was especially the Pauline texts which caused problems, and Augustine (first at *Gen. ad Litt.,* 3.22.34, then in the *De Trinitate,* 12.7.10) was the first patristic writer to confront 1 Corinthians (which many took to be scriptural evidence against woman's creational status as image) head-on, explaining it in terms of Genesis as actually supporting the view that woman was so created[22]—but apparently to an inferior degree, since the purpose of her creation itself was procreation (cf. *Gen. Litt.,* 9.5.9): qua helpmeet, woman is not an image of God, qua human being, she is. Other (possibly related) explanations of female inadequacy were also available: the idea that in the *saeculum,* the weaker mind should be subservient to the stronger (*Q. Hept.,* 1.153), or, more generally, that the male sex is more honorable: Jesus was male "since it was fitting that he should take the human nature of man, the more honorable of the two sexes" (*83 Questions,* 11).

Let us now return to Aquinas, whose extensive use of Aristotelian sociobiology separates him from many of his medieval predecessors.[23] Aquinas agrees

21. A glance at the translations and glosses on *andra* shows how the interpreters have felt obliged to fudge this extraordinarily obscure passage.

22. Cf. T. J. van Bavel, "Woman in the Image of God in St. Augustine's '*De Trinitate* XII,'" *Signum pietatis* (Würzburg: 1989), 267–88, esp. 269ff.; R. J. McGowan, "Augustine's Spiritual Equality: The Allegory of Man and Woman with regard to *imago Dei,*" *Revue des Etudes Augustiniennes* 33 (1987): 255–64; D. G. Hunter, "Augustinian Pessimism? A New Look at Augustine's Teaching on Sex, Marriage, and Celibacy," *Augustinian Studies* 25 (1994): 153–77; K. Børresen, "Patristic Feminism: The Case of Augustine," *Augustinian Studies* 25 (1994): 139–52.

23. For a brief summary of the relevant texts see K. E. Børresen, "God's Image, Is Woman Excluded? Medieval Interpretation of Gn 1:27 and 1 Cor 11:7," in *Image of God and Gender Models in Judaeo-Christian Tradition,* ed. K. E. Borresen (Oslo: Solum Forlag, 1991), 208–27, esp. 218–24. A more nu-

with Augustine that it is only (or at least "chiefly")[24] in his "mind" that man is created in God's image (*ST* I, q. 93, a. 4 and 6, s.c.; cf. I, q. 75, a. 2, ad 6, etc) and that the distinction of male and female relates only to the body. At this stage he seems to ignore the Aristotelian point that substantive bodily differences, in a hylomorphic account of man, must also affect the nature of the soul. Had he followed Aristotle closely, he might have argued here that since the soul of woman (and the virtue of woman) is different from that of man, it is likely that even though man and woman are both created in God's image, the two sorts of image are different. Indeed, he has already offered more scriptural reasons for coming to this very conclusion (*ST* I, q. 93, a. 4, ad 1): "God's image is found equally in both man and woman as regards that point at which the idea of 'image' is principally realized, namely an intelligent nature. . . . But as regards a secondary point, God's image is found in a male in a way in which it is not found in a woman." Of course he might have gone on to say—and, according to a recent interpreter, could have gone on to say[25]—that God's image is also found in a woman in a way in which it is not found in a man, but he does not do that. Rather he continues, "For man is the beginning and end of woman, just as God is the beginning and end of all creation" and proceeds to cite Paul in 1 Corinthians that "the male is the glory and image of God, while the woman is the glory of the man."[26] So like Augustine, Aquinas tries to evade a commonly accepted "misogynist" reading of 1 Corinthians without neglecting it altogether.

That, in effect, Aquinas more or less spells out the apparent Augustinian view of the inferior version of woman's imaging of God is hardly surprising— not least when we turn to his selective use of Aristotle—to whom Augustine, as I have noted, has no recourse in such matters. For Aquinas's adoption of hylomorphism (which might have encouraged him to see less inferiority in the female image than Augustine) is counterbalanced by the Aristotelian notion that there is a sense in which the male is the perfect type of human being, so that the psychological differences between the sexes which the hylomorphic theory demands are interpreted (as in Aristotle himself—and

---

anced treatment of some of the texts can be found in P. A. de Solenni, *Towards an Understanding of Woman as Imago Dei* (Rome: Edizioni Università della Santa Croce, 2003). Børresen's treatment is too harsh on Aquinas, de Solenni's is sometimes too anachronistically kind.

24. *"Principaliter,"* though a *repraesentatio* of the image also exists in the human body (*in corpore hominis*—therefore presumably both male and female). 4 *Sent.,* d. 49, q. 4, a. 5 b.

25. De Solenni, *Towards an Understanding.*

26. Cf. *On 1 Corinthians,* lectio 2 (*"vir specialius dicitur imago Dei secundum mentem"*).

despite a plausible reading of Genesis that both males and females are created in God's image) as implying the inferiority of one sex, namely, the female, to the other.

When Aquinas speaks of the actual creation of woman, he begins with the just-mentioned text of the *De generatione animalium* (1.737A27) where Aristotle argues that woman is formed as an incomplete male (*ST* I, q. 92, a. 1).[27] And this biology predictably issues elsewhere in a clearer account of female psychological inferiority.[28] Woman is by nature subordinate to man because among human beings *(in homine)* the power of rational discernment varies considerably (*ST* I, q. 92, a. 1, ad 2 and 3),[29] and again, "Woman is subject to man because of the weakness of her nature, of both the spirit and the body" (*ST,* supp., q. 81, a. 3, ad 2; cf. *SCG,* III, 122).[30] And she is more prone to concupiscence (*ST* II-II, q. 149, a. 4). This inadequacy of the incomplete male, as Aquinas spells it out, means not that women are defective in *their* nature (*ST* I, q. 92, a. 1, c.): nature as a whole needs a woman, as such, for the purpose of women is to assist in procreation (broadly understood as including domestic life; *ST* I, q. 92, a. 2, s.c., following Aristotle, *Nicomachean Ethics,* 1182A19). Nothing could do the job required better.[31] The incompleteness comes out when a woman is compared with a man, as the process of conception indicates, for "the active power in the seed of the male tends to produce something like itself, perfect in masculinity"—and various Aristotelian explanations are given for why, at times, the active power fails and an inferior female is produced. In brief, then, for Aquinas, woman is created in God's image, but despite the possibility that hylomorphic theory might offer a more radical complementarity, Aristotelian metaphysics and psychology give way to Aristotelian biology so as to reinforce the tradition—deriving partly from biblical texts urging that women not exercise authority over men (1 Tm 2:12; 1 Cor 7,

27. Cf *SCG,* III, 94, etc.; with A. Mitterer, "Mann und Weib nach dem biologischen Weltbild des hl. Thomas und dem der Gegenwart," *Zeitschrift für katholische Theologie* 57 (1933): 491–556.

28. Cf. *Scripta super libros sententiarum,* 2 d. 16, 1, 3, contra.

29. This sentence is often misconstrued as simply saying that in males (wrong for *in homine)* the power of reason is greater. But the sense is not changed by correcting the translation: the fact that among human beings some are more "reasonable" than others is offered as an explanation of male psychological superiority.

30. Cf. also *ST* II-II, q. 149, a. 4; and II-II, q. 156, a. 1, ad 1, c.

31. Cf. *In Sent.,* 4.44.1.3. The significance of the contrast between *natura particularis* and *natura universalis,* insofar as it affects Aquinas's conclusions about the "chance" incompleteness of each individual woman when viewed in an Aristotelian context, is exaggerated by M. Nolan, "The Defective Male: What Aquinas Really Said," *New Blackfriars* 75 (1994): 156–66. Nolan is followed too closely by de Solenni, *Towards an Understanding,* 101–3.

etc.) and partly from more general traditional interpretations of scriptural remarks about the image of God, not least that of Augustine—that the degree
of imaging (though not of intelligence) is unequal between the sexes.[32]

Some Limited Conclusions

My choice of themes has been selective, but granted the limited nature of
my survey the following variegated points should be taken into account in
some future more wholesale analysis of Aquinas's Augustinianism.

1. Aquinas's teaching on existence shows an unconscious tendency toward,
and a philosophically enriched clarification of, a genuinely Augustinian position.

2. Aquinas's teaching on grace and virtue (on the other hand) shares various Augustinian ambiguities (not least about whether philosophical analysis of human action relates to fallen or unfallen man), while at the same time
giving a more "Pelagian"—not doctrine, but—impression to contemporary
philosophical readers than Aquinas would probably have produced had he
been able to give Augustine the benefit of a more historical (and historicist)
reading. This is apparent not least in his controverted treatment of freedom,
where the relation between various old Augustinian difficulties and the anti-
determinism of Aristotelian accounts of human action in general is left rather
unclear. Is this a problem of amalgamating Aquinas the moral theologian and
Aquinas the "would-be" (I speak here with great hesitation) secular philosopher?

3. On woman and the image of God, Aquinas's selective resort to Aristotle
reinforces rather than corrects some of the more problematic parts of Augustine's position, not least because he is inclined (perhaps in defense of what he
takes to be Scripture) to give disproportionate weight to Aristotle's biological
assumptions over against his hylomorphic theses in metaphysics and psychology. (But note that there is also another unintegrated but more interesting
side to Aquinas on the nature of women.)

In the three themes I have discussed, I have discerned no consistent pat-

32. There are, however, indications elsewhere in Aquinas that a more serious complementarity
could be developed from his writings—in other words, that he is more inconsistent than I have been
able to outline here. De Solenni (*Towards an Understanding*) discusses the themes of the "equal friendship" of marriage and of a *consortio socialis* (106–22), of the superior love of Mary Magdalene (110–12;
also picked out by Augustine in this connection), and of receptivity (113–18) and of its importance in
perfect human thinking and human relationships with God.

tern in the effects of Aquinas's Aristotelianism on his Augustinian base. In one case, the new philosophy develops and elucidates Augustinian intimations, in another, its still undigested state confirms old prejudices while at the same time widening the philosophical debate, in the third, an opportunity is lost, insofar as Aquinas uses Aristotle selectively to confirm Augustinian confusion. Here then we have a sample of the successes and failures in the complex relationship between Augustine and Aquinas.

5

Imago Dei

A Test Case for St. Thomas's Augustinianism

John P. O'Callaghan

The topic of man as the *imago Dei* is a prominent theme in St. Thomas's major systematic works, including his Scriptum super libros sententarium Magistri Petri Lombardi (Commentary on the Sentences), the Quaestiones disputatae de veritate *(De veritate)* and the Summa theologiae *(Summa).* His theological approach to the theme is deeply informed by St. Augustine, in particular his De Trinitate. Thus, the topic presents a paradigm instance for considering St. Thomas as an Augustinian. In his exhaustive and excellent treatment of St. Thomas on the *imago Dei,* To the Image of the Trinity: A Study in the Development of St. Thomas's Teaching, D. Juvenal Merriell has argued that in St. Thomas's work there is a development in his treatment of the topic. He examines St. Thomas's discussion in the Commentary on the Sentences, the *Quaestiones disputatae de veritate,* and the *prima pars* of the Summa theologiae.[1] However, Merriell's treatment presents the development in almost entirely theological terms, without much discussion of any philosophical development in the underpinnings of St. Thomas's thought.

I will argue here that St. Thomas's theological discussion of the *imago Dei*

---

1. D. Juvenal Merriell, *To the Image of the Trinity: A Study in the Development of St. Thomas's Teaching* (Toronto: Pontifical Institute of Mediaeval Studies, 1990).

shifts over time in important respects precisely because he more fully developed his own understanding of the Aristotelian philosophical resources available to him, and as he moved away from some of the philosophical claims made about human nature by St. Augustine in the *De Trinitate*.[2] For brevity's sake and the purposes of this paper, I am interested in St. Thomas's discussions in question 10 of the *Quaestiones disputatae de veritate,* and the *prima pars* of the *Summa theologiae.* The *Quaestiones disputatae de veritate* were composed just after the Commentary on the Sentences, and the philosophical shift between the *De veritate* and the *Summa theologiae* is particularly sharp. My conclusion will be that the Aristotelian philosophical resources St. Thomas draws upon in the two discussions affect in different ways how he understands the central Augustinian thesis that a human being is an *imago Dei* in virtue of his or her rational nature. Thus, even as St. Thomas remains deeply committed to that theological thesis, his theological understanding of it evolves with the evolution of the underlying philosophical presuppositions.

I will proceed as follows. First, I will provide a sketch of the way in which St. Augustine presents the mind (mens) as the *imago Dei* in his *De Trinitate*. Second, I will describe how St. Thomas integrates St. Augustine's insights into his own discussion of the mind in question 10 of the *Quaestiones disputatae de veritate.* Third, I will note significant ways in which St. Thomas's discussion of human nature in the prima pars of the *Summa theologiae* departs from, and even quietly rejects certain Augustinian features of his own earlier discussion. Finally, I will point out how those shifts change important features of St. Thomas's theological discussion of man as the *imago Dei.*

St. Augustine's *Imago Dei*

The central theme of St. Augustine's *De Trinitate* is, of course, the divine Trinity, not the *imago Dei.* The *imago Dei* theme enters into the discussion much later in the second half of the work as St. Augustine searches for a created mirror within which he might catch a glimpse of the Trinity that he knows by faith, a mirror that may help him to understand that Trinity better. Pre-

---

2. I am using the term "philosophical" here as characterizing a rational discourse that takes its starting point from a reflection upon the material world around us, including our activities in that world, and that proceeds argumentatively without relying upon premises that can only be known to be true as a result of the gift of supernatural faith in the Divine Trinity revealing them. This use does not exclude the possibility that various philosophical theses, in this narrow sense, may well be prompted psychologically and historically by the content of supernatural revelation.

ceding the discussion of the *imago Dei* are systematic discussions of the doctrinal teaching of the Church on the divine Trinity that must be adhered to, as well as an extended scriptural analysis of texts that are to be understood in the light of that doctrinal teaching, and a philosophical discussion of how different words are said of God in light of certain claims that are traditionally asserted to hold of God, claims like those involving God's simplicity (that God is not composed of parts). So, one way to read the structure of the *De Trinitate* is that it begins with the Church's faith in the revelation of God as a Trinity, and then turns to an examination of human nature in that light, only to return to God in the last book as incomprehensibly beyond the created mirror in which the *imago Dei* is found. The justification for such a procedure is the text of Genesis in which it is written that man is made in the image and likeness of God. St. Augustine's procedure is not to discover features of creation that can then be applied to God, but, rather, starting with what he believes about the Trinity as his guide, to find vestiges or likenesses of God in creation and then the image proper in the human mind.

There are two central features of the doctrinal teaching on the Trinity that shape the structure of the *imago Dei* that St. Augustine discovers in the mind: the real unity of being of the divine nature amidst the real diversity of the three Persons. The real unity of the divine nature is adhered to against the Arians, while real diversity of Persons is adhered to against the Sabellians.[3] However, against the general background of ancient polytheism, the *unity of being* in one nature of the three divine Persons would seem to be the more difficult element of the Trinitarian formulation from Nicea—"God from God . . . , of one being. . . ." The three Persons of the Trinity are not said to be of one divine nature in the way in which three human persons might be said to be of one human nature, for the human beings are three distinct persons *and* three distinct beings or substances.[4] In the Nicean formulation there are three Persons, but only one divine being. St. Augustine solves the difficulty of the unity of being amidst the three distinct Persons by a theory of naming in which the term "God" is said absolutely of the one being while the personal names of "Father," "Son," and "Holy Spirit" are said relatively. While one divine be-

---

3. *S. Aurelli Augustini Hipponensi Episcopi de Trinitate,* in *Augustinis, Hipponensis Episcopi opera omnia, post Lovaniensium theologurum recensionem,* vol. 42 of *Patrologiae latinae,* ed. J. P. Migne (1865), esp. lib. VI, cap. IX, no. 10, against the Arians; and lib. VII, cap. IV, no. 9, against the Sabellians. See also Merriell, *To the Image of the Trinity,* 18–24.

4. De Trinitate, lib. VII, nos. 7–11.

ing, the Persons are said to be distinguished from one another as really related to one another.[5] My task here is not to examine whether this solution works, but to look at how it determines and shapes St. Augustine's later account of the human mind in which the image of God is found.

When we turn to the discussion of man as the *imago Dei,* we find that the prior Trinitarian solution determines very strongly the structure of the mind that St. Augustine describes in the second half of the work. St. Augustine first distinguishes the mind *(mens)* from the rest of human nature as what is essential or substantial in human nature or the soul *(anima).* Mind is also distinguished from all those activities we share in common with animals.[6] He writes:

Anything in our consciousness that we have in common with animals is rightly said to be still part of the outer man. It is not just the body alone that is to be reckoned as the outer man, but the body with its own kind of life attached, which quickens the body's structure and all the senses it is equipped with in order to sense things outside.[7]

The acts we share in common with animals are the acts of the outer man, while the activities of mind that are distinctive of our rational life constitute the life of the inner man. St. Augustine's stress upon these two different areas of our life is so strong that he comes close to suggesting two principles of life in human nature. The mind is one principle, and the other is this principle he refers to enigmatically as the principle that "quickens the body." I do not want to suggest that St. Augustine actually maintained that there are two souls in a human being, just that there is a certain ambiguity about how we are to understand the relationship between the mind and this principle that "quickens the body" having "its own kind of life attached." When we come to the discussion of St. Thomas in the *Summa theologiae* this ambiguity will play an important part in understanding his position.

St. Augustine is quite clear that these broad aspects of our lives must be

---

5. See *De Trinitate,* lib. V–VII, *passim.* And for St. Augustine's own general summary of his solution, the prologue to lib. VIII, no. 1.

6. Mind is preeminent in the soul. *De Trinitate,* lib. XV, no. 11. "Mind" signifies or "displays" essence or substance. Lib. IX, no. 2. Mind, as memory, intellect, and will is "one life, one mind, one substance." Lib. X, no. 18. The whole context of lib. X shows that it would be inappropriate to claim that the things "we have in common with animals" are "one life, one mind, one substance." While we may not want to say that they are another substance, they are not the substance that is the mind. All translations from the Latin are mine, unless otherwise indicated.

7. In the translation of Edmund Hill, O.P., *The Works of St. Augustine, A Translation for the 21st Century: The Trinity* (New York: New City Press, 1991), 322. *De Trinitate,* lib. XII, no. 1.

clearly distinguished, the animal from the rational or mental. This separation allows him to eliminate one of the possible Trinitarian likenesses he comes up with as not genuinely constituting the *imago Dei,* namely, the trinity of sensation, mental attention, and will. In St. Augustine's account, it is not sufficient that the sense organs should be acted upon by the world in order that sensation take place. It must also be the case that the mind attend to the state of the sense organs in order that it be aware of what is taking place in the sense organs, and thus of the sensible world that is affecting those organs. But this mental attention can only take place as a result of the activity of the will causing the mind to attend to sensation. Thus St. Augustine discerns three elements in sensation that might provide elements for the Trinitarian character of the *imago Dei,* the activity of the sense organs brought about by the world, the act of mental attention, and the activity of the will directing the mental attention to sensation.

However, according to St. Augustine this trinity cannot be a genuine *imago Dei* because sensation as part of the life of the "outer man" does not have the requisite underlying unity of nature or being with mental attention and will that could be an image of the divine unity of nature.[8] The activity of a sense organ is one of those activities we share with the animals, and must be attributed to the principle that quickens the body's functions, not the essence or substance of the soul which is the mind. For St. Augustine there appears to be a deep fissure in the unity of human nature. So there is not enough unity of being between sensation on the one hand and mental attention and will on the other hand. So, to pursue the *imago Dei* we must turn away from the life of sensation, inward toward the life of the mind to find a unity of being sufficient to form the basis of the *imago.* It is to be found in the essential and substantial unity of the mind. Here we see the anti-Arian doctrinal teaching on the divine unity shaping the image that is to be found in man.

Turning within then to the "inner man," St. Augustine tries out and abandons some other possible Trinitarian likenesses.[9] Perhaps the most important trinity that he initially abandons is the trinity of mind, understanding, and love. This trinity was attractive to St. Augustine because one can say that understanding and love proceed from the mind, as the Son and the Spirit

---

8. *De Trinitate,* lib. XI, no. 5 for the image involving these three having a certain unity, but not a unity of nature or being; no. 6 for the turning away from this image because it belongs to the outer man.

9. See ibid., lib. XI, *passim.*

proceed from the Father. However, he abandons this trinity because, while "understanding" and "love" are said relatively, that is, they are always *of* something, "mind" is said absolutely like "God," not like "Father." In other words, the trinity of mind, understanding, and love does not capture the Trinitarian solution he had come up with concerning God, in which "God" is said absolutely, and "Father," "Son," and "Holy Spirit" are said relatively.

Instead, St. Augustine settles upon the trinity of memory, intellect, and will as acts of the one mind. Here we have a genuine *imago Dei*. These three acts of mind are understood to be quite distinct from any act we share with animals. They are three different acts, and yet they are the one mind's acts. Indeed, St. Augustine does not hold that they are acts "of the one mind." Rather, he writes that "these three, memory, understanding, and will, are not three lives but one life; nor three minds but one mind; therefore it follows that they are not three substances, but one substance."[10] They are not acts *of* the mind, but simply the mind acting, that is, the mind remembering, knowing, and willing. Thus there is an adequate unity of being in their diversity for being the *imago Dei*. "Mind," like "God" is said absolutely, denoting the "essence" or "substance" of man as "God" denotes the one being of the divine nature, while "memory," "intellect," and "will" are all said relatively of that mind, insofar as they all take and are related to some formal object. In the image, "memory" corresponds to "the Father" as that from which understanding proceeds. "Intellect" corresponds to "the Son," as that in which understanding is expressed, particularly in the utterance of an inner *verbum*. "Will" corresponds to "the Holy Spirit" as expressing the love that proceeds from memory and intellect, but also binds them together.[11] Yet they are one mind. And the mind is the one essence or substance of the soul.

However, it is not enough that they are the one mind's acts each related to some formal object. In that case their unity would not be complete. St. Augustine argues that for this mental trinity to be a genuine *imago Dei,* it cannot simply image God on the part of the subject in which it exists, but it must image God on the part of the objects of the acts. In the first place, these acts cannot be concerned with exterior things. To be concerned with exterior things is to be caught up in the life of the "outer" and "lower man."[12] At the very least there must be an indwelling of the acts and objects, as there is an indwelling within the Trinitarian life. In other words, the mental trinity is

10. Ibid., lib. X, no. 18.   11. Ibid., lib. XIV, no. 13.
12. See ibid., lib. X, nos. 6–7. But especially, lib. XI, no. 8.

properly an *imago Dei* only when the acts take each other as their objects, the mind remembering itself, knowing itself, and loving itself in these three acts; knowing its loving, loving its knowing, and so on.[13] Even here it falls short of the genuine image, for it must be occupied with itself *as* the *imago Dei,* remembering itself, knowing itself, and loving itself *in God.* In that case, it becomes transparent to itself. St. Augustine had begun the discussion of the mind by asserting that nothing could be as present to the mind's understanding as it is to itself.[14] However, as the discussion ends it becomes clear that this claim is only verified in the mind's recalling to itself God's presence within it, expressing that recollection in its own self-understanding, and loving itself in that presence of God to the self.[15]

Finally, St. Augustine argues that in general for the mind to be an *imago* there can be no nature higher than it, that is, between it and that of which it is an *imago.*[16] Thus, insofar as the mind as a unity constituted by memory, intellect, and will, remembering, knowing, and loving itself in God is an *imago Dei,* there can be no nature higher than it that stands between it and God in the scale of being an image. Any other kind of creature that may be an *imago Dei* will be at best a creature of equal greatness to the human mind, but no greater. St. Augustine does not explicitly mention angels, that is, purely spiritual substances, when he makes this point. However, it does follow from it that the human rational nature, that is, the mind, which St. Augustine says is the essence and substance of the human soul and thus the essence or substance of the human being, is of equal greatness with the angels as images of God. Indeed, with this result in mind, while the soul may differ from a purely spiritual substance because of its involvement with the body and the principle that "quickens" the body, insofar as he says that the mind is the essence and substance of the human soul, excluding from that essence and substance the "outer" life of the body and all those activities we share in common with animals, it seems to follow that the essence and substance of the human soul, the mind, does not differ from the essence and substance of a purely spiritual substance. As minds we are "essentially" and "substantially" akin to angels. I have stated this last claim in a deliberately provocative way in order to highlight later a feature of St. Thomas's discussion.

In conclusion to this discussion of St. Augustine, we want to take from him the clarity of his discussion of the *imago Dei* with its emphasis upon the

13. Ibid., lib. X, no. 18.   14. Ibid., lib. X, no. 9.
15. Ibid., lib. XIV, no. 15.   16. Ibid., lib. XI no. 9.

unity of the mind amidst the diversity of memory, intellect, and will. We do not want to think of these acts as distinct from the mind, but as identical with it as its acts attending to the most appropriate object, namely, the divine Trinity and the mind itself *as* the image of the divine Trinity. In addition, we want to keep in mind that methodologically we attain to this vision of the *imago Dei* by an explicit turning away from the "outer man" as it is experienced in and through acts of sensation, and the life of the body generally.

The *imago Dei* in St. Thomas's *Quaestiones disputatae de veritate*

The standard English translation of St. Thomas's tenth disputed question on truth announces that it concerns "the Mind" simply.[17] This title is misleading, for the Latin text is explicit in detailing its Augustinian subject matter, namely, "the mind in which there is an image of the Trinity," where the first point of inquiry is "whether the mind, inasmuch as there is in it an image of the Trinity, is the essence of the soul, or one of its powers."[18] The Augustinian import of the question is clear from the fact that St. Augustine had in fact asserted that the mind, in which the *imago Dei* is found, is the essence of the soul. And the objections in article 1 are predominantly objections based upon texts from St. Augustine's *De Trinitate*.[19] This particular point of inquiry on the Augustinian theme, as well as many of the other articles throughout the question, is driven by the twelfth- and thirteenth-century influx of Aristotelian themes into the discussion of the human soul. Other articles address such topics as "can our mind know material things in their singularity," "does the human mind receive knowledge from sensible things," "does the human mind know itself through its essence or through some species," "is it through their essence or through some likeness that our mind knows habits which exist in the soul?" While Augustinian elements are always in the background of these particular discussions, for the most part they are driven by distinctive features of the broad Aristotelian account of the soul and cognition. On the

17. Thomas Aquinas, *Truth,* vol. 2, trans. James V. McGlynn, S.J. (Chicago: Henry Regnery Company, 1953).

18. "Utrum mens, prout in ea ponitur imago trinitatis, sit essentia animae." *Quaestiones disputatae de veritate,* X, *proemium.* All Latin texts will be taken from the Index Thomisticus CD-ROM. The translator of the English text provides a translation of this passage only after announcing the topic simply as the Mind, and includes it only after announcing the start of article 1.

19. Of nine objections, six are based explicitly or implicitly upon passages of the *De Trinitate.*

other hand, there are articles of a distinctly Augustinian cast against the background of Aristotelian theses, as for example "is there memory in the mind," "does the mind know material things," "is the image of the Trinity in the mind as it knows material things or only as it knows eternal things," "in this life can someone know that he has charity?"

Structurally it is significant that the question ends in a way that mimics St. Augustine's *De Trinitate,* which had ended with the incomprehensibility of God and thus the ultimate failure of the *imago Dei* as a mirror. St. Thomas finishes by asking "can the mind in this life see God through his essence" (no, in this life short of a miracle; but yes, in the next), "is God's existence self-evident to the human mind, just as first principles of demonstration, which cannot be thought not to exist" (it is self-evident *per se* but not *quoad nos*), and "can the Trinity of Persons in God be known by natural reason" (no). The first nine questions of the *De veritate* that preceded question 10 concerned Truth, particularly the Truth that is God, God's Knowledge, the Divine Ideas, the Divine Word, Divine Providence, Predestination, the Book of Life, and then two questions on the angels. Despite any particular differences of content and detail this broad structure follows St. Augustine's theological method from God to creation as we saw it in the structure of the *De Trinitate.*

St. Thomas's addition of the topic of the angels in questions 8 and 9 can be understood against the background of an Augustinian justification, despite the fact that St. Augustine did not consider them in the *De Trinitate.* St. Augustine in his interpretation of Genesis argues that the creation of the angels as spiritual natures preceded the creation of material reality, and the creation of the human mind, signified in Genesis by the creation of the "heavens" and the "light" of day before the sun and the earth were created.[20] However, St. Thomas does not in these questions describe angels as images of God. There is certainly no biblical warrant from Genesis for doing so, because it is only human beings who are described there as made to the "image and likeness" of God. Still, the broad structure is the theological structure embodied in St. Augustine's work of proceeding from God as font of creation and revelation to creatures. The rational movement from God as revealed to creatures in the light of that revelation is the method of theology according to St. Thomas, in contrast to the method of philosophy that proceeds from creatures to God and does not rely upon revelation but employs unaided reason.[21]

20. *De genesi ad litteram libri duodecim in corpus scriptorum Ecclesiasticorum Latinorum* (Prague: F. Tempsky, 1983), II, 8, pp. 43–45.

21. See *Summa theologiae* I, q. 1, aa. 7–8; and *Summa contra gentiles,* IV, 1.

Despite the Augustinian structure and theme of question 10, there are two features of St. Thomas's discussion of the mind as *imago Dei* of a distinctly Aristotelian cast. First there is the theme of the soul's self-knowledge, and second the heavy reliance upon the distinction between the powers and the essence of a substance. With regard to the soul's self-knowledge, St. Thomas denies the kind of self-transparency of the soul to itself that St. Augustine had posited. Yet St. Thomas argues that the mind in one way knows itself through its essence, and in another way does not. With regard to its mere existence, the mind can know that it exists by its activity. But it does not know what it is, since what it is is determined by what it knows. The mind as potentially knowing the world is like prime matter, and can only be known as actually informed by the forms of material things. The distinction here between these two modes of knowing the mind, that is, knowing *that it exists* and knowing *what it is,* is based upon Aristotle's distinction in the *Posterior Analytics* between knowing *that* something exists and knowing *what it is.*[22]

St. Thomas takes this position because he has adopted the Aristotelian thesis that the essence of something is known through its powers, which powers are known through their acts, which acts in turn are known through their objects. Given this principle, we should not expect a difference here between St. Augustine and St. Thomas with respect to the sense powers. St. Augustine had said that the activities of sense insofar as they are the acts of the outer man are shared in common with animals, and we ought to expect that our understanding of them will involve how they engage the "outer" world of the "outer man." But what of the rational powers of the soul? Here St. Augustine had said that we must turn away from the outer man and its engagement with the "outer" world, in order to turn undistracted within to find the light of truth in which the mind is transparent to itself. And yet St. Thomas argues in articles 4–6 that the proper object of the intellective faculty of the soul is the material being of material substances. Material substance is the proper object of the intellective faculty because it derives its knowledge from sensation and the way sensation engages the world. The mind is purely potential unless it is actually informed by the forms of things. And yet it is a basic Aristotelian thesis that something is known only insofar as it is in act. So the mind must be in act with regard to what it knows, if it is to be known in turn. But for it to be in act with regard to what it knows, it must be actually knowing material objects. So for the mind to be knowable, it must be knowing its proper ob-

22. See Aristotle, *Posterior Analytics,* II, 1, 89b32–35.

ject, material reality. Thus, even the mind, as well as the other powers of the soul, is known through its engagement with the material world.

Still, St. Thomas agrees with St. Augustine that the perfect *imago Dei* cannot be found in the mind knowing material things, but only in its knowing itself, and even more so in its knowing God. Thus with St. Augustine, the task of understanding the *imago Dei* requires a turning within of the soul to understand itself. But in opposition to St. Augustine, such a turning within cannot involve a turning away from what is outside and beyond the soul. So St. Thomas writes,

> our mind is not able to understand itself in such a way that it immediately apprehends itself; but from an apprehension of other things, it comes to an understanding of itself, just like the nature of prime matter is known from the fact that it is receptive of forms of a certain kind[23]

and

> to know what the soul is is very difficult; hence the philosopher writes that it is altogether very difficult to accept anything with assurance about it.[24]

"From a consideration of the nature of the species which is abstracted from sensible things, we discover the nature of the soul in which such a species is received."[25] Thus, methodologically St. Thomas's study of the *imago Dei* differs in an important respect from St. Augustine's. St. Thomas does not think that in one's knowledge of the mind one can engage in a fundamental separation from one's knowledge of material things to apprehend the mind in a kind of pristine clarity. In that case, there is no room for a robust methodological distinction between the "inner" and "outer" man.

In addition, we saw that St. Augustine had clearly stated that the mind is the essence or substance of the soul. But in the first article of question 10, St. Thomas rejects that thesis; the mind is a power of the soul. Merriell notes that this is a rejection on St. Thomas's part of his own earlier position in the *Sentences Commentary,* where he had identified the mind with the essence of the soul.[26] It is interesting that St. Thomas's argument here for this rejection is not a purely Aristotelian argument. It relies upon an etymology deriving the Latin *"mens,"* "mind," from *"mensurare,"* "to measure," which signifies an act. But an act proceeds from a power, and citing the authority of Dionysius,

---

23. *De veritate*, q. 10, a. 8.   24. Ibid., q. 10, a. 8, ad 8.
25. Ibid., q. 10, a. 8, ad 9.   26. Merriell, *To the Image of the Trinity,* 12.

St. Thomas writes "a power or potency is midway between essence and operation."[27]

This rejection of the Augustinian thesis that the mind is the essence of
the soul poses a distinct problem, however, for the Augustinian discussion of
the *imago Dei,* which had found the image of God's unity in the unity of the
mind as the substance or essence of the soul. How can St. Thomas maintain
the anti-Arian unity if the mind is just another power among all of the soul's
powers, in particular, just another power in addition to the soul's diverse powers of memory, intellect, and will?

In fact, St. Thomas appears to solve this difficulty in his responses to the
objections in article 1. The relevant objections, 7 through 9, are grounded in
Aristotelian theses about the nature of powers, particularly their defining acts
and objects. However, St. Thomas follows St. Augustine, and asserts that the
power of mind is constituted by memory, intellect, and will. But now these
three are primarily understood as particular powers of the mind, not acts.
Still, the mind itself is not a power over and above, or in addition to these
particular powers, but a kind of general and potential power constituted from
them, like a hand is constituted from its fingers, and the power of house-
building is constituted from the particular powers of stone-cutting and construction.[28] The unity of God is imaged in the unity of this general power
constituted from memory, intellect, and will, which three powers provide the
image of the Trinity.

Thus, St. Thomas neatly solves a problem he had raised for himself by rejecting St. Augustine's substantialist understanding of the mind against an Aristotelian ontology of powers. He is able to maintain the distinctive Augustinian thesis that the *imago Dei* is to be found in the mind consisting of memory,
intellect, and will.[29] And the unity of mind itself can very neatly preserve St.
Augustine's two main doctrinal concerns about the *imago,* preserving an image of the anti-Arian unity of the divine nature, and the anti-Sabellian diversity of the Trinitarian persons.

Here I disagree with Merriell's treatment of this point in the *De veritate.* Merriell suggests that the mind here is a general power in the sense of

---

27. "Ut patet per Dionysium, cap. XI *Caelest. Hierarch.*" *De veritate,* X, q. 10, a. 1.

28. See responses to objections 7–9.

29. Note, however, the added complication of St. Thomas's understanding of memory. Memory
is not itself a power. Primarily, it is a habitual state of a power. Secondarily, it is not a habitual state of
the intellectual power, but of sense. This complication about memory is too involved to pursue here.
However, St. Thomas treats it as an insignificant complication for his purposes.

"not one particular faculty, but a group of faculties."[30] He argues on the basis of the response to objection 8 that St. Thomas "locates" the image in the mind as this "group of faculties," and yet finds its subject in the soul insofar as the latter is called mind improperly. The problem with this analysis is that it leaves unclear the unity of the image. Is it to be found in the soul, or this "group of faculties"? If the image of the unity is to be found in the soul itself, what point was there to collecting the three powers into a mere group and calling that grouping mind?

There is no explicit evidence in St. Thomas's discussion for the thesis that the image of the unity is to be found in the essence of the soul rather than the mind. Indeed in response to the fifth objection, St. Thomas had written in agreement with St. Augustine that, "in the account of the image, mind holds the place of the divine essence, while memory, intellect, and will hold the place of the three persons."[31] So St. Thomas is concerned to preserve those two features of the image—the unity and the plurality. The sense of the term "mind" in response to objection 5 is clearly not the improper sense that applies to the soul itself, for in conclusion to the passage, St. Thomas writes, "[these three] are said to be one mind, insofar as [they are] taken as parts under a whole, just as sight and hearing are taken under the sensitive part of the soul." The unity of the mind containing the powers of memory, intellect, and will is compared to the unity of the sensitive part of the soul, not the unity of the soul itself. This sense is at play again in response to objection 8, when he writes, "mind, when it is taken for the power, is compared to intellect and will as whole to parts."[32] So the sense of "mind" at play in response to objection 5 is clearly mind as a part of the soul, not the soul itself. And the image of the divine unity is to be found in the unity of mind taken as a part, not the unity of soul. So, for the sake of argument, even if the soul is in some improper sense the subject of the image according to the response to objection 8, the soul does not actually account for the image of unity.

That unity must be found in the "group[ing] of faculties" as a whole containing memory, intellect, and will as parts. However, Merriell's analysis of the text does not adequately account for it. Objections 7 and 8 had established that the mind is a unity in at least the sense of a mere set, collection, or grouping. But Merriell treats the response to objection 9, which refers to the

30. Merriell, *To the Image of the Trinity,* 114–15.   31. *De veritate,* X, q. 10, a. 1, ad 5.
32. Ibid., X, q. 10, a. 1, ad 8.

mind as a "general power," as merely reasserting the point of the response to 8.[33] If Merriell is correct, it is difficult to see the point of the response to 9, for it then appears to say nothing more in describing the mind as a general power than in describing it as a whole consisting of parts, a point already made in response to 8; the response to 9 appears to be superfluous. On the contrary, objection 9 was designed to argue that on the supposition that the mind is a whole with the parts described in the response to 8, it cannot itself be a power, because powers do not have parts. St. Thomas's response to this objection, however, asserts that the mind is a different kind of power from memory, intellect, or will; it is a *general* power; they are *particular* powers. Because it is a different kind of power, it can have parts where they cannot.

In that case, the mind is not simply a grouping of those particular powers. Not any collection of powers can be called a "general power." Consider the collection of powers that consists in the power of reproduction and the power of hearing. There is no general power constituted from this group, or unity to it prior to our simply collecting the two powers into a set of interest to us. St. Thomas clearly wants to attribute a special unity to the powers of intellect, memory, and will that exists in them prior to our collecting them into a set of interest to us. So, in response to objection 9, St. Thomas compares the way in which the mind is constituted from the powers of memory, intellect, and will to the way in which a hand is constituted from the fingers, and, though St. Thomas does not mention it, presumably the palm. But of course a hand is not a mere grouping of its parts, the five fingers and the palm, in the way in which a box of marbles, for instance, is a group containing the marbles as parts. The hand is a whole that expresses an integrated unity of act. Similarly, here in the *De veritate* the mind is a whole that goes beyond the mere collection of particular powers as elements, to a power with its own appropriate unity of act, a unity of act that is not identical with the particular unity of act of any of its parts taken singly.

The point of the response to objection 9 is to defend against the objector's claim that a power cannot contain other powers. But clearly a collection or group can contain powers as parts, without itself being a power. Thus, Merriell's analysis cannot adequately account for St. Thomas's characterization of the mind as a "general power" in response to 9, or even the plausibility of the objector's claim. But the distinction St. Thomas had just made in

33. Merriell, *To the Image of the Trinity,* 114.

response to objection 7 between the sensitive part of the soul and the mental or rational part of the soul tracks very nicely the strong distinction St. Augustine had made between the mind constituting the activity of the "inner life" of the soul, and the activities of sensation, among others, that we share with animals constituting the "outer life" of the soul. The response to objection 9 is designed to guarantee that the mind is something to which we can attribute a robust unity of act, even if it is not the unity of the essence, namely, the unity of act appropriate to a power.

In other words, while St. Thomas rejects St. Augustine's position that the mind is the essence of the soul, he holds on to the unity that St. Augustine had found in the mind. St. Thomas's discussion in the response to the objections, including 5 and culminating in the response to 9, would be pointless unless read as attempting to preserve the unity St. Augustine had located in the mind amidst the diversity of memory, intellect, and will, and thus to preserve the image of the unity of the divine nature amidst the Trinity of Persons.

Finally, St. Thomas distinguishes two different senses in which we can consider the *imago Dei* in the mind, perfectly and imperfectly. The mind is a perfect *imago Dei* when we consider it with regard to its activity, that is, with regard to actually remembering, knowing, and loving. On the other hand, it is an imperfect *imago Dei* when we consider it with regard to the powers simply.[34] This distinction between imperfect and perfect allows St. Thomas to maintain St. Augustine's thesis that the *imago Dei* is most adequately found in the mind's knowing God:

The image of the Trinity is primarily and principally in the mind insofar as it cognizes God, but secondarily in a certain way insofar as it cognizes itself, in particular when it considers that it is an image of God, a consideration which does not stop with itself but carries itself to God.[35]

If we are thinking in terms of the imperfect sense of *imago Dei,* the powers themselves are sufficient to attribute the *imago Dei* to human beings. But if we are thinking of the perfect sense of *imago Dei,* they are not. In the perfect sense, St. Thomas agrees with St. Augustine that the mind as occupied solely with worldly matters risks becoming little more than a likeness of God, not an image, even if in the imperfect sense it remains an *imago Dei.* Here St.

34. See *De veritate,* q. 10, a. 3.
35. Ibid., q. 10, a. 7.

Thomas can make use of St. Augustine's phrase "the outer man" in a moral sense that does not involve the ontological connotations it appeared to have in St. Augustine. A man is living the life of the "outer man" when his mind is preoccupied solely with worldly things rather than with God and those worldly things in the light of God. He is then not as perfect an image as he could be.

St. Thomas Loses His Mind and Finds His Soul in the *Summa theologiae*

When we turn to consider St. Thomas's discussion of human nature and the *imago Dei* in the first part of the *Summa theologiae*,[36] we see that there is a certain amount of continuity with the discussion in the *De veritate*. We also see some distinct shifts in his thought that render his discussion of the *imago* much more complicated and nuanced. I will argue that apart from any larger theological motives, the shift is driven in part by the thirteenth-century Aristotelian controversy about the nature of the soul raging in the universities, a controversy that St. Thomas engages in the *Summa theologiae*, but that was absent in the *De veritate*.[37]

With regard to the continuity with the *De veritate*, there are several points of agreement. First, the structure of the first part of the *Summa theologiae* once again mimics the broad structure of the *De Trinitate*. It begins with a discussion of God and the Trinity. It proceeds to a general discussion of creation and the work of the six days of Genesis. There is an extended discussion of angels as intelligent creatures that precedes the discussion of human beings, which latter discussion culminates in the discussion of the *imago Dei*. Second, methodologically St. Thomas continues to maintain the Aristotelian principle that the essence of the soul is known through its powers, which are known through their acts, which are in turn known through their objects. Third, St. Thomas thus continues to maintain that the human soul can only be known in virtue of its embodied engagement with the world. Finally, he continues to maintain that the *imago Dei* is to be found in man qua rational

36. *ST* I, qq. 75–102.

37. The Aristotelian controversy finds expression in the *Summa contra gentiles* as well. However, there St. Thomas writes nothing about man as the *imago Dei*. So my choice of the *Summa theologiae* discussion is motivated by two considerations—the *Summa theologiae* is later, and it includes both the controversy concerning the soul, and the discussion of the *imago Dei*.

creature. What matters to us here for noticing the difference from the *De veritate* is the focus of his attention in discussing that rational nature, and what he now thinks the mind is, or better, is not.

The first and most significant difference to notice in St. Thomas's discussion of man's rational nature is his abandonment of the mind found in the *De veritate*. He continues to use the term "mind," but very rarely. Instead his focus now is upon the soul, and its powers of intellect and will.[38] When he uses the term "mind" now it is simply a synonym for "intellect," which primarily and properly refers to the power of thought and understanding in contradistinction to the will; as a power it does not include the will as a part.[39] Of course St. Thomas had begun the discussion in the *De veritate* by relating *"mens"* to *"mensurare,"* and associating the latter with the act of intellect. But we also saw that he then expanded the notion of mind beyond the particular power of intellect to include the particular power of will as constituting with intellect a general power that is not identical with either particular power. Now in the *Summa theologiae* "mind" is simply synonymous with "intellect," and there is no extension of it beyond that. Indeed, question 82, article 3, explicitly uses "mind" as a synonym for "intellect" in a way that positively excludes the power of will. Like "intellect" it is also occasionally used analogously and secondarily to refer to the whole soul, since St. Thomas says that the soul itself is named from its highest power, namely, *intellect.*[40]

This move away from the mind of the *De veritate* is no mere verbal shift on St. Thomas's part. In the *Summa theologiae* there is no discussion whatsoever, by any name, of the special general power that St. Thomas had discussed in the *De veritate.*[41] St. Thomas does not explicitly remark that he is abandoning his earlier position. But this feature of his discussion is not a simple oversight, for there is a principled and very good philosophical reason why St. Thomas would abandon it. The power of mind described in the *De veritate* does not do anything. Both here and in the *De veritate,* St. Thomas accepts the Aris-

38. Again memory plays a subordinate role as the habit of intellect from which understanding proceeds.

39. See *ST* I, q. 75, a. 2.

40. St. Augustine holds a similar principle when he says that "it is customary to name the whole from its better part, that is, to name both body and soul, which is the whole man from the soul. Thus it is written that with Jacob there went down to Egypt seventy-five souls, meaning that number of men and women." *De Trinitate,* lib. VII, no. 7.

41. I have discussed this shift in much greater detail than I can here in my "Aquinas's Rejection of Mind, Contra Kenny," *Thomist* 66 (2002).

totelian principle that powers are specified by their acts, which are specified by their objects. It follows from this that there is no reason to posit a power in a substance when there is no formal object for it to attain by its act. When we look back at the *De veritate* discussion, it is evident that the object of the intellect is Truth. The object of the will is The Good. Intellect is the power by which we respond to the intelligibility of being, and arrive at the truth. By memory we recall what we have already come to know. Will is the power by which we move toward the goodness or desirability of being. Now, consider St. Thomas's analogy to the hand. The hand does actually have an act integrating the fingers. However, in providing this analogy St. Thomas made no attempt at all to tell us what the mind does. It is a power, so it must have an act. While it includes in some sense the powers of memory, intellect, and will, it is not identical to any of them. Specifying their objects and acts is not sufficient for specifying its object and act. So what is it?

In effect, St. Thomas did not tell us what the mind does. Given that failure, he had no philosophical reason for thinking there is any such thing. Thus, his positing of it in the *De veritate* looks excessively ad hoc. It looks as though he was searching for a way to continue to affirm in words what St. Augustine had said about the mind as the image of God, given the fact that he had abandoned a cornerstone of St. Augustine's analysis, namely, that the mind is the essence or substance of the soul. The soul does not have sufficient unity to be the image of God, because of the fissure St. Augustine had placed within the soul between the activities we share in common with animals and those we do not. So a new unity had to be found, and St. Thomas found it.

The sole justification in the *De veritate* for identifying the mind as a general power constituted from memory, intellect, and will, with a unity that goes beyond a mere collection of powers, was the desire to respond to Augustinian objections motivated by the loss of the image of unity in talking about the three separate powers. We saw that desire explicitly in his response to the fifth objection of article 1 in question 10, when he explained how the image of the divine unity is to be found in the mind. But in the *Summa theologiae* the mind does no work helping us to understand the "essence, power, and operation" of the human soul, the subject matter that St. Thomas specifies at the beginning of the so-called "Treatise on Human Nature" in the *Summa theologiae* that leads directly into the discussion of the *imago Dei*. It does no work, because it has nothing to do.

It might be objected that St. Thomas did tell us in the *De veritate* what the act of the mind was when he began by assigning the task of the mind to "measure" reality, which led him to reject St. Augustine's substantialist thesis. But here we have an equivocation on the term "mind" between its use at the beginning of the discussion and at the end. The task of measuring reality is actually the task of the intellect alone. At that point St. Thomas's mind does not appear to be akin to St. Augustine's mind at all; the term is simply being used as a synonym for "intellect." However, St. Thomas then proceeds to expand the notion of the mind to make it look quite a bit like St. Augustine's without the substantialist underpinning, by making it a general power including within it memory and will. But when St. Thomas makes that move he has abandoned the initial account of its act, and thus also the reason for having argued that it could not be the essence or substance of the soul. This all smacks of an ad hoc and somewhat wooden effort to maintain the words of St. Augustine without the substance, involving equivocation at the cost of coherence. To his credit, St. Thomas abandons that discussion of the general power of mind in the *Summa theologiae.*

This loss of mind is very significant. The discussion of human nature in the *Summa theologiae* is directly ordered toward its culmination in question 93 on the *imago Dei.* In the *De veritate* St. Thomas had broken loose the essence or substance of the soul from the unity of the mind. Now, lacking a mind, it would seem that he has no locus for that unity. In other words, he has apparently lost his primary tool for preserving the Augustinian image of anti-Arian unity that St. Augustine had been concerned to promote in calling the mind the essence or substance of the soul. In effect, St. Thomas's solution in the *De veritate* was ad hoc and philosophically unjustified once he had rejected in the first article St. Augustine's substantialist account of the mind. Here in the *Summa theologiae* St. Thomas is proceeding in a fashion that is simply more philosophically cogent given that fateful step, but also perhaps theologically more difficult.

The Unity of the Soul

It is not merely or primarily philosophical cogency against the background of the *De veritate* that is driving the absence of mind in the *Summa theologiae.* One of St. Thomas's central concerns in the *Summa theologiae* discussion is to argue for the simple unity of the soul. This is a concern that was not evident in the *De veritate* discussion, but is of central importance in the *Summa theologi-*

ae because of the Plurality of Substantial Forms debate raging in the universities. The so-called Pluralists argued that there must be more than one substantial form in human nature, or at the very least a "form of corporeity," that is, a special form of the body that gave it its distinctive material structure, in addition to the properly human soul which is rational. According to the Pluralists, the human soul either stands apart from these other substantial forms, or consists of a kind of nesting of substantial formal parts hierarchically arranged. If it stands apart, its relation to the body appears to be that of a mover to the moved, lacking substantial unity with the body.[42] If it is a nesting or collection it has no obvious intrinsic unity insofar as the other non-human substantial forms within it are shared with other creatures. In either case, the soul has no intrinsic unity as the form of the body. In addition, the Pluralists were often universal hylomorphists, that is, they thought that all creatures, even purely spiritual creatures, were composites of matter and form. Stressing that matter is the principle of potency, they held that even purely spiritual creatures are composites of form and matter, because of the potency within them; the matter was of a special sort, namely, "spiritual matter." Thus also the human soul must contain this spiritual matter insofar as it is a rational nature that has a principle of potency within it.

Against the Augustinian background that they all shared, it is easy to see the appeal of these positions. In the first place, the plurality of substantial forms allows one to concentrate upon the distinction between the rational form of the mind, and the non-rational but living form of the body. We saw that St. Augustine had made a distinction in *De Trinitate* between the mind which is the substance or essence of the soul, and the principle that "quickens the body" with "its own life attached." One way of understanding the Pluralists' position is that it is making that Augustinian distinction in the Aristotelian language of substantial form that was becoming increasingly dominant among all parties in the twelfth and thirteenth centuries. If the life of the outer man is as distinct from the life of the inner man as St. Augustine said it was, it appears philosophically warranted to recognize at least two substantial forms of life, the animal and the rational; two distinct forms of life require at least two distinct substantial forms.

There can then be a distinct focus upon the substantial nature of the rational form or mind, which we know St. Augustine identified as the substance or

---

42. "Ut posuit Plato." See *ST* I, q. 76, a. 3.

essence of the human soul. Insofar as even angels are composed of form and spiritual matter, so also the mind or rational substantial form is composed from a certain form and spiritual matter. In that regard the mind is substantially little different from an angelic intelligence, other than that in this life it is also united with a substantial form of the animal body. Earlier I suggested somewhat provocatively that St. Augustine's thesis about there being no nature higher than the mind as *imago Dei* suggested little substantial difference from angelic substances qua rational creatures.

Finally, it is easy to see that upon death it is this rational substantial form, the mind, with its own substantial life that can be said to survive while the other lower forms, or the form of corporeity, remain and decompose with the body.[43] In these several ways, the Pluralists would appear to have a clear route to preserving St. Augustine's discussion against the background of the Aristotelian account of the soul that had made its way into the university discussions of the thirteenth century. It is no surprise then that we see such medieval Augustinians as Robert Grosseteste, John Pecham, Robert Kilwardby, St. Bonaventure, and later figures like Scotus, and Ockham adopting one or another of the Pluralist positions, which is not to deny the philosophical role of the arguments employed by the Pluralists for the positions they adopted.

St. Thomas, on the other hand, thoroughly rejects any sort of plurality of substantial forms in human nature. In addition, he rejects universal hylomorphism with regard to both the angels and the human soul.[44] A soul is entirely formal, and the human being is a composite of a simple soul and particular matter. St. Thomas argues that the soul is the substantial form of the body and qua form is act. But act cannot have potency as a part of itself qua act. Thus, the soul is a simple unity composed of no parts.[45] In addition there is no form of corporeity, unless it is nothing other than the rational soul itself as informing matter.[46] The form, as act, along with matter as the principle of potency constitutes one being. As constituting with matter one being, it is not at all essentially or substantially the same as an angel.[47]

---

43. See *ST* I, q. 76, a. 3, obj. 1, and ad 1.   44. *ST* I, q. 75, a. 5.
45. Ibid.

46. For a thorough discussion of the Plurality of Forms in St. Thomas, see John F. Wippel, *The Metaphysical Thought of Thomas Aquinas* (Washington, DC: The Catholic University of America Press, 2000), 327–51. See also James A. Weisheipl, O.P., "Albertus Magnus and Universal Hylomorphism: Avicebron," in *Albert the Great: Commemorative Essays*, ed. Francis J. Kovach and Robert W. Shahan (Norman: University of Oklahoma Press, 1980); and "The Origins of the Problem of the Unity of Form," *Thomist* 24 (1961): 257–85.

47. *ST* I, q. 75, a. 7.

Even the soul's powers are not ontological parts of it. St. Thomas's position in question 10 of the *De veritate* was that the "mind" as a unity was in fact constituted from the powers of memory, intellect, and will, though the mind was neither the soul itself, nor its essence. Here in the *Summa theologiae*, St. Thomas rejects the position that the soul is constituted from these or any powers at all. The soul is a simple act from which the powers flow as *propria* or necessary accidents.[48] Though St. Thomas often writes in the common fashion of "sight seeing," or "intellect thinking," or "will loving," he also corrects himself by writing that properly speaking it is not a power that sees, understands, loves, and so on, but the substance, the man himself, who engages in these acts in virtue of these powers. Like "the eyes seeing," "intellect thinking" is a mere secondary manner of speaking.[49] Consequently, the relation of the powers to the simple soul is direct, and unmediated by any other power or form. They "flow" from it according to a certain "natural necessity," are ontologically dependent upon it, and thus do not make up its parts.[50]

St. Thomas's rejection of the plurality of substantial forms is driven by substantive Aristotelian theses. In an objection he considers this argument for Pluralism:

The Philosopher says that the genus is taken from matter, and the difference from the form. But *rational,* which is the constitutive difference of a man, is taken from the intellective soul, while he is called *animal* because he has a body animated by a sensitive soul. Therefore the intellective soul is related to the body animated by the sensitive soul as form to matter. Therefore the intellective soul is not of the same essence as the sensitive soul in a man, but presupposes it as a material supposit.[51]

The picture we are presented with in this objection is of an animal body that is already animated by a living sensitive soul and complete in that nature, to which a rational soul is superadded, so that the rational soul does not animate matter as such, but, rather, a living non-rational animal.[52] Against the background of the *De Trinitate*'s statement about the principle that quickens the

48. For an account of so-called necessary or inseparable accidents, see St. Thomas's commentary on Aristotle's *Physics,* lib. 1, lect. 6; as well as *De ente et essentia,* cap. 5.

49. *ST* I, q. 75, a. 2; and q. 76, a. 1. Also *ST* II-II, q. 58, a. 2. For a general discussion of the way acts belong to individual substance see Stephen Brock, *Action and Conduct* (Edinburgh: T&T Clark, 1998), 16–29.

50. *ST* I, q. 76; and in particular ad 3.

51. *ST* I, q. 76, a. 3, obj. 4.

52. The use of "already" here is not temporal, but expresses an ontological priority—"the intellective soul is related to the body animated by the sensitive soul as form to matter."

body with its own life attached, it is easy to read this objection as an Augustinian objection couched in the Aristotelian logical apparatus of *species, genus,*
and *difference.* And we saw that in the *De veritate,* St. Thomas appeared to
preserve this distinction simply in terms of the "sensitive part" of the soul and
the mental or "rational part" of the soul which is the mind.

However, St. Thomas rejects the argument of the objection. He writes
that:

It is not necessary that there be a diversity in the nature of things following upon the
diverse notions and logical classifications that attend our mode of understanding those
things. One and the same thing can be apprehended in different ways.[53]

The morning star is the evening star, Cicero is Tully, and so on. One and the
same soul can be understood in many ways. In particular, it is known *through*
the powers that derive from it. So, it can be understood insofar as powers of
sensation and bodily life derive from it. It can also be understood insofar as
the powers of intellect and will derive from it. These are diverse powers leading to diverse ways of knowing the soul. These different ways of knowing the
soul do not, however, entail that two or more things are being known. One
and the same soul is understood in these different ways.

Moreover, in the actual body of the response St. Thomas gives several arguments for the simple unity of the substantial form. The first stresses the simple unity of human life. A substantial form is the principle of unity in a being. Diverse substantial forms would imply diversity of substantial being; in
other words, if a human being had two or more substantial forms, he would
in fact be two or more substances leading two or more substantially different
forms of life. On the contrary, a human being displays a unity of life in his or
her acts integrating reason as the form of the acts that a human animal engages in, even if those acts share a description that at a certain level does not distinguish them from the acts of other animals, like eating, or reproducing, and
so on. We can describe the act of a dog and of a man as eating or reproducing, and so on. But we have not adequately or fully described the human act
until we have specified it formally as rational eating or rational reproduction.
St. Thomas gives the classic Aristotelian example of *a white man.*[54] He holds
that on the Pluralist's position the life of reason would be no more united to
the animate life of the human animal than is *being white* united to the life of

53. *ST* I, q. 76, a. 3, ad 4.
54. See Aristotle, *Metaphysics,* bk. 7, ch. 4, 1029b12–1030b25.

a human being, that is, merely accidentally. This position he thinks is manifestly false.

The second argument follows closely upon the first in arguing from the
mode of essential predication, which is of course the supposed basis for the
Pluralist's objection. St. Thomas's response makes use of Aristotle's distinctions in the *Posterior Analytics* among the four modes of *per se* predication.[55]
The classical definition of a man is *a rational animal.* This involves essential
predication. Such essential predications are necessarily true. But there is no
essential predication where there is a diversity of forms.[56] If there were a diversity of forms here, the predication would be *per accidens,* and not necessary. Then the statement that *a man is a rational animal* would be no more
necessary than the *per accidens* statement *a man is a white animal,* that is, not
at all. On the contrary, the unity of form is the ground of the necessary truth
of the definition. It is the necessity of self-identity for forms, which is simply
unity taken as a transcendental feature of being.[57]

With both of these arguments in article 3, St. Thomas is concerned to preserve the unity of human life, the principle of which is the unity of the human soul as the substantial form of the body. He argues that the function of
substantial form is to provide the unity of being of the substance,[58] with no
mediating principle blocking the intimate union of the soul as the substantial
form of the body.

Indeed, it is precisely because of this unity of substantial form in the rational animal that our intellect is called "rational." St. Thomas asks in question
79, article 8, whether reason is a power other than intellect. His answer is negative. Rationality, which is characterized by the back and forth of argument
proceeding from one thing known to another, and so on, is the form that intellect takes in our lives. It has this discursive mode because of its engagement
with sensation. Its actuality is not the actuality of a bodily organ; nonethe-

---

55. *Posterior Analytics,* I, 73a34–b26.

56. Strictly, St. Thomas argues in the response that the only essential predication involving diverse
forms is in what Aristotle distinguishes as the second mode of *per se* predication. In such a predication, the subject is actually included in the definition of the predicate; the predication one is considering is not itself a definition of the subject. "But *man* is not predicated in the definition of *animal,*
but conversely *animal* is in the definition of *man.*" Thus there is no case of the second mode of *per se*
predication here. Insofar as the definition is a *per se* statement, it must be in the first mode, in which
there is no diversity of forms.

57. *Quaestiones disputatae de veritate,* I, q. 1, a. 1, on the transcendental features of being, *unity* in
particular.

58. *ST* I, q. 76, a. 3.

less it draws its content from sensation and the engagement of the body with the material world. Thus, it is always getting partial insight into the features of the world, leading to many items of partial insight that must be integrated into judgments, which judgments may be related discursively to other judgments that reason has made. But as a power it has this defining relation to the powers of sensation precisely because there is but one simple substantial form which is the actual substantial unity of sensation and reason. So intellect or mind in us is the power of reason because it is the power of a living body. It follows from this, of course, that neither angels nor God are rational even though they are intellectual.[59] *Rational* is the form of the animal acts we engage in. Our acts of eating, reproduction, and so on are not primarily *preceded* by acts of reason. Reason is their form.[60] Therefore, reason is not a power or second essence or substance within us that separates or distinguishes us *from* animals. It distinguishes us *as* animals.

The unity of the general power of the mind in the *De veritate* appeared to allow St. Thomas to hold on to St. Augustine's anti-Arian unity in the Trinitarian *imago Dei.* If St. Thomas were to hold on to the power of mind here in the *Summa theologiae* that he held on to in the *De veritate,* he would leave himself open to the charge of ad hoc inconsistency. Given the Dionysian principle he used in the *De veritate* that a power is midway between act and essence, as well as the absence of any act of the mind, and *a fortiori* the absence of the power of mind, if St. Thomas wanted in the *Summa theologiae* to continue to hold on to the special character of mind as a distinct unity, a unity other than the unity of the soul itself, he would have to maintain that it is an inner essence of the soul. But the consequent leads very quickly to the Pluralist position, since such an inner essence of the soul would leave the essence of the soul as substantial form of the body unaccounted for, as St. Thomas believes it is unaccounted for by the Pluralists.

---

59. Of course, "intellectual" must itself be said by analogy of human beings, angels, and God.

60. Here we might make the kind of distinction St. Thomas often makes between priority of time and priority of nature. There may well be acts of reason that precede a particular act of eating or reproduction in priority of time. But it does not follow that the particular act of eating or reproduction is by nature devoid of the form of reason. I am claiming that by a priority of nature in a human being acts of eating, reproduction, and so on have reason as their form, even if they are also preceded by particular acts of reason in deliberative processes leading up to them. We do not reason and then do something that other animals do. We reason and then reasonably do something only human animals do, but something that shares a basic level of description with things other animals do. Reason both precedes and informs.

If there is to be any unity to the mind of man, it is not going to be an ad hoc and unjustified unity of a special power, nor is it going to be the unity of a special substance, essence, or substantial form within the essence of a human being. It is going to be none other than the unity of the soul of a human being. But the human soul is the substantial form of a human body.[61] So, that unity of substantial form is nothing other than the unity of the human being, that is, the substantial unity of the living human body. Thus, St. Thomas cannot make a substantive ontological distinction between the life of the *outer man* and the life of the *inner man* based upon a distinction between the life of the mind and the bodily activities we share in common with other animals, as St. Augustine had. And St. Thomas cannot rely upon a supposed unity of mind to sustain St. Augustine's desire for an anti-Arian image of the divine unity. His only option is the unity of soul, that is, the unity of the human being as such that he had defended against the Pluralists.

The *imago Dei* in the *Summa theologiae*

It is now appropriate to examine how these philosophical positions on mind, soul, and unity alter St. Thomas's theology of the *imago Dei*. The rejection of the mind, and emphasis upon the unity of the soul complicates St. Thomas's discussion of the *imago Dei* in question 93 of the first part of the *Summa theologiae* in a number of ways. The *Summa theologiae* discussion of the *imago Dei* is as manifestly engaged with the Augustinian discussion as was the *De veritate*. Almost all of the nine article headings refer directly to topics in St. Augustine—"whether the Image of God is in a human being" (a. 1), "whether the Image of God is to be found in irrational creatures" (a. 2), "whether the Image of God is found in every human being" particularly with regard to whether it is in women (a. 4, obj. 1),[62] "whether the Image of God is in a human being according to the Trinity of Persons" (a. 5), "whether the Image of God is in a human being as regards the mind only" (a. 6), "whether the Image of God is to be found in the acts of the soul" (a. 7), "whether the Image of the Divine Trinity is in the soul only by comparison with God as its object" (a. 8), and "whether likeness is properly distinguished from image" (a. 9). The objections in these articles overwhelmingly come from St. Augustine's

---

61. *ST* I, q. 76, a. 1.
62. For St. Augustine's discussion see *De Trinitate,* lib. XII, esp. nos. 10–21.

De Trinitate. Finally, the term "mind" is often used throughout here along with "soul," particularly in article 6, where in questions 75 through 89 the use of "soul" had predominated.[63]

Yet there are notable differences. We saw that "mind" is used in the first part of the *Summa theologiae* simply as a synonym for "intellect," whether in its proper application to the power of intellect, or analogously to the whole soul in virtue of its highest power. That use remains in play in question 93. In addition, St. Thomas nowhere asks the opening question of the *De veritate* discussion, that is, whether the mind as containing the image of the Trinity is the essence or substance of the soul, or a power of the soul, the question directly prompted by St. Augustine's claim in the *De Trinitate* that it is the essence or substance of the mind. This absence of the topic is well accounted for by the fact that St. Thomas had just finished an extended discussion over fifteen questions of the essence, powers, and operations of the soul in which no distinct power of mind, other than the intellect, played a part. The soul can be called mind just as it can be called intellect from its highest power, because "mind" is just a synonym for "intellect." But the first article of question 77 had established that no power of any kind can be the essence of the soul, from which it follows trivially in the first article of question 79 that the intellect is merely a power of the soul, not its essence.

The first objection to that article in question 79 had quoted St. Augustine to the effect that the mind is the essence of the soul. In response, St. Thomas deals with the objection very briefly as involving the manner of speaking in which the soul can be named from its highest power "intellect"; and he asserts that St. Augustine is using "mind" in that sense, namely, as synonymous with "intellect." That cursory treatment is the extent of his discussion of the thesis that had formed the entire first article of his discussion in the *De veritate,* the thesis that had been so important to St. Augustine. Now, St. Thomas sees no

---

63. "Mens" is used a total of 398 times in question 10 of the *De veritate,* while "intellectus" is used a total of 188 times, for a factor of 2 to 1 in favor of "mens." "Mens" is used a total of 261 times in the first part of the *Summa theologiae,* as compared to 1,900 times for "intellectus"—a factor of 7 to 1 in favor of "intellectus." In questions 75–89, the so-called "Treatise on Human Nature," "mens" is used a total of 74 times, while "intellectus" is used 885 times—a factor of 12 to 1 in favor of "intellectus." But in question 93 on the *imago Dei* "mens" is used 42 times, while "intellectus" is used only 7 times—a factor of 6 to 1 in favor of "mens." In the "Treatise on Human Nature" "anima" is used 1,143 times for a ratio of 15.5 to 1 in favor of "anima," while "anima" is used 37 times in question 93 for a ratio of 1.14 to 1 in favor of "mens." It is difficult to know how much stock to put into such comparisons, however interesting they may appear, as they provide no context. However, the use of "mens" jumps out in question 93 against its relative absence in the so-called "Treatises on Human Nature."

reason at all for considering the topic when he turns to the discussion of the *imago Dei* in question 93.

We saw that in the *De veritate* discussion St. Thomas's rejection of St. Augustine's substantialist thesis was the fateful step that led him to the ad hoc and philosophically unjustified positing of the mind as a general power of the soul to preserve the image in the mind of the anti-Arian unity of the divine nature. We have seen here, however, that in the discussion of the essence, powers, and operations of the soul constituting questions 75 through 89, St. Thomas has no place for this ad hoc power because he has no philosophical job for it to do. Any suggestion of such a mediating unity between the powers of intellect and will and the unity of the soul would too easily make St. Thomas subject to the Pluralist position on substantial forms, a position that he rejects. So here in the *Summa theologiae* discussion the image of divine unity is rendered more complicated by the fact that now the only candidate for unity of the image is the unity of the essence of the entire soul, which essence is not to be a mind but to be a substantial form of a body, a substantial form in the Aristotelian sense as St. Thomas understands it.

According to St. Thomas, the human soul is not strictly speaking a substance, even though it is unique in being subsistent as an essential constituent principle of a substance.[64] Consequently, since "essence" properly speaking applies to a substance, the use of "essence" as in "the essence of the soul" is by analogy. A soul is a principle in the essence of a material substance along with matter. In that sense we can speak of the essence of the soul with regard to the role it plays in the essence of the substance properly speaking. And in that sense, the essence of the soul is to be the substantial form of some living human body. So the unity of that soul, which is the only candidate for the image of the divine unity, is nothing other than the unity of the material substance of which that soul is the substantial form.[65]

Still, in question 93 St. Thomas does want to hold on to many of the the-

---

64. Throughout his works St. Thomas very often calls the soul an intellectual substance simply. However, under the influence of his commentaries on Aristotle, in particular *Commentaria in libros de anima* and *Commentaria in libros metaphysicorum,* he begins to call the soul substance by analogy, insofar as the soul as a substantial form is reduced to the category of substance, being one principle with matter of what is properly speaking a substance, a particular material composite complete in its nature or essence. See *ST* I, q. 29, a. 1, ad 5; and q. 75, a. 2, ad 1; I-II, q. 110, a. 2, ad 2. Also *Quaestio disputata de anima,* no. 1, and ad 3; q. 2, ad 11. *De unitate intellectus contra Averroistas,* ch. 1, no. 3. *In libros de anima,* bk. 2, lectio 1, nos. 213, 214, 221; lectio 4, no. 275. *In libros metaphysicorum,* bk. 5, lectio no. 10, nos. 898–899; bk. 7, lectio no. 10, nos. 1484, 1487; lectio no. 11, nos. 1523, 1532.

65. *Commentaria in libros metaphysicorum,* bk. 8, lectio no. 5, no. 1767.

ses St. Augustine had held in the *De Trinitate*. In particular, he preserves St. Augustine's distinction between a *likeness, trace,* or *vestige* and an *image* proper. In articles 1 and 2 of the question, St. Thomas makes clear that "image" is a likeness of an exemplar that is both copied from the exemplar (a. 1), and also attains in some fashion to the *species* of the exemplar (a. 2). It is these latter features that narrow the broader notion of a likeness to the more narrow notion of image.[66] Of course human nature does not share any strict *species* with God, so this also must be understood by analogy.[67] But with the notion of *species* in play, St. Thomas brings in the structure of Aristotelian logic to analyze why a human being is made to the image of God, while other creatures are made simply to his likeness. In Aristotelian logic a *species* definition is constituted by a *genus* limited or informed by a *specific* or *ultimate difference*. We have already seen an example in the case of the definition of man in the Plurality of Forms argument, *a man is a rational animal.* There *animal* was the *genus,* and *rational* was the *specific* or *ultimate difference* informing or limiting the *genus* to that *species.*

In the case of the *imago Dei* it is *likeness* that plays the role of the *genus,* and the ability to know or understand that is the *specific* or *ultimate difference.* St. Thomas writes:

> If a likeness is only according to the *genus,* . . . then this is not sufficient for something to be an image of something else. . . . The intelligible character *(ratio)* of an image requires likeness according to the *species.* . . . However, it is manifest that a likeness of *species* follows according to an *ultimate difference.* Now some things are like God in the first place and most commonly simply because they exist; in the second place because some [that exist also] live; and in the third place, because [some that exist and live] also know and understand. . . . Therefore, it is intellectual creatures alone, properly speaking, who are said to be to the image of God.[68]

Notice the structure of this argument. All things that exist are likenesses of God; here existing is a common *generic* feature of likeness. Life as a *difference* serves to limit or contract that broad *genus* of likeness to a narrower notion. The *genus* of *likeness* is determined by existing simply, or existing and living. But life is not a *specific* or *ultimate* difference, so we do not yet have a *species* of likeness that can be called an *image of God.* The *ultimate difference* is constituted by knowledge and understanding. Thus knowledge and understanding

---

66. *ST* I, q. 93, a. 2.   67. *ST* I, q. 4, a. 3.
68. *ST* I, q. 93, a. 2.

contract the *genus* of likeness even further to an *image,* so that only existing, living, intelligent creatures are made *to the image of God.* So the definition of an image of God is *an existing living thing that knows and understands.*

This is a crucial argument for St. Thomas. In the first place, it sets up the next article in which he asks whether angels are more to the image of God than human beings are. We saw that St. Augustine had not considered this question. We also saw that St. Thomas had not raised the issue in the *De veritate,* even when he was writing particularly about the angels in questions 8 and 9. After all, Genesis, from which the text of the "to the image of God" is taken, by itself provides no straightforward theological warrant for attributing that dignity to angels, as the text involving *"imago Dei"* is confined to the creation of man, "male and female."[69] But according to this definition of an *image of God* in the *Summa theologiae,* angels must also be images of God because they are existing living things that know and understand. That conclusion is so obvious to St. Thomas that he does not bother to draw it in article 3. Instead, he simply argues that absolutely speaking angels are greater images of God than are human beings, because he had argued back in question 75, article 7, in response to the third objection, that "from the fact that a soul requires a body in a certain way for its operation, it is clear that the soul holds an inferior grade of intellectuality than an angel does which is not united to a body." Recall that it is because the soul is a substantial form of a body that human beings are rational, and angels are not. By contrast, St. Bonaventure, who held a particularly robust version of the Plurality of Substantial Forms position, held that angels and human souls, as spiritual substances, are equal images of God.[70] So St. Thomas's argument here about angels versus human beings locates the difference and priority of image between them squarely in the difference between an angel as a spiritual substance and a soul as the substantial form of a material substance. I will return to this discussion below for an important qualification that St. Thomas makes, again on the basis of the soul being the substantial form of a body.

A more important point for my argument at this point is that we can see the parallel with the Plurality of Substantial Forms debate in the discussion of the *imago Dei.* In that earlier debate, St. Thomas argued that the Pluralists

---

69. Following St. Augustine, St. Thomas argues in a. 4, ad 1, that the image is found indifferently in all male and female human beings, as opposed to the objection that it is found only in males.

70. See A. Schaefer, "The Position and Function of Man in the Created World According to Saint Bonaventure," *Franciscan Studies* 21 (1961): 335–42.

fallaciously held that when we have a plurality in a description there must be a plurality in the thing described. "Living," "sensate," and "rational" in *a man is a living, sensate, rational being* must track three distinct substantial forms in a human being. St. Thomas argued that, on the contrary, in a definition there is only one form that is signified in different ways. Thus, the *generic* descriptions that point to life and sensation, captured by the term "animal" in the definition, involve the very same form captured by the term signifying the *ultimate difference,* that is, "rational." The form in a human being that is the animal form just is one and the same as the rational form; there is no diversity of forms here.

Now suppose we apply that analysis analogously to the question of whether there is a difference between the likeness of God in a human being, and the image of God in a human being. The human being is said to be a likeness because he exists, and lives. He is said to be an image because he knows and understands. So, echoing the Pluralists, one might argue that there are two different mirroring features of being human in relation to God, the likeness and the image. After all, Holy Scripture says "image *and* likeness of God." On the contrary, St. Thomas, by introducing into the discussion the language of essential definition in terms of *genus, species,* and *ultimate difference* that he had used earlier to defeat the Pluralists, can block this effort to draw apart the likeness and the image in a human being. The features characteristic of being an image are compared to the features characteristic of being a likeness as *ultimate difference* to *genus* in constituting the definition of the *species* of image. So the image just is the likeness specific to being human, as the rational form just is the animal form in a human being.

So, there are not two representations of the divine within us, the existing living likeness, and the rational image; there is only one, the existing living likeness that is the rational image. In article 6, St. Thomas writes just that—"while in all creatures there is some likeness of God, in a rational creature alone is there found a likeness in the mode of an image, as was said above," that is, a likeness that in the case of a rational being just is an image. When Genesis says that human beings were made to the "image *and* likeness of God" it does not imply that we are two things, a likeness and an image, but one thing, a likeness which in us is an image. If St. Thomas had held that there is a "likeness" distinct from the "image," it would be very difficult for him to maintain that the angels are greater images of God, except *per accidens*. For the image in both would be based simply upon intellect excluding bodily life, a position clearly reminiscent of St. Augustine's. But it is not St. Thomas's. By identifying the image with the likeness, St. Thomas includes within the human image the mode of existence and life appropriate to the human being, that it is *embodied* as the life of an animal.

The point I want to draw from this particular discussion is that we know from the Plurality of Forms discussion that it is one and the same soul in virtue of which a human being exists, lives, knows, and understands. Thus, from this discussion in question 93, the principle of our being a likeness that is an image of God is none other than the principle of simple unity that St. Thomas had argued for in the Plurality of Forms debate. A human being *exists* by his one soul, *lives* as an animal by that one soul, and *knows* and *understands* as a human animal by that one soul. The powers that characterize human life, moving, growing, reproducing, sensing, knowing, and loving, all proceed from the simple unity of that soul. So the image of God is to be found in a human being according to the unity of that life which is the soul. For this reason St. Thomas will refer to the image being found in a human being according the "intellectual nature," as in the first line of the response to article 4, "a man is said to be to the image of God according to the intellectual nature."[71] The intellectual nature is the soul, not the power of intellect or mind.

Now when St. Thomas turns to the fifth article on "whether the image of God is in a man according to the Trinity of Persons," he makes a distinction between two ways that we can consider the image of God. The signification of *"imago Dei"* does not immediately distinguish between the image of divine unity and the image of Trinitarian plurality. St. Thomas had just responded to an objection in article 5 that the principal signification of *"imago Dei"* is "the intellectual nature."[72] The point of article 5 is to argue that the intellectual nature is an image of both the unity of the divine nature and the trinity of divine Persons; the image can be considered according to the divine nature or according to the Trinity of Persons, just as one can consider the soul either according to the powers of sensation or reason that proceed from it. In making this argument, St. Thomas is not introducing multiple images in a human being, one for the divine nature and one for the Trinity of Persons. It is a consideration of the one image, the intellectual nature, in two different ways. "It ought to be said that in a man there is an image of God with respect to the

71. See *ST* I, q. 93, aa. 3 and 4.

72. He does this in the context of asking whether the image of God is found in all human beings, particularly in women. Ibid., q. 93, a. 4, ad 1.

divine nature and the Trinity of Persons, for in God there exists one nature in three Persons."

That the image of the unity of the divine nature is also the image of the Trinity of Persons follows, according to St. Thomas, because:

To be to the image of God according to the imitation of the divine nature does not exclude that it would be an image of God according to the representation of the three Persons; rather it is that the one follows from the other.

Because it is according to the being of the one divine nature that there are three divine Persons, being an image of the Trinity of Persons follows from being an image of the unity of the divine nature. But it is according to the unity of the soul that it is an image of the unity of the divine nature. St. Thomas is able to maintain St. Augustine's desire for an anti-Arian image of the divine nature in the unity of the soul without the ad hoc unity of St. Augustine's mind found in the *De veritate*. And it is in virtue of being an image of the divine unity that it will also be an image of the Trinity of Persons, though in this article St. Thomas does not tell us how it is an image of the Trinity.

If we turn to article 6 in which St. Thomas asks "whether the image of God is in a man only according to the mind," he argues that indeed, "the image of God is not discovered in the rational creature [man] except according to the mind." Could article 6 be the basis for an objection to the position I have been arguing here? I have been arguing that the image of God is to be found in the human soul. The unity of the human soul is the basis for that image being an image of the unity of the divine nature, from which St. Thomas had argued that the image of the Trinity must also be found in the soul. But a well-known English translation of the passage I quoted here translates *"nec in ipsa rationali creatura invenitur Dei imago, nisi secundum mentem"* as "this image of God is not found even in the rational creature except in the mind."[73] This translation lends itself to an imaginative picture in which we think of the soul as a kind of inner space in which we search about to find a more precise location for the image of God. So in a sense, it might remain true to say that the image of God is in the soul, but in something like the way in which a pen is in my office. You are not really telling me much of interest in telling me the pen is in my office. It is really in my desk drawer. That is the locus where it

73. See *Basic Writings of Saint Thomas Aquinas,* vol. 1, trans. Laurence Shapcote, O.P., ed. Anton C. Pegis (New York: Random House, 1944), *ST* I, q. 93, a. 6, p. 893.

is to be found. Even St. Augustine could say that the image of God is found in the soul, because it is *really* found in the essence of the soul which is the mind. So, conceiving of the soul as a kind of inner space with various parts, we might say that while it is trivially true that the image of God is in the soul, it is genuinely in the mind, not really in the soul as such.

However, there are several problems with reading article 6 this way. In the first place, to say that something is "in the soul" or "in the mind" should not be thought of along the lines of spatial metaphors. The sense of the Latin preposition *"in"* in contexts involving the soul is one of existential dependence, not spatial location.[74] So a thought exists "in the soul" because of its existential dependence upon the soul, not because it is located in some inner space. A power exists "in the soul" because of its existential dependence upon the soul, and so on. Thoughts, beliefs, desires, deliberations, choices, and so on are not the "furniture of the mind." They depend upon the soul for their existence, but are not inside it as parts. In the second place, it is clear from the body of the article that St. Thomas does not intend to exclude the soul and its unity as the basis for the image. "Mind" is being used here in its proper and restrictive sense to refer only to the power of intellect. This is made clear when St. Thomas says that the contrast class that is excluded by focusing upon the mind is "the other parts" of the soul, when he writes "a vestigial likeness [not image] is found in the other parts which the rational creature may have." Thus "mind" here does not refer to the soul itself in the secondary sense in which its synonym "intellect" does, but, rather, to a part of the soul in contrast to other parts. The other parts of the soul are excluded, not the soul itself.

That this discussion is not intended to exclude the soul as the basis for the image is made clear when St. Thomas once again argues "with regard to the image of the divine nature, rational creatures seem to attain to a representation of the *species* insofar as they not only exist and live, but also insofar far as they understand." The point of this passage, as we saw in its use in earlier articles, is not to exclude existing and living from the image, but to include understanding as what specifies the human mode of life as a likeness which attains to an image. Existing and living are included within the image of the divine nature, not excluded from it as if only the activity of intellect and the

---

74. See John P. O'Callaghan, *Thomist Realism and the Linguistic Turn: Toward a More Perfect Form of Existence* (Notre Dame, IN: University of Notre Dame Press, 2003), 164–65.

power that gives rise to it form the basis for the image. It is the soul that determines the mode of existing, living, and understanding appropriate to the human *imago Dei*, the rational animal.

Finally, the actual text of the article does not support the thesis that the mind is the locus of the image in contrast to the soul. The heading of the article was *"utrum imago Dei sit in homine solum secundum mentem,"* that is "in a man" "according to the mind." The response held that the image is found in the rational creature "according to the mind," that is, *"secundum mentem."* It does not say *"in mente."* The conclusion of St. Thomas's response is "a likeness of God is discovered in a man in the manner *(per modum)* of an image according to the mind *(secundum mentem),* but in the manner of a vestige according to his other parts *(secundum alias partes eius)."* The "according to" here has to be read against the logical background of the *genus, species,* and *difference* that St. Thomas has specified as the appropriate means for understanding how a likeness that is an image differs from a likeness that is a vestige, the conceptual tools he had given us back in article 2. In the example *a man is a rational animal,* a man is an animal *according to* reason. Reason does not specify a self-contained part of the human being in which one can find a separate form of life; human life is not found "in reason," but in animal life "according to reason."

The mode of existence and life that would otherwise be a mere vestigial likeness of God in a human being, just as it is vestigial in other animals, is an *image* of God in a human being because that mode of life takes place "according to" reason—not because reason is distinct from that mode of life, but because it specifies it. Thus, the *imago Dei* is not found "in the mind" as opposed to the soul, but in the soul "according to reason." What St. Thomas is arguing here is that if the mode of existence and life we have were only specified by those powers we share with other animals, particularly sensation, the likeness in us would only be vestigial, not an image. But such a specification of our animal life as sensitive, while true, is not complete. It is only complete when reason informs that specification. So the sense in which we must understand the claim that the image is not "in the other parts" *(in aliis . . . partibus)* and not "according to its other parts" *(secundum alias partem eius)* is that the existence and life of a man is not specified as an image by reference to those parts. Instead, the very same likeness that would otherwise be a mere vestige is specified as an image with reference or "according to" the power of the mind, that is, the intellect.

This is not an ad hoc analysis. The Aristotelian use of *genus, species,* and *difference* is St. Thomas's, and it provides him with rich resources for sorting through the issues involved in this discussion. It is a clear parallel to the earlier Plurality of Forms discussion in question 76. The vary same existence and life in us that is described as the life of an animal is ultimately specified as human animal life insofar as it is "according to reason." Human life is not "in reason," but "according to reason." Reason does not distinguish us *from* animals. It specifies us *as* animals; it specifies the form that animal life takes in us. Similarly, understanding does not distinguish the image in us *from* a vestigial likeness found in our existence and animal life. It specifies the likeness of our existence and animal life; it specifies the form that that likeness takes in us—an *imago Dei* "according to" our rational nature.

This analysis of how "mind" is being used in article 6 is immediately confirmed by the questions posed in article 7, which is "whether the image of God is found in the soul *(in anima)* according to its acts," and article 8, which is "whether the image of the divine Trinity of Persons is in the soul *(in anima)* only by a comparison to God as its object." In neither case does he use *"in mente."* While article 6 had used *"in homine secundum mentem,"* these articles use *"in anima."* However, there is no conflict in his use of *"in homine"* in article 6 and *"in anima"* here; I pointed out earlier that for St. Thomas, following Aristotle, the unity of the human soul is none other than unity of the human animal. The human form or soul just is the man being actually human; a man and his soul are not two things, but one, since the being of the man and the being of his soul are the same. If St. Thomas had meant to "locate" the image of God in the mind in an exclusive and primary sense that places the soul, indeed the human animal, in a secondary external position, it would no longer be appropriate for him to inquire in both of these questions about the soul. Instead, he ought now to be asking, "whether the image of God is found in the mind according to its act" and "whether the image of divine persons is in the mind only by comparison with God as its object."

Finally, it is in article 6 that St. Thomas specifies *how* the image of God in the soul is both an image of the unity of the divine nature and the trinity of divine Persons. In article 5 he only argued the fact that the image is an image not only of the unity of the divine nature, but also of the Trinity of Persons. But that argument did not tell us *how* the soul is an image of the Trinity of Persons. If the image were found only "in" the mind, rather than in the soul "according to" the mind, the image of the divine unity would be trivial, since the power of intellect or mind just is one unified power. The problem would be that there would be no image of the Trinity in the power of "intellect or mind" as such.

At this point the question arises about how St. Thomas maintains the image of divine plurality. Hasn't his Aristotelianism made him sacrifice the image of plurality for the image of unity? If the image of unity is to be found in the soul, there no longer seems to be any reason to distinguish the powers of memory, intellect, and will from all the other powers of the soul, the powers of the animate life of an animal. In fact, St. Thomas does tend to drop the power of memory from the image. He had actually had problems all the way back in the *De veritate* integrating memory into the image, since he held that memory is actually the habit of a power, not a power itself or the act of that power. It is the habitual retention of knowledge present in the mind. In that sense it is not really a power distinct from the intellect. Now in the *Summa theologiae,* he tends to drop it from the image. Instead, he focuses upon the way in which understanding proceeds from the intellect and expresses itself in a mental word, a *verbum mentis.* I do not have the space here to go into this feature of the image in detail. However, from the expression of the mental word expressing understanding an act of will then follows.

So, St. Thomas analyzes the image of the Trinity of Persons in terms of the interplay between intellect and will. The image of the unity of the divine nature is according to the existence, life, and understanding of the soul. But the image of the Trinity of Persons is found according to the way in which "in rational creatures, [there] is found a procession of an [inner][75] word according to the intellect, and a procession of love according to the will." Later he clarifies this claim by reference to other creatures in which there is no "principle of the [inner] word, [inner] word, and love." The image of plurality is found *according to* the mind or intellect, the principle from which the inner word springs, which then proceeds to love as an expression of the will informed by understanding. What is interesting about this image is that we saw how St. Augustine had considered it in the *De Trinitate,* before rejecting it in preference for what he took to be the more adequate image of mind, memory,

---

75. Again, "inner" here should not be taken according to a spatial metaphor. It simply serves to distinguish the expression of understanding that depends existentially upon the act of intellect from the expression of that understanding by the voice, the "outer" word. The "outer" word depends existentially upon both the act of understanding and the activity of the vocal chords. Thus the outer word is "in" the intellect *and* the mouth.

intellect, and will. In this way, St. Thomas is not simply abandoning St. Augustine's theological analysis, but, rather, affirming in him what he thinks is best.

Now, in article 7 he asks "whether the image of God is found in the soul according to acts" *(Utrum imago Dei inveniatur in anima secundum actus)*. Here again, with the use of the English "in" for *"secundum,"* the translation I referred to earlier has "whether the image of God is to be found in the acts of the soul." The translator seems intent upon hunting down the image for where it may be hiding. On the contrary, St. Thomas has already found it in the unity of the soul which is the unity of the living human being. He is now describing or "specifying" what he has already found. St. Thomas will write that the image of the divine Trinity is primarily "according to the acts *(secundum actus)*, as namely from knowledge had [by the soul], by actual thinking we form an interior word, and from this we break out into love." From the knowledge possessed habitually by the intellect, it proceeds in actual thought to express an act of understanding which is the inner word or *verbum,* and from that expression of an inner word the will proceeds to express an act of love, presumably directed at the object of understanding. The principle from which understanding proceeds looks to be the correlate of the Father, while the *verbum* is the correlate of the Son of God, the Divine *Verbum,* and the springing forth of love is the correlate of the Holy Spirit who proceeds from both. St. Thomas then concludes that in a secondary fashion, the image of the Trinity is according to *(secundum)* the powers from which these acts proceed.[76]

Love proceeds from the will. But the will is a power of the soul, and is only a power of the mind insofar as "mind" is taken in the secondary sense as applying to the entire soul. It is not a power of intellect or mind in the proper

76. My text of the *Summa theologiae* has for the entire passage "Et ideo primo et principaliter attenditur imago Trinitatis in mente secundum actus, prout scilicet ex notitia quam habemus, cogitando interius verbum formamus, et ex hoc in amorem prorumpimus." The *"in mente"* here might suggest that I am wrong in centering the image in the soul and not in the mind. However, the entire context makes it clear that *"in mente"* must be taken in the secondary sense in which it applies to the soul, not the power of intellect. The title of the article uses *"in anima";* in beginning his response St. Thomas writes, "si ergo imago Trinitatis divinae debet accipi in anima"; the sentence immediately before the one containing *"in mente"* has "Verbum autem in anima nostra"; and the sentence immediately after it has "secundario, et quasi ex consequenti, imago Trinitatis potest attendi in anima." Thus, the entire context makes it quite clear that St. Thomas is writing about the image of the Trinity in the soul according to the acts of the powers of intellect and will; and *"mente"* here is taken in its secondary sense, in which it signifies the entire soul.

sense. If the image of God is only to be found "in" the mind in the proper sense, that is, the power of intellect, it cannot be an image of the Trinity of Persons. So the only way to achieve an account of the image of God as an image of the unity of the divine nature *and* the Trinity is to establish it in the soul "according to" the intellect and the will.[77]

This part of the discussion mirrors St. Thomas's rejection of the Plurality of Forms. The soul is known through the powers that flow from it. A plurality of powers flow from the soul. But that plurality of powers does not imply a plurality of souls, or a plurality of ontologically constitutive parts of the soul. Nonetheless, in defining the nature of which the soul is the formal principle, the *genus* animal is further specified "according to" the ultimate *difference, rational,* taken from the power of mind or intellect. This ultimate specification does not exclude the sensitive part and the other parts of the soul from what is included within the *genus* animal. It simply does not specify the *human* animal *according to* those other parts. Likewise, those parts of the soul are not excluded from the likeness of God; in fact insofar as they express the generic manner in which a human being "exists and lives," they specify it as a *likeness.* They simply do not specify that likeness as an *image* of God "according to" those parts. Understanding, which proceeds from intellect or mind, does.

How Like an Angel

I want to return now to an earlier point, namely, St. Thomas's argument that angels are greater images of God than human beings are, in order to display the depth of St. Thomas's placing the image not in the mind, but in the soul, and thus in the incarnate human being as such. In the beginning of the discussion on the mind in the *De veritate,* St. Thomas considers the objection that the mind is the essence of the soul, because mind has the same definition in us and in the angels, and the essence of an angel is its mind. We know that St. Thomas rejects the conclusion. In response to the objection he then also rejects the premise that is supposed to lead to that conclusion; he writes that an angel is called a mind not because its essence is the power of mind, but because mind is its highest power. In the *De veritate,* the case is similar

---

77. We have to be careful in St. Thomas's use of the term "part" here in describing the "parts of the soul," since the sensitive and intellectual "parts" of the soul are not constitutive of the soul. This talk of parts is for mere collections of powers of the soul. But those powers themselves are not constitutive elements of the soul, but, rather, derive from it as different from it.

for the soul, except that it has other powers besides mind, and so St. Thomas says that "one cannot call the soul a mind in the way in which one calls an angel a mind."[78] This argument accords well with his rejection of St. Augustine's substantialist thesis; but the rejection of the substantialist thesis does not particularly distinguish angels from the soul, as for St. Thomas it is equally true of angels that the mind is not their essence either, in the primary sense of "mind." But the discussion is very brief and says only what needs to be said to reply to the objection. St. Thomas does not pursue any further in the *De veritate* question how we are to think of the relative intellectual natures of angels and human beings, in particular, with respect to the *imago Dei.*

In the *Summa theologiae,* we know that St. Thomas thinks the soul can be called "mind" from its highest power of "intellect or mind." By contrast with the *De veritate* discussion, however, in the *Summa theologiae* he is at pains to explain that the soul is not of the same intellectual species as an angel; he devotes an entire article of question 75 to the topic.[79] It is not of the same species because the soul is the substantial form of a body. This is a detailed rejection in St. Thomas of what I claimed was an admittedly provocative thesis to be attributed to St. Augustine, namely, that the mind of man is substantially or essentially the same as an angel. Thus, having argued that angels and the soul are not of the same intellectual species in question 75, now, in question 93, St. Thomas devotes an entire article, number 3, to the issue "whether the angels are more to the Image of God than a man is."

St. Thomas did not ask this question in the *De veritate* discussion, even though he did devote two other extended questions to angels. He did, however, ask it in an even earlier work, his *Commentary on the Sentences of Peter Lombard.* There he said that even though strictly speaking angels are higher images of the divine Trinity, in a way a man could be considered a higher image of God insofar as he was the active principle of the generation of all other human beings, after the fashion in which God by the act of creation is the principle of all beings other than Himself. Here St. Thomas must mean Adam, since in the medieval setting it is only Adam who could be considered the principle responsible for the generation of all other human beings. St. Bonaventure appears to have made a similar point in his *Sentences* commentary, when he wrote that the human soul could be considered a higher image of

78. *De veritate,* q. 10, a. 1, ad 4.
79. *ST* I, q. 75, a. 7.

God insofar as the soul is joined to a body, and "as from one God all things come, so from one man all men come."[80] However, in this sense St. Thomas has then shifted away from the question of the image of the divine Unity in Trinity, since the image of external creation has little to do with the image of the intrinsic unity in plurality of the Trinity itself. It has to do with being an image of God as Creator.

St. Thomas's response to the article in question 93 of the *Summa theologiae* is in fact more complex than I indicated earlier. St. Augustine's claim about the human mind being the highest image of God is brought up in the first two objections to the article in order to argue that an angel cannot be a greater image of God than a human being is. The first objection cites a sermon of St. Augustine's to the effect that according to St. Augustine "God gave his image to no other creature than man." So it would seem that angels are not to be counted images of God at all. The second objection cites another work of St. Augustine's to make the same point he had made in the *De Trinitate*. "According to Augustine, . . . a man is so much to the image of God that he is formed by God with no creature interposed [between the man] and God. . . . Therefore an angel is not more to the image of God than a man."

In response to the first objection, St. Thomas points out that St. Augustine only intends to exclude animals lacking intellect from the image, not intellectual beings in general. Thus, angels can be taken to be images of God without going against St. Augustine. In response to the second, he argues that if one considers the soul and angels at the broad level of simply describing them as "intellectual creatures" then there is a certain kind of equality between them; considered in that way, one is not higher than the other. But of course that point says very little, since it is akin to saying that at a certain broad level dogs and human beings are equally animals. It fails to address whether angels and the soul are equal considering them as what they specifically are, angelic versus human; St. Thomas writes that such a consideration "does not exclude that an angel may be more to the image of God" in some other way. It is on that specific point that he argues that angels, when considered absolutely with regard to their specific natures, are indeed greater images of God.[81] St. Thomas's response presupposes that the image is to be found in the nature, though the ranking of the one as greater than the other is "according to" the power of

---

80. See Schaefer, "The Position and Function of Man," 346–49, esp. n. 157. My translation of the Latin.

81. See *ST* I, q. 58, a. 3; and q. 79, a. 8.

intellect in each. "The image of God is in angels more than in men because the intellectual nature is more perfect in them."

But then St. Thomas makes a startling move in the response. He says that one can consider the *imago Dei* in a secondary fashion with regard to the way in which one can find in human beings a certain imitation of God. The imitation he has in mind is with regard to the production of one human being from another. He writes that this imitation is "insofar namely as man is from man, as God is from God" *(inquantum scilicet homo est de homine, sicut Deus de Deo).* "And according to this [consideration] . . . , the image of God is in a human being more than in an angel" *(Secundum haec . . . magis invenitur Dei imago in homine quam in angelo).* The reference to the generation of God from God calls to mind the Nicene creed, and pertains to the unity of nature, that is, to the anti-Arian creedal affirmation of unity, while in man it pertains to reproduction. Thus St. Thomas is turning away from the image of God as Creator that he stressed in the *Commentary on the Sentences,* to return to the image of the intrinsic unity in plurality of the Divine nature itself. Notice also that St. Thomas is talking about human nature as such, not a particular human being, Adam, who might be considered responsible for the generation of all other human beings. The production of man from man pertains to reproduction. Thus the claim pertains to all human beings in their reproductive capacity.

We saw that there are not multiple images of God in a human being. There is the one image in human nature that can be considered with respect to different aspects of the divine Trinity in Unity. Thus it is in human nature as such, not in the mind, not even in the soul alone, but in the composite nature of soul and body that we see the image of the divine Unity in Trinity, an image that can be considered in at least two ways "according to" two features of human life, the intellectual-volitional, *and* the reproductive. So contrary to his earlier discussion in the *Sentences* commentary, by placing the image in human nature as such, St. Thomas makes it an image that pertains to all human beings alike, male and female.[82]

This move toward a secondary consideration of the *imago Dei* is striking for a number of reasons. First, it pertains to the essence of the soul as substantial form of the body. But recall St. Thomas's rejection of "spiritual matter" that could function to differentiate one angel from another within a *species.*

---

82. In fact, St. Thomas argues in *ST* I, q. 93, a. 4, ad 1 that the image is equally in male and female alike.

Insofar as an angel is completely free of matter, the principle of multiplicity within a *species*, even free of "spiritual matter," it completely exhausts its *species*. There can be only one member of any angelic *species*, and thus an angel cannot produce another of the same nature as if angel from angel. In other words, it cannot be an image of God in this way.

Second, it is striking because it does not reduce this imitation to the level of a mere trace or vestige. It is a genuine, though secondary, way of considering the image of God in man. Nonetheless, considering the image of God in this way is still "according to reason." This likeness "[does] not belong *per se* to the notion *(ratio)* of the divine image in man, unless the first imitation is presupposed, which is according to the intellectual nature." No doubt other animals reproduce members of their own nature, dog from dog, salmon from salmon, and so on. However, presumably such reproduction is not an image of God, but remains merely a vestigial likeness because it is not according to reason. In the human case, it is genuinely an image because it is "according to reason." In other words, other kinds of creatures that reproduce members of their kind do not count here as images according to this secondary sense, because lacking intellect their natures do not count as images in the primary sense. Thus what we see here in the discussion of angels confirms the earlier discussion of the Plurality of Forms debate in the *Summa theologiae*. There we saw that St. Thomas rejects a plurality of substantial forms in a human being, and maintains that reason is the form of our bodily acts. Of particular interest now is the way in which it is the form of the act of human reproduction. Our generation of members of our kind counts as a genuine image because of the way in which it is informed by our reason. These two ways in which we may consider the image must come together as one in the existing image, much like the way in which the two ways of considering a human being according to the genus *animal* and the difference *rational* must come together as one in the existing human being.

Third, it is striking because it pertains to what St. Augustine had described as the life of the outer man, and we saw that he argued that no image of God can be found in that outer life because of its lack of unity of being or substance with the life of the inner man, that is, the life of the mind. And yet we have seen in St. Thomas his determination to stress the absolutely simple unity of the soul precisely qua substantial form of the living body. Thus, St. Thomas's earlier rejection of the Plurality of Forms has allowed him to extend the notion of image to this secondary sense. According to this secondary consideration there is no question that the essence of the soul is a genuine *imago Dei*.

Finally, the most striking feature of his answer is that he argues that in this respect a human being is a greater image of God than an angel is. Though it is a secondary consideration, it is precisely insofar as the soul is incarnate as the substantial form and unity of a body that a human being can be said to be a greater image of God than an angel is. God cannot say to an angel "be fruitful and multiply." Thus in question 93 on the *imago Dei* we can see the *telos* of St. Thomas's earlier detailed discussion of the unity of the soul as the substantial form of the human body, providing it with a simple unity of life. Because of his emphasis upon that unity of embodied life, he has found a way of reaffirming St. Augustine's theological insight that man is the highest *imago Dei,* but clearly not in the way in which St. Augustine affirmed that truth, as St. Thomas presupposes very different philosophical underpinnings on the rational nature of human beings.

Conclusion

What is to be said then of St. Thomas as Augustinian in the *Summa theologiae* discussion of the *imago Dei?* If we take the discussion of the *imago Dei* in question 93, together with the questions that preceded it on the essence, powers, and operations of the human soul, beginning with question 75, we can see that he manages to develop St. Augustine's insight about how the image of God is to be found in a man in a way that preserves St. Augustine's emphasis upon the anti-Arian unity of the divine nature amidst the anti-Sabellian plurality of persons. He does so, however, against the background of a shift in his own understanding of the philosophical resources he draws upon, a shift away from the unity of the mind drawn from St. Augustine toward a more robust Aristotelian emphasis upon the unity of the incarnate human person from which the powers of intellect and will proceed. St. Thomas's defense of the incarnate unity of the human person, against the background of the Plurality of Forms controversy, plays its role in question 93 precisely when he argues that the image of God is in a man "according to" the mind, not in the mind itself, and most strikingly when he finds an image of God in human nature according to the reproduction of "man from man as God from God."

Theologically St. Thomas retains and pursues the Augustinian insight into the image of God in man in virtue of his rational nature. Indeed, having re-

jected St. Augustine's substantialist thesis in the *De veritate,* St. Thomas effectively returns to it, and adopts it here in the *Summa theologiae*—it is indeed
in the substance or essence of a human being that the image of God is to be
found. But that substance or essence of being human is not divorced from the
activities we share in common with animals. It is the life of a particular kind
of animal, a rational one that has one form of life, and is one image of God.
He has also found a way of affirming St. Augustine's claim that a human being is the highest *imago Dei,* but precisely in that place where he differs most
markedly from St. Augustine's philosophical presuppositions about the rational nature of human beings, the rational life of the animal body each of us
is. Thus theologically he follows St. Augustine with the underpinnings of an
enriched Aristotelian philosophical anthropology that does not posit a fissure
at the heart of human life between our acts as embodied persons and our acts
as images of God. This is the form that St. Thomas's Augustinianism takes on
the test case of the *imago Dei.*

6

Augustine and Aquinas on Original Sin

Doctrine, Authority, and Pedagogy

Mark Johnson

My interest in this topic stems from my graduate school days, when I began studying the Fathers and then the moral teaching of Thomas Aquinas. When it came to assessing the reach and influence of Augustine's teachings in the thirteenth century, our teachers instructed us always to remember that Augustine's principal conduit was the *Libri sententiarum* of Peter Lombard, who had gathered together quotations from many theological figures but most especially from Augustine and had placed them into his "book of opinions," arranging them dogmatically, in order to cover the Christian religion.[1] The success of Lombard's text, both inside the schools and in the religious orders—Dominicans of Thomas's day and before were told to have and to study

---

1. For more on Lombard see Marcia Colish's definitive *Peter Lombard,* 2 vols. (Leiden: E. J. Brill, 1994); or her more accessible "Peter Lombard," in *The Medieval Theologians,* ed. G. R. Evans (Oxford: Blackwell Publishers, 2001), 168–83. See also Ignatius Brady's "Prolegomena" to the Quarrachi edition of Lombard's *Sententiae in IV libros distinctae,* vol. 1, part 1 (Grottaferrata: Collegium Sanctae Bonaventurae, 1971), 8*–45* 117*–29*. The articles of Michel Barnes and Wayne Hankey in this volume also touch upon how the teaching of Augustine was mediated to Thomas's age. All references to Lombard's *Sentences* come from the Quarrachi edition, *Magistri Petri Lombardi parisiensis episcope sententiae in iv libros distinctae,* 3rd ed., vol. 2, ed. Ignatius Brady, O.F.M., et al. (Grottaferrata: Collegium Sanctae Bonaventurae, 1971).

their *Summa,* and that meant Lombard's *Summa sententiarum*[2]—meant that the teaching of Augustine, if only in abbreviated form, would be on hand for almost any doctrinal topic and would indeed have a prominent place in the establishment or explanation of that topic.[3]

Now this all is verified in the case of the fall and of original sin in Lombard; his primarily biblical account of the fall and of original sin from book 2, distinctions 20–35, in the *Sentences,* features Augustine over any other author, and by a wide margin (*De genesi ad litteram, De peccatorum meritis, De Trinitate,* etc.). Such a strong Augustinian presence in his account of original sin meant in turn that the various *scripta* on the *Sentences* from the thirteenth century (including those more loosely based, such as William of Auxerre's *Summa aurea* and the *Summa fratris Alexandri*) would have to make room for, or otherwise deal with, the authority and very phraseology of Augustine. And so they did.[4] More than that, Augustine's teaching and choice quotations make their way into other texts, not immediately associated with Lombard, such as disputed questions, quodlibetal questions, *summae,* and so on.

Given this omnipresence of Augustine as regards the doctrine of original

2. Writing in the 1260s Humbert of Romans, the former master of Thomas's Dominican Order instructed all the librarians in the order to have a copy of Lombard's *Sententiae* in a centralized location in each convent's library (see Humbertus de Romanis, *Opera de vita regulari,* vol. 2, ed. J. J. Berthier [Turin: Marietti, 1956], 256). For more on the book practices of the Dominicans, see K. W. Humphreys, *The Book Provisions of the Medieval Friars (1215–1400)* (Amsterdam: Erasmus Booksellers, 1964), 18–45, esp. 36 and 43; and for Dominican use of Lombard throughout their educational system, and not simply in the university setting, see M. Michele Mulchahey, *"First the Bow is Bent in Study . . . " Dominican Education Before 1350* (Toronto: Pontifical Institute of Mediaeval Studies, 1998), 134–38.

3. Sometimes texts masquerading as those of Augustine are brought to bear, as when Lombard explains Christ's sinlessness by using the spurious *De fide ad Petrum* in *Sentences,* lib. II, dist. 31, cap. 7 (*Magistri Petri Lombardi,* vol. 2, 509).

4. See Albertus Magnus, *In II Sent.,* in *Opera Omnia,* vol. 27, ed. A. Bourgnet (Paris: Vivès, 1894), d. 20–35, pp. 339–579; Albertus Magnus, *Quaestio de peccato originali,* in *Opera Omnia,* vol. 25 (Münster im Westfalen: Aschendorff, 1993), 2.189–203; *Summa fratris Alexandri,* in *Alexandri de hales summa theologica,* vol. 3 (Quaracchi: Collegium S. Bonaventurae, 1930), lib. 2, inq. 2, tract. 3, q. 2, pp. 230–282; Bonaventura, *In II Sent.,* in *S. Bonaventurae opera theologica selecta,* vol. 2 (Quaracchi: Collegium S. Bonaventurae, 1938), dd. 30–35, pp. 734–870; Guillelmus Altissiodorensis, *Summa Aurea,* in *Guillelmi Altissiodorensis Summa Aurea,* vol. 2.2, ed. J. Ribaillier (Grottaferrata: Collegium Sanctae Bonaventurae, 1982), lib. 2, tract. 14, pp. 510–547; Guerricus de Sancto Quentino, *Quodlibetum IX,* in *Guerric of Saint-Quentin Quaesetiones de quolibet,* ed. W. H. Principe (Toronto: Pontifical Institute of Mediaeval Studies, 2002), a. 5a, pp. 387–88. One would also have to add the earlier, but famously "Augustinian" St. Anselm, whose *De conceptu virginali et originali peccato* was often cited; see *Obras completas de San Anselmo,* ed. P. Julian Alameda, vol. 2 (Madrid: Biblioteca de autores christanos, 1953), 4–77.

sin, one might share my puzzlement at a certain text on the topic in Thomas Aquinas's *Summa theologiae.* In the *Summa theologiae* generally, Thomas quotes Augustine as much as he ever did in his other writings. There are places where Augustine's authority simply settles a question.[5] But in one text, *prima secundae,* question 81, article 1, on whether and how the first sin of our first parents is carried over to us who draw our origin from them—Augustine's texts on this topic would seem to be legion—Thomas's use of Augustine is almost non-existent. At the very least this encourages an investigation.

My presentation is in three sections. First, I will explain the order and placement of texts in the *secunda pars* of Thomas's *Summa theologiae,* and more precisely, the *prima secundae,* which covers the most general presentation of moral issues, or moral matter, as Thomas calls it.[6] Second, I want to put on display the earliest options Thomas had when it came to pressing Augustine into service on the issue of original sin. Third, and finally, I wish to examine the text from the *prima secundae* and suggest some reasons for Augustine's relative silence in Thomas's text; what was it about Thomas's pedagogical goals that led him not to invoke explicitly the doctrine and authority of Augustine here?[7]

The Placement of Original Sin in Thomas's Moral Pedagogy

Although Thomas consistently maintained the ubiquitous priority of the intellect over the will in his teaching—the former, indeed, is the "source" or principle of the latter[8]—we should not downplay the importance, indeed

5. See, for instance, *ST* I-II, q. 55, a. 4, s.c.; q. 71, a. 6, s.c.; q. 100, a. 4, s.c. All references to the *Summa theologiae* will be taken from the Ottawa edition, *Sancti Thomae de Aquino Summa theologiae,* 5 vols. (Ottawa: Medieval Institute, 1948).

6. At the outset of the *secunda secundae* of the *Summa theologiae,* Thomas refers to the *prima secundae* just completed (*Summa theologiae,* II-II, prologus): "Post communem considerationem de virtutibus et vitiis et aliis ad materiam moralem pertinentibus, necesse est considerare singula in speciali; sermones enim morales universales sunt minus utiles, eo quod actiones in particularibus sunt."

7. The source apparatus in the Ottawa *Summa* and the Pauline edition (which appropriated the Ottawa edition's apparatus) suggest that, at *ST* I-II, q. 81, a. 1, c., the sources for Thomas's personal teaching in the article *"initium sumit apud Augustinum,"* whereupon they cite J.-B. Kors's *La justice primitive et le péché originel d'apres S. Thomas. Les sources.–La doctrine* (Kain: Revue des sciences philosophiques et théologiques, 1922), 33 and 147, as well as the *Dictionnaire de théologie catholique* article on "péché original" (vol. XII, 390–95). To anticipate: it is true that one sees the phrase *"omnes ille homo fuerant"* in Augustine, but Thomas's tack here is different from the way that either Augustine uses it or Lombard uses it (following or using Augustine).

8. See *ST* I, q. 19, a. 1; I, q. 87, a. 4, esp. ad 1.

primacy, of the will when we enter the domain of morals. For it is by will that man does anything, insofar as he is a *human* being. Even God does not "cause" save to the extent that will is conjoined to his knowledge.[9] We who are interested in the domain of morals should celebrate, therefore, the singular and central contribution of the will.[10]

Now, as is well known, Thomas in the second part of the *Summa theologiae* divides his treatment of morals into two main sections: the *prima secundae* and *secunda secundae*. The former part is the more general treatment of moral matter, the "common consideration," Thomas calls it,[11] while the latter part addresses things in greater detail.

Scholars often bypass the short introductions Thomas provides before the various sections of his *Summa,* but it is there in those introductions, the prologues, that he spells out the order of treatment of things, and the rationale for that order. By consulting these prologues for the *prima secundae,* these ligaments, if you will, we get a sense of how Thomas has structured the thing.[12] The image of God is made for beatitude, and this beatitude, though manifold, exists above all in seeing God face to face in the beatific vision. But humans cannot just make this vision happen; they must earn it, through concrete acts they perform, meritorious acts, specifically as human beings. The will is the source of the human acts that they perform, and so Thomas, after spelling out just what human happiness or beatitude is, devotes a long discussion to the will and its acts, turning next to a consideration of the emotions, which, while being acts we humans do have, are acts we also share with other animals, and so are less immediately human. After this lengthy treatment (up to q. 48 of the *prima secundae*) Thomas turns to "the sources of human acts," the *principia actuum humanorum.* Now these sources of human action can be internal or external (Thomas uses the words "intrinsic" and "extrinsic"). The intrinsic sources for Thomas are the powers of the human soul and its dispo-

---

9. *ST* I, q. 14, a. 4, c., on whether the knowledge of God is the cause of things: "Unde necesse est quod sua scientia sit causa rerum, secundum quod *habet voluntatem coniunctam.*"

10. See *In II Sent.,* d. 24, q. 3, a. 2, c.: "ibi incipit genus moris ubi primo dominium voluntatis invenitur"; and *ST* I-II, q. 24, a. 4, c.: "[aliquae] pertinent ad genus moris, prout scilicet participant aliquid de voluntario et de iudicio rationis." But the will does not constitute the domain of morals, nor can it act without the influence of intellect. See Michael Sherwin, "The Will's Role in Practical Reasoning," chap. 2 in *By Knowledge and by Love* (Washington, DC: The Catholic University of America Press, 2005), 18-62.

11. *ST* II-II, prol. See *ST* I-II, q. 114, a. 10, ad 4 *in fine:* "et haec de moralibus in communi dicta sufficiant."

12. See especially the prologues for *ST* I-II, q. 6; I-II, q. 18; I-II, q. 22; I-II, q. 49; and I-II, q. 90.

sitions, which otherwise go by the name of "habits." These habits are in turn divided into good habits and bad habits, the virtues and the vices. Thomas closes out the *prima secundae* with a consideration of the extrinsic sources of human actions, namely God and the devil. Thomas had dealt with the devil's influences in the first part of the *Summa,* so he devotes his time henceforth to God's salutary influence, first addressing God's instructing us through law (hence the treatise on law, qq. 90–108), and second addressing God's helping us through grace (qq. 109–114).[13] All of these disparate topics are treated because they have some connection, some proximate, others more remote, to the act of the will.

What is the place of original sin in this larger scheme? Thomas turns to the topic of sin (remembering that it is an intrinsic principle of bad human action) in question 71 of the *prima secundae,* promising a full treatment under six separate headings. The fifth of these headings addresses "the causes of sin," and Thomas breaks this treatment up into three parts, interior causes (ignorance, weakness, and malice), exterior causes (God, the devil, and man), and sin itself (which can also cause other sins). Our text of interest, then, concerns the way in which a man, namely Adam, is able to be the cause of the existence of sin in us. Adam is exterior to all other human beings, for sure, but how his sin comes to be in us, to be our sin, poses a problem, a problem left to us by St. Paul's teaching in Romans 5.

The Received Teaching of Augustine

While I do not wish at this point to address how Thomas chooses not to use Augustine in his treatment in the *Summa theologiae,* question 81, article 1, I do wish to emphasize that he appropriates Augustine's teaching *that* there is such a thing as original sin; Thomas followed Augustine in this, as did all his contemporaries, and as did Lombard, thinking of course that they were being faithful to Christian teaching. All these were embracing a common understanding of the letter to the Romans. To phrase it in the terminology of the *Summa theologiae*'s account of original sin, Thomas holds Augustine's teach-

---

13. Why the treatment of law *before* that of grace? I have not been satisfied by the research into this that I have done to date, but my sense is that law should be treated first, because its seat *(materia in qua,* its *subiectum)* is the intellect, which is more causal with respect to the will than is the subject for grace, which is the essence of the soul *(ST* I-II, q. 110, a. 4, esp. ad 1), since for Thomas the essence of the soul is not per se operative, while the powers that flow from the essence of the soul are per se operative.

ing *that* Adam's original sin is in us in a real, genuine way, such that the sacraments of the Church, and the passion of the Church's founder, are needed. The question will be, "What is the best way to explain *how* this sin of Adam makes its way to us, and remains a sin?"

J. Patout Burns, in his book on Augustine's teaching on grace, discusses Augustine's teaching on original sin under three headings: the primacy of Christ, the communication of original sin through carnal concupiscence, and the origin of the soul.[14] Each of these elements of Augustine's total teaching, he emphasizes, was affected by controversy, especially by the Donatists and the Pelagians.[15]

Regarding the teaching on Christ's primacy, Augustine takes seriously the teaching of Paul, especially as it is found in the letter to the Romans, chapter 5, where Paul repeatedly contrasts the graces of Christ with the disobedience of Adam. The key text for the doctrine of original sin is Romans 5:12: *"sicut per unum hominem in hunc mundum peccatum intravit et per peccatum mors et ita in omnes homines mors pertransiit in quo omnes peccaverunt."* While the *"in quo omnes peccaverunt"* becomes a key theological particle—just what does it mean that all are "in" either Adam or Adam's sin?—the reason to investigate this text arises because of Augustine's consistent belief that faith and baptism are absolutely necessary in order to enter the Kingdom of Christ.[16] He even wondered whether the good thief in the Gospel of Luke, who had faith, might somehow have been baptized.[17] Even children who have not yet attained the age of reason stand in need of the cleansing power of Christ through baptism, despite the fact that personally committed sin is for them as yet impossible.[18] This omnipresent need therefore implies some pre-existent sin found in each member of the human race.

So what would account for the presence of some sin in every human being, upon birth? Augustine here turns to the teaching of Romans *("In quo omnes peccaverunt")*. Adam's original sin fractured the primal state of grace in which he and Eve had been created, bringing upon him and her the primary punishment of death, although Augustine came later to emphasize that carnal concupiscence (the unruly desires of the body) is also an effect of the fall,

---

14. J. Patout Burns, *The Development of Augustine's Doctrine of Operative Grace* (Paris: Études augustiniennes, 1980), 96–109.

15. Mary T. Clark's more recent *Augustine* (Washington, DC: Georgetown University Press, 1994), 51–53, is also useful.

16. *De gen. ad litt.*, 10:14–16.   17. *De anima et eius origine*, 1:9,11.

18. *De pecc. mer.*, 1:23, 33.

and the proximate source of inherited guilt in those who come from Adam.[19] This disobedient inclination in humans, especially in the sexual powers, is a persistent inclination to sin and a disinclination to do the will of God. More importantly, after the fall, even baptized Christians of good will bring forth other humans through carnal lust—mere rational choice does not stir the sexual members into reproduction—and that carnal lust and the other features of concupiscence are transmitted to their offspring, through which they in turn are inclined to sin. This concupiscence in children is sinful, so they stand in need of forgiveness.[20] All the more so, if we take the passage *"in quo omnes peccaverunt"* to suggest some sort of pre-existence of all human beings in Adam.[21]

The origin of the human soul doubtless has a role to play here, especially if one were able to follow a traducian account of the soul (for this would more easily allow the passing on of sin in the soul of Adam to his posterity). However, Augustine had abandoned all considerations of the human soul as a material reality, and therefore had to contend with two possible spiritual accounts of its origin: either by direct creation from God, or through some sort of creation from the soul of one's parents. The first approach had the benefit of avoiding traducianism altogether. Yet in this approach a soul, presumably pure at its creation, would be made sinful by its contact with sinful flesh. Moreover, this approach seemed to run afoul as regards justice, for God would at times be creating souls destined for damnation, as when babies die without baptism. Augustine entertained the second view, which had the benefit of keeping the soul spiritual and yet providing a common lineage of both flesh and soul, tainted by Adam's original sin, as it courses its way through Adam's descendents, all the way to us. In the end, he left that question unsettled.

This overview so far has been based upon scholarship that consults directly the texts of Augustine where he treats of these topics. Yet his teaching gets intensified, even telescoped, in Lombard's *Libri sententiarum,* where Lombard, to suit his pedagogy, quotes the teaching of Augustine to the extent that it helps him cover a series of items, a doctrinal checklist. On whether there is original sin, Lombard quotes the *De baptismo parvulorum* (that is, *De peccatorum meritis*) to the effect that not adhering to the fact that there is a propa-

---

19. *De fide et symb.,* 10:23; and *De lib. arb.,* 3:18, 52–62. See also *De nupt. et concup.,* 1:5–7; 2:30.
20. *Contra Iul.,* 2:5,12; *Contra Iul. op. imp.,* 4:41, 5:20.
21. See Patout-Burns, *The Development,* 106–7.

gation of original sin, but merely rather its imitation, is Pelagianism. This sin goes from parent to child through flesh stained by concupiscence.[22] Is original sin a fault, a *culpa,* chapter 7 asks? Yes it is; Augustine, in the *De natura et gratia,* points to the apostle's text that all have *sinned: "omnes peccaverunt."* The Augustine of the book called the *Hypognosticon* says that Adam's sin harmed both himself and all, because from him we all receive damnation and fault *(culpa).*[23]

Having established that original sin is *culpa,* Lombard turns to address how we understand the phrase of Paul, "in whom all have sinned" *(in quo omnes peccaverunt).*[24] Here again the leading text is Augustine's *De baptismo parvulorum* (1:10), which insists that Paul covered all the bases by the phrase *in quo,* because, says Augustine, whether we are speaking about Adam *(in quo homine)* or his sin *(in quo peccato),* all are present. Lombard then adds a significant comment, taken from the *De baptismo parvulorum,* which summarizes and intensifies the doctrine of communal guilt; in Adam all were as one man *(omnes ille unus homo fuerant),*[25] and Lombard, for good measure and with help from the *glossa ordinaria* adds a fateful line: *"id est, in eo materialiter erant."* Augustine's teaching is given a decidedly material slant, which, even if consonant with the reconstituted "real" teaching of Augustine, is now destined to begin discussion on a range of other issues (such as the truth of human nature questions).[26] For our purposes, it lessens focus on the soul as a possible and practical source of the transmission of original sin. It is our fleshly derivation from Adam that becomes key, and the defects of his flesh that become ours.[27]

Fitting Doctrine and Authority to Pedagogical Exigency

This matter-centered approach dominates the various *scripta* on the *Libri sententiarum,*[28] and Thomas in his *scriptum* on *Libri sententiarum,* book 2, dis-

---

22. Lombard, *Libri sententiarum* II, d. 30, caps. 4–5.

23. Ibid., citing *Hypognosticon,* 2:4.   24. Ibid., cap. 10, no. 2.

25. *Libri sententiarum,* II, dist. 30, cap. 10.

26. See Walter H. Principe, "*De veritate humane naturae:* Theology in Conversation with Biology, Medicine, and Philosophy of Nature," in *Knowledge and the Sciences in Medieval Philosophy: Proceedings of the Eighth International Congress of Medieval Philosophy,* ed. Reijo Tyorinoja et al. (Helsinki: Annals of the Finnish Society for Missiology, 1990), 486–94.

27. *Libri sententiarum,* II, cap. 14, no. 3.

28. See the texts cited above, note 4.

tinction 30, begins his treatment of original sin with the question: "does a defect coming down to us through our origin have the character of fault *(culpa)?*" From the outset Thomas seizes on the fact that *culpa* is a defect via will; in other words, there is no *culpa* where there is no will. Armed with the distinction between person and nature (emphasized here in particular by Anselm's *De conceptu virginali,* 2:23), Thomas allows there to be a fault of the person and a fault of the nature. What is needed is a will that regards not just the person, but the whole human nature. Now Adam was, in an odd way, both person and nature, since he was an individual who had a certain power over all human nature; before the fall special graces were given to him with which to merit heaven, which would also be transmitted to his progeny, had he remained sinless (this is the doctrine of original justice, coming proximately from Anselm). Now, by freely sinning, Adam lost those graces for himself and for human nature, such that the defect of those graces does have the character of fault in the nature (and in those who are of the nature), with an act of will, namely Adam's, as its cause.[29]

In addressing an objection Thomas spells out the mechanism of original sin in a vivid way, which appears to me to have Augustine's teaching clearly in mind, although Thomas does not say so. A very strong objection to the notion of derived guilt says this: no accident (that is, no property) can be handed on or transferred unless its subject is handed on. Now the subject of fault (that is, its location) is the rational soul, and since we are agreed that the soul itself is not transmitted, we preclude the possibility that fault or *culpa* is trans-

---

29. *In II Sententiis,* d. 30, q. 1, a. 2, c.: "Sciendum est igitur, quod haec tria, defectus, malum, et culpa, ex superadditione se habent. Defectus enim simplicem negationem alicujus boni importat. Sed malum nomen privationis est; unde carentia alicujus, etiam si non sit natum haberi, defectus potest dici; sed non potest dici malum, nisi sit defectus ejus boni quod natum est haberi; unde carentia vitae in lapide potest dici defectus, sed non malum: homini vero mors est et defectus et malum. Culpa autem super hoc addit rationem voluntarii: ex hoc enim aliquis culpatur quod deficit in eo quod per suam voluntatem habere potuit. Unde oportet quod secundum hoc quod aliquid rationem culpae habet, secundum hoc ratio voluntarii in ipso reperiatur. Sicut autem est quoddam bonum quod respicit naturam, et quoddam quod respicit personam; ita etiam est quaedam culpa naturae et quaedam personae. Unde ad culpam personae, requiritur voluntas personae sicut patet in culpa actuali, quae per actum personae committitur; ad culpam vero naturae non requiritur nisi voluntas in natura illa. Sic ergo dicendum est, quod defectus illius originalis justitiae quae homini in sua creatione collata est, ex voluntate hominis accidit: et sicut illud naturae donum fuit et fuisset in totam naturam propagatum, homine in justitia persistente; ita etiam et privatio illius boni in totam naturam perducitur, quasi privatio et vitium naturae; ad idem enim genus privatio et habitus referuntur; et in quolibet homine rationem culpae habet ex hoc quod per voluntatem principii naturae, idest primi hominis, inductus est talis defectus."

mitted, too.[30] Thomas agrees that the soul is not transmitted, of course, so his response to this objection will have to allow that the matter of human reproduction, the semen, is able somehow to cause the existence of *culpa* in the soul of the offspring of Adam. He notes that there were both moral and physical defects in Adam after his fall, and that the physical defects in Adam are able to be propagated by his seed, and, importantly, because the soul is meant to animate this sort of body (the now-fallen human body) it also acquires the deformation of fault because it is this sort of body's form. Thomas illustrates this by noting that, at a bodily level, the leper begets the leper, and one with gout begets another with gout. At a rational level one can, through the body, cause defects in the soul, as in those who are stolid from birth. He quotes no authority here—in fact he quotes no one in his positive teaching in the article—but I am confident that he took his explanation to accord with Lombard's *littera,* and, through it, with Augustine.[31]

Thomas deals with original sin in the middle years of his writing, in book 4 of the *Summa contra gentiles* (chs. 50–52) and in the *Compendium theologiae* (1.156). He also deals with original sin in a finely wrought treatment in the *De malo* (q. 4; cf. q. 5). But, as often happens, his mature and sustained treatment is that of the *Summa theologiae* I-II, question 81, to which I now finally turn.

Remember that the pedagogical location of this text in the *Summa theologiae* is among the ways in which one man can cause sin in another man. Our text, in article 1, therefore, asks whether the first sin of our first parents can be transmitted to those who come after them, their posterity. The various objections make their case, and Thomas quotes the passage from Romans 5 in the *sed contra:* "Through one man sin entered into this world." In many ways, things here are a streamlined recasting of prior texts.

30. Ibid., obj. 3: "Praeterea, nullum accidens potest traduci, nisi subjectum suum traducatur. Sed subjectum culpae est anima rationalis, quae cum non sit ex traduce, ut supra probatum est, videtur quod nec aliquid per originem tractum rationem culpae habere possit."

31. *In II Sent.,* d. 30, q. 1, a. 2, ad 3: "Ad tertium dicendum, quod peccatum originale non traducitur per traductionem sui subjecti, quod est anima rationalis, sed per traductionem seminis: quia ex quo anima patris per peccatum infecta fuit, sequitur etiam inordinatio in corpore, subtracto illo ordine quem natura instituta prius acceperat: et ita etiam ex semine illo generatur corpus tali ordine destitutum; unde et anima quae tali corpori infunditur, deordinationem culpae contrahit ex hoc ipso quod hujusmodi corporis forma efficitur; cum oporteat perfectionem perfectibili proportionatam esse: sicut propter aliquam corruptionem seminis contingit non tantum defectus in corpore prolis ex illo semine generatae, ut lepra, podagra, vel aliqua hujusmodi infirmitas; sed etiam defectus in anima, ut patet in his qui a nativitate naturaliter sunt stolidi."

In his *responsio* Thomas begins his doctrinal presentation by stating that it is a matter of the faith that Adam's sin comes down through posterity. For this reason we baptize our infants so as to clean them in some way from the infection of fault, of *culpa*. He continues. To hold otherwise is to hold the Pelagian heresy, as Augustine says "in so many of his books" *(in plurimis libris suis)*—this being the only time Thomas mentions Augustine in the text of this article.

Now Thomas must teach. He notes that two different approaches emerged as attempts to explain how the sin of the first parents is transmitted originally to posterity. Some writers focused on the soul, since the soul is the subject of sin, and held that the soul itself was transmitted along with the human seed, such that infected souls produced infected souls: a classic traducian account.[32] Now others, holding this prior traducian effort to be false, sought to explain how the sin of the parent could be passed on without the passing on of the soul, and so they worked to explain how the bodily defect of the parent is passed to the child, like the way in which the leper begets a leper and one with gout begets another with gout. Since defects on the part of the body can redound to the soul, in this way it is possible that *culpa* in the flesh can be transmitted through human seed to the offspring, and thereby infect the soul[33] (note to the reader: your are correct if this sounds to you exactly like Thomas's own teaching in his commentary on the *Sentences,* which I said above consciously accords with his understanding of Augustine).

But these two approaches, Thomas continues, are insufficient: *"sed omnes huiusmodi viae insufficientes sunt."* Even if we grant that bodily defects are passed on from parent to child, and even if we grant that some defects of the soul's operation are consequent upon those indispositions of the body (like mental retardation), still, the fact that these defects come from another seems to preclude the notion of fault, or *culpa,* which is characterized first and fore-

---

32. *ST* I-II, q. 81, a. 1, c.: "Ad investigandum autem qualiter peccatum primi parentis originaliter possit transire in posteros, diversi diversis viis processerunt. Quidam enim, considerantes quod peccati subiectum est anima rationalis, posuerunt quod cum semine rationalis anima traducatur, ut sic ex infecta anima animae infectae derivari videantur."

33. Ibid.: "Alii vero, hoc repudiantes tanquam erroneum, conati sunt ostendere quomodo culpa animae parentis traducitur in prolem, etiam si anima non traducatur, per hoc quod corporis defectus traducuntur a parente in prolem, sicut si leprosus generat leprosum, et podagricus podagricum, propter aliquam corruptionem seminis, licet talis corruptio non dicatur lepra vel podagra. Cum autem corpus sit proportionatum animae, et defectus animae redundent in corpus, et e converso; simili modo dicunt quod culpabilis defectus animae per traductionem seminis in prolem derivatur, quamvis semen actualiter non sit culpae subiectum."

most by its being voluntary. Even if we were to grant a traducian account of the soul and of original sin, the fact that the infection of the soul of the child was not by his own will blows away the notion of a fault that obliges one to punishment *("amitteret rationem culpae obligantis ad poenam")*. As Aristotle notes in the *Ethics* (III), we do not reproach the one born blind; we pity him.[34]

And so Thomas, leaving behind his prior teaching, and his understanding of Augustine's teaching, sets out a different course. All those who come from Adam can be considered as one man, to the extent that they all are of one nature, which they receive from the first parent. In this way the many human beings who derive from Adam can be considered members of one body. Thomas now adds a key difference from the earlier, rather homogeneous unity of the collective that one noted in Lombard. The act of one member of a body, say the hand, is not voluntary by the will of the hand (of course), but by the will in the soul, which as prime mover moves the hand (note the introduction of heterogeneity, the one has primacy over the other, is the source of the other's action). Thus the homicide that a hand might commit is not imputed to the hand (if the hand were separated from the body), but it is imputed to the hand as being some part of a man that is moved by a first motive principle of the man. And so the disorder that is in a man, derived from Adam, is not in that man by his own will but rather by Adam's, who by the motion of human generation moves others—you and me—who derive their origin from him.[35] And this is why it is called "original sin," while the sin de-

---

34. Ibid.: "Sed omnes huiusmodi viae insufficientes sunt. Quia dato quod aliqui defectus corporales a parente transeant in prolem per originem; et etiam aliqui defectus animae ex consequenti, propter corporis indispositionem, sicut interdum ex fatuis fatui generantur, tamen hoc ipsum quod est ex origine aliquem defectum habere, videtur excludere rationem culpae, de cuius ratione est quod sit voluntaria. Unde etiam posito quod anima rationalis traduceretur, ex hoc ipso quod infectio animae prolis non esset in eius voluntate, amitteret rationem culpae obligantis ad poenam, quia, ut philosophus dicit in III *Ethic.,* nullus improperabit caeco nato, sed magis miserebitur."

35. Ibid.: "Et ideo alia via procedendum est, dicendo quod omnes homines qui nascuntur ex Adam, possunt considerari ut unus homo, inquantum conveniunt in natura, quam a primo parente accipiunt; secundum quod in civilibus omnes qui sunt unius communitatis, reputantur quasi unum corpus, et tota communitas quasi unus homo. Porphyrius etiam dicit quod participatione speciei plures homines sunt unus homo. Sic igitur multi homines ex Adam derivati, sunt tanquam multa membra unius corporis. Actus autem unius membri corporalis, puta manus, non est voluntarius voluntate ipsius manus, sed voluntate animae, quae primo movet membra. Unde homicidium quod manus committit, non imputaretur manui ad peccatum, si consideraretur manus secundum se ut divisa a corpore, sed imputatur ei inquantum est aliquid hominis quod movetur a primo principio motivo hominis. Sic igitur inordinatio quae est in isto homine, ex Adam generato, non est voluntaria voluntate ipsius sed voluntate primi parentis, qui movet motione generationis omnes qui ex eius origine

riving from the soul to a bodily member is called "actual sin." And so, the actual sin that is committed by a bodily member is not to be attributed to that member except to the extent that it is a member of this man (we call this "human sin"). In a like way, the original sin cannot be a sin of this person except to the extent that this person receives his nature from the first parent (and hence has the "sin of nature"). Original sin, then, is more a sin of the nature than of the person. And with that, Thomas finishes this treatment.[36]

Conclusion

So what has Thomas done? It seems to me that—I believe Cajetan saw this, too[37]—Thomas had the sense that prior attempts to explain the transmission of original sin (his own, and Augustine's, included) were unable to explain how *culpa* could justly be attributed to this person, to you or to me,

---

derivantur, sicut voluntas animae movet omnia membra ad actum. Unde peccatum quod sic a primo parente in posteros derivatur, dicitur originale, sicut peccatum quod ab anima derivatur ad membra corporis, dicitur actuale." The analogy Thomas is employing here is that the will is to the hand as Adam is to all other humans.

36. Ibid.: "Et sicut peccatum actuale quod per membrum aliquod committitur, non est peccatum illius membri nisi inquantum illud membrum est aliquid ipsius hominis, propter quod vocatur peccatum humanum; ita peccatum originale non est peccatum huius personae, nisi inquantum haec persona recipit naturam a primo parente."

37. It was pleasant to learn that Cajetan had suspicions similar to mine. See his commentary *in hoc locum*, in *Sancti Thomae de Aquino opera omnia iussu impensaque, Leonis XIII. P.M. edita,* vol. 7 (Romae: Ex Typographia Polyglotta S. C. de Propaganda Fide, 1882), 89: "In eodem articulo, adverte quod Auctor positionem, quam in II *Sent.,* dist. xxx, secutus est, licet non totaliter, arguere videatur: Si tamen diligentius consideretur littera, dum arguitur insufficientiae secunda via, positio illa olim sua reprehenditur. Nam ibi tenuit peccatum originale contrahi per originem sicut podagram vel stoliditatem, redundant in formam conditione materiae; et habere rationem culpae propter voluntatem parentis. Hic autem licet de isto voluntario non fiat mentio referendo illam opinionem subintelligitur tamen, ut puto, tanquam commune confessum ab omnibus, quod hoc est voluntarium aliena voluntate. Reprehenditur autem haec positio tanquam insufficiens quia non salvat rationem voluntarii etiam aliena voluntate, sic quod sufficiat ad rationem culpae in hoc genito. Quoniam totum hoc quod illa positio dicit accepta tum verificatur de Socrate secundum se: est namque secundum se habens conditiones formae coaptatas materiae conditionibus, voluntarie Adae voluntate contractas ab eo. Et tamen defectus iste non est culpa Socratis secundum se. Quia ergo oportet ad salvandum voluntarium requisitum ad culpam huius absque propria voluntate, ponere hunc hominem esse aliquid alienae voluntatis, ut sic sit voluntarius defectus voluntate propria non secundum se, sed secundum quod membrum alterius, a quo inchoat haec culpa; et hoc non positum est a praedictis positionibus: ideo arguuntur. Et ponitur alia via, qua salvatur sufficienter ratio voluntarii per hoc quod ponitur in Socrate hoc peccatum ut est membrum Adae, et ex consequenti in ipso secundum se." Santiago Ramírez, in his commentary on Thomas's text here (*De vitiis et peccatis,* in *Opera Omnia* [Salamanca: Dominicos provincia de España, 1990], book 8, vol. 2, p. 554), notes that Cajetan, Conrad Köllin, and Johannes Capreolus caught this evolution in Thomas's teaching.

at all. And yet the constant practice of the Church in baptizing, built upon the texts of St. Paul, took for granted that there *was* some sort of fault, but a fault that of course was not from the proper will of the child to be baptized. The accounts of human unity deriving from Augustine in Lombard gave one the sense that, in the homogeneous whole that was humanity in Adam, the infection of original sin in any part of the entity was the same, the *culpa* the same. But Thomas sets aside his prior teaching and does not invoke Augustine (and, likely, the expected interpretations that his invocation would produce). Instead Thomas's *alia via* makes Adam the primary motive power, by will, in the whole human body. In this body we are not just members materially, but members such as can be moved by his will in performing that original sin. The sin is his, primarily, and ours only through origin. His was the mortal sin, calling for damnation; ours is a fault of our nature, calling for the cleansing and rebirth in the Lord, but for which no one is liable to the fires of hell.[38]

So in the end Thomas sought to safeguard the reality of original sin in a way that fit his moral pedagogy, wherein will is the source, really, of genuine, imputable, moral actions and blame. The Augustine as presented and interpreted in Thomas's milieu could not provide him with an *"unus homo"* of sufficient differentiation to detail the causal flow of Adam's will to us, members by our nature, of his body. Thomas's *alia via* does do this. And for this reason Thomas can close his treatment here in the *Summa* with the passage from the letter to the Ephesians, where Paul says, "by nature, we were all sons of wrath."[39] God help us all.[40]

---

38. This all touches upon the doctrine of eternal punishment for those infants who died without the benefit of the sacrament of baptism, which Christopher Beiting has treated thoroughly. See Christopher Beiting, "The Idea of Limbo in Thomas Aquinas," *Thomist* 62 (1998): 217–44, and "The Nature and Structure of Limbo in the Works of Albertus Magnus," *New Blackfriars* 85 (2004): 492–509.

39. *ST* I-II, q. 81, a. 1, *in fine* c.: "ita peccatum originale non est peccatum huius personae, nisi inquantum haec persona recipit naturam a primo parente. Unde et vocatur peccatum naturae; secundum illud Ephes. II, 'eramus natura filii irae.'"

40. A more extended treatment of this topic would want to incorporate Thomas's discussion of the issue of original sin in his comments on St. Paul's letter to the Romans, ch. 5, lectio 3, which Thomas revised with some care, and which Fr. Torrell is inclined to date to Thomas's last years in Naples (see J.-P. Torrell, *Saint Thomas Aquinas*, vol. 1, *The Person and His Work*, trans. Robert Royal [Washington, DC: The Catholic University of America Press, 1996], 250–53, 340). That treatment can be found in *S. Thomae Aquinatis super epistolas S. Pauli lectura*, vol. 1, ed. R. Cai (Torino: Marietti, 1953), 73–76 (nos. 408–410) and is similar in content to what is found in the *Summa theologiae*.

7

"Without Me You Can Do Nothing"

St. Thomas with and without St. Augustine on John 15:5

Guy Mansini, O.S.B.

Both St. Augustine and St. Thomas commented on the Gospel according to John. As we might expect, St. Thomas learned much about the fourth gospel from St. Augustine. In his own commentary, St. Thomas cites him more than any other patristic writer. However, and again as we should expect, he had lights of his own in meditating on the Light that shone in the darkness, the Light that neither St. Augustine nor St. Thomas supposed they could comprehend. "As Augustine says, to attain to God with the mind is a great blessing, but to comprehend Him is impossible."[1] This essay takes up a place, John 15:5, where both the indebtedness and the originality of St. Thomas, vis-à-vis St. Augustine in attaining to, if not comprehending, the Light, are evident. "Without me," the Lord says to the disciples, "you can do nothing." St. Augustine takes John 15:5 to declare the necessity of the grace of Christ for good works. St. Thomas discerns also a more comprehensive claim about the universal causality of the Word. Both, again, lay the foundations for hearing

---

1. St. Thomas Aquinas, *Super Evangelium S. Ioannis lectura,* ed. Raffaele Cai (Turin/Rome: Marietti, 1952), 1:5 (no. 102): "Illud enim dicitur comprehendi, cuius fines concluduntur et conspiciuntur. Quia, sicut dicit Augustinus, attingere Deum mente, magna beatitudo est: comprehendere vero, impossibile est."

in John 15:5 a word about the theology of orders. We conclude with a brief reflection on the identity of revelation within the continuity of interpretations.

I. St. Augustine, John 15:5, and Grace

St. Augustine preached or dictated his *In Johannis evangelium tractatus* between 406 and 420, but those tractates on chapters 13 to 21, to which our text belongs, can be more narrowly dated to the last two of these years, after 418.[2] Tractate 81, therefore, our text, was dictated not long after the Council of Carthage, 418, well after *On the Merits and Remission of Sins and on Infant Baptism* (411), *On the Spirit and the Letter* (412), and *On Nature and Grace* (415), just after the production of *On the Grace of Christ and on Original Sin* (418), in the years in which he was writing the first book of *On Marriage and Concupiscence* (418–419) and just before *Against Two Letters of the Pelagians* (421). In other words, tractate 81 was written in the fullness of the maturity of his response to Pelagianism. The ease with which he takes up the cudgel is therefore not surprising.

"As the branch cannot bear fruit of itself, except it abide in the vine, no more can you except you abide in me" [Jn 15:4]. A great encomium on grace, my brothers, one that will instruct the souls of the humble and stop the mouths of the proud! Let those now answer it, if they dare, who, ignorant of God's righteousness and going about to establish their own, have not submitted themselves to the righteousness of God. Let those who are self-complacent answer it, who think they have no need of God for the performance of good works. Don't they fight against such a truth, those men of corrupt mind, reprobate concerning the faith, whose reply is only full of impious talk, when they say: "It is of God that we have our existence as men, but it is of ourselves that we are righteous"? What is it you say, you who deceive yourselves, and, instead of establishing free will, cast it headlong down from the heights of self-elevation through the empty regions of presumption into the depths of the ocean grave? For your assertion that man, of himself,

2. Marie-François Berrouard, "L'exégèse de saint Augustin prédicateur du quatrième Evangile," *Freiburger Zeitschrift für Philosophie und Theologie* 34 (1987): 311–14; more conveniently, Allan D. Fitzgerald, following Berrouard, "Johannis evangelium tractatus," in *Augustine through the Ages. An Encyclopedia,* ed. Allan D. Fitzgerald (Grand Rapids, MI: William B. Eerdmans Publishing Company, 1999), 474b–475a. A "tractate" for Augustine can be the same as a sermon or homily. Tractates 1–16 were preached in the winter of 406–407; tractates 17–19 and 23–54 in 414; tractates 20–22 after late 419; and tractates 55–124 were more likely dictated first then preached in 419–420. For Augustine as preacher and exegete in the *Tractates,* see John M. Norris, "The Theological Structure of Augustine's Exegesis in the *Tractatus in Evangelium Ioannis,*" in *Augustine: Presbyter Factus Sum, Collectanea Augustiniana* II, ed. Joseph T. Lienhard, Earl C. Muller, and Roland J. Teske (New York: Peter Lang, 1993), 385–94.

works righteousness, *that* is the height of your self-elation. But the Truth contradicts you, and declares: "The branch cannot bear fruit of itself, unless it abide in the vine." Away with you now over your giddy precipices, and, without a spot whereon to take your stand, vapor away at your windy talk. These are the empty regions of your presumption. But look well at what is tracking your steps, and, if you have any sense remaining, let your hair stand on end. For whoever imagines that he is bearing fruit of himself is not in the vine, and he that is not in the vine is not in Christ, and he that is not in Christ is not a Christian. Such are the ocean depths into which you have plunged.

Ponder again and again what the Truth has still further to say: "I am the vine," he adds, "you are the branches: he who abides in me, and I in him, brings forth much fruit; for without me you can do nothing" [Jn 15:5]. For just to keep any from supposing that the branch can bear at least some little fruit of itself, after saying, "he brings forth much fruit," his next words are not, without me you can do only a little, but "you can do nothing." Whether then it be little or much, without him it is impossible; for without him nothing can be done. For although, when the branch bears little fruit, the vinedresser prunes it that it may bring forth more; yet if it does not abide in the vine and draw its life from the root, it can bear no fruit whatever of itself. And although Christ would not have been the vine, had he not been man, yet he could not have supplied such grace to the branches, had he not also been God. And just because such grace is so essential to life that even death itself ceases to be at the disposal of free will, he adds, "If anyone does not abide in me, he shall be cast forth as a branch and wither; and they shall gather him into the fire, and he is burned [Jn 15:6]."[3]

3. *In Iohannis Evangelium Tractatus* LXXXI, 2–3; Corpus Christianorum, Series Latina, vol. 36 (Turnhout: Brepols, 1954): "'Sicut palmes non potest ferre fructum a semetipso, nisi manserit in vite, sic nec vos, nisi in me manseritis.' Magna gratiae commendatio, fratres mei: corda instruit humilium, ora obstruit superborum. Ecce cui, si audent, respondeant, qui ignorantes Dei iustitiam, et suam volentes constituere, iustitiae Dei non sunt subiecti. Ecce cui respondeant sibi placentes, et ad bona opera facienda Deum sibi necessarium non putantes. None huic resistunt veritati, homines mente corrupti, reprobi circa fidem, qui respondent et loquuntur iniquitatem, dicentes: A Deo habemus quod homines sumus, a nobis ipsis autem quod iusti sumus? Quid dicitis, qui vos ipsos decipitis, non assertores, sed praecipitatores liberi arbitrii, ex alto elationis per inania praesumtionis, in profunda submersionis? Nempe vox vestra est, quod homo ex semetipso facit iustitiam. Hoc est altum elationis vestrae. Sed veritas contradicit, et dicit: 'Palmes non potest ferre fructum a semetipso, nisi manserit in vite.' Ite nunc per abrupta, et non habentes ubi figamini, ventosa loquacitate iactamini. Haec sunt inania praesumtionis vestrae. Sed quid vos sequatur videte, et si est in vobis ullus sensus, horrete. Qui enim a semetipso se fructum existimat ferre, in vite non est; qui in vite non est, in Christo non est; qui in Christo non est, christianus non est. Haec sunt profunda submersionis vestrae.

"Etiam atque etiam considerate quid adhuc veritas adiungat et dicat: 'Ego sum,' inquit, 'vitis, vos palmites. Qui manet in me, et ego in eo, hic fert fructum multum; quia sine me nihil potestis facere.' Ne quisquam putaret saltem parvum aliquem fructum posse a semetipso palmitem ferre, cum dixisset: 'hic fert fructum multum,' non ait, quia sine me parum potestis facere; sed; 'nihil potestis facere.' Sive ergo parum, sive multum, sine illo fieri non potest, sine quo nihil fieri potest. Quia etsi parum adtulerit palmes, eum purgat agricola ut plus afferat; tamen nisi in vite manserit et vixerit de radice, quantumlibet fructum a semetipso non potest ferre. Quamvis autem Christus vitis non esset, nisi homo

"His words are not, without me you can do only a little, but you can do nothing." A great encomium on grace, indeed, and I mean Augustine's text. The Johannine verse, for its part, is nicely suited to indicate that grace is not law, not teaching, not good example, not even the exterior manipulation of the vinedresser, but rather an interior reality, like sap, like life.[4]

The anti-Pelagian virtues of John 15:5 were well-known to Augustine by the time he came to it in tractate 81. It was an important locus for him. The index of texts to volume 5 of the Edinburgh edition of the *Nicene and Post-Nicene Fathers,* first series, *St. Augustine: Anti-Pelagian Writings,* includes every anti-Pelagian work except his *Answer to Julian* and the *Unfinished Work in Answer to Julian.* It lists twenty-two biblical texts cited ten times or more. John 15:5 is not the favorite text making the same point—Philippians 2:13 occurs twenty times and 1 Corinthians 4:7 occurs twenty-one times.[5] Still, John 15:5 is cited fourteen times and is ninth on the list—six times before the composition of the later tractates to which our text belongs, three times during the period of their composition, and five times after.[6] If one consults the index to the new translation of the *Contra Julianum opus imperfectum,* not included in the Edinburgh translation, John 15:5 mostly retains its place, with eight citations making it the eleventh most cited scriptural text of the work. John 15:5 is also cited seven times within the tractates themselves, three times for rebuke of the Pelagians.[7]

---

esset, tamen istam gratiam palmitibus non praeberet, nisi etiam Deus esset. Verum quia ita sine ista gratia non potest vivi, ut et mors in potestate sit liberi arbitrii. 'Si quis in me,' inquit, 'non manserit, mittetur foras sicut palmes; et arescet; et colligent eum, et in ignem mittent, et ardet.'" And he adds: "Unum de duobus palmiti congruit, aut vitis, aut ignis: si in vite non est, in igne erit; ut ergo in igne non sit, in vite sit." I have modified the translation of John Gibb and James Innes in *The Nicene and Post-Nicene Fathers,* first series, vol. 7 (Grand Rapids, MI: William B. Eerdmans Publishing Company, 1888, 1983), 345–46.

4. See tractate 80, no. 2: Insofar as he is the vine, which is to say, insofar is he is incarnate, Christ is not the vinedresser, but rather is his Father. On the other hand, insofar as "I and the Father are one," which is to say, insofar as Father and Son are the one God, he is the vinedresser: "And yet not such a one as those, whose whole service is confined to external labor; but such that He also supplies the increase from within." In *On the Spirit and the Letter,* 42 (25), John 15:5 is used together with 2 Corinthians 3:6 to make the point that grace is interior and so something different from the exteriorly written law. *De spiritu et littera, Corpus scriptorum ecclesiasticorum Latinorum,* 60, 153–229.

5. For some reason I do not know, there is never any appeal made to Isaiah 12:26 ("O Lord, you have wrought for us all our works"), which would also make St. Augustine's point admirably.

6. The indexing of the *Nicene and Post-Nicene Fathers* is at least sometimes more accurate than that of the more recent Rotelle edition, *The Works of Saint Augustine, A Translation for the 21st Century: Answer to the Pelagians I–IV* (Hyde Park, NY: New City Press, 1997–), which, however, has the advantage of including the *Answer to Julian* (in vol. 2) and the *Unfinished Work in Answer to Julian* (all of vol. 3).

7. I mean 15:5b, not 15:5a; in addition to tractate 81, see tractate 53, no. 10, composed in 414; and tractate 86, no. 3, composed in 418–420.

It is not always pressed into service in exactly the same way; this shifts according to the shifting focus of the controversy.[8] In 412, at the outset of the controversy, according to Augustine what cannot be done without Christ is "good works" or "righteousness" or the fulfillment of the commandments, and the aid required to do these things is a grace interior to the will, variously described as the love of the Holy Spirit poured into our hearts (Rom 5:5) or God's giving us both to will and to work (Phil 2:13) or a grace that "cures the will whereby righteousness is freely loved."[9] In the first of these places from *On the Spirit and the Letter,* in chapter 42, 2 Corinthians 3:6 establishes the differences between the Old and New Covenants: the letter that can but teach leads to death, as for example the command not to covet (Ex 20:17) awakens desire as the Apostle teaches (Rom 7), but only the Spirit gives life interiorly by the gift of charity (Rom 5:5) so that the command may be kept. The grace of Christ is by no means exterior teaching, for God works in us both to will and to do (Phil 2:13), and John 15:5 serves nicely not simply to affirm the fact of interior grace, but in addition to confirm its necessity: "without me you can do nothing." This remains the context for the other two appeals to John 15:5 in *On the Spirit and the Letter.*

In 415, in *On Nature and Grace,* Augustine states that the branch cannot bear fruit and nothing can we do unless grace both goes before and follows, healing before and following with health and strength, calling us before, following with glory. Or more simply, the fruit we are to bear means being without sin, being just, which requires grace helping free will.[10]

In 418, in *On the Grace of Christ,* St. Augustine applies himself to Pelagius's threefold distinction of capacity, will, and performance *(possibilitas, voluntas, actio).*[11] Philippians 2:13 shows that grace is not simply the created capacity of freedom, but is a matter of both the good will and the performance St. Paul speaks of. A good will is charity (ch. 22), and charity is shed abroad in our hearts by the Holy Spirit who has been given to us (Rom 5:5).[12] Pelagius ad-

---

8. For the course of the controversy, I rely on J. Patout Burns, *The Development of Augustine's Doctrine of Operative Grace* (Paris: Études Augustiniennes, 1980).

9. *On the Spirit and the Letter,* 42 (25), 50 (29), 52 (30).

10. *On Nature and Grace,* 35 (31), 73 (62) (*De natura et gratia,* in *Corpus scriptorum ecclesiasticorum Latinorum,* 60, 231–299). See close to this time, in 414, tractate 53, no. 10, where unless one believes that the grace of Christ is necessary for good works, one cannot believe in the one who said "without me, you can do nothing."

11. *On the Grace of Christ,* 4 (3), in *Corpus scriptorum ecclesiasticorum Latinorum,* 42, 123–206; see 127: "Tria . . . distinguat . . . : possibilitatem scilicet, qua potest homo esse iustus, voluntatem, qua vult esse iustus, actionem, qua iustus est."

12. *On the Grace of Christ,* 22 (21), 27 (26).

mits that grace helps us accomplish more easily what we may accomplish by will alone, but John 15:5 has it not that without Christ we cannot perform good works easily, but that without Christ we can do nothing.[13]

The year 418 also marks St. Augustine's discovery of the necessity of an interior operative grace for conversion, as unfolded in *Letter 194*.[14] Conversion is also the context of *Against Two Letters of the Pelagians* in 419–420, where the discovery of *Letter 194* is confirmed by God's conversion even of those who resist him.[15] Concordantly with *Letter 194*, we learn that the very desire of the good is included in what we cannot do without Christ. It is not said, Augustine observes, that without him we can perfect nothing, but rather without him we can do nothing: grace is needed for both the beginning and the ending.[16] Moreover, even thinking the good prior to justification—that, too, is included in what we cannot do without Christ. For the Apostle says, "Not that we are sufficient to think anything as of ourselves, but our sufficiency is of God" (2 Cor 3:5). We are not sufficient "to think anything"; "to which," Augustine says, "'nothing' is the contrary." "And this is the meaning of what the Lord says, 'Without me ye can do nothing.'"

The text of *Against Two Letters* continues in a sort of extended meditation on John 15:5. Book II, chapter 20 (9), notes both that it is man's part to prepare his heart (Prv 16:1) and that, once we open our mouth, God will fill it (Ps 80:10). Augustine comments: "for although, save by his assistance without whom we can do nothing, we cannot open our mouth, yet we open it by his aid and by our own agency, while the Lord fill its without our agency."[17] But the Lord also says, "I will open thy mouth," and therefore, "Why is this, except that in one of these cases He cooperates with man as the agent, in the other He does it alone." So the next chapter (ch. 21) begins: "Wherefore God does many good things in man which man does not do; but man does none which God does not cause man to do." Both parts are included in the scope of John 15:5. So, the desire of the good, which is love—that is, the desire of the good because of delight in the good—is God's work in us without us, but

13. Ibid., 30 (29), and see the appeal to Romans 5:5 in the very next chapter, 31(30). The point of 30 (29) together with the appeal to John 15:5 is repeated in the fifth canon of the Council of Carthage (418).

14. Burns, 142, 145–50.

15. Ibid., 142, 150–55.

16. *Against Two Letters of the Pelagians,* II, 18 (8) (*Contra duas epistolas Pelagianorum, Corpus scriptorum ecclesiasticorum Latinorum,* 60, 421–570).

17. *Nicene and Post-Nicene Fathers,* vol. 5, trans. Robert Ernest Wallis, 400.

since it is *our* desiring, it falls under John 15:5. "For, if without Him we are able to do nothing actually, we are able neither to begin nor to perfect, because to begin, it is said, 'His mercy shall prevent me' (Ps 49:10); to finish, it is said, 'his mercy shall follow me' (Ps 23:6)."[18]

The last use of John 15:5 in *Against Two Letters* occurs in a passage of great force to the effect that no one makes himself good, but God can convert even those who resist Him. Pride, he says, has stopped the ears of the Pelagians, and they do not hear:

they do not hear: "for what have you that you did not receive?" (1 Cor 4:7); they do not hear: "without me you can do nothing" (Jn 15:5); they do not hear: "love is of God" (1 Jn 4:7); they do not hear: "God has dealt the measure of faith" (Rom 12:3); they do not hear: "the Spirit blows where it will" (Jn 3:8) and "they who are led by the Spirit of God, they are the sons of God" (Rom 8:14); they do not hear: "no one can come unto me unless it has been given him by my Father" (Jn 6:65).[19]

Augustine appeals to John 15:5 for the same things in the latter part of the controversy. So, in *On Grace and Free Will* (426–427), it again embraces both operative grace as well as God's assistance of our agency, as in this allusion to the text in chapter 33:

He operates, therefore, without us, in order that we may will; but when we will and so will that we may act, He cooperates with us. We can, however, ourselves do nothing to effect good works of piety without Him either working that we may will or co-working when we will.[20]

Moreover, while *Against Two Letters* used John 15:5 to assert the impossibility of merit prior to justification, it is now used to show the need for grace for merit after justification.[21] Our good works, Augustine says, are grace.[22]

Also in 426–427, *Rebuke and Grace* reasserts the need for grace for works after justification, since "without me you can do nothing."[23] But it also treats

---

18. Ibid., 401.

19. *Against Two Letters,* IV, 14 (6); I have altered the Wallis translation in *Nicene and Post-Nicene Fathers,* vol. 5, 422. See Burns, 154–55.

20. *On Grace and Free Will,* 33 (17) (*De gratia et libero arbitrio, PL* 44, 881–912; see 901): "Ut ergo velimus, sine nobis operator; cum autem volumus, et sic volumus ut faciamus, nobiscum operatur: tamen sine illo vel operante ut velimus, vel cooperante cum volumus, ad bona pietatis opera nihil valemus."

21. Ibid., 13 (6).

22. Ibid., 20 (8).

23. *On Rebuke and Grace,* 2 (1) (*De correptione et gratia, PL* 44, 915–946).

of the grace of perseverance. For Adam before the fall, perseverance would have required an *auxilium sine quo*. For us who are in Christ, perseverance is a stronger grace, an *auxilium quo*.

For not only did he [the Lord] say, "Without me ye can do nothing"—by which Augustine envisages Adam's actualization of the possibility of not sinning—but he also said, "Ye have not chosen me, but I have chosen you and ordained you that ye should go and bring forth fruit and that your fruit should remain" (Jn 15:16). By which words he showed that He had given them not only righteousness, but perseverance therein.

This is the *auxilium quo* of the predestined.[24] While the *Two Letters* made John 15:5 to govern also the operative graces of conversion, including them in what we cannot do apart from Christ, in *Rebuke and Grace,* in the last citation in the work, it is rhetorically convenient for John 15:5 to envisage a cooperative grace only. The *sine quo* suggests a *quo,* and that proposes a way for allocating the verses of John 15, verse 5 to the first, verse 16 to the second.[25]

The long and sprawling *Unfinished Work in Answer to Julian,* composed from 427 to 430, deploys John 15:5 eight times, as noted above, but for no new purpose. Twice, the issue is the avoidance of sin.[26] Four times, it encompasses works of piety or "doing good."[27] Once, it is very narrowly invoked for willing the good, together with Philippians 2:13 and Proverbs 8:35, and once for justification.[28]

Summing up, it must be said, therefore, that St. Augustine takes full advantage of the plasticity of the text, the comprehensiveness of all "doing," of any "doing," and the absoluteness of "nothing." Good works, all merit, keeping the law, staying free of sin, desiring the good and even thinking the good, staying upright and persevering in the good: none of these things can be done without the grace of Christ. Could there be imagined a broader scope for the import of the text?

---

24. Ibid., 34 (12), Wallis translation.

25. See tractate 86, no. 3, on John 15:16: the fruit he has chosen us to bear is not produced without him, Augustine points out, appealing to 15:5; thus, 15:16 seems to indicate an operative (and prevenient) grace and 15:5 a cooperative grace, as in tractate 81.

26. *Answer to the Pelagians, III: Unfinished Work in Answer to Julian,* trans. Roland J. Teske (Hyde Park, NY: New City Press, 1999), I, 98; IV, 122 (*Contra Julianum opus imperfectum, PL* 45, 1049–1608).

27. Ibid., I, 86; III, 118, 119, 120, and here whether to do the good is in thought, word, or action.

28. Ibid., I, 97, and II, 198. In the *Answer to Julian* of 421, included in *Answer to the Pelagians II,* trans. Roland J. Teske (Hyde Park, NY: New City Press, 1999), the nothing we can do without Christ is to govern sexual desire, book V, 16 (66) (*Contra Julianum, PL* 44, 641–874).

II. St. Thomas, John 15:5, and Creation

The *Lectura* on the Gospel of John are a product of St. Thomas's second Paris regency, 1269–1272. They were a *reportatio,* but one corrected by St. Thomas himself.[29] One, at least, of St. Thomas's readings of St. Augustine's *Tractates* was relatively proximate to the composition of his own *Lectura.* For the *Catena Aurea* was finished in 1267, and the *Tractates* are reported from the beginning to the end for the Gospel of John.[30] Furthermore, St. Thomas's reading of the *Tractates* was foundational to the composition of his *Lectura,* for St. Augustine is St. Thomas's favorite authority, referred to 426 times, and much beyond St. John Chrysostom in second place at 259 references.[31] Augustine is not quoted by Thomas at 15:5 in the *Lectura,* though he contributes to the *Catena* there. The reminiscence of St. Augustine is, however, patent enough, as will appear presently.[32]

St. Thomas reads John 15:4b–8 as giving four reasons why the branches, Christians, should remain in the vine, Christ: so that God may be glorified (vs. 8); so that we may receive what we pray for (vs. 7); so that we may avoid punishment (vs. 6); and, in the first place, so that we be sanctified (vss. 4b–5).

29. James A. Weisheipl, O.P., introduction, in St. Thomas Aquinas, *Commentary on the Gospel of St. John,* part I, trans. James A. Weisheipl, O.P., and Fabian R. Larcher, O.P. (Albany, NY: Magi Books, 1980), 3. Jean-Pierre Torrell, *Saint Thomas Aquinas,* vol. 1, *The Person and his Work* (Washington, DC: The Catholic University of America Press, 1996), 199, doubts the report of Bartholomew of Capua and Tolomeo of Lucca that St. Thomas himself corrected the text, and attributes the quality and extent of the text to Reginald of Piperno. Torrell thinks the *lectura* were given in 1270–1272.

30. Indeed, St. Thomas may well simply have used the *Catena* in composing the *Lectura* as he did for the *tertia pars* of the *Summa;* see Louis J. Batillon, "Saint Thomas et les Pères: De la *Catena* à la *tertia pars,*" in *Ordo Sapientiae et Amoris. Hommage au professeur Jean-Pierre Torrell, O.P.,* ed. Carlos-Josaphat Pinto de Oliveira, O.P. (Fribourg: University of Fribourg, 1993), 16–22.

31. Thereafter, we have Origen at ninety-one times, Gregory the Great at fifty-four, and St. Hilary at forty-six. See Gilles Emery (following Leo Elders), "Biblical Exegesis and the Speculative Doctrine of the Trinity in St. Thomas Aquinas's Commentary on John," in his *Trinity in Aquinas* (Ypsilanti, MI: Sapientia Press, 2003), 304. Emery notes that contemporaries are not cited at all, in contrast to the youthful work on the *Sentences,* and Aristotle hardly at all (fourteen times). Weisheipl, introduction, in Aquinas, *Commentary on the Gospel of St. John,* 12, comes to another count: Augustine, 373; Chrysostom, 217; Origen, 95. Augustine, and especially for the *Tractates,* is much the most cited author in the commentary of Rupert of Deutz, too; see the indices in Rupert Tuitiensis, *Commentaria in Evangelium Sancti Iohannis,* ed. Rhabanus Haacke (Turnhout: Brepols, 1969).

32. Wilhelmus G. B. M. Valkenberg, *Words of the Living God: Place and Function of Holy Scripture in the Theology of St. Thomas Aquinas* (Leuven: Peeters, 2000), 173, n. 101: "When comparing Aquinas's commentary with his *Glossa continua* on John, many of the explanations in his commentary prove to be derived from the Fathers. In many cases, Aquinas did no longer mention the sources he found when composing his '*catena*' on John."

Verses 4b–5a state the necessity of inhering in the vine in order to bear fruit. Verse 5b declares the efficaciousness of remaining in the vine: the first part of 5b states the fact of efficaciousness: not just fruit, but "much fruit" will be born, and the "much fruit" consists in abstaining from sin, in doing the works of sanctification, in edifying others, and in eternal life; the second part of 5b states the reason of this efficaciousness: "without me you can do nothing."

the reason of this efficaciousness is that "without me you can do nothing." In these words, he both instructs the hearts of the humble and stops up the mouths of the proud, especially of the Pelagians, who say that they can do the good works of the virtues and of the law from themselves, without the help of God: in saying which, they want to assert free will, but rather cast it down.

For behold, the Lord says here that without him we can do, not great works, neither the least works, but nothing. Nor is this surprising, since neither does God do anything without the Lord: above, 1:3: "nothing has been made without him." For our works are done either in virtue of nature, or from divine grace. If in virtue of nature, since all motions of nature are from the Word of God himself, no nature can be moved to do something without him. But if in virtue of grace: since he himself is the author of grace, since "grace and truth have come through Jesus Christ," as is said above, 1:17, it is manifest that no meritorious work can be done without him: 2 Corinthians 3:5: "Not that we are sufficient to think anything of ourselves as if from ourselves; but our sufficiency is from God." If therefore we cannot even think unless from God, much less can we do other things.[33]

Evidently, St. Thomas is following St. Augustine's homilies on the Gospel of John closely in composing his own commentary. He not only follows his predecessor in reading John 15:5b against the Pelagians, but borrows some of the very rhetoric of St. Augustine: as St. Augustine after verse 4, so St. Thomas at verse 5 reports that this teaching instructs the hearts of the humble and stops the mouths of the proud. He observes with St. Augustine that though the Pe-

---

33. *In Ioannem*, 15:5 (no. 1993): "Ratio autem huius efficaciae est, 'qui sine me nihil potestis facere.' In quo et corda instruit humilium, et ora obstruit superborum, et praecipue Pelagianorum, qui dicunt bona opera virtutum et legis sine Dei adiutorio ex seipsis facere posse: in quo dum liberum arbitrium asserere volunt, eum magis praecipitant.

"Ecce enim Dominus hic dicit, quod sine ipso non solum magna, sed nec minima, immo nihil facere possumus. Nec mirum quia nec Deus sine ipso aliquid facit; supra, 1:3, 'Sine ipso factum est nihil.' Opera enim nostra aut sunt virtute naturae, aut ex gratia divina. Si virtute naturae, cum omnes motus naturae sint ab ipso Verbo Dei, nulla natura ad aliquid faciendum moveri potest sine ipso. Si vero virtute gratiae: cum ipse sit auctor gratiae, quia 'gratia et veritas per Iesum Christum facta est,' ut dicitur supra, 1:17: manifestum est quod nullum opus meritorium sine ipso fieri potest; 2 Cor 3:5, 'Non quod sufficientes simus aliquid cogitare ex nobis quasi ex nobis; sed sufficientia nostra ex Deo est.' Si ergo nec etiam cogitare possumus nisi ex Deo, multo minus nec alia."

lagians want to uphold free will, they rather destroy it. We should note, too, that just as St. Augustine had often used 2 Corinthians 3:5 in relatively close conjunction with John 15:5—although not in tractate 81—so here also does St. Thomas.[34]

Beyond the dogmatic concern he shares with St. Augustine, however, St. Thomas is a "systematic" theologian.[35] St. Thomas has, as Gilles Emery has it, a properly "speculative" concern, and this also in the *Lectura* on John.[36] From St. Augustine's teaching that God so acts in Christians as to produce their own production of those good works that lead to salvation, St. Thomas generalizes: God acts in all human works, producing the human production of any work, whether of grace or of nature.[37] It can be observed, too, that calling on nature as the work of God, where nature is the first and internal principle of the operations of a substance, ensures that we will understand grace as a similarly internal principle of human operation.

The analogy can be spelled out more closely. Suppose we put Augustine's arguments as follows: If existence alone comes from God, but "good works" (keeping the commandments, acting virtuously, loving God and neighbor) come from us, then so far as those works go, we are not in Christ, we are not dependent on Christ, and so are not Christians. Therefore, such works cannot really be good in the relevant sense; they cannot lead to salvation, they cannot lead to Christ because they do not spring from Christ. St. Thomas's point can be put similarly. If existence alone comes from God, but our willings and workings come from ourselves, then so far as those works go, we are not dependent on God. But God is Being. And so, just as our acts are not Christian acts if they are not really Christ's work in us, so also if any of our acts (whether natural or unto salvation) are not God's work in us then they are not in being. That is, they are not; such acts are impossible. Christian acts are impossible except they be Christ working in us and through us. Any act is impossible simply speaking, that is, it cannot be except it be God working in us

34. *On the Grace of Christ*, 26 (25) and 30 (29); *Against Two Letters of the Pelagians*, II, 18 (8); *On Grace and Free Will*, 13 (6) and 16 (7).

35. I mean in the sense, for instance, that Bernard Lonergan gives that title in *Method in Theology* (New York: Herder and Herder, 1982), ch. 13.

36. Emery, "Biblical Exegesis and the Speculative Doctrine of the Trinity," 293–94, 312–13.

37. This should not be understood as finding a double literal sense for John 15:5, but as taking advantage of the comprehensiveness of "nothing." See Leo J. Elders, "Aquinas on Holy Scripture as the Medium of Divine Revelation," in *La doctrine de la révélation divine de saint Thomas d'Aquin*, ed. Leo Elders, S.V.D. (Rome: Pontificia Accademia di S. Tommaso e di Religione Cattolica, 1990), 148–50.

and through us. Augustine's point is that insofar as one performs a human act
independently of Christ, one is not a Christian. Thomas's point is that, insofar as one performs an act independently of God, one does not . . . exist. We
appreciate at this point the truth in the sobriquet G. K. Chesterton proposes,
"St. Thomas of the Creator," or Josef Pieper's contention that the doctrine of
creation is the "hidden key" to St. Thomas's thought.[38]

The appeal St. Thomas makes to John 15:5 is not isolated. Using the indexes
of the Leonine edition of the *Opera omnia*, one easily locates three places in the
Summa theologiae, two in the *Summa contra gentiles*, and one in the *Quaestiones
disputatae de veritate*.[39] Charles Lohr's index of the *Sentences* commentary gives
one more.[40] Three times, the text is invoked to make a typically Augustinian
point: we cannot prepare for grace unless God moves us, we cannot avoid sin
of incontinence without the help of God, and we cannot merit divine help
without divine help.[41] Three times, the text is invoked in an argument whose
point is to diminish human agency.[42] In all three replies, St. Thomas universal-
izes and, as it were, transcendentalizes John 15:5: it is not only we who cannot
act apart from God, no created agent can; and this does not diminish the reality of the agency of the created cause. Here, we might say, St. Thomas makes
the same reflection apropos of John 15:5 as he does in the *Lectura*.[43] And this
is so also in the *Summa contra gentiles*, book 3, 67, which is addressed to the
transcendental and universal agency of God, the cause of the operation of all
things that operate. Here, as is typical for the *Contra gentiles*, the six arguments
of reason for the truth of the proposition are confirmed in the last paragraph
by the authority of Scripture: John 15:5, Isaiah 26:12, and Philippians 2:13. That
is, the authority of the Scriptures has already provided the theological, doctrinal truth that St. Thomas first manifests also by reason.[44] It is these other vers-

38. G. K. Chesterton, *Saint Thomas Aquinas* (New York: Sheed & Ward, 1933), 141, and see also 30,
93, and 121; Josef Pieper, *The Silence of St. Thomas*, trans. John Murray and Daniel O'Connor (New
York: Pantheon, 1957), "The Negative Element in the Philosophy of St. Thomas Aquinas," 44–71.

39. None in the *Quaestiones disputatae de potentia, de malo, de anima, de spiritualibus creaturis;*
none in the *Expositio in Iob*, and none in the *Quodlibets*.

40. Charles H. Lohr, *St. Thomas Aquinas, "Scriptum super Sententiis": An Index of Authorities Cited*
(Amersham: Avebury, 1980).

41. *Summa theologiae* I-II, q. 109, a. 6, ad 2; II-II, q. 156, a. 2, ad 1; *Summa contra gentiles*, bk. 3,
149, no. 3.

42. *In II Sententiis*, d. 28, q. 1, a. 1, arg. 1, and ad 1; *De veritate*, q. 24, a. 1, arg. 9; and *Summa theologiae* I-II, q. 6, a. 1, arg. 3.

43. And in the *Sentences* commentary as in the *Lectura*, with the aid of 2 Corinthians 3:5.

44. See Valkenberg, *Words of the Living God*, 138–39, for a similar procedure in the *Summa theologiae*.

es, practically equivalents of John 15:5, that are invoked in crucial places as the authoritative settlement of a question: Isaiah 26:12 for the *sed contra* in *Summa theologiae* I, q. 8, a. 1; I, q. 105, a. 5; and *Quaestiones disputatae de potentia* q. 20, a. 1; and Philippians 2:13 for the *sed contra* in *Summa theologiae* I, q. 105, a. 4; and I-II, q. 9, a. 6.[45]

To return to the *Lectura*. It was suggested above that when St. Thomas expands St. Augustine's argument to include the order of nature and creation, his commitment to a properly systematic and speculative task is to be discerned. But this should not be understood to mean a corresponding distancing of himself from the exegetical and expository task of the *Lectura*. In the first place, to pick out the role of Christ not only in the works of grace but also in the works of nature is nothing but to advert more fully and completely to the divinity of Christ, who is responsible for creation as for grace. And in doing this, St. Thomas follows the intention he set forth for himself at the beginning of the *Lectura,* an intention he thinks most concordant with the nature of the fourth gospel itself: "since the other evangelists treat principally of the mysteries of the humanity of Christ, John specially and preeminently brings forward the divinity of Christ in his gospel."[46] The divinity of Christ is manifested in the fourth gospel first in the life of Jesus, chapters 2 to 11, and then in his dying, according to St. Thomas's division of the text. Within the life of Christ, his divinity is shown first in his dominion over nature, chapter 2 and Cana, and then in the order of grace, beginning with chapter 3 and as declared in the conversation with Nicodemus.[47]

In the second place, that St. Thomas does not depart from his exegetical and expository task in bringing out the agency of Christ in the works of nature is clear in that it is accomplished by invoking John 1:3: the expansion of the argument is warranted precisely by the exposition of the gospel text.[48] What St. Thomas does at this point, John 15:5, which St. Augustine does not, is call on John 1:3. And in fact, the argument is more strictly Trinitarian—that

---

45. For this authoritative and non-dialectical use of the *sed contra,* see Valkenberg, *Words of the Living God,* 36, 136; and Leo Elders, "Structure at fonction de l'argument 'sed contra' dans la *Somme théologique* de Saint Thomas," *Divus Thomas* (Piacenza) 80 (1977): 245–60. Notice that Isaiah is deployed when it is a matter of all created causes as second causes and Philippians when it is matter of the human will. Philippians is invoked also at *Summa theologiae* I, q. 83, a. 1, arg. 3; III, q. 13, a. 4, ad 3; and III, q. 18, a. 1, ad 1; *In IV Sententiis,* d. 1, q. 1, a. 1, arg. 3. Isaiah is invoked also at *In II Sententiis,* d. 25, q. 1, a. 1, arg. 3, and ad 3.

46. *In Ioan.,* prologus (no. 10).

47. *In Ioan.,* 2:1 (no. 335).

48. See Emery, "Biblical Exegesis and the Speculative Doctrine of the Trinity," 298–303.

is, respectful of the distinction of Persons—than has thus far been indicated: not only do we do nothing apart from Christ, in the order of either nature or grace, but neither does God the Father do anything apart from him: John 1:3. Not that the Father is moved by the Son, but rather the reverse: the causality of the Word stands between that of the Father and every created agent. Not only is grace the grace of Christ, but creation is in Christ: and "all motions of nature are from the Word of God himself."

The explanation at John 1:3 is very full. The preposition "through" *(per)* can indicate three quite distinct manners in which its object is a cause. According as the operation proceeds from the agent, the object signifies either the efficient cause by which the agent does what he does, as a bailiff does what he does by (through) the authority of the king, or the formal cause, as a fire heats by (through) heat. In neither of these ways does the Father make all things through the Son, for the Son is not the efficient cause of the Father, and the formality by which the Father makes all things, the divine wisdom, is not distinct from the divine essence, although it is rightly appropriated to the Son. Additionally, however, the preposition can signify the operation, not as proceeding from the agent, but as terminating in the worked thing, as when we say a carpenter makes a bench by (through) a hand axe: the action does not terminate in the worked thing except through the axe. The point of the elaborate circumlocution of this third way of signifying causality is to avoid saying that *per* indicates instrumentality. For it is expressly to be denied that the Son is the instrument or minister of the Father, since to say so implies a subordination of inequality. An instrument works by the power of the principal agent and produces something beyond the proportion of its nature.[49] But in God, the same power by which the Father works is given to the Son, and in this way, to say that the Father does all things through the Son "is not appropriated to the Word, but is proper to him, because this that he is the cause of creatures he has from another, namely, from the Father from whom he has being."[50]

There is this difference then between saying that God does nothing without the Word and saying that we branches do nothing without the vine: the Word of the Father is not the Father's instrument; we, on the other hand, are instruments of the Word. But it is because the Father does nothing without the Word that, in our own fashion, we do nothing without Christ.

49. See, for example, *De veritate,* q. 27, a. 4, c.
50. *In Ioan.,* 1:3 (no. 76).

Furthermore, St. Thomas explains at John 1:3, while the Son is said by appropriation to be the wisdom by which the Father makes all things, he is said most properly to be the Word by which He makes all things, "for whoever makes something, it is necessary that he preconceive it in his wisdom," and "the preconceived form in the mind of the artificer is the *ratio*" of what is to be made. "Therefore thus does God do nothing except through the concept of his intellect, which is wisdom conceived from eternity, namely, the Word of God." And as Augustine says, the Word is the Art of all things, in whom the *rationes* of things live.[51]

The last reference reminds us, however, that when St. Thomas calls on such service from John 1:3, he is calling for service it has already rendered to St. Augustine.

So, dearly beloved, because the Wisdom of God, by which all things have been made, contains everything according to design before it is made, therefore those things which are made through this design itself are not forthwith life, but whatever has been made is life in Him.[52]

And again:

For no form, no structure, no agreement of parts, no substance whatever that can have weight, number, measure, exists but by that Word and by the Creator Word to whom it is said, "Thou hast ordered all things in measure and in number and in weight" (Wis 11:21).[53]

When he reads John 15:5, St. Augustine thinks first of graced operation, of our performance in Christ, of our doing work that bears fruit unto salvation. St. Thomas readily recognizes this, but adds that no created agent operates independently of the creative Word for whatever work, on the ground that the operation of a created agent is itself created. Branches of Christ certainly do not operate unto his and his Father's glory and their own souls' salvation except in virtue of his divine power. But also, neither does the grapevine on the trellis in the backyard bear its fruit except as moved, because created, by the

---

51. Ibid., 1:3 (no. 77); the reference is to the *De Trinitate*.

52. *Tractate* 1, no. 17 (Gibb-Innes translation).

53. Ibid., no. 13 (Gibb-Innes translation). See Gilles Emery, "Trinity and Creation: The Trinitarian Principle of the Creation in the Commentaries of Albert the Great, Bonaventure, and Thomas Aquinas on the *Sentences*," in *Trinity in Aquinas*, 37–39, 62, for the Augustinian warrant for the Trinitarian processions as cause of the emanation of creation in St. Thomas.

divine power, just as neither does a human being perform even a naturally virtuous act except as moved by God.[54]

In both ways, created agents can be called instruments of God; in the second, a natural instrument for a natural end; in the first, a supernatural or supernaturalized instrument for a supernatural end. In each case, however, the notion of an instrument is strictly verified: the instrument operates as an instrument only as moved by the principal agent; and it produces something beyond the proportion of its nature and within the proportion only of the principal agent. So, in the case of created natures, nothing moves except as moved by the First Mover; and whatever is produced is some being. But the production of being is within the proportion of only one nature, the divine nature, whose nature is not distinct from its being. Therefore, the creaturely production of whatever being, substantial or accidental, must be instrumental.[55]

When the issue is human operation within the economy of grace, the instrumentality of the creature is equally clear once we know how to read the Scriptures as taught by St. Augustine. For "from his fullness have we all received, grace upon grace" (Jn 1:16), nor is there grace that does not come through Jesus Christ (Jn 1:17). Now, grace is a participation of the divine nature (2 Pt 1:4), and "therefore it is impossible that any creature should cause grace."[56] *Auctoritative*, God alone causes grace, but instrumentally, the humanity of Christ causes grace, and especially in his passion.[57] As the universal cause of grace,[58] Christ the head is the source of grace for all the members of the body.[59] It follows, furthermore that in what grace itself causes, we are instruments of the author of grace, whether for justification, moved by operative grace,[60] or for merit, moved by cooperating grace.[61] While in the order of grace, the created agent is given, as it were, a new nature, another, or, we can say, a modifying, elevating principle of operation, so that now we can love God, not just above all things, but as friends called to share in his very own beatitude,[62] it remains that every operation in virtue of this new nature is first set in motion by God.[63]

54. *Summa theologiae* I, q. 105, a. 5 and I-II, q. 109, a. 2.

55. *De potentia*, q. 3, a. 7; and see Bernard Lonergan, *Grace and Freedom: Operative Grace in the Thought of St. Thomas Aquinas*, ed. J. Patout Burns (New York: Herder, 1971), 76–88; and Lonergan, "On God and Secondary Causes," in *Collection*, ed. Frederick Crowe (New York: Herder, 1967), 54–67.

56. *ST* I-II, q. 112, a. 1, c.

57. *ST* I-II, a. 1, ad 1; III, q. 49, a. 1, c and ad 1; III, q. 64, a. 3, c; *De veritate*, q. 27, a. 4, c.

58. *ST* III, q. 49, a. 1, ad 4.   59. *ST* III, q. 8, a. 1, c.

60. *ST* I-II, q. 113, a. 3.   61. *ST* I-II, q. 114, aa. 2 and 6.

62. For grace as a new nature, see *Quaestio disputata de virtutibus in commune*, a. 10; for charity as friendship founded on the hope of beatitude, see *ST* II-II, q. 23, a. 1.

63. *ST* I-II, q. 109, a. 2, c.

III. John 15:5 and Apostolic Office

We have seen that within the created order and, universally, for whatever work of nature, we can do nothing without Christ. And we have seen that within the economy of salvation, equally universally, for whatever work of grace, we can do nothing without Christ. There is yet another way to take John 15:5, and that is ecclesially-ministerially, and to say that, for whatever work of ministry there be in the Church, the ministers can do nothing without Christ. It is not just that, as members of the Body, we are instruments of the author of grace as regards the effects of grace for our own souls' salvation, but also, Christ's headship itself can, in a certain way, be shared. The sacraments are instrumental causes of grace; also, those who cause the sacraments can be instrumental causes of grace.[64] Principal and instrumental cause can be compared as follows:

> other ministers of the Church do not dispose or do anything unto spiritual life as if from their own power, but rather by the power of another; Christ does so, however, from his own power. Hence it is that Christ could offer the effect of the sacraments through himself, because the whole efficacy of the sacraments was in him as in its origin.[65]

The minister acts by the power of another without whom, evidently, he can do nothing.

John Paul II and Joseph Cardinal Ratzinger (now Benedict XVI) invoke John 15:5 very prominently for this last sort of instrumentality. So John Paul II says in *Pastores dabo vobis,* number 14:

> just as "the Son can do nothing of his own accord" (Jn 5:19) such that his teaching is not his own but the teaching of the One who sent him (cf. Jn 7:16), so Jesus says to the apostles: "Apart from me you can do nothing" (Jn 15:5). Their mission is not theirs but is the same mission of Jesus. All this is possible not as a result of human abilities, but only with the "gift" of Christ and his Spirit, with the "sacrament": "Receive the Holy Spirit. If you forgive the sins of any, they are forgiven; if you retain the sins of any, they are retained" (Jn 20:22–23). And so the apostles, not by any special merit of their own, but only through a gratuitous participation in the grace of Christ, prolong throughout history to the end of time the same mission of Jesus on behalf of humanity.

And it is clear that this mission encompasses the offices of teaching, ruling, and sanctifying.

---

64. Sacraments: *ST* I-II, q. 112, 1, ad 2; III, q. 49, a. 1, ad 2 and ad 4; III, q. 62, a. 1, c; *De veritate,* q. 27, a. 4, c and ad 2; ministers: *ST* III, q. 64, a. 1; *De veritate,* q. 27, a. 4, ad 18.

65. *De veritate,* q. 29, a. 4, ad 2.

Ratzinger, in *Called to Communion,* likewise connects John 15:5 and 5:19 in order to show the connection of apostolic office with Christological mission, not simply as to the content of the mission insofar as that can be parceled out in the functions or *munera* of preaching, sanctifying, and ruling, but also as to its interior structure. Christological mission makes manifest the procession of the Word from the Father, in which procession everything the Father has is granted the Son, and in which the Son has nothing of his own, but all is from the Father. In the same way, for both John Paul II and Cardinal Ratzinger, apostolic office is so much the reception of the word and agency of another, of the mission of Christ, that the office bearer does "nothing" of his own, apart from Christ.

On their own, by the force of their own understanding, knowledge, and will, they [the apostles] cannot do anything they meant to do as apostles. How could they possibly say "I forgive you your sins"? How could they conceivably say "This is my body" or impose their hands and pronounce the words "Receive the Holy Spirit"?[66]

This seems to tilt things exclusively in the direction of sanctifying, but Ratzinger in fact includes the totality of apostolic mission here: "Nothing that makes up the activity of the apostles is the product of their own capabilities." Rather—and here he renders the importance of what I have called the structural identity of Christological and apostolic mission—"it is precisely in having 'nothing' to call their own that their communion with Jesus consists, since Jesus is also entirely from the Father."[67]

Furthermore, Ratzinger finds in this structure the sense of what it means to say orders is a sacrament.

Sacrament means: I give what I myself cannot give; I do something that is not my work; I am on a mission and have become the bearer of that which another has committed to my charge.[68]

In other words, the sacramentality of orders and the sense in which the priest, as such and in all his activities, is a sacrament of Christ acting "in the person of Christ" are intimately connected. This way of reading John 15:5, the use to

---

66. Joseph Cardinal Ratzinger, *Called to Communion: Understanding the Church Today* (San Francisco: Ignatius Press, 1996), 114. The German edition was published in 1991; *Pastores dabo vobis* was issued in 1992.

67. Ratzinger, *Called to Communion,* 114.

68. Ibid., 115.

which John Paul II and Cardinal Ratzinger put it, is well prepared for in the readings of St. Thomas and St. Augustine.

One might expect to find John 15:5 so invoked in St. Augustine's anti-Donatist writings. But it is not so. John 15:5a is used several times to point out that baptism inserts one into the vine that is Christ and not into the minister who baptizes. Just as Christ is the one who really baptizes, baptizes unto the remission of sins, so does he, by this real and true washing of the soul, insert the baptized into himself, the true vine, and make them members of the body of which he is Head.[69]

It is rather in tractate 80 that 15:5, "without me you can do nothing," is pressed into the service of understanding apostolic ministry as precisely that—ministry. The point of departure of the following is John 15:3, "you are already made clean by the word which I have spoken to you." Augustine continues:

Here, you see, he is also the one who prunes the branches—a work which belongs to the vinedresser [namely, his Father, in Jn 15:2], and not to the vine; and more than that, he makes the branches his workmen. For although they do not give the increase, they afford some help, although not of themselves: "For without me," he says, "you can do nothing."[70]

And he continues the citation of 1 Corinthians 3:5–7: the workmen, Apollos and Paul, are ministers who by their preaching plant and water, but only God gives the increase, for "he works not by them, but by Himself, for work like that exceeds the lowly capacity of man . . . and rests solely and entirely in the hands of the Triune Vinedresser."[71]

We can summarize by saying, first, the ministers are made ministers by Christ. Second, the minister does something as minister—there is a proper ministerial activity. Third, what the minister does as minister is not done without Christ. Fourth, only God gives the increase.[72]

69. *Answer to the Letters of Petilian,* I, 5 (6); III, 42 (51), in *Nicene and Post-Nicene Fathers,* first series, vol. 4 (Grand Rapids, MI: William B. Eerdmans Publishing Company, 1983) (*Corpus scriptorum ecclesiasticorum Latinorum,* 52, 1–227).

70. *In Ioannis Evangelium Tractatus* LXXX, 2: "Ecce et ipse mundator est palmitum, quod est agricolae, not vitis officium, qui etiam palmites operarios suos fecit. Nam etsi non dant incrementum, impendunt tamen aliquod adiumentum; sed non de suo, 'Quia sine me,' inquit, 'nihil potestis facere.'" I have modified the Gibbs-Innes translation.

71. Ibid.: "non per illos, sed per seipsum facit [= incrementum dare]; excedit hoc humanam humilitatem, excedit angelicam sublimitatem, nec omnino pertinet nisi ad agricolam Trinitatem."

72. For three and four, see further *Answer to Petilian,* III, 54 (66): "Now I am willing to ask whether it be true that the minister of Christ is nothing. Who will say so much as this? . . . For ministering

St. Thomas, too, is willing to see the "fruit" of the vine as embracing apostolic works. In the *Lectura,* at 15:5, it includes the edification of others; at 15:8, it includes not only holiness of life but teaching well *(bene docere),* not only charity but *fructum doctrinae.*[73] Without Christ, therefore, these works cannot be done, and apart from him the apostles do nothing.

St. Thomas does not elaborate a view of apostolic ministry at John 15:5, but elsewhere, he expresses what Augustine does in tractate 80, in the more technically developed language of instrumentality. In the sacraments, the minister is truly an instrument of grace, but only an instrument, for God alone as principal agent is competent to work the interior effect of grace.[74] The minister is just one in a chain of three links: first, the humanity of Christ, especially in his passion; second, the minister; and third, the sacrament itself. All are instruments of the divinity for the production of grace.

Without Christ, no natural agent or member of his Body or minister of his word and sacraments does anything. Also, without Christ, none of this can be seen, either, and it will be useful to conclude this study by noting the verification of John 15:5 in the order of the manifestation of its meanings.

In the first place, would it be true to say that, without St. Augustine, St. Thomas sees nothing at John 15:5, or that whatever he sees there has already been shown him by Augustine? Arguably, this is substantially true. The question is not what would St. Thomas have seen if St. Augustine had never existed or produced the *Tractates.* For even so, there is already the invitation in the text of the gospel to read the "nothing" that is done without Christ in John 15:5 with the "nothing" that is made without him in John 1:3. The question is what he did see, already seeing what St. Augustine saw. And answering this question is easy if we remember the Augustinian teaching apropos of such passages as John 1:3 on creation through the Word. There is furthermore the example St. Augustine provides of making John 1:3 the interpretative key at other places in John.[75]

---

and dispensing the word and sacrament, he is something, but for purifying and justifying, he is nothing, seeing that this is not accomplished in the inner man, except by him by whom the whole man was created and who while he remained God was made man" (King translation).

73. *In Ioan.* 15:5 (no. 1992), 15:8 (no. 1996).

74. Ibid., 1:33 (no. 276), where there is also influence of Augustine's tractate 5, and most conveniently *Summa theologiae* III, q. 64, a. 1, c. In the q. 64, a. 1, notice the appeal to tractate 80 in the third argument to express a view of sacramental causality rejected in the corpus along the lines of tractate 80 but without citing Augustine. Tractate 80 shows up five times in qq. 60–64 of the *tertia pars.*

75. For instance, at John 5:19; see tractates 18, 19, 20, and 23.

Should we say, second, that John Paul II and Cardinal Ratzinger see nothing not already seen by St. Thomas and St. Augustine? As to St. Thomas and St. Augustine, it is difficult to see that the notion of instrument St. Thomas deploys in his sacramental theology is anything else than a more technical expression of what St. Augustine had already determined in tractate 80 to be the roles of Christ and the minister in the sacrament. On the other hand, Cardinal Ratzinger's formula for sacramentality, "I give what I myself cannot give; I do something that is not my work," nicely captures the idea of an instrument as producing an effect beyond its proportion, but in more personalist terms, terms closer to the text of Scripture.[76]

Third, should we say that Augustine himself and for his own part sees anything at John 15:5 not given him to see by the Evangelist? The Evangelist declares Christ the author of grace from the outset of the gospel, at 1:16–17. John 6:44 lent itself to St. Augustine as evident indication that grace is interior. The very image of the vine itself, as noted above, indicates grace as Augustine, and not as Pelagius, took it. Augustine takes John 15:5 to be saying something about apostolic office as well as the life of grace of every Christian member of the Body. In this he is followed especially by the Holy Father and Cardinal Ratzinger. This is to pick up on the commissioning of verse 16 ("I chose you and appointed you that you should go and bear fruit"), so that the fruit of the vine is at once and undividedly personal holiness and the holiness that, in fulfillment of one's mission, connects another person to the person of Christ. Such mission may, of course, be that of sharing in apostolic office.

Last, there is the question of what John himself saw, or what he heard of the Word he touched with his hands and saw with his eyes. Here, we return to the reading of John Paul II and Cardinal Ratzinger: there is a relation to be noted between John 5:19 and 15:5. So, giving his disciples an extension of his mission, sending them to bear fruit, he indicates that Christian mission really is his mission, in that it repeats the structure of his own mission: as I do nothing apart from Him who sent me, so you will do nothing apart from me, I who send you, and that will be the guarantee of the reality, the purity, and the success of the mission. It cannot be more real than to be caused by and imitate as caused the mission of the Son, itself the translation in time of the eter-

---

76. All we would need further is to show that John 5:19 does not similarly make of the Word an instrument of the Father: the Son receives all, but doing so, it is his "own." Or, if the words Christ speaks are not his (Jn 14:1), we must understand that they are not originally his. The words of the priest, on the other hand, are neither originally his nor do they become his.

nal procession of the Word. Its purity is maintained by its limits, absolute and exigent: you can add, not a little, not somewhat to the mission, but nothing. On the other hand, we cannot despair of its bearing less fruit than what is appointed to the Son himself.

From the incarnate Word to St. John, therefore, and from Evangelist to Church Father to Common Doctor, and ending with contemporary authoritative witness, the same light shines. As we *do* nothing apart from Christ, so we do not *see* this apart from him. Which is to say, by Christ, his light, we see him work the work of creatures, go before and complete by his grace the work of Christians, and give life to the Body also through the service of Christian ministers.

8

Aquinas, Augustine, and the Medieval Scholastic Crisis concerning Charity

Michael S. Sherwin, O.P.

One of the dangers of applying the scholastic method of dialectical questioning to the study of theology is that one may pose a question that one's culture does not yet know how to answer, or at least not answer well. This is precisely what happened when the early scholastics of the twelfth century started to pose questions about Augustine's portrayal of charity.[1] The crisis was perhaps inevitable. The twelfth century witnessed a remarkable blossoming of interest in the nature of love, especially of love as desire.[2] It was a unique historical moment. With the marriage of Eleanor of Aquitaine to Louis VII of France, troubadour culture from the south, with its theories of courtly love (fin'amor), moved to the heart of France and spread through the works of the trouvères.[3] At the same time, the twelfth century saw the ascendance of new

1. Robert Wielockx, "La discussion scolastique sur l'amour d'Anselme de Laon à Pierre Lombard d'après les imprimés et les inédits" (Ph.D. diss., Catholic University of Louvain, 1981), xx–xxii.

2. Denis de Rougemont famously and controversially affirmed that the modern conception of love as a passion emerges in the twelfth century. *Love in the Western World* (Greenwich, CT: Fawcett, 1969).

3. Eleanor of Aquitaine would later marry Henry II of England and bring troubadour culture to the British Isles. For Eleanor of Aquitaine's influence on the spread of troubadour culture, see Rita Lejeune, "Rôle littéraire d'Aliénor d'Aquitaine et de sa famille," *Cultura Neolatina* 14 (1954): 5–53; Marcus Bull and Catherine Léglu, eds., *The World of Eleanor of Aquitaine: Literature and Society in Southern France Between the Eleventh and Thirteenth Centuries* (New York: Boydell Press, 2005); John Parsons and Bonnie Wheeler, eds., *Eleanor of Aquitaine: Lord and Lady* (New York: Palgrave Macmillan, 2002).

monastic orders (the Cistercians and the Carthusians)—peopled by adult vocations schooled in the ways of secular love—whose members were in the process of producing an abundant monastic love literature.[4] A feature common to the literature both of the monks and of the court troubadours and trouvères was the focus on love as desire.[5]

It was also during the twelfth century that schools of theology, distinct from the monastic schools, began to emerge and to apply the dialectical tools of logic and argument to the scriptural and patristic heritage they had received. Although by century's end Paris was the primary center of this theological reflection, during the first half of the twelfth century the cathedral school in the fortified city of Laon still predominated.[6] Scholars are currently unable to determine the influence of secular and monastic love literature on the schoolmen at Laon. One thing, however, is certain. At the very moment that this literature was blossoming, an anonymous scholastic writer penned a treatise (titled *De caritate*) that attacked the very thing these literary traditions

---

4. Jean Leclercq, *Monks and Love in Twelfth-Century France* (Oxford: Oxford University Press, 1979), 8–26, 109–36. Leclercq contrasts the traditional medieval Benedictine communities, whose members were mostly drawn from the ranks of their child oblates, and the Cistercians and Carthusians (as well as the various communities of canons regular), whose communities were principally composed of adult vocations. See ibid., 9–12.

5. On love as desire in the writings of the troubadours, see Michel Zink, *Littérature française du Moyen Age* (Paris: Presses Universitaires de France, 1992), 102–4; Moshé Lazar, *Amour courtois et "fin'amors" dans la littérature du XIIe siècle* (Paris: Klincksieck, 1964); and Lazar, *"Fin'amour,"* in *A Handbook of the Troubadours,* eds. F. R. P. Akehurst and Judith M. Davis (Berkeley: University of California Press, 1995), 61–101. On love as desire in monastic literature, see Jean Leclercq, *Love of Learning and the Desire for God* (New York: Fordham University Press, 1982), and *Monks and Love,* 99–108. The twelfth century also saw the growing presence of the Cathars, who likewise were confronting the nature of true love. Scholars have attempted to establish direct links between the troubadour and Cathar conceptions of love. Denis de Rougemont early affirmed this link, while Roger Boase has asserted that "Courtly Love and the Cathar Heresy were both inspired by Eros: the soul's nostalgic and insatiable desire to dissolve itself in the Unity whence it sprang" (*The Origin and Meaning of Courtly Love* [Manchester: Manchester University Press, 1977], 78). The Cathars' understanding of love, however, remains obscure. The Cathars famously viewed sexual desire as an evil placed in humans by an external evil principle. Yet what were the Cathars' views on true love? Was it a purified desire or did they view it as free of all desire? The Cathars' notion of the spiritual marriage between the soul and Spirit seems to point to the latter view, but existing evidence does not allow scholars to offer a definitive judgment on this issue. For more on the Cathars, see Michel Roquebert, *La religion cathare: le Bien, le Mal et le Salut dans l'hérésie médiévale* (Paris: Perrin, 2001); Jean Duvernoy, *Le catharisme: la religion des cathares* (Paris: Privat, 1976). For a study that notes the focus on desire by both the literature of courtly love and the "theologians" of the twelfth and thirteenth centuries, see Charles Baladier, *Éros au Moyen Âge: amour, désir, et "delectatio morosa"* (Paris: Cerf, 1999).

6. Richard Southern, *Scholastic Humanism and the Unification of Europe,* vol. 1, *Foundations* (Oxford: Blackwell, 1995), 198–204.

shared in common. It attacked the view that charity entails desire. This little work seems to have provoked a crisis in the medieval scholastic understanding of charity. The issue was this: to what extent does charity consist in the desire for God as our beatitude? At stake was the danger of defining charity in terms of self-love, and thus reducing God to a means toward our own fulfillment. Moreover, if charity is desire for God, in what sense can God be said to love us from charity, and how are we able to love our neighbor from charity? As we shall see, questions such as these led Aquinas, a century later, to develop a psychology of love that integrated desire more successfully into the dynamics of love and thereby offered an account of charity more faithful to the biblical witness. To understand Aquinas's achievement we must first consider the definition of charity Augustine offers in *On Christian Doctrine,* because the controversy was shaped by Augustine's portrayal. Indeed, in some respects the controversy was a dispute over how to interpret Augustine. From this perspective, Aquinas can be viewed as saving Augustine's insights from the distortions of later interpreters, friend and foe alike.[7]

Augustine's Definition of Charity

Augustine states in the early chapters of *On Christian Doctrine* that "some things are to be enjoyed, others to be used, and there are others which are to be enjoyed and used."[8] He then explains, "Those things which are to be enjoyed

---

7. Scholarship on the medieval conceptions of love has been deeply influenced by the studies of Pierre Rousselot and Anders Nygren. These studies, however, present the medieval literature from within dichotomous frameworks that are foreign to it. Rousselot portrays the medievals as developing two mutually opposed conceptions of love: a physical conception and an ecstatic conception (Pierre Rousselot, "Pour l'histoire du problème de l'amour au Moyen Age," *Beiträge zur Geschichte der Philosophie des Mittelalters, Texte, und Untersuchungen* 6 [1908]: 1–104; for a revised English edition, see Pierre Rousselot, *The Problem of Love in the Middle Ages: A Historical Contribution* [Milwaukee: Marquette University Press, 2001]). Nygren presents the medieval literature from within a larger dichotomy between pagan and Christian conceptions of love (*eros* and *agape,* respectively) and the influence of what Nygren sees as Augustine's attempt to offer a "*caritas*-synthesis" (Anders Nygren, *Agape and Eros,* trans. Philip S. Watson [New York: Macmillan, 1939]). The discomfort caused by the binary vision of these two works has been enormously productive, provoking a number of scholars to read Augustine, the medievals, and even the Scriptures with greater care. An aspect of this more careful reading is to present the medieval discussions from within the context of their own questions. As Robert Wielockx has shown, the scholastics at Laon were asking their questions about charity from within the context of their reading of Augustine's definition of it.

8. *De doctrina christiana,* 1.3 [3]: "Res ergo aliae sunt, quibus fruendum est, aliae quibus utendum, aliae quae fruuntur et utuntur."

make us blessed. Those things which are to be used help and, as it were, sustain us as we move toward blessedness in order that we may gain and cling to those things which make us blessed."[9] Augustine then defines what he means by enjoyment and use. "To enjoy something is to cling to it with love for its own sake. To use something, however, is to employ it in obtaining that which you love, provided that it is worthy of love."[10] He next informs the reader that God alone is to be enjoyed, while all other things are to be used. This is true, he explains, even with regard to the love of self and of our neighbor. In both cases our love should have the character of use: we should use ourselves and our neighbor by ordering our love for each toward the enjoyment of God.[11]

Augustine does not wish to imply that we should treat others in a purely utilitarian or exploitative fashion. The Latin verb "to use" *(uti)* was richer than this. It was a standard way to describe friendly human relations.[12] Nevertheless, as Oliver O'Donovan has observed, Augustine himself seemed uncomfortable with the term and settles instead upon the notion that we should "enjoy one another in him."[13] This revision is reflected in the definition of charity Augustine subsequently offers in a later section of *On Christian Doctrine*, a definition that was to become popular among medieval authors. Augustine affirms: "I call 'charity' the soul's motion toward enjoying God for his own sake, and enjoying one's self and one's neighbor for the sake of God."[14]

9. Ibid., 1.3 [3]: "Illae quibus fruendum est, nos beatos faciunt. Istis quibus utendum est, tendentis ad beatitudenem adiuvamur et quasi adminiculamur, ut ad illas, quae nos beatos faciunt, pervenire atque his inhaerere possimus."

10. Ibid., 1.4 [4]: "Frui est enim amore inhaerere alicui rei propter se ipsam. Uti autem, quod in usum venerit, ad id, quod amas obtinendum referre, si tamen amandum est."

11. See ibid., 1.22 [20–21].

12. Oliver O'Donovan, *"Usus* and *Fruitio* in Augustine, *De Doctrina Christiana I,"* Journal of Theological Studies* 33 (1982): 365. See, for example, Lewis and Short, who tell us that *uti* can mean *"to enjoy the friendship of* anyone; *to be familiar* or *intimate with, to associate with* a person" (*A Latin Dictionary Founded on Andrews's Edition of Freund's Latin Dictionary,* rev. Charlton Lewis [and Charles Short] [Oxford: Clarendon Press, 1991], 1947). Hence, Cicero can describe the man he introduces to the proconsul of Cilicia as "quo multos annos utor valde familiariter," which the Loeb translation renders, "who has for many years been a very intimate friend of mine." Marcus Tullius Cicero, *Letters to His Friends* (Cambridge, MA: Harvard University Press, 1972–1979), 1.3.1.

13. *De doctrina christiana,* 1.32 [35]: "nobis etiam invicem in ipso perfruamur." The phrase appears to be influenced by the Vulgate of Paul's letter to Philemon, where he states his desire to "enjoy you in the Lord" *(te fruar in Domino).* See John Rist, *Augustine: Ancient Thought Baptized* (Cambridge: Cambridge University Press, 1994), 165. See also Raymond Canning's treatment of this question in *The Unity of Love for God and Neighbour in St. Augustine* (Heverlee-Leuven: Augustinian Historical Institute, 1993), 79–115.

14. *De doctrina christiana,* 3.10 [16]: "caritatem voco motum animi ad fruendum deo propter ipsum et se atque proximo propter deum."

Any analysis of this definition hinges on how one interprets the phrase "for his own sake" *(propter ipsum)*. One way of interpreting it would be that charity's desire finds its final fulfillment only in God. In other words, the emphasis is on desire, with the *propter ipsum* signifying that nothing else is the final object of desire. We desire God and do not refer that desire to anything else. This interpretation does capture an aspect of the passage. Augustine elsewhere affirms that "the whole life of a good Christian is a holy desire."[15] Moreover, Augustine defines love *(amor)* as an appetite or desire *(appetitus)* and holds that this love is charity when it is directed to God.[16] These passages give the impression that Augustine reduces charity merely to a love of desire. As we shall see, however, what Augustine says elsewhere about charity reveals a richer view. It suggests that while desire is an aspect of charity, it is not the whole of charity. It suggests that for Augustine the *rhetor*, expressions such as *propter deum* or *propter ipsum* are meant to cover a range of meanings. The problem, however, is that this richness is not easily apparent to the reader of *On Christian Doctrine*, especially if he is only reading snippets of it as contained in a collection of sentences. However this may be, a number of twelfth-century authors, among both Augustine's defenders and detractors, read Augustine as portraying charity simply as desire for God.

Twelfth-Century Critics and Defenders of Augustinian Charity

Robert Wielockx in his masterful study of the scholastic love literature of this period shows that the author of the *De caritate* begins his critique of Augustine by modifying the Augustinian definition of charity in a seemly innocuous fashion.[17] For the *De caritate*, "Charity is the soul's motion toward lov-

---

15. *Tractatus in epistolam Joannis*, 4.6: "Tota vita Christiani boni, sanctum desiderium est."

16. *De diversis quaestionibus 83*, 35.1: "Nihil enim aliud est amare quam propter se ipsam rem aliquam appetere." Ibid.: "Deinde cum amor motus quidam sit, neque ullus sit motus nisi ad aliquid; cum quaerimus quid amandum sit, quid sit illud ad quod moveri oporteat quaerimus." Ibid., 35.2: "Amor appetitus quidam est."

17. Wielockx, "La discussion scolastique sur l'amour," 179. The authorship of the *De caritate* cannot be determined with certainty. The *De caritate* appears in a manuscript collection attributed to Anselm of Laon and in a collection attributed to William of Champeaux. Odon Lottin, who edited several versions of the *De caritate*, was uncertain whether it was a work of Anselm's or of William's (Odin Lottin, *Psychologie et morale aux 12 et 13 siècles*, vol. 5 [Gembloux, Belgique: Duculot, 1959], 62). Wielockx employs internal evidence to show that neither author could have penned it. Instead, he suggests that the most likely author of the *De caritate* was Gauthier de Mortagne. See Wielockx, "La discussion scolastique sur l'amour," 142–58.

ing God for God's own sake and loving oneself and one's neighbor for the sake of God."[18] As Wielockx notes, the author has removed "enjoying" *(fruendum)* from the definition and replaced it with the more generic term "loving" *(diligendum).*[19] The *De caritate* then explains that to love God for God's own sake means serving him without desiring any recompense or reward for doing so. "We should love God, not for the sake of any reward we might expect from Him, but for his own sake alone, that we might serve Him."[20] The author interprets self-love and neighbor love in the same way: "That we should love ourselves for God's sake means this alone: that we should love God and serve him."[21] Thus, the injunction to love our neighbor as ourselves means only this: "just as we love ourselves that God may be served, likewise should we love our neighbor that God may be served."[22] This phrase parallels closely the famous text from *On Christian Doctrine* where Augustine states that God "has mercy on us that we may enjoy Him, and we have mercy on our neighbor so that we many enjoy Him."[23] Here again, however, the *De caritate* has replaced the notion of enjoyment with that of service. In all these passages the author of the *De caritate* asserts that the goal of charity is not enjoyment, but service.[24]

The author subsequently portrays those who seek enjoyment as mercenaries. "Some serve God from fear, and these are called servants; others serve him because of rewards, and these are called mercenaries; while others serve him from love, and these are called sons."[25] While he grants that some mercenaries are at least seeking eternal rewards, he nonetheless affirms that "those who

18. *De caritate,* 1: "Caritas est motus animi ad diligendum Deum propter Deum et se et proximum propter Deum." Wielockx, "La discussion scolastique sur l'amour," 56. Imperfect but more accessible editions of the *De caritate* can be found in Lottin, *Psychologie et morale,* vol. 5, 61–64.

19. Wielockx, "La discussion scolastique sur l'amour," 179.

20. *De caritate,* 3: "Deum enim debemus diligere, non propter aliquod praemium quod ab eo expectemus, sed propter ipsum solum, cui ut serviamus." Wielockx, "La discussion scolastique sur l'amour," 56.

21. *De caritate,* 8–9: "Seipsum quoque debet unusquisque diligere propter Deum, id est: ad hoc tantum, ut Deum diligat et ei serviat." Wielockx, "La discussion scolastique sur l'amour," 56.

22. *De caritate,* 18–19: "Ut sicut se diligit ad serviendum Deo, ad idem diligat proximum." Wielockx, "La discussion scolastique sur l'amour," 57.

23. *De doctrina christiana,* 1.30 [33]: "Ille nostri miseretur, ut se perfruamur, nos vero invicem nostri miseremur, ut illo perfruamur."

24. Wielockx, "La discussion scolastique sur l'amour," 180–81.

25. *De caritate (Tria sunt genera,* 1–4): "Alii enim Deo serviunt pro quocumque timore et hi dicuntur servi; alii pro mercede et hi dicuntur mercenarii; alii pro amore et hi dicuntur filii." Wielockx, "La discussion scolastique sur l'amour," 63. On the *Tria sunt genera* as the original introduction to the *De caritate,* see Wielockx, "La discussion scolastique sur l'amour," 61–79.

seek eternal rewards desire to see Christ and to be in heaven for the sake of their own enjoyment."[26] He thus concludes cuttingly that "those who seek what is their own [namely their own enjoyment] do not seek what is Christ's, and consequently neither will they attain Christ."[27]

Wielockx convincingly traces the effect of the *De caritate* on the schoolmen at Laon by presenting an impressive collection of scholastic texts from the period that react directly against it. This collection shows that many of the defenders went far beyond the letter of Augustine's texts to affirm unabashedly that charity is the desire to enjoy God. Several examples from Wielockx's collection suffice to reveal the character of these reactions. First, there is a collection of sentences titled *Principium et causa*. When the author of this work defines charity, he affirms that the definition comes from Augustine. He too, however, modifies the text, changing two key phrases: "Charity is the soul's desire to have God for his own sake; it is the love of God for his own sake and the love of neighbor for the sake of God."[28] The author of a similar work, the *De conditione*, offers an analogous reformulation: "Augustine defines charity in *On Christian Doctrine* as follows: 'charity is the soul's desire to enjoy God and to love oneself and one's neighbor for the sake of God.'"[29] Both these texts have replaced Augustine's neutral *"motus animi"* with *"appetitus animi."* Also, the first text refers to charity as a desire "to have God," not just enjoy Him, while the later portrays it as a desire to enjoy God without the modifying clause "for his own sake" *(propter ipsum).* Another contemporary author takes the bolder step of redefining service (the heart of the *De caritate*'s view of charity) in terms of enjoyment as our reward (the very thing the *De caritate* denies): "Divine service is to place God before everything else, to love Him more than everything else and for Himself, that we might have Him as our

---

26. *De caritate* (*Tria sunt genera*, 6–8): "Qui vero quaerunt aeternum, hi sunt qui propter propriam delectationem Christum videre desiderant et in paradise esse optant." Wielockx, "La discussion scolastique sur l'amour," 63.

27. *De caritate* (*Tria sunt genera*, 8–9): "Hi ergo quaerunt quae sua sunt, non quae Jeusu Christi. Propterea nec illud habebunt." Wielockx, "La discussion scolastique sur l'amour," 63.

28. *Principium et causa:* "Caritas est appetitus animi ad habendum Deum propter seipsum, id est amor Dei propter ipsum, et amor est proximi propter Deum"; Franz Bliemetzrieder, *Anselms von Laon systematische Sentenzen,* Beiträge zur Geschichte der Philosophie des Mittelalters 18 (Münster: Aschendorff, 1919), 81. Wielockx, "La discussion scolastique sur l'amour," 185.

29. *De Conditione:* "Caritatem vero definit Augustinus in libro De doctrina christiana dicens: 'Caritas est appetitus animae ad fruendum Deo et se diligendum et proximum propter Deum'" (Y. Lefèvre, "Le *De conditione angelica et humana* et les *Sententiae Anselmi,*" *Archives d'Histoire Doctrinale et Littéraire du Moyen Age* 26 [1959]: 273). Wielockx, "La discussion scolastique sur l'amour," 186.

reward."[30] Perhaps most radically, one florilegia collection contains the assertion that our love for God is based on self-love: "There is a love about which
no precept is made, namely, the love of self, and it is the cause of our love for
God and neighbor."[31] This author then describes love for God and neighbor
as analogous to the way we love our hands or any other body part. We love
our members because we do not want to lose them. We are similarly attached
to God and neighbor, not wanting to lose them either.[32]

If we move from Laon to Paris, we find a similar reaction in the work of
Hugh of Saint-Victor. He defines love in the following terms: "what does it
mean to love except to desire and to will to have and possess and enjoy?"[33]
Elsewhere, he states this more succinctly: "what is it to love except to will to
have?"[34] Without hesitation Hugh applies this definition to charity's love for
God: "What is it to love God? It is to will to have Him. What does it mean to
love God for his own sake? It is to love so that you might have Him."[35] Hugh
also attacks directly the views expressed in the *De caritate:*

> Certain fools say: 'we love God and serve Him, but we do not seek any reward. We are
> not mercenaries. Nor do we seek Him. . . . We cast out of hand any payment so that we
> don't seek the one we love. For we love with a pure, gratuitous and filial love, not seek-
> ing anything. We love Him without seeking anything, not even seeking the one we love.'
> Those who say these things do not understand the character of love.[36]

30. *Deus est sine principio:* "Divina servitus est Deum cunctis rebus praeponere, plus omnibus diligere, et hoc propter ipsum, ut ipse habeatur in praemio"; Klagenfurt Universitätsbibliothek (Studien-
bibliothek) Parchment 34, folio 20r. Wielockx, "La discussion scolastique sur l'amour," 186.

31. *Florilegium* (Lottin, no. 216): "Est una dilectio de qua non fit preceptio, scilicet dilectio sui, et
ipsa est causa dilectionis Dei et proximi"; Paris, Bibliothèque nationale, MSS Latin 12999, folio 56va.
Wielockx, "La discussion scolastique sur l'amour," 188. Lottin, *Psychologie et morale,* vol. 5, 138.

32. *Florilegium* (Lottin, no. 216): "Diligit item se homo qui non vult amittere manum vel pedem
vel aliquid aliorum membrorum. Quia ita vero se diligit, diligit et ipsum creatorem qui ei tam pul-
chra membra que non vult perdure dedit"; Paris, Bibliothèque nationale, MSS Latin 12999, folio 56va.
Wielockx, "La discussion scolastique sur l'amour," 188. Lottin, *Psychologie et morale,* vol. 5, 138.

33. Hugh of Saint-Victor, *De sacramentis* (PL 176: 534): "Quid est diligere nisi concupiscere, et habere velle et possidere et frui?" Wielockx, "La discussion scolastique sur l'amour," 190.

34. Hugh of Saint-Victor, *De sacramentis* (PL 176: 534): "Quid est enim diligere nisi ipsum velle
habere?" Wielockx, "La discussion scolastique sur l'amour," 190.

35. Hugh of Saint-Victor, *De sacramentis* (PL 176: 528–529): "Quid est Deum diligere? Habere
velle. Quid est Deum diligere propter seipsum? Ideo diligere, ut habeas ipsum." Wielockx, "La discussion scolastique sur l'amour," 191.

36. Hugh of Saint-Victor, *De sacramentis* (PL 176: 534): "Dicunt . . . stulti quidam . . . : Diligimus Deum et servimus illi, sed non quaerimus praemium, ne mercenarii simus: etiam ipsum non
quaerimus. . . . In tantum enim excutimus manus ab omni munere, ut etiam ipsum non quaeramus
quem diligimus. Pura enim et gratuita et filiali dilectione diligimus, nihil quaerimus. . . . Diligimus
ipsum sed non quaerimus aliquid, etiam ipsum non quaerimus quem diligimus. . . . Qui hoc dicunt
virtutem dilectionis non intelligent." Wielockx, "La discussion scolastique sur l'amour," 194–95.

With Hugh of Saint-Victor the battle lines are clearly drawn. One side portrays charity as service of God without involving the desire to attain or enjoy Him as our fulfillment. The other side pictures charity simply as the desire to posses and enjoy God. While on the surface the defenders of desire might appear closer to Augustine, their exclusive emphasis on desire distorts Augustine's fuller view. Medieval readers of Augustine, however, are not alone in interpreting Augustine in this way. The twentieth century saw a venerable line of critics who read Augustine in a similar manner, but who did so to critique him. They saw Augustine as forging an unholy alliance with desire in his portrayal of charity. One need only think of Anders Nygren's classic study.[37]

Augustine's Richer View

A number of scholars have responded to Nygren and his colleagues by showing that Augustine has a fuller account of charity.[38] An extended exploration of the many facets of Augustine's theology of charity is beyond the scope of this brief essay. Several features of it, however, deserve to be noted. First, Augustine's theology of charity as enjoyment becomes intelligible only within the context of Augustine's confrontation with Platonism. Second, Augustine portrays the enjoyment proper to charity as drawing the Christian into the dynamics of God's love for his creatures and ultimately into the dynamics of the Trinity's love for itself. Thus, the motion of the soul toward enjoying God for Himself is not ultimately self-regarding but other-regarding. In other words, the self finds its desired fulfillment in an other-regarding love. As we shall see, for Augustine, the delight proper to charity is rooted in the worship of God and the service of our neighbor. Third, Augustine sketches a psychology of love that portrays love's act as entailing more than simply desire.

In book 8 of *The City of God,* Augustine depicts classical moral philosophy as seeking the "highest good," which he describes as the good that makes us

---

37. Anders Nygren, *Agape and Eros,* trans. Philip S. Watson (New York: Macmillan, 1939); see also Karl Holl, *Gesammelte Aufsätze zur Kirchengeschichte,* vol. 3 (Tübingen: Mohr, 1928–1932), 54–116. For studies of Protestant and Catholic reactions and appropriations of Nygren's thesis, see Gene Outka, *Agape: An Ethical Analysis* (New Haven, CT: Yale University Press, 1972). See also Timothy P. Jackson, *The Priority of Love: Christian Charity and Social Justice* (Princeton, NJ: Princeton University Press, 2003), and *Love Disconsoled: Meditations on Christian Charity* (Cambridge: Cambridge University Press, 1999).

38. See especially Raymond Canning, *The Unity of Love for God and Neighbour in St. Augustine* (Heverlee-Leuven: Augustinian Historical Institute, 1993); and Oliver O'Donovan, *The Problem of Self-Love in St. Augustine* (New Haven, CT: Yale University Press, 1982).

blessed when we seek it "for itself and not for anything else."[39] He then praises the Platonists for discovering that we become blessed not by enjoying the body or the mind, but by enjoying God. Augustine even credits them with discerning something of the character of this enjoyment. We become blessed not by enjoying God "as the soul does the body or itself, or as one friend enjoys another, but as the eye enjoys light."[40] Augustine subsequently reveals that this depiction of enjoyment of God comes from Plotinus, who discovered that the source of both human and angelic happiness is "a certain intelligible light."[41] This light "illumines them that they may be penetrated with light and enjoy perfect happiness in the participation of God."[42] The context of the Plotinian teaching to which Augustine alludes here is significant. Plotinus prefaces his portrayal of this mystical vision by considering the relationship between enjoyment and the good. Would we still pursue the good even if it was not enjoyable?[43] The question leads Plotinus to depict enjoyment as something that accompanies the good. We desire the good because of its objective character. Even though a soul that is united to the good cannot help but enjoy it, the soul desires the good because of what the good objectively is.[44] The analogy with the eye's enjoyment of light is apt precisely because sight focuses on the object seen and not on itself. Aristotle, therefore, in a passage to which Plotinus seems to allude, describes sight as one of the activities that we would engage in even if it did not bring us pleasure.[45] Far from being an egocentric possession of the good, therefore, Plotinus's mystical union with the divine light draws the soul out of itself into the reality that underlies

39. *De civitate Dei*, 8.8: "Ubi quaeritur de summo bono, quo referentes omnia quae agimus, et quod non propter aliud, sed propter se ipsum adpetentes idque adipiscentes nihil, quo beati simus, ulterius requiramus."

40. Ibid.: "Non sicut corpore vel se ipso animus aut sicut amico amicus, sed sicut luce oculus."

41. Ibid., 10.2: "Quodam lumine intellegibili."

42. Ibid.: "A quo inlustrantur, ut clareant atque eius [Dei] participatione perfecti beatique subsistant."

43. Plotinus, *Enneads* VI, 7 [38] 24.5–18: "Does the good hold that nature and name because some outside thing finds it desirable? May we put it that a thing desirable to one is good to that one and that what is desirable to all is to be recognized as the good? . . . The question comes to this: Is goodness in the appropriate or in something apart, and is the good good as regards itself also or good only as possessed?" See also *Enneads* VI, 7 [38] 27.28 and 29.1.

44. Plotinus, *Enneads* VI, 7 [38] 25.16: "The good must, no doubt, be a thing pursued, not, however, good because it is pursued, but pursued because it is good." *Enneads* VI 7, [38] 30.9, 24–25: "It would follow merely that intellect is the good and that we feel happy in possession of that good. . . . This state produces the most enjoyment and should be chosen above all: for lack of an accurate expression, we hear it described as 'intellect in conjunction with enjoyment.'"

45. Aristotle, *Nicomachean Ethics*, 10.3 (1174a4–10). See Pierre Hadot, introduction, in *Les écrits de Plotin: traité 38 (VI, 7)* (Paris: Éditions du Cerf, 1999), 64–66.

all good.[46] This contemplative union is so absorbing that "the self is put out of mind in the contemplation of the supreme."[47] Moreover, Plotinus affirms that this "commerce" with God inclines the soul toward "justice" and "moral good," because "the soul is pregnant with these when it has been filled with God."[48] Indeed, the enjoyment of God can push the soul to "report to others this communion." Plotinus offers the example of Minos, whose "contact with the divine inspired him to legislate." Being a "friend of Zeus," he shared with others the pattern of this divine communion by crafting laws that were "the image of it."[49]

Plotinus, however, views generosity toward others as only an optional consequence of one's love for God.[50] It is at this point that Augustine begins his critique of the Plotinian perspective. The Platonists discovered something of the nature of God, but did not love Him as He deserved. The love of God, Augustine explains, entails the true service that is worship *(latreia)*.[51] He describes this worship as a sacrifice of humility and praise offered to God by the fire of our charity.[52] This love moves us to consecrate and offer ourselves to God.[53] Moreover, by clinging to God in this way, we are purified from sin[54] and receive the virtues that move us to work for our neighbor's salvation.

> It is by spiritually embracing Him that the intellectual soul is filled and impregnated with true virtues. We are enjoined to love this good with all our heart, with all our soul, with all our strength. To this good we ought to be led by those who love us, and to lead those we love.[55]

46. Plotinus, *Enneads* VI, 9 [9] 11: "It was a going forth from the self, a simplifying, a renunciation, a reach toward contact and at the same time a repose, a meditation toward adjustment. This is the only seeing of what lies within the holies." John Rist describes this aspect of Platonic desire as pertaining to what he calls an "ethics of inspiration" where the morally beautiful *(kalos)* leads to a self-forgetful love of God and service of others that nonetheless fulfills us. See Rist, *Augustine: Ancient Thought Baptized*, 153.

47. Plotinus, *Enneads* VI, 9 [9] 7.   48. Ibid., 9.

49. Ibid., 7.17–28.

50. Ibid., 7.28. See Dominic O'Meara, *Plotinus: An Introduction to the "Enneads"* (Oxford: Clarendon Press, 1993), 109.

51. *De civitate Dei,* 10.3: "Huic nos servitutem, quae latreía Graece dicitur, sive in quibusque sacramentis sive in nobis ipsis debemus . . . eum suavissimo adolemus incenso, cum in eius conspectu pio sanctoque amore flagramus."

52. Ibid.: "Ei sacrificamus hostiam humilitatis et laudis in ara cordis igne fervidam caritatis."

53. Ibid.: "Ei dona eius in nobis nosque ipsos uouemus et reddimus."

54. Ibid.: "Ad hunc videndum, sicut videri poterit, eique cohaerendum ab omni peccatorum et cupiditatum malarum labe mundamur et eius nomine consecramur. Ipse enim fons nostrae beatitudinis, ipse omnis appetitionis est finis."

55. Ibid.: "Illi cohaerere, cuius unius anima intellectualis incorporeo, si dici potest, amplexu veris impletur fecundaturque virtutibus. Hoc bonum diligere in toto corde, in tota anima et in tota virtute praecipimur; ad hoc bonum debemus et a quibus diligimur duci, et quos diligimus ducere."

Augustine further reveals the character of charity's enjoyment of God by describing what it would mean for an angel to love us: "he must will for us to become blessed by submitting ourselves to Him, in submission to whom he himself is blessed."[56] Enjoyment of God, therefore, entails a pious submission of our hearts and minds to God.

Augustine further criticizes the Platonists for thinking that they can attain happiness by their own unaided efforts.[57] For our purposes, however, the interesting aspect of Augustine's account is that he accepts Plotinus's portrayal of enjoyment as an attainment that leads us out of ourselves toward the contemplation of God. The soul is perfected in an enjoyment that is a type of self-forgetfulness. Ultimately, this love is a participation in the Trinity's own love for itself, which implies neither need nor unfulfilled desire.[58] In this life, our participation in God's Trinitarian love also implies imitating Christ's love, even to the point of dying on the cross for love of the Father and of our neighbor.[59]

In several places, Augustine also offers the rudiments of a psychology of love. For example, in book 14 of the *City of God,* Augustine prefaces his argument that two loves have built two cities (the earthly and the heavenly), by showing that the Scriptures employ *amor* and *dilectio* in both positive and negative senses. When these terms signify a good love, they are interchangeable with *caritas,* which he describes as the love by which "a man seeks to love God not according to man but according to God, and to love his neighbor as himself."[60] Augustine is attempting to establish a generic notion of love so that he can subsequently present the specific contrast between the good and evil loves that build the two cities: there is well-ordered love that loves all things as ordered to the love of God, and there is disordered love that loves all things toward the love of self. He then offers a further clarification.

56. Ibid.: "Ei uult esse subditos, ut beati simus, cui et ipsa subdita beata est."

57. See Gerard O'Daly, *Augustine's "City of God": A Reader's Guide* (Oxford: Clarendon Press, 1999), 199.

58. *De Trinitate,* 15.31–32: "Sanctus itaque spiritus de quo dedit nobis facit nos in deo manere et ipsum in nobis. Hoc autem facit dilectio. Ipse est igitur deus dilectio. . . . Ipse ergo significatur ubi legitur: 'Deus dilectio est.' Deus igitur spiritus sanctus qui procedit ex deo cum datus fuerit homini accendit eum in dilectionem dei et proximi, et ipse dilectio est. Non enim habet homo unde deum diligat nisi ex deo. . . . Dilectio igitur quae ex deo est et deus est proprie spiritus sanctus est per quem diffunditur in cordibus nostris dei caritas per quam nos tota inhabitet trinitas."

59. *Tractatus in evangelium Ioannis,* 64.4 (*PL* 35.1807); 81.4 (*PL* 35.1846–1847); 84.2 (*PL* 35.1848). See Raymond Canning, *Unity of Love for God and Neighbour in St. Augustine,* 72–73.

60. *De civitate Dei,* 14.7: "Nam cuius propositum est amare Deum et non secundum hominem, sed secundum Deum amare proximum, sicut etiam se ipsum."

A righteous will, then, is a good love; and a perverted will is an evil love. Therefore, love yearning to possess what it loves is desire; love possessing and enjoying what it loves is joy; love fleeing what is adverse to it is fear; and love undergoing such adversity when it occurs is grief. Accordingly, these reactions are bad if the love is bad, and good if it is good.[61]

There are three things to notice in this passage. First, Augustine introduces the notion of *voluntas* as signifying a good or bad love depending on whether the will is *"recta"* or *"perversa."* Second, he asserts that desire and joy *(laetitia)* are two different forms of love. Lastly, he holds that desire and joy are good or bad depending on the love that underlies them. This mini-psychology of love establishes the following progression in the motion of love: will, desire, joy. Moreover, although Augustine styles both desire and joy as forms of love, as "love desiring" and as "love enjoying," he seems to reserve love properly so called to *voluntas.*[62] Good love is *voluntas recta,* evil love is *voluntas perversa.* What are the characteristics of love as *voluntas?* Does Augustine wish to affirm that *voluntas* has two acts: desire and enjoyment, or does he see *voluntas* as something more general, as, for example, the principle that underlies both desire and enjoyment?

The nature of will in Augustine is a large and controversial question that cannot be pursued in these pages. I wish only to suggest that for Augustine, although desire and enjoyment are both forms of *voluntas, voluntas* is not reducible to them. In fact, Augustine, in several works, attempts to explain the will's love by appealing not to desire but to good will *(benevolentia).* For example, in his commentary on 1 John, Augustine asserts that "all love contains an element of good will toward those who are its object."[63] He distinguishes the love we have for things such as food or clothing from the love proper to persons by grounding the latter in the experience of friendship: "friendship entails a certain good will, as when we do things for those whom we love.

---

61. Ibid.: "Recta itaque voluntas est bonus amor et voluntas perversa malus amor. Amor ergo inhians habere quod amatur, cupiditas est, id autem habens eoque fruens laetitia; fugiens quod ei aduersatur, timor est, idque si acciderit sentiens tristitia est. Proinde mala sunt ista, si malus amor est; bona, si bonus."

62. See, for example, the following quotation from the *De Trinitate,* where he equates *voluntas* with *amor* and *dilectio. De Trinitate* 15.41: "De spiritu autem sancto nihil in hoc aenigmate quod ei simile videretur ostendi nisi voluntatem nostram, vel amorem seu dilectionem quae valentior est voluntas, quoniam voluntas nostra quae nobis naturaliter inest sicut ei res adiacuerint vel occurrerint quibus allicimur aut offendimur ita varias affectiones habet."

63. *In epistolam Ioannis,* tr. 8.5 (*PL* 35.2038): "Omnis dilectio, fraters charissimi, utique benevolentiam quamdam habet erga eos qui diliguntur."

Even if we cannot do things for them, the good will alone suffices for the lover."[64] In one of his later sermons, Augustine explicitly considers what this implies in relation to God.

Let your charity principally be displayed as a love of friendship, which should be gratuitous. You should not have or love a friend in order to receive something from him. If you love him because he gives you money or some other temporal commodity, you love not him, but the goods he gives you. A friend should be loved gratuitously, for himself, and not for anything else. If the rule of friendship encourages you to love man gratuitously, how much more gratuitously should you love God, who commands that man be loved? Nothing is more delightful than God. . . . You do not worship him gratuitously if you do so in order to receive something from him. Worship him gratuitously and you will receive him.[65]

It would seem, therefore, that when Augustine defines charity as the soul's motion toward enjoying God "for his own sake [*propter ipsum*],"[66] the *"propter ipsum"* is meant to convey that this enjoyment loves God gratuitously. Our enjoyment of God consists in loving Him for Himself and not for any reward we might receive from Him, not even for the enjoyment that comes from loving Him in this way. In other words, in *On Christian Doctrine*, Augustine attempts to express through the rich Plotinian notion of enjoyment the same truth he will preach in a sermon by means of the more prosaic Aristotelian understanding of friendship: charity loves God for Himself.[67]

When we read these passages from Augustine in light of the twelfth-century scholastic controversies on love, they all suggest that Augustine's definition of charity was meant to convey a richer conception of charity than either his twelfth-century defenders or detractors were able to grasp. As we have seen, the issue centered on the role of desire in charity. The extreme positions

64. Ibid.: "Amicitia quaedam benevolentiae est, ut aliquando praestemus eis quos amamus. Quid, si non sit quod praestemus? Sola benevolentia sufficit amanti."

65. *Sermo* 385.3.4 (*PL* 39.1692): "Videat enim caritas vestra primum amicitiae amor qualiter debeat esse gratuitus. non enim propterea debes habere amicum vel amare ut aliquid tibi praestet. si propterea illum amas ut praestet tibi vel pecuniam vel aliquod commodum temporale non illum amas sed illud quod praestat. amicus gratis amandus est propter sese non propter aliud. si hominem te hortatur amicitiae regula ut gratis diligas, quam gratis amandus est deus qui jubet ut hominem diligas? Nihil delectabilius Deo . . . colis non gratis, ut aliquid ab ipso accipias. gratis cole, et ipsum accipies."

66. *De doctrina christiana*, 3.10 [16].

67. Gerald Schlabach, in reviewing Raymond Canning's study of Augustine's theory of love, has noted the importance of the different contexts in which Augustine considers charity. See Gerald W. Schlabach, review of *The Unity of Love for God and Neighbour in St. Augustine*, by Raymond Canning, *Augustinian Studies* 26 (1995): 157.

advanced during this twelfth-century debate failed to see 1) that Augustine's charity was meant to shift the focus from the self (and one's own fulfillment) to God; 2) that it contained an element of affective appreciation that did not imply desire; and 3) that it also had an aspect of benevolence, whereby we wish good to the beloved, even though Augustine was not exactly sure what this could mean in relation to our love for God. As we shall see, Aquinas's mature conception of charity enables him to preserve Augustine's insights by grounding them in a more adequate psychology of love.

Aquinas's Solution

The present state of scholarship does not permit us to identify with certitude the influence of twelfth-century controversies on St. Thomas's theology of love. To what extent were the authors at Laon known to Aquinas? To what extent did he know the work of Hugh of Saint-Victor? Nothing in the texts of Aquinas enables us to establish that he knew any of these authors. Aquinas, however, was confronted with an analogous challenge. He was confronted with the task of offering a coherent conception of charity in light of the biblical and Augustinian heritage he had received. When we study Aquinas's theology of charity from the context of the twelfth-century controversies concerning the nature of charity, we discover that Aquinas introduces five innovations that ground charity in a more adequate psychology of love. First, he portrays love properly so called as the principle of every appetitive power, underlying both desire and enjoyment. In other words, although desire presupposes love, love is not reducible to desire. Second, he presents this principle as an affective affinity for the loved object: a *complacentia.* Third, he presents this *complacentia* as having a twofold tendency: toward the beloved *(amor amicitiae)* and toward the good we will for the beloved *(amor concupiscentiae).* To love, he explains, is always to will some good for the beloved from a union of affections. Thomas then explains how charity elevates this psychology. Charity's *complacentia* has the character of friendship *(amicitia).* God communicates his life to us and upon this *communicatio* a union of affections and a mutual well-wishing, which are essential to friendship, are established. This is his fourth innovation: he portrays the virtue of charity as a type of friendship. Lastly, Aquinas holds that properly speaking the desire for God belongs to the theological virtue of hope, whereby we desire God's eternal beatitude as our fulfillment. In other words, while hope's act is a concupiscible love *(amor concupiscentiae)*, charity's act is a love proper to friendship *(amor amicitiae)*. When we love God from charity we will his good in the sense that we celebrate his goodness. In the remaining sections of this essay, we shall consider each of these features.

Love as *Complacentia boni*

Aquinas introduces his mature psychology of love in his study of the passions. This is appropriate because in Aquinas's view we know the spiritual through the physical.[68] In the case of love, the bodily transmutations proper to the passion of love are more evident to us than the spiritual acts proper to love in the will.[69] Aquinas thus describes spiritual love by analogy with emotional love.[70] Aquinas begins his analysis of love by quoting the exact passage from *The City of God* cited earlier: "Augustine says that all the passions are caused by love: since 'love yearning to possess what it loves is desire; love possessing and enjoying what it loves is joy.'"[71] Drawing on the Aristotelian analysis of motion, Aquinas then explains what this means.

> Good has the aspect of an end. . . . Now it is evident that whatever tends to an end, first has an aptitude or proportion to that end, for nothing tends to a disproportionate end; second, it is moved to that end; third, it rests in the end, after having attained it. And this very aptitude or proportion of the appetite to good is love, which is complacency in good [*complacentia boni*]; while movement toward good is desire or concupiscence; and rest in good is joy or pleasure.[72]

Aquinas subsequently adds that when Augustine describes desire and joy as love, he does so because love is their cause.[73] Aquinas thus makes explicit what

68. *ST* I, q. 84, a. 7, ad 3.

69. See *ST* I, q. 85, a. 1; *ST* I, q. 87, aa. 1–3.

70. *ST* I, q. 82, a. 5, ad 1: "Amor, concupiscentia, et huiusmodi, dupliciter accipiuntur. Quandoque quidem secundum quod sunt quaedam passiones, cum quadam scilicet concitatione animi provenientes. Et sic communiter accipiuntur, et hoc modo sunt solum in appetitu sensitivo. Alio modo significant simplicem affectum, absque passione vel animi concitatione."

71. *ST* I-II, q. 25, a. 2, s.c.: "Augustinus dicit, in xiv de Civ. Dei, quod omnes passiones ex amore causantur, 'amor enim inhians habere quod amatur, cupiditas est; id autem habens, eoque fruens, laetitia est.'"

72. *ST* I-II, q. 25, a. 2: "Bonum autem habet rationem finis. . . . Manifestum est autem quod omne quod tendit ad finem aliquem, primo quidem habet aptitudinem seu proportionem ad finem, nihil enim tendit in finem non proportionatum; secundo, movetur ad finem; tertio, quiescit in fine post eius consecutionem. Ipsa autem aptitudo sive proportio appetitus ad bonum est amor, qui nihil aliud est quam complacentia boni; motus autem ad bonum est desiderium vel concupiscentia; quies autem in bono est gaudium vel delectatio."

73. *ST* I-II, q. 26, a. 1, ad 2: "Amor dicitur esse timor, gaudium, cupiditas et tristitia, non quidem essentialiter, sed causaliter."

is only implicit in Augustine: love is the first change in the appetite, from which desire and joy spring. For something to be the goal of an agent's action, that agent must somehow already be apt or proportioned for attaining that goal. This aptitude is love.

But why employ the word *complacentia* to describe this aptitude? One possible reason is that the term can connote both affect and approval. Once Aquinas had defined love as the principle underlying desire and enjoyment, he had to find a term that could express the way in which this principle is present in both of them. Moreover, since love is the principle of an appetite, the term had in some way to express the affective element essential to love.[74] Aquinas apparently judged that *complacentia,* as a word that literally signifies "with pleasing assent" *(cum + placentia),* could convey these meanings. When we desire and enjoy, we do so from an underlying *placentia* that is present throughout.

There is perhaps another reason this term seemed appropriate to Aquinas. In the Vulgate of Matthew's Gospel, God the Father employs the verbal form of *complacentia* to express his attitude toward the Son. Both during Jesus' baptism and his transfiguration, the voice from heaven refers to Jesus as "my beloved Son in whom I am well pleased." The term used in each case is *complacui(t).*[75] We should also note that *complacentia* is here linked to *dilectio.* The beloved Son *(dilectus)* is pleasing to the Father. Implicit in this account is the affirmation that the Father's love entails a certain *complacentia* in the Father's will. Aquinas, therefore, seems to draw on the biblical account of the Father's love for the Son and on Aristotle's theory of causality to ground Augustine's psychology of love on a firmer foundation.

Love's Act as Willing Good to Another

As we have seen, after describing love as the principle underlying desire and enjoyment, St. Thomas distinguishes intellectual from sensual love. Intellectual love is the love proper to the will. He next offers a further refinement not present in Augustine. He distinguishes *amor,* a general term applicable even to brute animals or inanimate objects, from *dilectio,* which, he explains,

---

74. On *"affectus"* or *"affectio"* as an essential element of love in the will, see *ST* II-II, q. 27, a. 2: "in dilectione, secundum quod est actus caritatis, includitur quidem benevolentia, sed dilectio sive amor addit unionem affectus"; *De caritate,* 2: "amor est principium omnium voluntariarum affectionum"; *ST* I-II, q. 56, a. 3, ad 1: "Verbum Augustini intelligendum est de virtute simpliciter dicta non quod omnis talis virtus sit simpliciter amor; sed quia dependet aliqualiter ab amore, inquantum dependet a voluntate, cuius prima affectio est amor."

75. "Hic est Filius meus dilectus in quo mihi complacui(t)." Mt 3:17; Mt 17:5; see also 2 Pt 1:17.

is a love proper only to intellectual or rational creatures, and is the result of the agent's free choice: "because *dilectio* implies, in addition to love, a preceding choice [*electionem praecedentem*], as the word itself denotes."[76]

But what is the nature of the acts of will that flow from this freely chosen complacency in the good? In other words, what is the nature of the will's desire? Drawing on Aristotle, Aquinas affirms that "to love is to will good to someone."[77] As such, "love has a twofold tendency: toward the good that a person wishes to someone (to himself or to another) and toward the one to whom he wishes some good."[78] Love is essentially love for someone.[79] To explain this dynamic Aquinas employs a distinction developed earlier in the thirteenth century, during controversies over whether angels naturally love God more than themselves. It is the distinction between *amor concupiscentiae* and *amor amicitiae,* which can best be translated as "the love proper to desire" and "the love proper to friendship," respectively. As Guy Mansini has shown, Aquinas appropriates this distinction to explain the twofold dynamic present in spiritual love.[80] The love proper to friendship *(amor amicitiae)* is the act of willing good to the beloved. This willing, however, must also be oriented toward the good we will for our friend and, thus, entails as an integral component an *amor concupiscentiae* for the good we will for him. This, in Aquinas's view, is the essence of the love of friendship. When we love a person we are always affirming some good for that person. These are not two separate loves. Rather, human love always has two components, one of which is subordinated to the other.[81] Love of concupiscence is contained within the dynamism of

76. *ST* I-II, q. 26, a. 3: "Addit enim dilectio supra amorem, electionem praecedentem, ut ipsum nomen sonat."

77. *ST* I-II, q. 26, a. 4: "Amare est velle alicui bonum."

78. Ibid.: "Sic ergo motus amoris in duo tendit, scilicet in bonum quod quis vult alicui, vel sibi vel alii; et in illud cui vult bonum."

79. *ST* I, q. 20, a. 2, ad 3: "Amicitia non potest haberi nisi ad rationales creaturas, in quibus contingit esse redamationem, et communicationem in operibus vitae, et quibus contingit bene evenire vel male, secundum fortunam et felicitatem, sicut et ad eas proprie benevolentia est."

80. Guy Mansini, "*Duplex amor* and the Structure of Love in Aquinas," in *Recherches de Théologie Ancienne et Médiévale,* supplementa, vol. 1, *Thomistica,* ed. E. Manning (Leuven: Peters, 1995), 137–96.

81. *ST* I-II, q. 26, a. 4: "haec autem divisio est secundum prius et posterius. nam id quod amatur amore amicitiae, simpliciter et per se amatur, quod autem amatur amore concupiscentiae, non simpliciter et secundum se amatur, sed amatur alteri. sicut enim ens simpliciter est quod habet esse, ens autem secundum quid quod est in alio; ita bonum, quod convertitur cum ente, simpliciter quidem est quod ipsum habet bonitatem; quod autem est bonum alterius, est bonum secundum quid. et per consequens amor quo amatur aliquid ut ei sit bonum, est amor simpliciter, amor autem quo amatur aliquid ut sit bonum alterius, est amor secundum quid." *ST* II-II, q. 25, a. 3: "Per amicitiam autem

our love of friendship for ourselves or for someone else.[82] Most fundamentally, the good we will for the beloved is simply the good of existence. "The first
thing that one wills for a friend is that he be and live."[83] Only subsequently
do we then will particular good things for our beloved and direct our actions
accordingly.[84] In relation to God, charity's proper act is to love God for Himself, which means to celebrate his existence and goodness.[85]

Aquinas concludes his analysis of love by underlining that love is the principle of all that the agent subsequently does. "Every agent acts for an end, as
stated above. Now the end is the good desired and loved by each one. Thus, it
is evident that every agent, whatever it be, does every action from some kind
of love."[86] Our actions, therefore, flow from our freely chosen love: from our
love for the goods we affirm and from our love for those to whom we affirm
them. In other words, before love is a principle of action, love is a response to
goodness. It is a response to God's goodness, to rational creatures' fellowship
in this goodness, and to the goodness proper to non-rational creatures in their
ordered relationship to God and our fellowship with Him.

Charity as *Amicitia hominis ad Deum*

St. Thomas begins his analysis of charity by defining charity as a type of
friendship with God. "Charity is a certain friendship [*amicitia*] of the human
person toward God."[87] Thomas's definition of charity as an *amicitia* marks the

---

amatur uno quidem modo, amicus ad quem amicitia habetur; et alio modo, bona quae amico optan-
tur." See also *ST* II-II, q. 25, a. 2.

82. Since friendship is founded on union, not unity, we do not have friendship *(amicitia)* for ourselves, but something more than friendship (*ST* II-II, q. 25, a. 4). Nevertheless, the love we have for
ourselves is the type of love that is proper to friendship (*ST* I-II, q. 28, a. 1, ad 2).

83. *ST* II-II, q. 25, a. 7: "Unusquisque enim amicus primo quidem vult suum amicum esse et vivere."

84. We see this progression described when we read the above-cited sentence from *ST* II-II, q. 25,
a. 7, in its larger context: "unusquisque enim amicus primo quidem vult suum amicum esse et vivere;
secundo, vult ei bona; tertio, operatur bona ad ipsum; quarto, convivit ei delectabiliter; quinto, con-
cordat cum ipso, quasi in iisdem delectatus et contristatus." See also *ST* I, q. 20, a. 2: "Amor noster,
quo bonum alicui volumus, non est causa bonitatis ipsius, sed e converso bonitas eius, vel vera vel aes-
timata, provocat amorem, quo ei volumus et bonum conservari quod habet, et addi quod non habet,
et ad hoc operamur."

85. *ST* II-II, q. 31, a. 1, ad 1: "Nostrum non est deo benefacere, sed eum honorare, nos ei subiici-
endo, eius autem est ex sua dilectione nobis benefacere."

86. *ST* I-II, q. 28, a. 6: "Omne agens agit propter finem aliquem, ut supra dictum est. finis autem
est bonum desideratum et amatum unicuique. unde manifestum est quod omne agens, quodcumque
sit, agit quamcumque actionem ex aliquo amore."

87. *ST* II-II, q. 23, a. 1: "Caritas amicitia quaedam est hominis ad Deum."

culmination of over a hundred years of scholastic reflection on the nature of charity.[88] The Scriptures describe the love existing between God and his people in various ways, among which is the theme of friendship. "I no longer call you servants, but friends" (Jn 15:15).[89] St. Thomas appears to choose friendship as his preferred description of charity because of the light Aristotle's analysis of friendship can shed on our relationship with God when this analysis is applied to charity.[90] In essence, Aquinas seems to intuit that Aristotelian *amicitia* offers a powerful analogy for understanding the unique *complacentia* that is charity. Thomas employs Aristotle's treatment of friendship in the *Nicomachean Ethics* to affirm that friendship has the following characteristics. First, friendship entails mutual benevolence. Friendship is more than merely a solitary expression of the love that exists in friendship. Friendship requires at least two who love each other with this love, whereby they will good to each other.[91] Thomas adds that in charity this act also entails a union of affections, for simple well-wishing is not enough for friendship.[92]

Aquinas emphasizes, however, that the foundation of this mutually benevolent affection is a certain communion in the good *(communicatio in bono)*. On the natural human level, *communicatio in bono* signifies for Aquinas both an active sharing of goods and a more basic participation in the same qualities, circumstances, or origins.[93] For Aquinas, the first meaning of *communicatio in bono*—the active exchange of goods and services—is rooted in the second more basic meaning. The second meaning refers to some fellowship in goodness. Two people share at least the goodness of their common humanity, but they can also be from the same country or town, have the same

88. See Guy Mansini, "*Similitudo, Communicatio,* and the Friendship of Charity in Aquinas," in Manning, *Thomistica,* 1–26; Joseph Bobik, "Aquinas on Friendship With God," *New Scholasticism* 60 (1986): 257–71.

89. *ST* II-II, q. 23, a. 1, s.c.: "Ioan. xv dicitur, 'iam non dicam vos servos, sed amicos meos.' sed hoc non dicebatur eis nisi ratione caritatis. ergo caritas est amicitia."

90. See A. Stévaux, "La Doctrine de la Charité dans les commentaires des *Sentences* de saint Albert, de saint Bonaventure, et de saint Thomas," *Ephemerides Theologicae Lovanienses* 24 (1948): 86–87; Anthony Keaty, "Thomas's Authority for Identifying Charity as Friendship: Aristotle or John 15?" *Thomist* 62 (1998): 594.

91. *ST* II-II, q. 23, a. 1.: "Sed nec benevolentia sufficit ad rationem amicitiae, sed requiritur quaedam mutua amatio, quia amicus est amico amicus."

92. *ST* II-II, q. 27, a. 2: "In dilectione, secundum quod est actus caritatis, includitur quidem benevolentia, sed dilectio sive amor addit unionem affectus."

93. See Joseph Bobik, "Aquinas on *Communicatio,* the Foundation of Friendship, and *Caritas,*" *Modern Schoolman* 64 (1988): 1–18; and Mansini, "*Similitudo, Communicatio,* and the Friendship of Charity in Aquinas," 1–26.

profession, belong to the same family, or have developed a similarly virtuous character. Each of these shared goods is a *communicatio vitae* or *communicatio in bono* upon which those who share this good can found a friendship: "all friendship is founded on some fellowship in life [*communicatio vitae*]."[94] Aquinas believes that these characteristics of human friendship are analogously present in charity. The foundation of the analogy rests on Aquinas's understanding of grace as a type of divine *"communicatio,"* whereby God begins to share *(communicare)* his life with us.

Since there is a *communicatio* between humans and God, inasmuch as God communicates his beatitude to us, some kind of friendship must be based upon this *communicatio*. . . . The love that is based on this *communicatio* is charity. Hence it is clear that charity is the friendship of the human person for God.[95]

After establishing this analogy between charity and human friendship, Aquinas employs Aristotle's analysis of friendship to illuminate the very aspect of charity that Augustine had struggled to explain: the object and order of its love.[96] For our purposes, however, the more interesting feature is how Aquinas uses the analogy of friendship to distinguish charity from the theological virtue of hope.

Charity and Hope

In relation to hope, St. Thomas first employs the analogy of friendship to explain charity's dependence on both faith and hope. Since communion with God in the good is a prerequisite for friendship with Him, unless we believe that such a communion is possible and unless we hope for this good as something attainable by us through God's assistance, we could never live the friendship that is charity.[97] Thus, charity depends for its existence on faith in

94. *ST* II-II, q. 25, a. 3: "Omnis amicitia fundatur super aliqua communicatione vitae." See also *De Regno,* 1.11: "Omnis autem amicitia super aliqua communione firmatur. eos enim qui conveniunt, vel per naturae originem, vel per morum similitudinem, vel per cuiuscumque societatis communionem, videmus amicitia coniungi."

95. *ST* II-II, q. 23, a. 1: "Cum igitur sit aliqua communicatio hominis ad deum secundum quod nobis suam beatitudinem communicat, super hac communicatione oportet aliquam amicitiam fundari. . . . Amor autem super hac communicatione fundatus est caritas. unde manifestum est quod caritas amicitia quaedam est hominis ad deum."

96. *ST* II-II, qq. 25 and 26. See Stephen J. Pope, *The Evolution of Altruism and the Ordering of Love* (Washington, DC: Georgetown University Press, 1994).

97. *ST* I-II, q. 65, a. 5: "Caritas non solum significat amorem dei, sed etiam amicitiam quandam ad ipsum; quae quidem super amorem addit mutuam redamationem cum quadam mutua communicatione, ut dicitur in VIII *Ethic.* Et quod hoc ad caritatem pertineat, patet per id quod dicitur 1 Ioan.

the intellect and hope in the will. Charity, however, is more perfect than hope because charity responds to God as a friend who is present, while hope responds to Him as an arduous absent good.

Love and hope differ in this way: love implies a certain union between lover and beloved, while hope implies a certain motion or tending of the appetite toward an arduous good. Union, however, is with something distinct, and therefore love is directly able to consider the other, with whom we are united by love, regarding him as we regard ourselves. Motion, however, is always toward a terminus properly proportioned to the moved object, and thus hope directly considers one's own good, and not that which pertains to another.[98]

Aquinas subsequently appeals to the distinction between *amor amicitiae* and *amor concupiscentiae* to explain how charity both animates but differs from hope. "Hope presupposes love of him whom one hopes to attain, which love is a love of concupiscence, by which one more loves oneself, desiring a good, than willing a good to another. Charity, however, entails a love of friendship, toward which hope flows."[99] In charity we say to the beloved, "It's good that you exist."[100] As noted above, when we love God, we are merely affirming or celebrating the goodness that is in Him. On the other hand, in Aquinas's view, the desire for God as our fulfillment is not properly an act of charity, but of hope. Aquinas recognizes that we can desire this fulfillment from charity, because it is according to God's love for us: God also desires that we be

IV, qui manet in caritate, in deo manet, et deus in eo. Et ad 1 Cor. I dicitur, fidelis deus, per quem vocati estis in societatem filii eius. Haec autem societas hominis ad deum, quae est quaedam familiaris conversatio cum ipso, inchoatur quidem hic in praesenti per gratiam, perficietur autem in futuro per gloriam, quorum utrumque fide et spe tenetur. Unde sicut aliquis non posset cum aliquo amicitiam habere, si discrederet vel desperaret se posse habere aliquam societatem vel familiarem conversationem cum ipso; ita aliquis non potest habere amicitiam ad deum, quae est caritas, nisi fidem habeat, per quam credat huiusmodi societatem et conversationem hominis cum deo, et speret se ad hanc societatem pertinere. Et sic caritas sine fide et spe nullo modo esse potest."

98. *ST* II-II, q. 17, a. 3: "Amor et spes in hoc differunt quod amor importat quandam unionem amantis ad amatum; spes autem importat quendam motum sive protensionem appetitus in aliquod bonum arduum. Unio autem est aliquorum distinctorum, et ideo amor directe potest respicere alium, quem sibi aliquis unit per amorem, habens eum sicut seipsum. Motus autem semper est ad proprium terminum proportionatum mobili, et ideo spes directe respicit proprium bonum, non autem id quod ad alium pertinet."

99. *ST* II-II, q. 66, a. 6, ad 2: "Spes praesupponit amorem eius quod quis adipisci se sperat, qui est amor concupiscentiae, quo quidem amore magis se amat qui concupiscit bonum, quam aliquid aliud. Caritas autem importat amorem amicitiae, ad quam pervenitur spe, ut supra dictum est."

100. Josef Pieper, *About Love,* trans. Richard and Clara Winston (Chicago: Franciscan Herald Press, 1972), 22.

united to Him as our fulfillment.[101] Nevertheless, strictly speaking, the love of desire by which we desire to enjoy God is the love proper to hope. Aquinas further describes this contrast in terms of perfect and imperfect love.

Perfect love is that by which someone is loved for himself, as when one wills him good, the way a man loves his friend. Imperfect love is that by which one loves something not for itself, but because of the good that comes to the lover from it, as when a man loves something he desires. The first love of God pertains to charity, by which we cling to God for Himself, while hope pertains to the second love, because one who hopes intends to obtain something for himself.[102]

The love by which we desire God as our perfection, therefore, properly belongs to hope. Although charity both animates this desire and enables it to attain the desired end, properly speaking charity loves God for Himself, willing and celebrating God's goodness.

These quotations from Aquinas place Augustine's texts in a new light. They suggest that Augustine's theology of love is primarily a theology of hope. This might seem paradoxical since Augustine himself says little about hope and what he does say often merely paraphrases the Scriptures.[103] Nevertheless, when Augustine in *On Christian Doctrine* defines charity as a *motion toward* enjoying God instead of as simply the enjoyment of God, he underlines an aspect of charity that exists only in this life. He is defining charity in terms of the imperfect and temporal act of loving God as an absent good. In other words, from the perspective of Aquinas, Augustine's theology of love emphasizes the component of temporal charity that properly belongs to hope.[104] This is understandable in light of Augustine's concern to show that perfect happiness (and thus also the perfect enjoyment of God) is possible only in heaven. As a consequence, however, Augustine underemphasizes charity's other aspects, especially its proper act of benevolent well-wishing. However this may be, one implication of Aquinas's psychology of love is that Augustine's

101. See *ST* II-II, q. 25, a. 4.

102. *ST* II-II, q. 17, a. 8: "Perfectus quidem amor est quo aliquis secundum se amatur, ut puta cui aliquis vult bonum, sicut homo amat amicum. Imperfectus amor est quo quis amat aliquid non secundum ipsum, sed ut illud bonum sibi ipsi proveniat, sicut homo amat rem quam concupiscit. Primus autem amor dei pertinet ad caritatem, quae inhaeret deo secundum seipsum, sed spes pertinet ad secundum amorem, quia ille qui sperat aliquid sibi obtinere intendit."

103. For a brief presentation of Augustine's theology of hope that notes the influence of Augustine's conception of charity on his theology of hope, see Francesco Russo, "Espérance," in *Encyclopédie saint Augustin,* ed. Allan D. Fitzgerald (Paris: Editions du Cerf, 2005), 538–41.

104. See *ST* II-II, q. 28, a. 1, ad 3.

confrontation with classical culture can be fruitfully reinterpreted from within a theology of hope. The deepest desires of the human heart and of human societies are not necessarily in vain. When healed and elevated in the grace of conversion they can attain their goal. Nevertheless, even when these desires are well directed, they are lived in hope.[105] The desires of the human heart find perfect fulfillment only in heaven in the eternal kingdom. In this life, therefore, an aspect of charity's love will always be lived in hope.

Conclusion

Early in the twelfth century, scholastic authors at both Laon and Paris began to question the biblical and patristic heritage they had received. They began especially to question the Augustinian account of charity. Although the extent to which Thomas Aquinas was aware of this questioning remains uncertain, he was clearly aware of the difficulties posed by the Augustinian heritage. Employing tools drawn from Aristotle and his reading of the Scriptures, Aquinas developed a psychology of love and a definition of charity that enabled him both to preserve Augustine's deepest insights and to remain more faithful to the biblical witness. In this way, Aquinas was able to save Augustine from the extreme views of some twelfth-century Augustinians.

105. *De civitate Dei* 19.20: "Quam tamen quicumque sic habet, ut eius usum referat ad illius finem, quam diligit ardentissime ac fidelissime sperat, non absurde dici etiam nunc beatus potest, spe illa potius quam re ista." See also *De civitate Dei* 19.4.

9

Augustine and Aquinas on the Good Shepherd

The Value of an Exegetical Tradition

Matthew Levering

How does the patristic-medieval tradition of biblical interpretation flow from and shape a Christological understanding of ecclesial authority? In seeking to answer this question, this essay will focus upon exegesis of Jesus' depiction of himself in John's Gospel as the "good shepherd" (Jn 10:1–18). I will proceed in three steps. First, I will summarize two recent attempts by biblical exegetes, one Catholic and one Protestant, to expose the meaning of John 10:1–18. Second, I will survey Augustine's reading of this passage in his commentary on John's Gospel. Third, I will examine in detail Aquinas's exegesis of this passage, in order both to trace his engagement with Augustine's interpretation and to compare the Augustinian-Thomistic tradition of exegesis with the approaches and results of contemporary exegetes. The goal is to begin to imagine more fully the path required for ecclesial integration of contemporary biblical exegesis with the Augustinian-Thomistic exegetical tradition.

I. Moloney and Witherington:
Contemporary Exegesis of John 10:1–18

Francis Moloney's commentary on John 10:1–18 focuses upon how Jesus transforms "the traditional messianic expectation of a Davidic shepherd-mes-

siah gathering one flock under one shepherd."[1] Although Moloney agrees with
other commentators in finding no "direct citation" of the Old Testament texts
regarding the figure of the shepherd, he is able to point to numerous sources,
largely from the prophets, that compose a "strong biblical tradition" behind
John 10:1–18, and he also identifies a significant deployment of the theme of
the shepherd in non-canonical Second Temple Jewish writings.[2] In the Gospel of John, Moloney points out, the figure of the shepherd is sharpened by
Jesus' interchange with the man born blind and the Pharisees that immediately precedes his depiction of himself as the "good shepherd." The man born
blind, whom Jesus has healed, worships Jesus, whereas the Pharisees reject Jesus on the grounds that he is arrogating divine prerogatives to himself. Jesus
tells the man born blind, who has been cast out of the synagogue, that "for
judgment I came into this world, that those who do not see may see and that
those who see may become blind" (Jn 9:39). In Moloney's view, the "judgment" is that the Pharisees claim a sufficiency that leaves no room for messianic fulfillment, and thus leaves no room for the "life" offered by Jesus to
those who follow him in faith.[3]

The actual practice of tending sheep provides the characters and dramatic
form of Jesus' parable: the door, the sheepfold, the doorkeeper, the shepherd,
the sheep, the familiar voice, as well as the sheep-stealers.[4] The Pharisees are
the sheep-stealers (Jn 10:6), because they do not hear Jesus' voice and therefore oppose his messianic work. Jesus is the "door" (10:7) who gives "right access" to the sheep and who opens to the good pasture.[5] Jesus rejects the Jewish
leaders who came before him:

"The Jews" who came before Jesus have rejected Jesus and rejected all who move toward
his revelation. This has been dramatically portrayed in 9:1–34. The claims of "the Jews"

1. Francis J. Moloney, S.D.B., *The Gospel of John* (Collegeville, MN: Liturgical Press, 1998), 306.
2. Ibid., 301.
3. Ibid., 302. Moloney observes, "There is increasing scholarly consensus that 9:1–39 and 10:1–21
form a literary unity" (308, n. 39).
4. Moloney mentions with regard to John 10:3 that some "allegorical readings of this passage attempt to identify the doorkeeper with some figure in the conflict between Jesus and 'the Jews'" (308,
n. 3), but he considers this interpretation improbable. Regarding John 10:1–5, he comments, "Allegorical readings of verses 1–5 are myriad. Most interpret the passage in an ecclesiological sense. Christ the
shepherd creates a new community (Temple, etc.) over against bankrupt Judaism" (309, n. 6).
5. Ibid., 303. Moloney observes, "A pastoral practice exists in the Near East, which has no literary
support, wherein the shepherd is the door. He lies down across the door-space and is thus both shepherd and door" (309, n. 7). He also points out that the Jewish wisdom literature links "shepherd" and
"door."

to be the leaders of God's people are false. They are thieves and robbers, purveyors of a messianic hope of their own making.[6]

In contrast, as the door of the sheepfold, Jesus is "the mediator" who gives life to the sheep, something that the Jewish leaders cannot give; Moloney sees here allusions to Ezekiel 34.

At this point Jesus identifies himself as "the good shepherd" (10:11). The mark of the "good" shepherd is radical gift of self by willingness to die for the sheep. Moloney affirms, "This self-gift of the shepherd unto death for his sheep has no parallel in the Jewish texts that speak of the messianic shepherd," and so Jesus' self-portrait does not fit Jewish messianic expectations.[7] Jesus then compares himself to the false shepherd or "hireling," a figure well known in the prophetic literature as well as non-canonical Second Temple texts such as 1 Enoch.[8] Moloney notes that the reader will connect "the Jews" with the "hireling," because the self-interested attachment of "the Jews" to the "former gift that came through Moses" prevents them from accepting Jesus' new gift of life, the fulfillment but also the transformation of Moses' gift.[9]

This context of conflict—Jesus versus "the Jews"—falls away in verse 14, where Jesus again proclaims that he is the good shepherd.[10] The context now is instead that of Jesus' (and his Father's) relationship to his followers. Moloney identifies a play on the word "to know" that unites Jesus, his sheep, and the Father in a relationship of mutual and intimate knowledge. On this ba-

6. Ibid., 303. Moloney remarks that the word "robbers" was applied elsewhere to the Zealots (see 308, n. 1). He states, "It has long been suggested that 'all who came before me' refers to the long history of God's people and its leadership. This is difficult as it implies criticism of the patriarchs, prophets, and righteous of the Old Testament era. There are a number of textual variations here as different manuscript traditions attempted to soften the criticism of the great figures from Israel's past" (309, n. 8). Moloney suggests that the verse most probably refers to the first-century Jewish leadership.

7. Ibid., 304. Moloney does recognize in a footnote, however, that "there are several Old Testament passages where the self-gift of the Messiah is possibly present (for example, Is 53:12; Zec 13:7)" (310, n. 11). He cites a study that argues for an "Isaian background" to verse 11.

8. Ibid., 304.

9. Ibid. Regarding verses 12–13, which depict the flight of the hireling, Moloney speculates, "The flight of Jewish leadership to Jamnia prior to the destruction of Jerusalem in A.D. 70 and subsequent events might form the background for this accusation. . . . Under the leadership of Johanan ben Za-kkai some managed to escape besieged Jerusalem to establish postwar Jamnia. In this interpretation the Pharisees of John 9:1–10:21 would represent postwar Judaism, 'the Jews' who preserved their own lives while the people of Jerusalem, the sheep of the flock, were snatched and scattered. The pain of the separation between the synagogue and the Johannine community is still keenly felt (cf. also 9:22; 12:42; 16:2)" (310, n. 12).

10. Moloney points out that most scholars divide the text at verse 11 and do not notice the transition at verse 14 (310, n. 14). Augustine and Aquinas, like Moloney, divide the text at verse 14.

sis, Moloney argues that although the image of the "shepherd" has its roots in Jewish messianic traditions, the Gospel of John adds a powerful new element, namely the grounding of the shepherd's identity and mission in his "oneness with God."[11] Given this intimate communion in knowledge of Jesus and his divine Father, it makes sense that Jesus will have to lay down his life for his followers—in accord with the Father's will—because "the Jews" will reject as blasphemous Jesus' claim: "It is precisely this issue that 'the Jews' will not accept. Indeed, they seek to kill Jesus because he makes such a claim (cf. Jn 5:16–18)."[12] Second, Jesus radically transforms the biblical image of the messianic "shepherd" also by suggesting that the "sheepfold" of the "shepherd" will include some "sheep" who do not belong to the chosen people of Israel. In order to bring them in, Jesus, embraced in the Father's love that he now manifests for his sheep, will lay down his life.

Moloney notes that this sacrificing of the good shepherd's life raises numerous questions that are taken up in the remainder of the Gospel of John:

How can death be the action of the Good Shepherd (v. 14)? How is it that he shows the Father's love for him as he lays down his life for the sheep (v. 15)? How can this death lead to a gathering of others who are not yet of this fold (v. 16)? What does it mean to say that God's love is shown in a free giving of one's life, only to take it again (v. 17)?[13]

For now, however, Jesus is content with simply making clear (v. 18) that his suffering and death will flow fundamentally from his own free will, not from the violent schemes of others and that the final outcome will not be death but life (his resurrection). His free will, moreover, does not autonomously guide these events; rather, he acts in obedience to the will of his Father. Moloney describes verses 15–18 as thus taking a circular pattern, beginning with Jesus' union in knowledge with the Father (v. 15) and ending with Jesus' union in will with the Father. Jesus' suffering, death, and resurrection, as the salvific actions of the messianic shepherd, manifest his union with the Father and enable others to share in this union.[14]

Ben Witherington III begins his discussion of John 10:1–18 by reflecting

---

11. Ibid., 305. Moloney here argues against Bultmann, who holds that the emphasis on knowledge indicates Gnostic sources (310, n. 14).

12. Ibid., 305.

13. Ibid.

14. Ibid., 306. Moloney notes, "Unlike most New Testament authors, who refer to the resurrection of Jesus as the action of God, the author of the fourth Gospel here presents Jesus as the agent," although in chapter 20 God the Father's agency is indicated (311, n. 17).

upon whether John intends for the reader to understand Jesus' discourse as occurring during the Feast of Tabernacles (Jn 7:2) or the Feast of Dedication (Jn 10:22). Drawing upon 2 Maccabees 1:9, he points out that the Jews considered the Feast of Dedication to be a winter version, as it were, of the Feast of Tabernacles; and so either way, John may have had the Feast of Dedication in mind as the primary context for the discourse. He then observes that John 10:1–18, with its theme of the good shepherd, would be particularly fitting for the Feast of Dedication, a festival celebrating the military triumph of the Maccabees. In the first century, in which the Maccabean victory was still powerfully recollected, Jesus' words would resonate with the reality that some of the Maccabees had indeed laid down their lives for God's people Israel, as Jesus suggested a true shepherd must do. Yet Jesus' words add further elements to this Maccabean context:

instead of many heroic shepherds, Jesus speaks of only one true shepherd for God's people; and when he speaks of his death, he is talking about not only a martyr's self-sacrificial act but a death that amounts to both the lifting up of the Son and his return to the glory from whence he came.[15]

In speaking of only *one* shepherd, and in referring to other shepherds under the rubric of "thieves and robbers" and "hirelings," Jesus evokes Ezekiel 34, which not only condemns Israel's false shepherds, but also prophesies that God, and a Davidic messiah, would be the one shepherd who would feed and establish Israel. In other words, Jesus is challenging Israel's present and past leadership by claiming to undertake the divine/messianic action that goes far beyond what is celebrated in the Maccabean festival.

Having laid out this religious/political context, Witherington identifies Jesus' mode of speech as rooted in Israel's wisdom literature, aiming both to reveal and conceal. Jesus names himself as "good shepherd" and "door." Witherington warns that "[w]e must not look for consistency in the development of the images. Despite protests from scholars, in early Jewish wisdom literature there was a sliding scale between parable and allegory."[16] According to Witherington, here following C. H. Dodd, the goal of such shifting imagery was to stimulate the audience to think deeply about the speaker's teaching. At stake is whether his audience will follow him or will follow the false leaders;

15. Ben Witherington III, *John's Wisdom: A Commentary on the Fourth Gospel* (Louisville, KY: Westminster John Knox Press, 1995), 187.

16. Ibid.

thus the discourse has both a political and an evangelical or missionary dynamic, marked by Jesus' presentation of his intimate relationship to each follower ("he calls his own sheep by name"; Jn 10:3).[17] As the "door," Jesus is the exclusive path to abundant "life" (v. 10), to salvation, to the Father. Yet this uniqueness does not imply a rejection of the great leaders of Israel; rather it evokes the prophetic condemnation of the false leaders (cf. Ez 34, Zec 11:4–9), including those in controversy with Jesus. Witherington observes that the condemnation equally applies to the later synagogue leaders who were contending with the evangelist and his followers over the status of Jesus. As Witherington says, "It is clear enough that the evangelist thinks the very spiritual lives of God's people are at stake."[18] Similarly, when Jesus condemns the hireling who flees when the sheep are in danger, Witherington sees a possible allusion to leaders who failed the evangelist's community (cf. 1 Jn 4; 2 Jn).

This is so because, as the introduction of the "good shepherd" makes evident, Jesus is presenting himself, and/or being presented by the evangelist, as the messiah, the Davidic king. Witherington cites here the texts from the Psalms and prophets that provide the background to the use of "sheep" and "shepherd" in this discourse. Furthermore, not only is Jesus the messiah, but he also has power over life and death, to the point of being able to "take it again" (Jn 10:17, 18) after death. In Witherington's view, "This is part and parcel of the attempt of the evangelist to portray Jesus as a divine agent of God who has eternal life in himself, the sort of life that cannot be brought to a halt by physical death."[19] As a divine agent, Jesus can enjoy a profound mutual knowledge with his followers: "I know my own and my own know me" (Jn 10:14). This mutual knowing, while parallel with Jesus' knowledge of his Father, is for Witherington a deliverance rather than a deification that would *absorb* human beings into God. Witherington differentiates this relationship between distinct persons from the absorption—what he terms "apotheosis or deification of the human individual"—present in the concept of salvation held by "various ancient pagan cults."[20]

When Jesus speaks in verse 16 of "other sheep, that are not of this fold," Witherington finds another allusion to the engagement of the evangelist's community in the mission to the gentiles. For Witherington this is a crucial point because he views the entire Gospel of John as a missionary handbook

17. Ibid., 188.
19. Ibid.

18. Ibid., 189.
20. Ibid.

or "evangelistic tool."[21] The evangelist's community, like Paul's, would have been composed of both Jews and gentiles, understood as *one* people of God united by the one messianic shepherd Jesus. Jesus creates this one people of God by means of his death and resurrection (vv. 17–18). Witherington raises the possibility that the second half of verse 17, "I lay down my life that I may take it again," means that Jesus locates the central meaning of his death not in the taking away of sins, but in attaining resurrected life that he could give to others; but whether or not this is the case, Witherington emphasizes that Jesus, as the divine Word, makes clear that death cannot be the end of his story. This aspect of the discourse again has evangelistic purpose for Witherington:

> For a non-believing audience, it was crucial to convey the point that Jesus was the master of his own fate.... The overall image here is of Jesus as a powerful and deeply caring shepherd who can provide for, protect, and even rescue his sheep. It is the image of a universal shepherd, whose ambition is to have one flock made up of Jewish and gentile sheep.[22]

The universality of Jesus' authority as shepherd grounds and justifies the particularity of his mission, since he alone, in contrast to the false leaders, is the "good shepherd" and the "door" who brings human beings to eternal life in relationship with God.

In sum, Moloney reads John 10:1–18 by focusing on the context of Jesus' debate with "the Jews" (the Pharisees), who are presented as having self-interestedly clung to the Torah in a way that prevents their acceptance of any messianic fulfillment (that is, their "seeing"). Moloney finds that Jesus' presentation of himself as messiah diverges from what the Pharisees would have expected in three crucial ways: his radical self-gift in laying down his life, his oneness with God, and his inclusion of gentiles in his community. Moloney also gives special attention to the context of the tending of sheep as the background to the intelligibility of the parable's terms and to the shift that occurs in verse 14, as the conflictual context drops away. Finally, Moloney notes that Jesus explains that his coming death will be the result of his own free will, rather than the result primarily of the violence of others, and that his death will lead to resurrected life, both for himself and for those who share in his intimate union with the Father. In contrast, Witherington reads the passage in the context of Maccabees and the Jewish festivals, as well as the rhetorical re-

21. Ibid., 190.
22. Ibid.

sources of Jewish wisdom literature and the rhetorical needs of the evangelist's missionary community. Witherington points out that Jesus presents a model of the "shepherd" that goes far beyond the Maccabean leaders and the Maccabean martyrs, because Jesus is shown to be the divine messiah who will deliver his people by giving them true communion with God and by establishing a community of Jews and gentiles united to God (though not absorbed into him or "deified") in Jesus. For Witherington, John 10:1–18 thus has a rightful rhetorical/missionary urgency, as both Jesus and the evangelist's community seek to call hearers to faith in Jesus, who by his particular mission universally calls human beings to salvation.

Before moving on to Augustine and Aquinas, therefore, we can identify certain theological concerns that play a role in contemporary exegesis as represented by Moloney and Witherington. Moloney interprets the discourse with significant attention to the communal/ecclesial aspect, both that of "the Jews" and that of the new "sheepfold" that contains Jews and gentiles who participate through the self-gift of Jesus in his communion with the Father. Witherington interprets the discourse with an emphasis on the missionary urgency of following and proclaiming Jesus, who rather than being a leader/ martyr on the merely human Maccabean level is the divine messiah who has accomplished the deliverance of all human beings. One can see in these two examples of exegesis the influence of currents of contemporary Catholic and evangelical theology. Yet, both authors are generally careful to avoid asking theological questions that cannot be answered by direct appeal to the text itself or to its historical context, even if such questions arise, as they do, from the text itself. Similarly, neither author applies theological understandings either from elsewhere in Scripture or from the Church's doctrinal tradition to the interpretation of John 10:1–18.

II. Augustine on John 10:1–18

Augustine, in his *In Ioannis Evangelium* or series of sermons that make up a full commentary on the Gospel of John, treats John 10:1–18 in three tractates or sermons.[23] He divides the text into commentary on verses 1–10, 11–13,

---

23. For studies of Augustine's biblical interpretation, see, for example, John M. Norris, "The Theological Structure of Augustine's Exegesis in the *Tractatus in Euangelium Ioannis*," in *Augustine: Presbyter Factus Sum* (New York: Peter Lang, 1993), 385–94; *Augustine and the Bible*, ed. and trans. Pamela Bright (Notre Dame, IN: University of Notre Dame Press, 1999); Frances Young, *Biblical Exegesis and*

and 14–21. In his reading, verses 1–10 have largely to do with faith; verses 11–13 with the Church as guided by Christ and the Holy Spirit as well as secondarily by bishops; and verses 14–21 with communion with Christ and the Father, as well as the significance of Christ's death.[24]

He begins, like Moloney, by connecting John 10:1–18 with the preceding discourse involving the man born blind and the Pharisees. For Augustine the point of this story in John 9, read through the lens of Jesus' teaching in John 10, is that in order to "see" one must be a sheep, a follower of Christ. The goal of teaching is to enable one to "see" truth. Augustine takes note of other teachers—pagan philosophers and heretics—in the ancient world. Neither pagan philosophers nor heretics properly know the "end." The end or goal of human life is to rest in the inexhaustible Truth that is the triune God. This goal is attainable through the reconciliation accomplished by Christ, the incarnate Word, but in order to share in this reconciliation one must have faith in Christ. Teachers who do not direct, by word and deed, their students to Christ fail ultimately to direct their students to truth, the goal of teaching and the goal of life. Pagan philosophers, heretical Christian teachers, and the Pharisees all display for Augustine therefore the lesson that, in Jesus' words, "he who does not enter the sheepfold by the door but climbs in by another way, that man is a thief and a robber" (Jn 10:1). This condemnation does not

---

the *Formation of Christian Culture* (Cambridge: Cambridge University Press, 1997), 265–84; *Engaging Augustine on Romans: Self, Context, and Theology in Interpretation,* ed. Daniel Patte and Eugene TeSelle (Harrisburg, PA: Trinity Press International, 2002). In his essay "Augustine's Reading of Romans, a Model for the Practice of 'Scriptural Criticism,'" Daniel Patte observes that "as we read Romans with Augustine, he cannot fail to call our attention to the hermeneutical frames of our respective interpretations. Augustine used a *regula fidei* in order to select what was for him the most appropriate interpretation. And so do we, whether we admit it or not. . . . Our interpretations have hermeneutical frames which presuppose certain views of religious experience; we approach the text in terms of specific theological categories and questions which directly reflect our convictions (in the proper sense of 'truths we hold as self-evident'), a kind of collective or individual *regula fidei*" (Patte, "Augustine's Reading of Romans," in Patte and TeSelle, *Engaging Augustine on Romans,* 262). On Augustine's mode of exegetical "reading in," see Thomas F. Martin, O.S.A., "*Vox Pauli:* Augustine and the Claims to Speak for Paul: An Exploration of Rhetoric at the Service of Exegesis," *Journal of Early Christian Studies* 8 (2000): 237–72.

24. For further discussion of how Augustine relies upon the "rule of faith" in his biblical interpretation, see Bryan M. Litfin, "The Rule of Faith in Augustine," *Pro Ecclesia* 14 (2005): 85–101. Litfin emphasizes the role of the *regula fidei* in Augustine's exegesis: "It has demarcated the field of play on which orthodox interpreters have room to run. On matters of non-essential doctrine, good exegetes can and should tolerate one another's differences. Likewise, multiple levels of spiritual interpretation are acceptable, so long as they stay in bounds. It is the Church's *regula fidei* which keeps the interpreter within safe limits" (100). Cf. Michael Cameron, "The Christological Substructure of Augustine's Figurative Exegesis," in Bright, *Augustine and the Bible,* 74–103.

mean that pagan philosophers, heretical Christian teachers, and the Pharisees fail to perceive and teach any truth. Rather, it means simply that their teaching, even while containing some truth, lacks the key to attaining eternal union with Truth, and thereby does not lead ultimately, in itself, to human happiness. They leave their students in the slavery of sin and falsehood, cut off from the very goal of teaching.

Seeking to apply the point to the lives of his hearers, Augustine focuses not on the Pharisees, but instead on the pagan philosophers and the Christian heretics. Although elsewhere he acknowledges a profound debt to pagan philosophers such as Cicero and the Neoplatonists, he warns against them here because their teachings may falsely seem adequate to attaining the goal. He holds that the same is true for heretical Christian teachers: "he [Arius] preaches a Christ such as he fabricates for himself, not such as the truth declares him [Christ]. Thou hast the name, thou hast not the reality."[25] How is it that a preacher of Christ, not a pagan, could have made such a mistake? Augustine suggests that the answer is twofold. First, faith in Christ is mediated and authoritatively taught by the Church, not autonomously by individual teachers. Augustine notes that those who wish to hold onto true teaching should "keep hold of this, that Christ's sheepfold is the Catholic Church."[26] Second, those teachers who, in teaching Christ, seek their own glory will find themselves separated from the truth of Christ, since Christ is humble. As Augustine puts it, "For Christ the Lord is a low gateway: he who enters by this gateway must humble himself, that he may be able to enter with head unharmed."[27] The theme throughout Augustine's treatment of verses 1–6, in short, is that one must believe in order to understand (cf. the Septuagint's translation of Is 7:9, quoted by Augustine).[28] Only faith will enable one to "see" the true mean-

---

25. Augustine, *Augustin: Homilies on the Gospel of John, Homilies on the First Epistle of John, Soliloquies,* ed. Philip Schaff, trans. John Gibb and James Innes (Peabody, MA: Hendrickson, 1888, 1995), "Tractate 45," 250.

26. Ibid.

27. Ibid., 250–51.

28. Luke Timothy Johnson points out in *The Future of Catholic Biblical Scholarship* (Luke Timothy Johnson and William Kurz, S.J. [Grand Rapids, MI: William B. Eerdmans Publishing Company, 2002]), 109–10, that the status of the Septuagint is an important, and unresolved, issue for theological biblical interpretation; cf. Josef Lössl, "A Shift in Patristic Exegesis: Hebrew Clarity and Historical Verity in Augustine, Jerome, Julian of Aeclanum and Theodore of Mopsuestia," *Augustinian Studies* 32 (2001): 157–75; Martin Hengel, *The Septuagint as Christian Scripture: Its Prehistory and the Problem of Its Canon,* trans. Mark E. Biddle (Grand Rapids, MI: Baker Academic, 2002). Augustine preferred the Septuagint.

ing of Christ's words, because Scripture is "pregnant with sacramental signs" that, because they speak of divine realities, can only be properly interpreted in faith.[29]

If Christ is the door (vv. 2 and 7) through whom the humble "sheep" can contemplate divine realities in faith, what about people who lived before Christ? Are they excluded from such realities, or can they too have faith? Augustine treats this question as it regards Jesus' comment in verse 8, "All who came before me are thieves and robbers; but the sheep did not heed them." Augustine explains that this condemnation does not apply to the prophets and other holy men and women: "Before his coming came the prophets: were they thieves and robbers? God forbid. They did not come apart from him, for they came with him."[30] How so, if Christ was not yet born? They came with the eternal Word, who spoke truth about divine realities through them. Citing John 14:6, "I am the way, the truth, and the life," Augustine reasons that all came "with" or through Jesus (the door) who were truthful.[31] So long as they did not, in pride, claim to set up a sufficient path to happiness, but instead understood that human beings awaited salvation from God, they taught "with" Christ. With particular (but not exclusive) reference to the holy people of ancient Israel, Augustine observes, "Before the advent of our Lord Jesus Christ, when he came in humility in the flesh, righteous men preceded, believing in the same way in him who was to come, as we believe in him who has come. Times vary, but not faith."[32] Faith is possible in all times, due to the ongoing presence of the Word in history.

Jesus says, however, that the sheep "did not heed" the "thieves and robbers" (Jn 10:8). For Augustine, this statement raises questions about people such as himself who heeded not only the pagan philosophers, but also heretical Christian teachers such as the Manicheans. Can people such as Augustine be "sheep," given that Augustine spent so many years heeding "thieves and robbers"? Augustine responds to this question by deepening his theological reflection on faith in two directions. First, in accord with Jesus' call to repentance and faith, Augustine speaks of conversion to Catholic faith and also of re-conversion on the part of fallen-away Catholics. Second, citing a number

---

29. Augustine, *Homilies on the Gospel of John,* 251. Cf. James Gaffney, S.J., "Believing and Knowing in the Fourth Gospel," *Theological Studies* 26 (1965): 215–41.

30. Augustine, *Homilies on the Gospel of John,* 252.

31. Ibid.

32. Ibid.

of biblical passages, he observes that Jesus may be speaking of "sheep" in the sense of God's eternal predestination.[33] A similar problem arises in the next verse, where Jesus says, "I am the door; if anyone enters by me, he will be saved and will go in and out and find pasture." Faith clearly flourishes when one "goes in" by Christ "the door"; but how is faith assisted by going "out"? Augustine suggests that Jesus' words open up more fully the dynamic of faith, which not only requires contemplative prayer (going "in"), but also, in normal circumstances, bears fruit in external actions (going "out"). He also offers another possible interpretation: perhaps the going "in" is our entrance into the Church through faith, and the going "out" is the completion of faith in our heavenly inheritance of eternal life. On this reading, the "pasture" described by Jesus is "eternal life," which Christians experience already on earth but fully in heaven.

In his sermon on verses 11–13, Augustine delves more fully into this ecclesial dimension of faith. He begins by reviewing the terms of the parable established in verses 1–13: door, doorkeeper, shepherd, sheep, thieves and robbers, hireling, and wolf. The first four, he notes, all apply in different ways to Jesus himself. Jesus says he is the door and the shepherd of the parable; he is also a "sheep" (as the Lamb of God) and the "doorkeeper," the latter because Jesus himself reveals himself and thereby opens for us, by enabling us to understand, the "door" to Truth. The Holy Spirit also brings us to faith and therefore can, according to Augustine, be recognized as the "doorkeeper."[34] The Church as the community of faith is therefore entirely Christological and pneumatological. Yet, the Church also has an outward apostolic structure. As Augustine is well aware, this visible structure means that some will hold office in the Church who do not truly belong, by faith and charity, to Christ. Why does Christ permit this scandal in his Church, whose very purpose is to mediate faith?

Augustine makes clear that Christ shares his unique role as "good Shepherd" with "good shepherds" who are his members.[35] Precisely because the Church is established by the "doorkeeper"—Christ and the Holy Spirit—the Church is not bereft of good shepherds who "enter by the door" as members of Christ's body not only externally but also internally, who in faith mediate the gift of faith.[36] This structure of mediation belongs to the dignity

33. Ibid., 253–54.
35. Ibid., "Tractate 47," 260.

34. Ibid., "Tractate 46," 256–57.
36. Ibid.

of Christ's members, who are configured to Christ by sharing in the mediation of the one Mediator. Such sharing is possible, Augustine affirms, because Christ in the preacher speaks to Christ in the hearer:

> Christ, therefore, is my [Augustine's] gate to you: by Christ I get entrance, not to your houses, but to your hearts. It is by Christ I enter: it is Christ in me that you have been willingly hearing. And why is it you have thus willingly hearkened to Christ in me? Because you are the sheep of Christ, purchased with the blood of Christ.[37]

The Word in the preacher of Truth speaks to the Word in the hearer who has been made faithful to Truth by Christ's sacrificial humility that takes away pride. What about, however, the unfaithful shepherds or "hirelings"? In other words, granting that Christ has called some good bishops, what about unfaithful bishops? Do they not invalidate the entire structure of ecclesial mediation?

Augustine first points out the nuances present in the word "hireling" (vv. 12–13) as opposed to the earlier terms "thieves and robbers." He notes, "The hireling does not here bear a good character and yet, in some respects, is useful; nor would he be called a hireling, did he not receive hire from his employer."[38] The employer has "hired" the bad shepherd. Just as Christ chose Judas to be one of the twelve, so also, Augustine observes, "There are some in office in the Church, of whom the Apostle Paul saith, 'Who seek their own, not the things that are Jesus Christ's.'"[39] Such self-seekers prize worldly gain over the eternal life offered in and through the self-giving Lord. Hirelings were present at the time of St. Paul and are still present in Augustine's time. Only the Lord who knows hearts can identify them with certitude, although times of trial draw some of them into the open.[40] Why does Christ allow them to remain in leadership positions in his body the Church? As in the case of Judas, Christ works through human weakness and even human sin. Augustine encourages his hearers to recognize that "even the hirelings are needful. For many indeed in the Church are following after earthly profit and yet preach Christ, and through them is heard the voice of Christ; and the sheep follow, not the hireling, but the Shepherd's voice speaking through the hireling."[41] The same situation occurred among the leadership of Israel: "Hearken to the hirelings as pointed out by the Lord himself: 'The scribes,' he saith,

37. Ibid.
38. Ibid., "Tractate 46," 257.
39. Ibid.
40. Ibid., 258.
41. Ibid.

'and the Pharisees sit in Moses' seat: do what they say; but do not what they do.'" Indeed, in all communities composed of human beings, some fall away and place their faith not in God but in earthly goods. Yet, this failure of some does not invalidate the whole structure of mediation, through which God is configuring his saints to the image of the "good Shepherd." As Augustine quotes St. Paul regarding such "hirelings" or false leaders, "What then? Only that in every way, whether in pretense or in truth, Christ is proclaimed; and in that I rejoice" (Phil 1:18).[42]

How then do the "hirelings" endanger the flock? They flee when the "wolf," or the devil, comes. Such flight differs from the flight encouraged by Christ elsewhere (cf. Mt 10:23) and practiced by Paul himself (2 Cor 11:33). Rather, the "wolf" comes by tempting the bad bishop or bad Christian to prefer worldly goods over God and God's people. Augustine gives the example of the bad bishop who exercises false prudence, in order to retain worldly honor and worldly peace. Such a "hireling," Augustine notes, "does not venture plainly to rebuke an offender. Look, some one or other has sinned—grievously sinned; he ought to be rebuked, to be excommunicated: but once excommunicated, he will turn into an enemy, hatch plots, and do all the injury he can."[43] In order to avoid the worldly injuries that could be thus inflicted, the bad bishop does not rebuke or excommunicate the scandalous sinner, and spiritual injuries to the flock result instead. As Augustine says, "Thou hast fled, because thou hast been silent; thou hast been silent, because thou hast been afraid. The flight of the mind is fear."[44] It is this spiritual flight of the "hireling" that exposes the flock fully to the workings of the "wolf" or devil, by appearing to condone behavior that is spiritually deadly and destroys true faith and charity, by leading the flock away from Truth.

In preaching upon verses 14–18, Augustine looks further into this relationship of preaching (ecclesial mediation) and faith. Discussing verses 14–15, "I am the good shepherd; I know my own and my own know me, as the Father knows me and I know the Father; and I lay down my life for the sheep," Augustine probes this relationship of "knowing" in terms of the earlier metaphor of the "door" and the "sheepfold" (v. 1): "He then knoweth the Father by himself, and we know the Father by him; so into the sheepfold he entereth by himself, and we by him."[45] To "enter" the "sheepfold" is to come to know the Word and the Father. This Word is not alien to us; rather we were created in

---

42. Ibid.
44. Ibid.

43. Ibid., 259.
45. Ibid., "Tractate 47," 261.

the Word, and by our rational light—itself a participation in the divine Light or Word—we can recognize in faith the Word as our source and goal. However, only Christ, the incarnate Word, is this source and goal. Problems arise when we misuse, in pride, our rational light and construct other "doors" to attain the Father. The one Shepherd and one Door has established one sheepfold in which we enter into him and rejoice with him in the knowing of the Father. This sheepfold can be identified by the fact that Christ, and no other, established it. Citing 1 Corinthians 1:12–13, Augustine gives the conclusion to his audience who, as citizens of Hippo, had to choose between the Catholic Church and the church whose self-understanding derived from the teachings of Donatus: "But of the one sheepfold and of the one Shepherd, you are now indeed being constantly reminded; for we have commended much the one sheepfold, preaching unity, that all the sheep should enter by Christ and that none of them should follow Donatus."[46]

Because of this divisive pride, Christ came to "lay down my life for the sheep" (Jn 10:15). This laying down of his life will result in "one flock, one shepherd" (Jn 10:16) through the mediation of his apostles, who preach to Jews and gentiles whereas Christ came only to the Jews. This mediation, Augustine emphasizes again, enables rather than impedes the gentiles' direct hearing of Christ's preaching. Citing 2 Corinthians 13:3 as an interpretive lens for John 10:16, Augustine affirms that "it is he himself who speaks by his servants, and it is his voice that is heard in those whom he sends."[47] In laying down his life and taking it again, Christ grounds our faith. Christ's death, then, is not primarily a result of the violence against him, nor is he passive in his resurrection. Rather, as the Word working through the instrumentality of his human nature, he accomplishes our salvation by his free will and according to his plan.[48] Yet, if we have faith in Christ who died and rose from the dead to free us from sin and bring us to eternal life, what kind of death is this? Is Christ's body separated from the Word of God, so that the Incarnation comes to an end at least for a time? On the contrary. Against the Apollinarians, Augustine affirms that our faith in Christ is not, during the time of his death, idolatrous. The Word remained united to both Christ's immortal soul and his dead body, even when his soul and body were separated in death.[49]

In interpreting Christ's parabolic discourse in John 10:1–18, Augustine thus places the emphasis on teaching and faith. The thematic center of the dis-

---

46. Ibid.
48. Ibid.

47. Ibid., 262.
49. Ibid., 263–65.

course, on Augustine's reading, comes in verses 14–15, "I am the good shepherd; I know my own and my own know me, as the Father knows me and I know the Father; and I lay down my life for the sheep." Here we find, placed firmly in the context of human beings' coming to share by faith in the intimate communion (of knowing) of the Father and the Son, the meaning of Christ's Cross and of Christ's relationship to us. Augustine explores these themes theologically through accounts of Christ the teacher, faith, pride and humility, the Church, history, conversion, predestination, contemplation and action, eternal life, the Holy Spirit, bishops, death and the immortality of the soul, and various heretical teachings.

How does Augustine's exegesis compare with Moloney's and Witherington's? Recall that Moloney highlights the contrast between "the Jews" and the new "sheepfold" of Jews and gentiles who share through Jesus' self-giving Cross in Jesus' communion with the Father, while Witherington emphasizes the missionary urgency of following and proclaiming Jesus, who contrasts with the Maccabean leaders and martyrs as well as with earlier wisdom teachers. Moloney and Witherington, thanks to the work of historical-critical scholars, give more weight to the "linear" historical context, both of Jesus' time and of the time of the evangelist: the role of "the Jews" vis-à-vis the new "sheepfold" is a point of tension, and similar tensions are generated by the evangelist's (and Jesus') missionary thrust and the need to distinguish Jesus from merely human leaders and teachers of Israel. Both Moloney and Witherington also recognize that the discourse in John 10:1–18 contains a powerful call to faith. As noted above, Moloney emphasizes the communal aspect of this call (the "sheepfold," the sharing in the communion of the Son with the Father), whereas Witherington emphasizes the individual aspect of the call (the missionary urgency, the need for deliverance).

Certainly, Augustine probes deeply into both the communal and the interior (individual) aspects of proclamation and faith. The reader of Augustine has no difficulty, then, in benefiting from the insights of Moloney and Witherington. Augustine's exegesis differs from Moloney's and Witherington's most clearly in two respects. First, Augustine engages Christ's discourse as a teaching that is ongoing in and through the Church. Whereas Moloney and Witherington occasionally hint at contemporary application, Augustine reads the discourse as shot through with contemporary application, because Jesus teaches not only directly to the Jews, but also to the Church directly through those whom he has sent, that is, through the apostles and their successors.

Thus Augustine has no problem in interpreting the discourse by reference to the historical structure (practices) and teaching of the Church and in contrast to teachings and practices that the Church has judged false, "heretical." In this regard, Augustine's exegesis is more "historical" in a different way than is "historical-critical" exegesis: Augustine insists upon including the history of the Mystical Body of Christ in interpreting the Word of God. The difference flows from a different understanding of history: linear *and* participatory, rather than strictly linear.

Second, Augustine contemplates Jesus' words in light of other scriptural teachings, both in the Gospel of John and in Scripture as a whole, and he seeks understanding in faith of these teachings by employing philosophical distinctions and clarifications. He thereby goes beyond what can be gleaned solely from John 10:1–18. For example, he draws in predestination (cf. Rom 8), the doctrine of the Word and our participation in the Word through our rationality (cf. Jn 1), death as the separation of soul and body (cf. Jn 19:30), and the immortality of the soul (cf. Mt 10:28). His reading of John 10:1–18 insists both upon the canonical dimension of Christ's teaching and upon the possibility of arriving not merely at the external coherence of Jesus' words, but their inner intelligibility as truth.

Exegesis according to Augustine's mode will be exegesis from within an ongoing ecclesial tradition. In his preface to his book, Moloney indicates an appreciation for the commentatorial tradition, albeit conceived in a rather eclectic manner:

The fourth Gospel has stirred minds, hearts, and imaginations from Christianity's earliest days. The second-century Gnostics used it in the construction of their systems, and its significance for mainstream Christianity is obvious from the time of Irenaeus (c. 130–c. 200). It was fundamental to the emergence of Christian theology, especially in the Trinitarian and Christological debates that produced the great ecumenical councils, from Nicea (325) to Chalcedon (451). Any interpreter of the fourth Gospel is the heir to rich and widely varied interpretative traditions. Indeed, it is my view that in 1, 2, and 3 John the Gospel received its first interpretation from within the communities for which it was produced. Such commentary has gone on unabated since then.[50]

Yet, Moloney cites Augustine only five times in 566 pages of commentary and offers only eighteen citations of other Fathers. To my knowledge, he leaves out all Christian thinkers who wrote between 430 and the nineteenth cen-

---

50. Moloney, *The Gospel of John*, xi.

tury; and among the numerous modern authors that he cites are no saints or bishops. The "unabated" commentary, in other words, seems to have in Moloney's view not produced much of notice before the nineteenth century and seems to have shifted from the ecclesial (and heretical) "interpretative traditions" of the first centuries to a strictly academic context. Witherington's commentary, for its part, lacks even the notice of the early Christian tradition that Moloney gives in his twenty-three citations and draws only implicitly, if at all, upon Protestant commentaries (for example, Luther, Calvin) written before the twentieth century.

From an Augustinian perspective it follows that while readers of Augustine can enjoy and learn from Moloney's and Witherington's exegesis, contemporary biblical interpretation needs to be re-inserted into the Church's tradition of contemplating the Word. Aquinas's commentary, with its rich engagement with the patristic tradition, offers a way of conceiving this task.

III. Aquinas on John 10:1–18

Aquinas organizes his treatment of John 10:1–18 in two main ways. On the one hand, he divides the text into four sections upon which to comment: verses 1–5, 6–10, 11–13, and 14–18. On the other hand, he proposes, as well, a two-fold division. Verses 1–10, in his view, show that Christ possesses life-giving power, while verses 11–18 address how Christ gives life. As we will see, his commentary on verses 1–10 thus revolves around deification and the mediation of deification in the Church, while his commentary on verses 11–18 reflects upon authority or power in Christ as self-giving (cruciform) love.

Lecture One: John 10:1–5—Divinization

Does Christ possess life-giving (deifying) power? Aquinas finds this question implicitly at the heart of the contrast presented by Christ in the parable, a contrast between the sheep, the door, the shepherd, and the gatekeeper, on the one hand, and the thieves and robbers on the other. Citing the Psalms and the prophets Ezekiel and Micah, Aquinas identifies the "sheep" as "the faithful of Christ and those in the grace of God."[51] This interpretation of "sheep" draws on a significant scriptural tradition of naming God's people; but what

---

51. Thomas Aquinas, *Commentary on the Gospel of St. John,* part II, trans. James A. Weisheipl, O.P., and Fabian R. Larcher, O.P. (Petersham, MA: St. Bede's Publications, 1999), ch. 10, lecture 1, no. 1365, p. 111.

about "the door"? The Old Testament does not give an account of God's action in terms of a door of a sheepfold, and so the meaning of "the door" must
be adduced from the passage. It is clear that much depends upon the nature
of "the door," since it provides the sole rightful way of going in to the sheep
(to God's people) and all other means of entering the sheepfold characterize sinners ("a thief and a robber," John 10:1). Yet, how should one interpret
"the door," since Scripture does not contain other clear passages in which the
naming of God's people as "sheep" is joined with reflection upon the "door"
of God's sheepfold?

Since he cannot turn directly to Scripture for an interpretation, Aquinas seeks assistance from the tradition of exegesis in which he works. From
among his patristic authorities, Aquinas chooses two: John Chrysostom and
Augustine. On the basis of texts from Colossians, Romans, John, Matthew,
and 1 and 2 Timothy, Chrysostom proposes that "the door" is Scripture,
through which human beings attain God's Truth, and without which human
beings fail, due to pride, to teach truly and fully. Pride is a kind of "climbing"
(John 10:1) that characterizes the rebel against God (the "thief") who claims
what does not belong to him and who causes the destruction of what should
have been God's "sheep," God's people. Furthermore, this reading concurs
with the preceding verse, where Jesus tells the Pharisees, "If you were blind,
you would have no guilt; but now that you say, 'We see,' your guilt remains"
(John 9:41). Jesus seeks to show the Pharisees that pride obstructs their reading of Scripture, whereas Jesus "enters by the door, by Sacred Scripture, that
is, he teaches what is contained in Sacred Scripture."[52] If they had understood
the Scriptures, they would have recognized Jesus as both the true Teacher and
the messiah (as the blind man does in chapter 9). When Jesus later teaches "I
am the door" (v. 9), he exposes the unity of Scripture as teaching about him.
As Aquinas says, "Now aside from Christ nothing is more fittingly called a
door than Sacred Scripture."[53] Since all Scripture teaches about Christ, and
since Scripture reveals Christ to us, it is "the door." In this way, the tradition
of exegesis enables Aquinas to expose Scripture as the Word of God and to
emphasize Scripture's role in teaching and forming God's people.

Aquinas also explores Augustine's interpretation, which we have already
examined above, of "the door" as Christ. Allowing the possibility that Christ's
understanding of "the door" had a multifaceted richness, Aquinas holds to-

52. Ibid., no. 1366, p. 112.
53. Ibid., no. 1367, p. 113.

gether Augustine's interpretation and Chrysostom's, without choosing between them. Just as Chrysostom draws his interpretation from scriptural texts and defends his interpretation on this basis, so also Augustine draws upon Revelation 4:1, "After this I looked, and lo, in heaven an open door!" That "open door" is Christ, the Lamb of God, corresponding with Christ's claim in John 10:9 to be the "door." The context of Revelation 4 gives the parable in John 10 a liturgical and eschatological significance, which Aquinas will emphasize throughout his treatment of John 10:1–18.

Aquinas then summarizes the reading that Augustine gives of Christ as the "door." Human beings cannot be brought to their final "end" by mere moral virtues (the philosophers) or ceremonial practices (the Pharisees); rather only faith in Christ can lead persons to their true fulfillment. This eschatological fulfillment in Christ is attained socially—liturgically—rather than individualistically. The "sheep" need the priestly mediation of "shepherds" in order to be fully united to Christ. Yet, to be a shepherd, just as to be a sheep, is a vocation dependent upon God's call, which must be received rather than arrogated. Aquinas quotes Hebrews 5:4, "And one does not take the honor upon himself, but he is called by God."[54] The shepherds, just like the sheep, must enter through Christ the "door." In other words, the bishops must possess the theological virtues and not practice "ambition and secular power and simony,"[55] the characteristics not of true shepherds but of "thieves and robbers" who do not recognize the "door."

54. Ibid., no. 1368, p. 113.

55. Ibid., no. 1368, p. 114. Raymond Brown notes that historical-critical biblical scholarship cannot determine Jesus' outlook toward ecclesial structure, and he argues that this ambiguity is ecumenically helpful (Brown, "The Contribution of Historical Biblical Criticism to Ecumenical Church Discussion," in *Biblical Interpretation in Crisis: The Ratzinger Conference on Bible and Church*, ed. Richard John Neuhaus [Grand Rapids, MI: William B. Eerdmans Publishing Company, 1989], 32–33). Yet, one would expect the Incarnation of the Son of God and the sending of the Holy Spirit to enable the community of Jesus' followers to constitute an ecclesial form not antithetical to Jesus' wishes. From this perspective, the reality depicted in the Bible participates historically in the past, present, and future reality that we name the "Church." Even if Catholics and Protestants disagree about some aspects of the Church, it seems that ecumenical dialogue would be fostered, not hampered, by agreement that the Church in the Bible is the Church today—in other words that there is a profound continuity, guided by the Holy Spirit, in the development of doctrine. This continuity is reflected upon sapientially by theological exegesis, which may theologically admit discontinuity as well. Brown remarks that "churches can take comfort if in examining their traditional stances [vis-à-vis "serious biblical criticism"] they can find a 'line of development' or 'trajectory' . . . from the Bible, making intelligible a biblical basis for the stances. But there were diverse lines of development coming out of the New Testament diversities, and so biblical criticism should force the Church to examine why it has chosen one line of development rather than another" (34–35). But this way of putting it makes the task one of demonstrating the

The true shepherd has faith in Christ and leads the flock to him; in so doing, such a bishop both enters in by the door of Scripture (Chrysostom), since Christ fulfills the Old Testament, as he teaches in Luke 24:44.[56] Yet, as Augustine says, the door is also Christ. As God, Christ is Truth, and as man Christ enters into beatitude through himself, through the "door" of Truth. Christ is thus the Head of the eschatological flock. Only Christ can enable others to enter; only Christ can call both "sheep" and "shepherds" (bishops). Christ enters beatitude directly, while all others enter by *participating* in Christ's Truth. Here Aquinas interprets verse 9, "I am the door; if any one enters by me, he will be saved," in terms of John 17:17, "Sanctify them in the truth."

Aquinas employs a similar approach to interpreting Christ's parabolic use of "gatekeeper." The task of the "gatekeeper" is to open to the good shepherd (v. 3), who enters by the door. Chrysostom, in keeping with his emphasis on Scripture, proposes that the "gatekeeper" that Christ has in mind is Moses, who writes of Christ, according to John 5:46. As Aquinas says, Moses "opens the way to a knowledge of Sacred Scripture" and thereby opens to Christ (the Word of God).[57] In tandem with this focus on scriptural teaching, Aquinas adds Augustine's emphasis on Christ, who not only is the "door" by which we

Church's continuity (at least via one "line") with the Church of the Bible. In faith, the task is a very different one. Far from attempting to prove the Church's lineage via a linear historical account, one seeks to enter into the biblical reality by sapiential pondering upon the theological mystery of the Church, a mystery that is alive and present today. In contrast to the notion that one must begin by a linear historical demonstration (whose outcome is perpetually in doubt and whose results can only be minimal), one begins with what, in faith, one knows as a mystery whose depths can be biblically illumined and explored. Despite Brown's affirmation of the ongoing work of the Spirit (49), his linear-historical model, in contrast to a model that appreciates historical-critical biblical research for the light it sheds upon the reality (the Church) that is participated in history, has reductionist consequences. Brown describes this process, "Evaluating the strength and directness of the line of development may also help a church to distinguish in the importance of traditional positions and thus to appreciate a 'hierarchy of doctrines'" (35). The point is that "the strength and directness of the line of development," as historically reconstructed, cannot function as a theological gauge for the mystery of the Church; once linear history serves as the gauge, the Church of every historical period will remain fundamentally extrinsic to the Church of every other historical period (in a nominalist non-participatory fashion), no matter what elements may be found to correlate between one period and another. Thus the primary question that Brown faces without being able to answer—the concern that arises continually, as it did at the Reformation, from the linear-historical mode—is that of "church teaching that goes beyond the Bible" (49), because "beyond" must mean "extrinsic" in this model. Participatory exegesis, it should be added, does not make the Church impenetrable to "challenges"; on the contrary, recognizing the Church as constituted not by linear progress but by participation in Christ (both of which categories are "historical") enables the most forceful challenges toward renewing the Church's holiness. See my *Participatory Biblical Exegesis* (University of Notre Dame Press, forthcoming).

56. Aquinas, *Commentary on John,* no. 1370, p. 114.

57. Ibid., no. 1371, p. 114.

enter beatitude, but also gives us the grace to enter beatitude. Following Augustine, this role of grace also connects the "gatekeeper" with the Holy Spirit, of whom Christ later teaches, "He will guide you into all the truth" (Jn 16:13). Moses, Christ, Scripture, and the Holy Spirit open the "door" to the "good shepherd," who leads to the beatitude that is our eternal participation in Truth. In other words, they are the "gatekeeper" to Truth, because they teach truly.

After the gatekeeper opens the door to the good shepherd, "the sheep hear his voice" (John 10:3). As Aquinas points out, this response of the sheep is the second mark (after the action of the gatekeeper) that identifies, in Christ's parable, the shepherd as good. The obedience of the "sheep" to the shepherd's "voice," Christ's teachings, raises the difficulty adduced by Augustine. Namely, what about converts or those who fall away? Like Augustine, Aquinas suggests that Christ may, in describing these "sheep," have in view the "elect," those God has predestined from all eternity (cf. Rom 8).[58] He also suggests that the image indicates, in its context, Christ's response to the Pharisees who have rejected him (Jn 9).[59]

As a third mark of the good shepherd, Aquinas observes the four actions taken by the shepherd in verses 3–4: calling (and knowing) the sheep by name, leading out the sheep, bringing them "out" into the world, and going before them. Aquinas interprets all these actions by recourse to other scriptural texts, and, as before, he focuses upon drawing out the movement of deification. Regarding Christ's knowledge of his flock, a knowledge required of all shepherds (including bishops), he cites Exodus 33:17, Proverbs 27:23, Psalm 147:4, and 2 Timothy 2:19. This knowledge or naming is deifying: as Aquinas says, "he knew them by name from eternity."[60] Regarding Christ's leading them out, he proposes, citing Psalm 107:14, that this signifies the removal from evil that is a condition of deification. Regarding Christ's bringing the sheep "out" of the sheepfold into the world, he compares this image to Matthew 10:16, where Christ says, "Behold, I send you as sheep in the midst of wolves." In the world, the sheep evangelize and "show the direction and way to eternal life."[61]

---

58. For an insightful recent discussion of Aquinas's understanding of "predestination," see Michal Paluch, *La profondeur de l'amour divin. La prédestination dans l'oeuvre de saint Thomas d'Aquin* (Paris: Vrin, 2004), as well as Jean-Pierre Torrell's preface to Paluch's book.

59. Aquinas, *Commentary on John,* no. 1373, p. 116.

60. Ibid., no. 1374, p. 116.

61. Ibid. Cf. Jésus Luzarraga, "Eternal Life in the Johannine Writings," trans. Silvia Anadon, *Communio* 18 (1991): 24–34.

Aquinas also cites here Isaiah 66:19 and Luke 1:79, both of which belong to the promise of deification. Lastly, regarding Christ's going before them, he notes (again citing scriptural texts) Christ's example in dying for truth and rising to everlasting life. Union with the Trinity by means of holy *imitatio Christi* in professing the Truth even unto death (Aquinas cites 1 Pt 2:21) is the goal of the "sheep" who follow the "shepherd," and it is this goal of sharing the divine life that fundamentally marks the shepherd as "good." In contrast, as Aquinas points out in commenting briefly upon verse 5, the sheep "will not follow" a "stranger" (Jn 10:5) because the stranger's "false and heretical" teaching is not Christ's. True sheep (the elect) do not "approve" of such teaching, because it leads not to deification but to death.[62] True teaching is life-giving, false teaching corruptive: "Bad company ruins good morals" (1 Cor 15:33).[63]

Lecture Two: John 10:6–10—the Church

If true teaching is life-giving, however, why does Christ here cloak his teaching in this set of parabolic images, rather than speak more directly? After all, Christ's audience did not understand his words: "This figure Jesus used with them, but they did not understand what he was saying to them" (Jn 10:6). Aquinas finds in this verse a transition that allows for a more full exposition, both by Jesus and by the commentator (Aquinas), regarding the role of the *Church* in the attainment of deification. This theme, while not absent before, is now amplified. Following Augustine, Aquinas argues that parables alienate the wicked and inspire the good, because the former cannot endure divine matters being beyond their ken, whereas the latter are awed and humble themselves before a truth that exceeds them. In humbling themselves, they constitute the Church, humbly bowing before the mysteries of faith rather than rationalistically demanding full comprehension and control. This posture of humility enables them to receive deeper insight into the mysteries that the arrogant have already cast aside as lacking meaning. First, Christ teaches them that he is the "door" described in the parable (Jn 10:7). Aquinas explains, "Now the purpose of a door is to conduct one into the inner rooms of a house; and this is fitting to Christ, for one must enter into the secrets of God through him: 'This is the gate of the Lord,' that is, Christ, 'the righteous shall enter through it' (Ps 118:20)."[64] Through this "door" enter both

---

62. Aquinas, *Commentary on John,* no. 1377, p. 117.
63. Ibid.
64. Ibid., lecture 2, no. 1382, p. 119.

the "shepherds" or bishops, and the "sheep" or faithful. All have access to "the secrets of God" through Christ.

Yet, what about the holy men and women of the Old Testament; are they not part of the Church, since they lived before Christ? Indeed, Jesus says, "All who came before me are thieves and robbers; but the sheep did not heed them" (Jn 10:8). Aquinas points out that the Manichees, themselves separated from the Church, taught that these words confirm the damnation of the men and women of the Old Testament. In contrast, Aquinas distinguishes between those who were sent by God and those who arrogated authority to themselves for purposes of self-aggrandizement. Authority in the people of God rests upon being "sent," having a mission from God. Those who truly are "sent" enter the "secrets of God" by the door of the Word. In a certain sense, therefore, they do not come "before" Christ the door. Although temporally they live before Christ, they already know him and enter "through" him, because the Word is always present. In making this point Aquinas combines Hebrews 13:8, "Jesus Christ is the same yesterday and today and forever," and Wisdom 7:27, "In every generation she [the Wisdom of God] passes into holy souls and makes them friends of God and prophets." As Aquinas says, many of "the people of Israel did listen to the holy prophets,"[65] and thus the true prophets and patriarchs could not be referred to by Jesus' phrase, "the sheep did not heed them."

The true prophets love the life-giving Word, the false prophets love their own death-dealing word:

it must be said that 'all who came before me,' that is, independently of me, without divine inspiration and authority, and not with the intention of seeking the glory of God but of acquiring their own, 'are thieves,' insofar as they take for themselves what is not theirs, that is, the authority to teach . . . , 'and robbers,' because they kill with their corrupt doctrine.[66]

Two themes merit special notice here. First, teachers must be "sent" and can be recognized as true by their participation in the Word who sends them, a participation that will be marked by humility. Second, Christ builds up his people in the world through this pattern of mediation, of "sending" human teachers. Aquinas explores these two aspects, Christ's authority and human participation in it, in his further analysis of Christ as the "door." When

65. Ibid., no. 1384, p. 120.
66. Ibid., no. 1385, pp. 120–21.

we enter through the "door," we enter into "the fellowship of the Church and of the faithful."[67] As the "door," which "safeguards the sheep by keeping those within from going out and by protecting them from strangers who want to come in,"[68] Christ guarantees that this community will not be overcome by false teachers and that those who follow him in the community will be "saved" (Jn 10:9) so long as, Aquinas adds, they persevere.[69] Christ is the guarantee, and yet "the fellowship of the Church and of the faithful"—as *what is guaranteed*—receives true teaching authority to proclaim truthfully the saving name of Christ.

Aquinas then ponders the meaning of Christ's affirmation that the elect who enter by Christ "will go in and out and find pasture" (Jn 10:9). Again he sees ecclesiological implications. Following Chrysostom, he notes that the security in which the elect "will go in and out" suggests the power of evangelization (cf. Acts 5:41), because the elect go outside the door and dwell among unbelievers and, instead of falling into error, "find delight in converting others, and find joy even when persecuted by unbelievers for the name of Christ."[70] Those who enter by Christ, are sent by him to share in his mission of the salvation of the world. Following Augustine, he observes that the passage can also indicate the fruitful union, in the spiritual development of the Christian, of the contemplative ("in") life and the active ("out") life. Augustine and Gregory the Great also read the passage as indicating more deeply the relationship of the person to the Church. The person goes "in" to the Church militant, the Church visible on earth, by enjoying the "pasture" of the "wonderful tabernacle" (Ps 41:5), the Eucharist; nourished in this way, the person is enabled to go "out" through Christ to the "pasture" (Ps 23) of the Church triumphant, the glory of heavenly union with God. To evoke this movement from the earthly to the heavenly "pasture," he quotes Song of Songs 3:11, "Go forth, O daughters of Zion, and behold King Solomon, with the crown with which his mother crowned him on the day of his wedding." Lastly, he identifies a fourth way of reading the text, from an anonymous patristic author: to "go in" means to contemplate Christ in his divinity, to "go out" means to contemplate Christ in his humanity, and "pasture," as "the joys of contemplation," is found in both.[71]

Aquinas concludes this section by briefly discussing verse 10, "The thief

67. Ibid., no. 1389, p. 121.

69. Ibid.

71. Ibid., no. 1393, p. 123.

68. Ibid.

70. Ibid., no. 1390, p. 122.

comes only to steal and kill and destroy; I came that they may have life and have it abundantly." In contrast to the "perverse teachings and evil practices" by which false teachers draw human beings to "everlasting destruction," Christ offers the fullness of life—eternal life—to those who enter "the Church militant through faith" and thereby receive "the life of righteousness," that is, charity (cf. Heb 10:38, 1 Jn 3:14).[72] The goal of Christ's *doctrina,* which unites believers through faith and charity in Christ's Church, is, as Aquinas has emphasized throughout, deification.

By dividing the text as he does (vv. 1–5 and 6–10), Aquinas is able to give special attention to the role of John 10:9, "if any one enters by me, he will be saved and will go in and out and find pasture," a text that is read over quickly by Moloney and Witherington as indicating the mediatorial role of Christ. Indebted to the Fathers, Aquinas takes the text as an opportunity to set forth the key elements of our "salvation" in Christ as a historical and eschatological reality: evangelization, martyrdom, conversion and purification of the soul by the contemplative and active life, the Eucharist and its eschatological "end," the everlasting glory of contemplating the Incarnate Lord.

We might pause and ask: Is this use of John 10:9 an example of patristic-medieval *eisegesis?* I think that the answer is both yes and no. It seems clear that the Fathers, followed by Aquinas, draw upon theological and ecclesial understandings not directly present in John 10:9. That they do so by continually referencing other biblical texts does not make their readings any less distinct from what John 10:9, or the parable in itself, directly conveys. In interpreting Christ's parable, however, why confine the meaning of Jesus Christ's words—even the meaning of Christ's words as conveyed by the evangelist John—solely to John 10:9 in the context of the parable or even the context of John's Gospel? Why could not Jesus' words express through the parable realities set forth elsewhere in the Bible and instantiated in the Church's life? Why should not the meaning of "saved" in John 10:9 have sufficient range as to include, in some way, the central elements of the Christian theology of salvation?

If the meaning offered by the parable can be expanded as in the Fathers and Aquinas, does such exegetical practice completely unhinge the text from its historical meaning and reference? I think not, once two points are recognized. First, the continuity of the missions of the Son and Spirit constitutes

72. Ibid., nos. 1395–1396, p. 123.

a central pillar of any Christian exegesis. There must be some continuity between the Church's understanding of the mysteries of faith and Christ's own teaching, as well as the teachings of the evangelists. Without this continuity in the tradition of Christian *doctrina,* it is unclear how one could see in the Bible itself, or in any Christian community, anything other than a random assortment of claims. What appears to be eisegesis thus belongs to a properly theological understanding of the history of the handing on of *doctrina.*

Second, Aquinas's appropriation of the Fathers, in exploring the literal sense of the text, proceeds without seeking to select one literal meaning and reject other possibilities. The four readings are offered ultimately with the intention not of pinning down the exact meaning, but rather of stimulating the reader's contemplation of the mystery of being "saved" and finding Christ's "pasture." In order to stimulate contemplation of the reality adverted to by Christ in the parable, the four readings draw upon resources other than the parable: other biblical texts as interpreting the ecclesial experience of Christians in history and the eschatological hope toward which Christians aim their strivings. In short, rather than unhinging John 10:9 from its historical meaning and reference, Aquinas's approach insists upon a Christologically and pneumatologically integrated understanding of historical meaning and reference. The meaning of the parable in its own context can be illumined and developed by reading the parable in light of the realities that believers know, in faith, about Christ and the Church. In other words, the parable's own historical context—presumably the question of "what John the Evangelist knew" and "what Jesus said and knew," the question of historical origins—cannot be separated from the pneumatologically integrated *historical* context of divine *doctrina,* ongoing in the Church's appropriation and teaching of revelation.[73]

Lecture Three: John 10:11–13—Authority

The themes of deification and the Church also characterize Aquinas's commentary on verses 11–13. In accord with the great theme of these verses—

---

73. Cf. Francis Watson, *Text, Church, and World* (Grand Rapids, MI: William B. Eerdmans Publishing Company, 1994), 260–61, although Watson—for whom the Church, while certainly present in historical communities, is a largely eschatological reality (the reality of "undistorted communication")—cannot, unless I have misunderstood him, account for an ongoing ecclesial participation in *sacra doctrina* beyond occasional(ist) moments of grace. See also, for a helpful account of the doctrine of revelation, John Lamont, "The Nature of Revelation," *New Blackfriars* 72 (1991): 335–45.

namely, Christ the good shepherd—Aquinas focuses his reflection here, however, upon *authority* in the Church.

Aquinas understands Christian authority in terms of the Church's participation in Christ's role as "shepherd." As Augustine teaches, since Christ is both "door" and "shepherd," Christ enters eternal life through himself, since in himself he knows the Father and manifests Him. All others enter eternal life, this deifying wisdom, *by participation* in Christ through faith and the sacraments of faith, above all the "spiritual food" of Christ's "own body and blood."[74] No one, Aquinas observes, can participate in Christ's status as the "door." Christ alone is the entrance point to heavenly life. But Christ enables others to participate in his authority as "shepherd." There are other shepherds or leaders in the Church, even though they are never autonomous or primary leaders.

Their participation in Christ's authority, a sacramental participation that constitutes the visible structure of the Church and whose purpose is to assist in the salvation of the world, is Christ's gift: the state of "being a shepherd he did share with others and conferred it on his members: for Peter was a shepherd, and the other apostles were shepherds, as well as all good bishops: 'I will give you shepherds after my own heart' (Jer 3:15)."[75] Following Augustine, Aquinas notes that, in one sense, all bishops are shepherds, but in another sense, Christ calls himself in verse 11 the *good* shepherd so as to indicate the necessity of charity for living up to the full meaning of "shepherd."

In this way, Aquinas ponders Christ's comparison in the parable of himself as the "good shepherd" (v. 11) with the "hireling" (v. 12). It is clear from the book of Acts and the epistles, as well as the gospels themselves, that Christ shared his authority with his disciples/apostles. Thus what Christ says about the "good shepherd" will apply also to those who "shepherd" the Christian community after Christ's ascension. Again following Augustine, Aquinas makes clear that such lesser "shepherds" are fully such only insofar as they participate in the pattern of Christ the "good shepherd" as his members. First, lest bishops be puffed up by their authority, he notes that they possess it as the Church's "children."[76] They are thus entirely dependent upon Christ and his Mystical Body for their authority, which is thus an authority constituted entirely by participation, not by autonomy or self-rule. Second, without char-

---

74. Aquinas, *Commentary on John,* lecture 3, no. 1398, p. 124.
75. Ibid., no. 1398, p. 125.
76. Ibid.

ity the bishop is only the shell of the "shepherd" he is called to be, because without charity the bishop lacks full union with Christ, the very source of the bishop's authority. Aquinas states, "For no one is a good shepherd unless he has become one with Christ by love and has become a member of the true shepherd."[77] Indeed, only as a "member" of Christ the shepherd—a member by the participation that is charity—can one effectively exercise a shepherd's "office" in the Church, because this authority (priestly, prophetic, and kingly) is none other than charity. Christ perfectly exercises his office of shepherd on the Cross, and all those who possess authority in the Church exercise the office properly only by participating in his Cross. Aquinas affirms, "The office of a good shepherd is charity; thus he [Christ] says, 'the good shepherd lays down his life for the sheep' [verse 11]."[78] The shepherd in the Church, as a child of the Church, must follow Christ the good shepherd in the perfection of charity, willingness to lay down one's life out of love for God and neighbor.

Authority is thus radical self-giving love, possible only as childlike participation in Christ. This is the very opposite of authority as conceived by the "hireling," who distorts his office by self-seeking love. As Aquinas points out, "This difference is touched upon by Ezekiel (34:2): 'Woe, shepherds of Israel who have been feeding yourselves! Should not shepherds feed the sheep?'"[79] He also notes that the difference is found likewise in Aristotle's distinction between a good king and a tyrant. Here once again Aquinas brings in the theme of deification. Good shepherds, for their service, merit a reward (Aquinas cites Sir 36:16, Is 40:10, and Lk 15:17). However, this reward is not, in Christ, a mere wage, which would be given to a servant, not a son. A son works for an inheritance. Those shepherds who are united to Christ in charity will exercise their office with a focus upon eternal life (the inheritance of deification), while those shepherds who distort the office will look instead for worldly wages. The true exercise of authority in the Church, in other words, requires understanding the "end" toward which the shepherd, following Christ in cruciform love, must lead, namely the "end" of deification. Such an "end" ensures that shepherds who exercise their authority truly will appear strange to the world, which judges all things in terms of worldly wages. Aquinas holds that "since everlasting life is our inheritance, anyone who works with an eye towards it is working as a child; but anyone who aims at something different

77. Ibid.
79. Ibid.

78. Ibid., no. 1399, p. 125.

(for example, one who longs for worldly gain or takes delight in the honor of being a prelate) is a hireling."[80] Shepherds who truly love the members of the Church will show their care by steadfastly calling them to radical self-giving love, because that is the path, marked by Christ, of deification. For Aquinas, Paul is the model of such a self-sacrificing shepherd in Christ's Church.[81]

Christ teaches in verse 13 that the hireling "sees the wolf coming and leaves the sheep and flees; and the wolf snatches them and scatters them." Who is the "wolf"? Aquinas suggests three answers: the devil, the heretic or false teacher (Mt 7:15, Acts 20:29), and the political tyrant (Ez 22:27). The shepherd—the bishop participating in Christ's office—must steadfastly oppose the works of all three. Following Augustine, Aquinas affirms that at times it is lawful for the bishop to flee from personal persecution, as in the case of St. Athanasius and in accord with Jesus' injunction in Matthew 10:23. Flight is not acceptable, however, when "the whole flock is sought" to undergo persecution.[82] Aquinas also recalls Augustine's point that flight of the body differs from flight of the soul, in which the cowardly shepherd refuses to defend and support the persecuted faithful.

Lecture Four: John 10:14–18—Jesus Christ

The final five verses of the Good Shepherd discourse draw together the above themes in a reflection upon Christ's authority and mission as Shepherd. Since Christ is the head of the Church, the path to deification, and the Shepherd in whom all ecclesial shepherds participate, it is fitting that the discourse concludes with exposition of *Christ's* authority and mission.

Verse 14, like verse 11, begins with "I am the good shepherd." Christ now grounds this office, and our participation in it, more deeply in his identity and mission. Christ says, "I know my own and my own know me, as the Father knows me and I know the Father; and I lay down my life for the sheep" (Jn 10:14–15). As regards Christ's knowledge of his members, Aquinas emphasizes that Christ knows "not just with mere knowledge only, but with a knowledge joined with approval and love: 'To him who loves us and has freed us from our sins' (Rv 1:5)."[83] Christ's knowing of his members is a *good shepherd's* knowing, that is, he knows us with love and saves us from destruction. Those who are Christ's "own" are, Aquinas holds, the elect "by predestination,

---

80. Ibid., no. 1403, p. 126.
82. Ibid., no. 1406, p. 128.

81. Ibid., no. 1408, p. 129.
83. Ibid., lecture 4, no. 1412, p. 130.

by vocation, and by grace."[84] Their knowledge of Christ, in turn, is therefore a faith alive with charity. In knowing him, they obey his will in charity.

Christ's knowing of his members is a *good shepherd's* knowing ultimately because it flows from his knowing of the Father. As Aquinas states regarding verse 15 (cf. Mt 11:27), "Our Lord says this because in knowing the Father, he knows the will of the Father that the Son should die for the salvation of the human race."[85] Because of his identity as the coequal Son of the Father and as the Mediator between God and man (related by "knowing" both to the Father and to the "sheep"), Christ knows how to lead his people to deification. True "authority" means sharing in the Father's authoring, or accomplishing, of his plan for the healing and deification of human beings, and this accomplishment occurs through self-giving love.

Christ's salvific death thus stands at the climax of the Good Shepherd discourse, with its themes of deification, true authority, communion in (divine) knowing, and self-giving love. But Christ's death itself is something of a mystery. What does it mean for Christ to "lay down" his life? Could it mean that the Word (Christ's "I," his Personhood) is parted from Christ's soul? Were this the case, Christ's death, far from being salvific, would break apart the Incarnation. Integrating scriptural exegesis and metaphysical analysis, Aquinas holds instead that Christ's soul and body are separated from each other, even while neither is separated from the Word. The key point is that the hypostatic union, the Incarnation, never ends.[86] Christ's death is not the negation of the Incarnation, but rather the way by which the Incarnate One repairs sin and death from within. In this way Christ's death, unlike merely human deaths, is able to bear salvific fruit. Aquinas affirms, "Then when he says, 'and I have other sheep,' he sets down the fruit of Christ's death, which is the salvation not only of the Jews but of the gentiles as well."[87] This ingrafting of the gentiles conforms, Aquinas points out, with the message of Psalm 2:8, among the central Christological psalms, and with Isaiah 49:6, the great "servant" song.[88]

The ingrafting of the gentiles also belongs to the Good Shepherd discourse's concern for authority, the Church, and deification. Aquinas notes that Jesus preached personally only to Israel (cf. Rom 15:8), by way of confirming the earlier covenants. The apostles preach Christ's word to the gentiles and there-

---

84. Ibid.

86. Ibid., no. 1415, pp. 131–32.

88. Ibid., no. 1417, p. 132.

85. Ibid., no. 1414, p. 131.

87. Ibid., no. 1416, p. 132.

by must share in Christ's authority (as shepherds to Shepherd). As Christ says in verse 16, those who "are not of this fold," that is, the gentiles, "will heed my voice. So there shall be one flock, one shepherd." The heeding of Christ's voice means observing his commandments (cf. Mt 28:20, Ps 18:43), summed up in the commandment of radically self-giving love. Such love produces "the unity of charity," which is historically constituted and visibly manifested as the "one Church of the faithful from the two peoples, the Jews and the gentiles" (cf. Eph 4:5, Eph 2:14).[89] The unity of charity is made possible because charity is a participation by faith in the love of the one good shepherd, Jesus Christ (cf. Ez 37:24). Thus Aquinas sees obedience, charity, and faith as constitutive of the Church of Christ the good shepherd. The visible community of the Church proclaims and nourishes this obedience, faith, and love, in which the saints' "righteousness,"[90] their sharing in Christ, is manifested.

Yet, why should Christ's death be so powerful? Would the Father, in eternity, be affected by the incarnate Son's death in time, as Jesus seems to imply by saying, "For this reason the Father loves me, because I lay down my life, that I may take it again" (v. 17)? Aquinas points out that "something temporal is not the cause of something eternal."[91] If not, then what does Jesus mean by hinging the Father's love for him upon his laying down of his life? Seeking to illumine the mystery of the Father's love in the Paschal mystery, Aquinas finds in other scriptural texts three ways of reading John 10:17. First, in saying that "the Father loves me," Jesus could be indicating that his resurrection is the Father's rewarding Jesus' perfect act of love on the Cross. This reading conforms with the testimony of Philippians 2:8–9, "He humbled himself and became obedient unto death, even death on a cross. Therefore God has highly exalted him and bestowed on him a name which is above every name." The problem with this reading is the issue of meriting God's love. On the basis of 1 Corinthians 13:3 and 1 John 4:10, Aquinas observes that God's "love precedes all our merit."[92] Thus one would need to be clear that Jesus as man merits not God's love per se, but the *effect* of God's love. God's love gives us the grace to merit reward; God rewards his own gifts—our graced actions. This first way of biblically reading Christ's death emphasizes its meritorious character, by which it accomplishes our salvation.

A second way of reading John 10:17 takes inspiration from Romans 8:32, "He who did not spare his own Son but gave him up for us all." Like Philip-

89. Ibid., no. 1419, p. 133.
90. Ibid.
91. Ibid., no. 1422, p. 133.
92. Ibid., no. 1422, p. 134.

pians 2, Romans 8 is a central biblical locus for understanding Christ's Cross. Aquinas proposes that Jesus' remark that "for this reason the Father loves me" could signify that *because* Jesus dies for our sins on the Cross, the Father loves him above all creatures. For in what way could the Father more profoundly love Jesus than to enable Jesus to be the one to save the world by his sacrificial death? By the deeds that he performs in the flesh, Jesus is the Savior of the world, thus revealing how much the Father loves and exalts above other creatures the incarnate Son. While this way of illumining John 10:17 emphasizes Jesus' headship, the third way emphasizes Jesus' humble obedience, the mark of the perfect charity by which Jesus frees the world from slavery to sin. Aquinas remarks that "an obvious sign of love is that a person, out of charity, fulfills the commands of God."[93] Jesus manifests in the world the Father's love by doing the Father's will.

The authority of the Good Shepherd Jesus thus takes the form of meritorious, cruciform obedience—an obedience which is construed not as mere submission to another's power, but rather as the incarnate Son's intimate communion with his loving Father. This relationship of supreme obedience (charity) makes Jesus the Head of all creation. Thus authority in Christ turns out to be the same as cruciform obedience, far different from images of authority as autonomous power. Such obedience (which the Church images) flows from and manifests communion with the God of love, and the ultimate fruit of this obedience is deification.

It would thus be a mistake to imagine Christ's death as primarily the result of human violence; rather, Christ has authority even over his death. Jesus makes this point in verse 18: "No one takes it from me, but I lay it down of my own accord. I have power to lay it down, and I have power to take it again; this charge I have received from my Father." Christ's Cross thus reveals that supreme power or authority coincides with supreme self-giving love. Aquinas notes that St. Paul "says in 1 Corinthians (1:18): 'For the word of the cross is folly to those who are perishing, but to us who are being saved it is the power of God,' that is, his great power was revealed in the very death of Christ."[94] True power or authority is found in self-giving love; it is by self-giving love that the "sheep" are led to "pasture," to the salvation that is deification. God's power is his love. In response to God's love, we must love God. In so doing, we become members of the obedient Head; we are configured in the Church

93. Ibid.
94. Ibid., no. 1425, p. 135.

to Christ's obedient image. This obedience, as a relationship of communion with the Wisdom and Love who unite us with the Father, is deifying. Aquinas thus concludes his commentary on the Good Shepherd discourse by quoting John 14:23: "If a man loves me, he will keep my word, and my Father will love him."

IV. Conclusion

The above examination of Augustine's and Aquinas's exegesis of John 10:1–18, in light of Moloney's and Witherington's contemporary exegesis, illumines, I hope, what it might mean to work within a theological tradition of biblical interpretation that takes the patristic-medieval tradition (with its deep awareness of the participatory dimensions of history) as its starting point and seeks to continue and develop this tradition in contemporary modes (attuned to history as linear). In a sense, the issue between pre- and post-historical-critical exegesis is what it means to engage "critically" with the text of Scripture.

Were "critical" to mean bracketing one's primary source of knowledge about the realities depicted in Scripture—namely, ecclesial faith[95]—then it would seem that one would have cut oneself off not only from the sense of interpenetrating realities that animates the patristic-medieval exegetical tradition, but also from the sense of realities that animates the Gospel of John. Neither can the lack of a "metaphysics" be the meaning of "critical," since the effort to exclude consciously one metaphysics always means that another metaphysics is entering (unconsciously) through the back door.[96] Neither can "critical" mean solely engaging particular "pericopes," leaving aside the context of the Gospel of John and of the entire Scriptures, since this would be precisely to deny Scripture's pneumatological character as an ultimately unified sacred teaching. Finally, neither can "critical" mean excluding the tradition of the Church's appropriation of the text, again because such narrowing would violate the Christological and pneumatological presuppositions, em-

---

95. As J. Augustine Di Noia, O.P., remarks, for the Christian, "faith and reason are interrelated levels of a single, unified theological inquiry, not subsequently correlated bodies of independently generated knowledge." Di Noia, review of *A Marginal Jew: Rethinking the Historical Jesus*, by John P. Meier, *Pro Ecclesia* 2 (1993): 125.

96. Cf. Di Noia's point in his review of Meier's book that the separation of doctrine and history "coincided with growing acceptance of the Kantian critique of metaphysics. The suspiciously metaphysical doctrinal formulae of the tradition were increasingly displaced in the articulation of faith in Christ or reinterpreted in moral, religious, and historical categories." Ibid., 124.

bedded in the texts themselves (written in communal/ecclesial contexts), that enable the Christian reader of the texts to read them as "Scripture."

I would suggest that Augustine's and Aquinas's readings of John 10:1–18, readings which explore and are inserted into the mediations of divine *doctrina,* invite us to reflect on a more fully Christian sense of "critical," one which allows for interpretive development as well as historical inquiry into the modes of scriptural *doctrina.* Augustine's focus on faith and the mediation of faith is further developed by Aquinas's exegetical emphases. On the one hand, Aquinas rarely strays far from Augustine. As will be clear, Aquinas's interpretation of the "door" as Christ alone, of Christ entering in through himself, of predestination, of the "gatekeeper," of Christ's knowledge of his sheep, of the prophets and patriarchs of the Old Testament, of contemplation and action, of the "pasture," of the abundant "life," of the "wolf" and the "hireling," of the participation of human "shepherds" in Christ the "good shepherd," of the "other sheep" as the gentiles, and of Christ freely willing his death—all bear the imprint of Augustine's exegesis.

On the other hand, Aquinas devotes less attention than Augustine to the "seeing" that is faith, and Aquinas leaves out certain elements that belong to Augustine's commentary on the passage, such as Augustine's illuminationist emphasis on Christ as the divine Light/Word speaking to the light/word in us. Aquinas tones down Augustine's critique of the pagan philosophers as "rattling jaws" for not knowing the "end" and does not take up Augustine's references to heretics such as the Donatists and the Apollinarians. Aquinas attends in more detail to the "end" of deification and how this "end" is attained. In this regard, he explores more deeply the authority of Christ as "good shepherd," an authority defined by self-giving love, and he explores the bishops' participation in this authority by being "sent." Similarly he explores more fully how Christ, knowing his "sheep," frees them from sin, sends them out as witnesses to the world, and enables them to move by *imitatio Christi* from meritorious suffering to glory (the pattern of deification). Influenced by Chrysostom and others, he pays more attention to the realities that *mediate* deification, such as Scripture, evangelization, Israel (Moses), the unity of the Church in charity and faith, and Christ's laying down his life—which is not to say, of course, that Augustine does not attend to these realities. In this regard Aquinas displays the influence of the Greek Fathers and the Dionysian-Proclan stream of Neoplatonic thought. Another evident difference lies in the mode by which the two doctors comment upon the text: Augustine's is more rhetorically sophisticated as befits a series of homilies preached in church, while Aquinas generally proceeds more dryly by setting forth the complementary opinions of patristic authorities or by exploring with Aristotelian precision the text in terms of signs, actions, and effects.

Yet were one to stop with the differences, one would miss the point in two ways. First, the similarities are far more extensive than the differences, and indeed the differences themselves are ones of nuance. Reading the two commentaries side by side, one finds a profound agreement between Augustine and Aquinas not only as regards the basic meaning of the text, but also as regards the realities of faith. This credal agreement both flows from and shapes their reading of John 10:1–18. For both, Christ is the incarnate Son of God; God is the Trinity; the Church is one, holy, catholic, and apostolic; the Church is visibly constituted by bishops who, as the successors of the apostles, are sent by Christ; God creates and predestines human beings from eternity; faith, charity, and the sacraments unite human beings to Christ; and so forth. Neither Augustine nor Aquinas could read Christ's words, or the words of the evangelist John, as if these realities were not true. To approach John 10:1–18 without knowing these realities would result in a misreading of almost all aspects of the text, as would—to varying degrees depending upon what truths were missing—bracketing some or all of these realities.

Second, the differences teach us how to read Scripture within a tradition—indeed within the patristic-medieval tradition which is the Catholic tradition of scriptural reading. By examining the differences in light of the similarities, one discovers both the openness of this tradition to development and the key doctrinal foundations that give the tradition its continuity and coherence as ecclesial reading. In developing Augustine's thought, Aquinas brings to bear the resources of the Greek Fathers, Aristotle, and Dionysian-Proclan Neoplatonism, along with his own insight and that of his contemporaries. It would seem reasonable that we might, in developing this patristic-medieval exegetical tradition, follow the same pattern of emphasizing certain points over others and of adding new historical insights (for example, Moloney's concern for the conflict of Jesus with "the Jews," Witherington's probing of the Maccabean overtones).

It will be clear that contemporary Catholic exegetes cannot enter into or develop the patristic-medieval tradition without adhering to the divine realities to which not only Augustine and Aquinas, but also the Catholic Church today, adheres. Indeed, identifying the text as canonical Scripture, in other words as ecclesially located sacred teaching, assists a truly "historical" and "critical" exegesis of Scripture, because of the historical locus of the mediations of God's teaching. Precisely because of this historical locus, every reading of Scripture implicitly or explicitly makes theological and metaphysical claims. No reading is neutral: one cannot bracket the Christological and pneumatological claims of Christian faith without separating one's reading of Scripture from the worldview of the New Testament authors themselves, a worldview rich in its participatory understanding of divine *doctrina,* the mediation of divine realities. As Luke Timothy Johnson has put it,

> The intellectual curiosity that drives the dissection of ancient cultures is in itself entirely legitimate. When the past culture is the world imagined by Scripture, however, something fundamental is revealed by an approach that so deliberately and decisively divides the world examined from the examiner's own world. The supreme virtue of the exegete within this scientific approach is detachment, which is thought to ensure the "otherness" of the text and enable its "objective" analysis. In contrast, the deadly vice of the exegete is subjectivity, a too passionate interest that can lead to the vice of eisegesis, understood as reading contemporary perspectives anachronistically into an ancient and alien world. The methodologically postulated distance between worlds enables the entire paradigm to work. That distance becomes more than methodological when the Bible is read mainly as an academic concern rather than as a matter of personal and community transformation. When read in the assembly of believers gathered in the name of the resurrected Jesus and in the power of the Holy Spirit, it is impossible to pretend that these texts speaking of the resurrected Jesus and the power of the Holy Spirit belong to a foreign and long-ago land. But when read simply as an exercise in historical research within an academy that banishes any explicit confessional stance or speech, the alien character of Scripture is reinforced. The community of readers who might have embodied the imaginative world of Scripture become themselves more and more disembodied—just as the texts of Scripture become more and more fragmented and evaporated into "ideas"—as the analysis of ancient texts is carried out in a context far apart from the practices of piety.[97]

For the patristic-medieval tradition, as we have seen, the "otherness" of the scriptural texts is fundamentally the profound, radical otherness of the divine realities that the texts proclaim. Augustine and Aquinas remind us that the biblical texts contain teachings about the realities of salvation that are more, rather than less, suggestively rich and complex than our own. Such teachings, posing a direct challenge to worldviews outside the influence of *sacra doctrina,*

---

97. Luke Timothy Johnson, "Imagining the World That Scripture Imagines," in Johnson and Kurz, *The Future of Catholic Biblical Scholarship,* 126–27.

must be engaged both "historically" and "critically," but in the fullest sense of those words. As Willie James Jennings observes in this vein, "Jesus' humanity as a fact of history cannot be established apart from a clear reckoning with his divinity."[98] The quest is ultimately not a quest for the texts' origins, but a quest for the Teacher through the participatory—and fundamentally ecclesial and sacramental—mediations of teachers and texts. By receiving the Scriptures ecclesially and thus from within the context of patristic-medieval biblical interpretation, exegetes and theologians may learn to knock more profoundly, in ecclesial and historical modes that are fully "critical," on the scriptural door through which we, as believers, enter the good shepherd's pasture.

98. Willie James Jennings, "Undoing Our Abandonment: Reading Scripture Through the Sinlessness of Jesus. A Meditation on Cyril of Alexandria's *On the Unity of Christ*," *Ex Auditu* 14 (1998): 95.

10

Reading Augustine through Dionysius

Aquinas's Correction of One Platonism by Another

Wayne J. Hankey

Nothing presents more problems for those who would enter the mentality of the medieval philosophical theologian than the task which has been set for this volume. Trying to judge the influence on Thomas Aquinas's doctrine of one of his authoritative ancient sources requires us to surrender, at least provisionally, what we think we know about the authority in question. As heirs of Renaissance and modern philology, and of the modern constructions of the history of philosophy, we will almost certainly have a different, perhaps even opposed, view of the source than a medieval theologian would have had. Ironically, our problem increases with the greater sophistication of the scholastics of the later Middle Ages because their sources became more rich and the mediations of what they understand about their authorities became more complex.

In the twentieth century, we have become aware of how much in form and content moderns impose when they construct their "histories" of philosophy—though mentioning Aristotle, Theophratus, Augustine, Proclus, Simplicius, Averroes, and Aquinas's *De unitate intellectus contra Averroistas* reminds us that the activity itself is part of philosophy and theology in antiquity and the Middle Ages. Our oppositions, for example, between Plato, Platonism, and Neoplatonism will not be made by as well informed a historian as Aquinas. In this he is following one of his most authoritative sources for the history of Platonism, Augustine. Both of them knew a good deal about Platonism but, with the exception of the *Timaeus* for Augustine, neither seems to have known the dialogues.[1] More importantly, in contrast to the tendency in modern histories, Aquinas follows the ancients who seek to make philosophical differences complementary and to see the historical movement as providentially guided. Without reducing them to one another, Aquinas will tend to incorporate the more kataphatic and intellectualist Augustine for whom we know by turning to the ideas in the divine Word within the systematic structures developed by theurgic and apophatic Neoplatonism, where the human soul is turned decisively toward the sensible and material. Thus, Proclus, mediated most authoritatively by the pseudo-Dionysius, helps construct the frame within which Augustine will make his crucially important contributions.[2] Perhaps, most importantly, although Aquinas is careful about the degrees of authority of different kinds of texts, he has little—which is not to say no—sense of the differences between genres, so texts of very different kinds are treated as if they were equally sources for conceptual propositions which figure as positions within the scholastic dialectic. We may indicate something of these problems and complexities by brief examples in respect to the three most important intellectual authorities for Thomas, all of whom are crucial to this paper: Aristotle, Augustine, and the pseudo-Dionysius.[3]

---

1. On Augustine, see Stephen Gersh, "The Medieval Legacy from Ancient Platonism," in *The Platonic Tradition in the Middle Ages: A Doxographic Approach,* ed. Stephen Gersh and Maarten J. F. M. Hoenen (Berlin and New York: Walter de Gruyter, 2002), 24–30; and F. Van Fleteren, "Plato, Platonism," in *Saint Augustine through the Ages: An Encyclopedia,* ed. A. Fitzgerald (Grand Rapids, MI: William B. Eerdmans Publishing Company, 1999), 631–54; on Aquinas, see R. J. Henle, *Saint Thomas and Platonism: A Study of the "Plato" and "Platonici" Texts in the Writings of Saint Thomas* (The Hague: Martinus Nijhoff, 1956), xxi; and my "Aquinas and the Platonists," in Gersh and Hoenen, eds., *The Platonic Tradition in the Middle Ages,* 279–324.

2. See R. D. Crouse, "Augustinian Platonism in Early Medieval Theology," in *Augustine: From Rhetor to Theologian,* ed. Joanne McWilliams (Waterloo, ON: Wilfred Laurier University Press, 1992), 109–20; Giulio D'Onofrio, "The *Concordia* of Augustine and Dionysius: Toward a Hermeneutic of the Disagreement of Patristic Sources in John the Scot's *Periphyseon,*" in *Eriugena: East and West,* ed. Bernard McGinn and Willemien Otten (Notre Dame, IN: University of Notre Dame Press, 1994), 115–40, is a useful survey. On their fundamental differences and the assimilation of Augustinian conceptions to a Dionysian logic, see W. J. Hankey, "Dionysian Hierarchy in St. Thomas Aquinas: Tradition and Transformation," in *Denys l'Aréopagite et sa postérité en Orient et en Occident,* ed. Ysabel de Andia (Paris: Institut d'Études Augustiniennes, 1997), 428–38.

3. For more on how Aquinas treats the history of philosophy and how he understood Aristotle and Dionysius, see my "Thomas's Neoplatonic Histories: His Following of Simplicius," *Dionysius* 20 (2002): 153–78.

Until 1268 and his reading of William of Moerbeke's translation of the *Elements of Theology* by Proclus, Thomas's Aristotle was the author of the *Liber de causis*, a compilation of propositions from the *Elements*, substantially modified by Plotinian retrievals and Islamic monotheism. His advanced education, which began in the syncretistic intellectual atmosphere in Naples, introduced Aquinas to Aristotle from within the long tradition which reconciled the Peripatetic and the Neoplatonic. This is no doubt why he initially judged that the pseudo-Dionysius followed Aristotle philosophically, and why although, later, when he had learned more about what we call Neoplatonism, he both recognized the Platonic character of the Dionysian corpus and, in contrast, judged that Dionysius and Aristotle were together more consonant with the Christian faith than were the *Platonici*. For him, Dionysius was not a sixth-century transmitter of the Neoplatonism of the late Athenian Academy developed in the Iamblichan tradition which he modified by Plotinian retrievals and Christian monotheism, but the first-century convert of St. Paul and the chosen conduit of his mystical wisdom.

Augustine was, with Aristotle, among the first sources of Thomas's knowledge of Platonism. From the beginning of his own writing, Thomas is clear that the bishop of Hippo was *imbutus* with the doctrine of the *Plato*, whom he "follows as far as the Catholic faith permits."[4] In consequence of this limit, he judges that Augustine may recite doctrines he does not assert.[5] Helpfully, unlike the pseudo-Dionysius, Augustine is explicit both about what he finds acceptable, superior to other philosophies, and even necessary for Christian faith within Platonism, and also about what he judges to be erroneous in it.

We need to ask what Aquinas knew about Augustine and how he knew it. Aquinas does not give us as much help in answering these questions as we would have if we were asking about his other greatest authorities. In contradistinction to the *Liber de causis*, the *Divine Names* of Dionysius, and much of Aristotle, Thomas commented on none of Augustine's works. Did he read any of them? One of the most important of his sources for Augustine was the

---

4. Aquinas, *Quaestio disputata de spiritualibus creaturis*, ed. J. Cos, vol. 24, part 2 of *Opera Omnia Sancti Thomae de Aquino* (Rome and Paris: Commissio Leonina-Éditions Du Cerf, 2000), 10, ad 8, 113, lines 515–516: "Augustinus autem, Platonem secutus quantum fides catholica patiebatur."

5. Aquinas, *Questiones disputatae de veritate*, ed. Fratrum Praedicatorum, vol. 22, part 3 of *Opera Omnia Sancti Thomae de Aquino* (Rome: 1973), q. 21, a. 4, ad 3; *Summa theologiae* (Ottawa: Piana, 1953), I, q. 84, a. 5, resp.; ibid., q. 77, a. 5, ad 3. Mark Jordan, *The Alleged Aristotelianism of Thomas Aquinas* (Toronto: Pontifical Institute of Mediaeval Studies, 1992), 40, compares Augustine's judgment of philosophy in *De civitate Dei* with Aristotle as a source for Thomas's relation to Platonism.

Sentences of Peter Lombard, whose character increases the problems involved in answering our questions.

The Lombard's textbook, which "did more than any other text to shape the discipline of medieval scholastic theology,"[6] was so deeply formed structurally, doctrinally, and through quotation by Augustine that Josef Pieper called it "a systematically organized Augustinian breviary."[7] Until the late Middle Ages, it was a principal source for the scholastic knowledge of Augustine; however, it is of the greatest importance to remind ourselves that Lombard had no direct knowledge of more than four of Augustine's books: *De doctrina Christiana,* the *Enchiridion,* the *De diversis quaestionibus 83,* and the *Retractationes.*[8] He depended largely on Augustinian *florilegia,* which were excerpts relative to the interests and needs of their authors and readers from the mountainous corpus of Augustine's writings. The first of these, the *Liber sententiarum,* 392 passages drawn from twenty-four of his writings, was produced by Prosper of Aquitaine, perhaps even before the great bishop of Hippo was dead.[9] Many were compiled as collections of proof texts; and by Thomas's time, eight hundred years and many controversies later, the *florilegia* of various kinds circulating among scholars, countless of them containing passages claiming the authority of Augustine, were so numerous that scholars have lost track of them. If these two Augustinian mountains were not enough to survey in an attempt to locate Thomas's sources, there was a third huge mountain of Augustinian texts which confronted Aquinas: the bastard treatises fathered onto the Latin Christian because his authority far exceeded any other.[10] These false works

6. Marcia Colish, "Peter Lombard," in *The Medieval Theologians,* ed. G. R. Evans (Oxford: Blackwell, 2001), 182.

7. J. Pieper, *Scholasticism: Personalities and Problems of Medieval Philosophy,* trans. R. and C. Winston (London: Faber and Faber, 1961), 98.

8. Jacques-Guy Bougerol, "The Church Fathers and the *Sentences* of Peter Lombard," in *The Reception of the Church Fathers in the West from the Carolingians to the Maurists,* vol. 1, ed. Irena Bachus (Leiden: Brill, 1997), 115. For the later shift, see Eric L. Saak, "The Reception of Augustine in the Later Middle Ages," in Bachus, *The Reception of the Church Fathers,* vol. 1, 367–404.

9. Prosper of Aquitaine, *Liber sententiarum* (Turnhout: Brepols, 1972); and see P.-I. Fransen, "D'Eugippius à Bède le Vénérable. A propos de leurs florilèges Augustiniens," *Révue Bénédictine* 97 (1987): 187–94; and E. Dekkers, "Quelques notes sur les florilèges Augustiniens anciens et médiévaux," *Augustiniana* 40 (1990): 27–44. Dekkers is summarized by J. T. Leinhard, "Florilegia," in *Saint Augustine through the Ages: An Encyclopedia,* 370–71.

10. See B. Blumenkranz, "La survie médiévale de saint Augustin à travers ses apocryphes," in *Augustinus Magister: Congrès international augustinien, Paris, 21–24 Septembre, 1954,* vol. 2 (Paris: Études Augustiniennes, 1954), 1003–18; M. de Kroon, "Pseudo-Augustin im Mittelalter. Entwurf eines Forschungsberichts," *Augustiniana* 22 (1972): 511–30; E. Dekkers, "Le succès étonnant des écrits pseudo-Augustiniens au Moyen Age," in *Fälschungen im Mittelalter. Internationaler Kongress der Monu-*

were often more popular than were the genuine ones. Lombard's *Sentences* contained quotations from these.

I wish to explore how Aquinas deals with a text on the Eucharist falsely attributed to Augustine in Lombard's *Sentences,* a text which expressed doctrines very different from Augustine's and which was drawn from a pseudonymous *florilegium,* the so-called *Sentences of Prosper.* How Thomas treats the pseudonymous text is of particular interest because he comes to a correct understanding of Augustine's doctrine, but, paradoxically, by way of an Aristotelian and Proclean epistemology which has the authority of Dionysius. There is an element of irony here, but it is as nothing compared to other moments in the history of this text: for example, John Wyclif supposed that he was quoting Augustine when he employed it in his invective against Lanfranc, but in fact he is quoting none other than Lanfranc himself![11]

I. The Pseudonymous Text

As I just indicated, the pseudonymous text is from Lanfranc, specifically from his *De Corpore et Sanguine Domini* (*PL* 150, 421–425). Lanfranc is responding to Berengar of Tours and in particular to Berengar's citation and interpretation of a portion of Augustine's *Letter to Boniface*. In consequence, the *De Corpore et Sanguine Domini* generally, as well as the pseudonymous passage we are considering, contain genuine quotations from Augustine.[12] M. Lepin has traced the process by which Lanfranc's work was chopped up, rearranged, abridged, and entered into the Eucharistic controversy for five hundred years, primarily, but not exclusively, as Augustine's *Sentences of Prosper.*[13]

menta Germaniae Historica München, *16–19 September 1986,* vol. 5, *Fingierte Briefe Frömmigkeit und Fälschung, Realienfälschungen* (Hannover, Germany: Hahnsche Buchhandlung, 1988), 361–68; J. Machielsen, "Contribution à l'étude de la pseudépigraphie médiévale en matière patristique. Problèmes d'attribution et de remaniement des textes homilétiques," in *Fälschungen im Mittelalter,* vol. 5, 345–59; J. Machielsen, *Clavis patristica pseudepigraphorum medii aevi,* vol. IA, vol. IIA, and vol. IIB (Turnhout, Belgium: Brepols, 1990–1994); and K. B. Steinhauser, "Manuscripts," *Saint Augustine through the Ages: An Encyclopedia,* 530.

11. For this ironic moment and a treatment of a considerable part of the history of this pseudonymous text from its origins in the eleventh century through to its use among the English Protestant controversialists and their Catholic adversaries of the sixteenth and seventeenth centuries, see my "'Magis . . . Pro Nostra Sentencia': John Wyclif, His Mediaeval Predecessors and Reformed Successors, and a Pseudo-Augustinian Eucharistic Decretal," *Augustiniana* 45 (1995): 213–45.

12. *Epistle* 98.9, PL 33, 363–364; *Corpus Scriptorum Ecclesiasticorum Latinorum,* vol. 34, part 2, ed. Al. Goldbacher (Vienna, 1898), 530–31.

13. M. Lepin, *L'idée du Sacrifice de la Messe d'après les théologiens depuis l'origine jusqu'à nos jours* (Paris: Beauchesne, 1926), 786–97.

Along with many others, Gratian's *Concordantia discordantium canonum,* or *Decretum,* in chapter 48, titled *Sacramentum, et res sacramenti sacrificium ecclesiae conficitur,* of his treatise *De consecratione,* reproduced a text from Lanfranc which Gratian, and almost all of those he followed and who would succeed him, credited to *Augustinus in libro Sentenciarum Prosperi.*[14] The decretum, together with the accompanying gloss, is known from its first words as "Hoc est." "Hoc est" was widely quoted and discussed in the Middle Ages and Early Modernity, and we mention Gratian in particular because Lepin judges that "Gratian, if not Lombard, himself dependent on Gratian, appears to be the source where St. Thomas has taken the beginning ... [of a sentence] from Lanfranc, which the Angelic Doctor attributes, like his predecessors, to St. Augustine."[15] Nonetheless, it was its use by the Master of the *Sentences* which required the scholastic theologians to confront the doctrine of "Hoc est." I translate the decretum as follows (see note 14 above for the Latin):

The sacrifice of the Church is made of two things, in two it remains: in the visible form of the elements and in the invisible flesh and blood of our Lord Jesus Christ; both in the sacrament and in the reality signified by the sacrament, that is the body of Christ, just as the person of Christ stands and is put together out of God and man, since he is true God and true man, for everything contains in itself the nature and truth of those things from which it is made. Now the sacrifice of the Church is made out of two things: the sacrament and the reality signified by the sacrament, that is, the body of Christ. Therefore there is both the sacrament and the reality to which the sacrament refers, that is, the

14. See *Corpus iuris canonici,* vol. 1, ed. A. Friedberg (Lipsis, 1879; Graz: Akademische Druck U. Verlagsanstalt, 1959), pars 3, *De consecratione,* dist. 2, cap. 48, columns 1331 and 1332: "Sacramentum, et res sacramenti sacrificium ecclesiae conficitur. Item Augustinus in libro Sentenciarum Prosperi. Hoc est, quod dicimus, quod omnibus modis approbare contendimus, sacrificium ecclesiae confici duobus, duobus constare: uisibili elementorum specie, et inuisibili Domini nostri Iesu Christi carne et sanguine; et sacramento, et re sacramenti, id est corpore Christi, sicut persona Christi constat et conficitur ex Deo et homine, cum ipse Christus uerus Deus sit, et uerus homo, quia omnis res illarum rerum naturam et ueritatem in se continet, ex quibus conficitur. Conficitur autem sacrificium ecclesiae duobus, sacramento, et re sacramenti, id est corpore Christi. Est igitur sacramentum, et res sacramenti, id est corpus Christi. Item: ?. 1. Caro eius est, quam forma panis opertam in sacramento accipimus, et sanguis eius, quem sub uini specie ac sapore potamus. Caro uidelicet carnis, et sanguis Sacramentum sanguinis; carne et sanguine, utroque inuisibili, spirituali, intelligibili, significatur corpus uisibile Domini nostri Iesu Christi, et palpabile, plenum gratia omnium uirtutum, et diuina maiestate. Item: ?. 2. Sicut ergo celestis panis, qui uere caro Christi est, suo modo uocatur corpus Christi, cum reuera sit sacramentum corporis Christi, illius uidelicet, quod uisibile, quod palpabile, mortale in cruce est positum, uocaturque ipsa carnis inmolatio, que sacerdotis manibus fit, Christi passio, mors, crucifixio, non rei ueritate, sed significanti misterio: sic Sacramentum fidei, quod baptismus intelligitur, fides est."

15. Lepin, *L'idée du Sacrifice,* 797.

body of Christ. Item: 1. There is his flesh, which we receive in the sacrament working in the form of bread, and there is his blood, which we drink under the form and taste of wine. Evidently flesh is sacrament of flesh, and blood is sacrament of blood. By flesh and blood, each invisible, spiritual, intelligible, is signified the body of our Lord Jesus Christ, visible and palpable, full by grace and by divine majesty of all virtues. Item: 2. Just as, therefore, the heavenly bread, which is the true flesh of Christ, is called in its own way the body of Christ, since in very truth it is the sacrament of the body of Christ, namely, of that body which being visible, palpable, and mortal was put on the cross, and just as that immolation of the flesh which is made by the priest's hands is called the passion, death, crucifixion of Christ, not in the very truth of the thing but in a signifying mystery, so the sacrament of faith, that is, baptism, is faith.

Happily, for the purposes of this paper, we do not need to explain the precise logic which compels and gives meaning to "Hoc est."[16] We must, however, follow Lanfranc this far: the mode of the similitude between the sacrament of the altar and the reality it signifies requires for him both a difference, so that the sacrament remains a signifying *figura,* and also an essential identity, so that it is effective *in veritate.* Thus, the sacrifice of the Church is not only of the sacrament as distinguished from its reality, but also of the reality itself of the body and blood of Christ, the *re sacramenti.* The immolation at the hands of the priest is in a signifying mystery, there is no new death of Christ in real fact, but the sacrifice is nonetheless of the reality, not just of the sacramental sign.[17] The second part says that the body is a sacrament of itself, an invisible thing is sacrament of another invisible reality. Or, to put it negatively, sacraments are not just outward and visible signs of inward invisible realities.

For Lanfranc, because of the relations to one another of the sacramental, the heavenly, and the earthly bodies of Christ—clearly distinguished for him—and because of the union in the Eucharistic sacrifice of the sacramental sign and the reality signified thereby—which he identifies as well as distinguishes—the representative, figurative, and mystical immolation in an exter-

---

16. For an explication, see J. de Montclos, *Lanfranc et Bérenger: La controverse eucharistique du xie siècle* (Leuven: Spicilegium sacrum Lovaniense, 1971), 404ff.

17. In so interpreting Lanfranc as teaching a real Eucharistic sacrifice, because of the identity of *sacramentum* and *res sacramenti,* yet a sacrifice which is also figurative and not carnal, I follow Montclos, *Lanfranc et Bérenger,* 410–15, who makes the point more strongly than H. Chadwick, *"Ego Berengarius,"* Journal of Theological Studies 40 (1989): 426–28. J. Pelikan, *The Christian Tradition,* vol. 3, *The Growth of Medieval Theology (600–1300)* (Chicago: University of Chicago Press, 1978), 184–204, gives a survey of the teaching and controversies concerning the real presence in this period and points to the emphasis on the sacrifice. Useful on what this means is G. H. Williams, "The Sacramental Presuppositions of Anselm's *Cur Deus Homo,"* Church History 26 (1957): 265.

nal liturgical action at the priest's hands effects a real sacrifice. In order that this sacrifice make effective and really present for the ever-recurring needs of the sinful world the historical, bodily death of Christ without slaying him again or affecting the impassibility of his glorious and ascended body, the distinction and the identity of liturgical mystery and sacramental reality are both required. He draws the consequences both that the Church offers as her sacrifice the reality to which the sacrament refers and that the body of Christ is a sacrament of itself, signifying and signified. From this derives his final consequence that the invisible is a sacrament of the invisible. All this of Lanfranc came to Bonaventure and Aquinas, as well as to many others, as the position of Augustine, and they perceived it to contradict other texts attributed to him.

The assertion in the first part of "Hoc est" is necessary in order to draw together diverse statements of Augustine. He certainly makes the distinction of sacrament and sacramental reality, and he certainly writes of an offering by the Church of her own reality as contained in Christ's offering of himself.[18] However, the two offerings are never drawn together in the manner of the *Sentences of Prosper.* The second of Lanfranc's assertions and the final consequences he draws do in fact contradict statements of Augustine well known to our authors, for example: "A sign is something which, over and above the specific form which it impresses on the senses, causes some further object to enter our cognition"; "The visible sacrifice is the sacrament, that is, the sacred sign, of the invisible sacrifice"; and "A sacrament is a visible form of invisible grace."[19] I propose to consider how Aquinas deals with the problem this contradiction presents, comparing it to Bonaventure's treatment of the matter in his *Commentary on the Four Books of Lombard's Sentences.*

18. See, for example, Augustine, *In Iohannis Evangelium* 26.11 (*CCSL* 36, 265); Sermon 292, *Ad Infantes de Sacramento* (*PL* 38, 1247); *De civitate Dei* 10.20 (*CCSL* 47, 294); and 22.10 (*CCSL* 48, 828).

19. Augustine, *De doctrina Christiana* 2.1.1 (*CCSL* 32, 32), "Signum est enim res praeter speciem, quam ingerit sensibus, aliud aliquid ex se faciens in cognitionem venire," is found in Lanfranc, *De Corpore et Sanguine,* cap. 12 (*PL* 150, 422 B–C); Gratian, *Decretum,* pars 3, *de cons.,* dist. 2, cap. 33 (Friedberg i, 1324); Lombard, *Sententiae in IV Libris Distinctae,* vol. 2 (Grottaferrata, Italy: Collegii S. Bonaventurae, 1981), lib. 4, dist. 1, quest. 3, 233; Aquinas, *Scriptum super Sententiis Magistri Petri Lombardi,* ed. M. F. Moos, vol. 4 (Paris: P. Léthielleux 1947), lib. 4, dist. 1, quest. 1, art. 1, quaestiuncula 3, arg. 1; Aquinas, *ST* III, q. 60, a. 1, obj. 2. A similar list could be given for Augustine, *De civitate Dei,* 10.5 (*CCSL* 47, 277): "Sacrificium ergo visibile invisibilis sacrificii sacramentum, id est sacrum signum est." There is an important bibliographical note at 232 of vol. 2 of the Grottaferrata edition of Lombard's *Sententiae* (1981). "Sacramentum est invisibilis gratiae visibilis forma" is equally well distributed. It becomes the standard definition and derives from Augustine, *Epistola* 105.3.12 (*CSEL* 34, 604). There are references at Gratian, *Decretum,* pars 3, *de cons.,* dist. 2, cap. 32 (Friedberg i, 1324); Lombard, *Sententiae,* lib. 4, dist. 1, quest. 2 and lib. 4, dist. 8, quest. 6 (Grottaferrata, ii, 232 and 284).

II. Aquinas, Augustine, and Dionysius

Aquinas was only beginning to develop his systematic theology when he commented on the *Sentences,* but, there, despite the use of the *quaestio,* the problematic texts deriving from Lanfranc masking as Augustine had to be dealt with somehow. Aquinas considered them in the *expositio textus* following on his theological questions in proper form and in his *Sentences* commentary. Bonaventure similarly dealt with them in *dubia (dubitationes circa litteram).* With the greater freedom of his *Summa theologiae,* St. Thomas used the Lanfranc texts, ascribing their source to Augustine and Gregory, but only so far as they were necessary for the complete formation of the theology of the sacraments.

Bonaventure certainly faced the contradictions squarely. It is wrong to say, he observes, that the flesh is sacrament of the flesh because nothing is a sign of itself, and if you should respond that in diverse states something can be both sign and what is signified—Lanfranc's way of thinking—Bonaventure draws your attention to the fact that a sign must be better known than that to which it points, so what is invisibly in the sacrament can hardly be a sign of the body which is visible in heaven. Again, if you should say—as Lombard does—that the flesh signifies flesh in the form of bread, Bonaventure observes that it is the bread which is visible and palpable. However, finally, and determinatively for Bonaventure, Augustine says that the visible flesh is signified by the invisible flesh (perhaps the most problematic statement from "Hoc est"). Bonaventure answers by a demonstration that there is a double, not a single, use of figurative speech: "because what belongs to the sign is attributed to the signified and what belongs to the signified is attributed to the sign."[20]

---

20. Bonaventure, *Commentaria in quatuor libros sententiarum Magistri Petri Lombardi,* vol. iv (Quaracchi, 1889), lib. 4, dist. 10, quest. 1, dubia 4, 226–227: "Item quaeritur de hoc quod dicit: 'Caro carnis et sanguis sacramentum est sanguinis.' Videtur enim male dicere, quia nihil idem est signum sui ipsius. *Si tu dicas mihi,* quod idem sub diversis statibus potest esse signum et signatum, ut caro, prout est sub Sacramento, sit signum sui, prout est in caelo, quod videtur dicere littera sequens; *contra:* signum debet esse notius sensibus quam signatum; sed caro, prout est sub Sacramento, est invisibilis et impalpabilis, in caelo visibilis et palpabilis; ergo non est signum eius. 'Si tu dicas,' sicut dicit Magister, quod caro accipitur pro signo carnis, scilicet pane; *contra:* species panis est visibilis et palpabilis; sed Augustinus dicit, quod carne invisibili significatur caro visibilis. Respondeo: Dicendum, quod tropologicus est sermo, nec tantum uno tropo, sed duplici, quia quod est *signi* attribuitur signato, et quod est *signati* attribuitur signo. Species enim panis est signum, quoniam est visibilis, sed caro interius contenta est signatum, quia est invisibilis. Dicere ergo, quod caro invisibilis signat, hoc est dicere, quod species panis, quae est signum carnis invisibilis, signat corpus Christi visibile et palpabile; et illa species panis est caro invisibilis, non quia non videatur, sed quia contentum eius, quod est

The key for him was what is contained in the sacrament. Thus, in the end, his solution was the same as Lanfranc's, and all the texts are saved. Bonaventure's determination was markedly different from what we shall find in Aquinas. Ironically, because the great Franciscan allowed intellectual intuition for humans, Bonaventure proceeded from an Augustinian view of human knowing to a doctrine of the sacraments which contradicts the genuine texts of Augustine.[21] Because Aquinas does not allow for such intuition, his result is the opposite.

As indicated above, in the *Sentences* commentary of Aquinas the problematic texts from Lanfranc posing as Augustine are addressed in the *expositio textus* at the end of distinction 10; they do not figure in his questions on the definition of sacrament in distinction 1. In the *expositio textus,* he gives less attention than does Bonaventure to addressing and reconciling all the texts. For him also there seem to be contradictions in what derives from Lanfranc. In another passage from Lanfranc, Thomas found the statement that "this is and this is not the body,"[22] and he agreed with Bonaventure that the part of "Hoc est" from which Bonaventure started seemed to be "false" because nothing is a sign of itself—for Bonaventure, it seemed to be "badly said" for the same reason. Their agreement is not surprising. Many of their predecessors had been equally troubled, and the gloss on "Hoc est" is occupied with the same problems: the notion of a self-signifying sacrament, a self-signifying body, indeed, with how, as "heavenly," the body signifies at all.[23] Lombard himself makes the fact of a problem evident. Nicholas Häring tells us that the Master of the

caro, est invisibile et intelligibile eatenus, qua ibidem continetur; quasi vellet Augustinus dicere: caro Christi visibilis et palpabilis signatur et continetur a specie panis invisibiliter et intelligibiliter."

21. On the complex, unresolved, unsystematic *"dualisme"* of Bonaventure as compared to Aquinas, see É.-H. Wéber, *Dialogue et dissensions entre saint Bonaventure et saint Thomas d'Aquin à Paris (1252–1273)* (Paris: Vrin, 1974), 140–42; Wéber, *La Personne humaine au xiiie siècle. L'avènement chez les maîtres parisiens de l'acception moderne de l'homme* (Paris: Vrin, 1991), 90–108; and Alain de Libera, "Une anthropologie de la grace. Sur *La Personne humaine au xiiie siècle* d'E.-H. Wéber," *Revue des sciences philosophiques et théologiques* 77 (1993): 241–54.

22. Aquinas, *Scriptum super Sententiis,* ed. Moos (1947), lib. 4, dist. 10, quest. 1, art. 4, quaestiuncula 5, expositio textus (no. 137, 426): "'Ipsum quidem et non ipsum corpus.' Videtur esse contradictio."

23. The gloss reads: "The heavenly sacrament, which truly represents the body of Christ, is called Christ's body, but not in plain speech. Therefore, it is called this 'in a certain way,' not in the truth of the thing, but by a signifying mystery; so this is the sense: it is called the body of Christ, that is, it signifies it" *(Coeleste sacramentum, quod vere repraesentat corpus Christi, dicitur corpus Christi, sed improprie. Unde dicitur, suo modo; sed non rei veritate, sed significante mysterio; ut sit sensus, Vocatur corpus Christi; id est, significat),* in these London printings of the *Decretals:* Francois Fradin (1533); *Apud Hugonem et Haeredes Aemonis à Porta* (1541); I. Ausultus (1559).

Sentences introduces our pseudonymous text with a formula which "generally heralds a troublesome text":

He goes on to tell us that St. Augustine was conscious of the obscurity of his own words *(quia obscure dixerat),* a fact which prompted him (that is, Augustine) to say that "the bread is called the body of Christ, although in reality, it is the *sacramentum* of Christ's Body . . . just as the *sacramentum* of faith is called faith."[24]

In his exposition of the text of the *Sentences,* Aquinas saves the problematic passage about an invisible sacrament of the invisible, not by anything as elaborate as a double allegory, but still by reference to the same key as Bonaventure used, that is, what is contained *(contenta)* in the sacrament. Aquinas writes: "these species [of bread and wine] with the flesh contained are called invisible flesh because under this form [the bread and wine] the flesh of Christ is not seen."[25]

In Thomas's *Summa theologiae,* a head-on confrontation with difficult texts like "Hoc est" could be avoided because the movement of theology was not from text to text, as in *lectio* or exposition, but from question to question. Logical structure, *ordo disciplinae,* dominated. Aquinas took up texts and placed them within his questions so as both to form his question as he willed and to bring out only that aspect of the text which served the completeness and movement of theology. At the height of his powers, he was disposing of a vast and complex philosophical logic which enabled him to balance one text and the position it represented against others, and in fact, the architecture of his thought is constructed by that balancing. When he takes up the question of the definition of sacrament, the changes he carried through in the structure of theological system and the complex balancing of positions in his philosophical logic allow him to put all the elements together in an especially interesting way.

In asking "What is a sacrament?" Aquinas seeks first to determine to which genus it belongs and inquires as to whether it belongs in the category of signs.

---

24. N. M. Häring, "A Study in the Sacramentology of Alger of Liège," *Mediaeval Studies* 20 (1958): 74.

25. Aquinas, *Scriptum super Sententiis,* ed. Moos, (1947), lib. 4, dist. 10, q. 1, a. 4, quaestiuncula 5, expositio textus (no. 139, p. 427): "'Caro carnis, et sanguis sacramentum est sanguinis.' *Videtur hoc esse falsum:* quia nihil est signum sui ipsius. *Et dicendum* quod carnem quae significat, nominat ipsas species, quae sunt signum carnis; et hoc tropice, ut Magister dicit: et ipsae species cum carne contenta dicuntur caro invisibilis, quia sub specie illa caro Christi non videtur. Carnem autem significatam nominat ipsam carnem Christi, secundum quod sub propria forma videtur; unde et 'visibiliter' dicitur."

He introduces, in objection 2 and the *sed contra*—that is, on both sides of the question—two of the very well-known statements of Augustine. One of them defines a sign as sensible, and the other makes sacraments visible signs.[26] This visibility creates problems for sacraments insofar as they are also hidden, and Aquinas determines the article by placing sacraments as "sacred secrets" in the genus of signs but without making sensibility essential.

The second article asks "Whether every sign of a sacred thing is a sacrament?" The question is forced by our text from Lanfranc's *De Corpore et Sanguine*, which lies behind the "some" who, in the *sed contra*, are the sources for this definition. Aquinas supposes them to be supported by the authority of Augustine.[27] Here what is essential about signs is not their sensible aspect, but rather that they lead us from the known to the unknown, and Aquinas emphasizes about sacraments that they make men holy.[28]

In article 3, as to "Whether sacraments are signs of one thing only?" Thomas uses the problematic decretal in order to strengthen further this aspect. The authority in the *sed contra* is *"Augustinus . . . in libro Sententiarum Prosperi."* Its point, taken from what is in fact Lanfranc, is that "in the sacrament of the altar the reality signified is twofold, namely, the true body of Christ and the mystical."[29] By this means, Aquinas introduces the threefold distinction of |the body of Christ necessary to the developments in Eucharistic theology where Lanfranc plays a crucial role: the Eucharistic, the historical, and the glorified body.[30] The effect of the article is to establish that the sacrament

26. *ST* III, q. 60, a. 1, "Quid sit sacramentum," the texts of Augustine are *De doctrina Christiana*, 2.1.1: "signum est quod, praeter speciem quam sensibus ingerit, facit aliquid aliud in cognitionem venire," and *De civitate Dei*, 10.5: "sacrificium visibile invisibilis sacrificii sacramentum, idest sacrum signum, est." Compare *Super Sententiis*, lib. 4, d. 1, q. 1, a. 1, qc. 2, co.: "signum importat aliquod notum quo ad nos, quo manuducimur in alterius cognitionem . . . etiam si non sit res cadens sub sensu."

27. *ST* III, q. 60, a. 2, s.c.: "Sed quidam definiunt sacramentum per hoc quod est sacrae rei signum, et hoc etiam videtur ex auctoritate Augustini supra inducta. Ergo videtur quod omne signum rei sacrae sit sacramentum."

28. *ST* III, q. 60, a. 2: "Signa proprie dantur hominibus, quorum est per nota ad ignota pervenire. Et ideo proprie dicitur sacramentum quod est signum alicuius rei sacrae ad homines pertinentis, ut scilicet proprie dicatur sacramentum secundum quod nunc de sacramentis loquimur, quod est signum rei sacrae inquantum est sanctificans homines." Compare *Super Sententiis*, lib. 4, d. 1, q. 1, a. 1, qc. 4.

29. *ST* III, q. 60, a. 3, s.c.: "Quod in sacramento Altaris est duplex res significata, scilicet corpus Christi verum et mysticum, ut Augustinus dicit in libro Sententiarum Prosperi."

30. Lepin, *L'idée du Sacrifice*, 765: "While for St. Augustine there are three manners of understanding 'the Christ': as God, as God made man, and as identified with the entire body of the Church, of which he is the Head, Paschasius speaks of three manners of understanding 'the body of Christ,' which is entirely different. And the explanation which he gives to his thought is in effect very divergent: the body of Christ is able to be: his natural body, his Eucharistic body, his mystical body: the Church."

is the cause of holiness and in what sense. The sacrament sanctifies because it stands in relation both to the historical body of Christ, where the passion and death securing our salvation occurred, and also to the glorious body, in mystical union with which our hope lies. The essence of sacramentality consists in its being a sanctifying cause:

The very fact that the term "sacrament" signifies the reality which sanctifies means that it should signify the effect produced. For this notion is understood in the very concept of sanctifying cause just as sanctifying.[31]

The fourth article of this question, "Whether a sacrament is always a sensible thing?" makes clear that, at this point, we have established only that a sacrament is a sign of a sacred thing, inasmuch as through it humans are sanctified. The question of its sensibility remains unsettled. It must now be faced. Augustine's authority is prominent here, but once again Aquinas places him on both sides of the question, in objection 3 and in the *sed contra!* Crucially, Aquinas's philosophical authority for understanding the relevant logic is Aristotle and the determining sacred authority is Dionysius the pseudo-Areopagite.[32] This is by no means the only place where Dionysius's Iamblichan Platonism is used in this context as an authority for the necessity of the human turn to the sensible. In his *Commentary on the Sentences,* when Aquinas is considering whether sacraments were needed before humans sinned, Dionysius is cited to the effect that knowing by way of the sensible is our natural way of cognition.[33] Again, near the end of his life in his *Exposition of John's Gospel,* when Aquinas is considering the words of our Lord to Nicodemus, "you must be born again of wa-

---

31. *ST* III, q. 60, a. 3, ad 2: "Dicendum quod sacramentum in hoc quod significat rem sanctificantem, oportet quod significet effectum, qui intelligitur in ipsa causa sanctificante prout est sanctificans."

32. *ST* III, q. 60, a. 4: "Est autem homini connaturale ut per sensibilia perveniat in cognitionem intelligibilium. Signum autem est per quod aliquis devenit in cognitionem alterius. Unde, cum res sacrae quae per sacramenta significantur, sint quaedam spiritualia et intelligibilia bona quibus homo sanctificatur, consequens est ut per aliquas res sensibiles significatio sacramenti impleatur, sicut etiam per similitudinem sensibilium rerum in divina Scriptura res spirituales nobis describuntur. Et inde est quod ad sacramenta requiruntur res sensibiles, ut etiam Dionysius probat, in I cap. caelestis hierarchiae."

33. *Super Sententiis,* ed. Moos (1947), lib. 4, d. 1, q. 1, a. 2, qc. 2, arg. 2 (no. 57, p. 17): "Praeterea. Dionysius in I cap. Eccles. Hierar., . . . assignat hanc causam institutionis hujusmodi sensibilium figurarum in sacramentis; quia per hujusmodi materiale elementum melius reducimur ad spiritualia, propter connaturalitatem cognitionis nostrae ad sensibilia. Sed homo in statu innocentiae materialis erat, et ex sensibilibus cognitionem accipiens, propter quod etiam in paradiso dicitur positus ad operandum, ut naturales vires rerum experiretur. Ergo et tunc indiguit hujusmodi sacramentis."

ter and the Holy Spirit," Dionysius reappears.[34] A sensible sign is necessary to
the sacrament of regeneration because "as Dionysius says, the divine wisdom
orders everything so that each is provided for according to its own condition."
Humanity is *"cognoscitivus,"* and "the natural mode of this kind of cognition is
that spiritual things should be known through sensible things, because all our
knowing begins from sense."

The question as to whether something sensible is essential to a sacrament
is not and could not have been settled for Aquinas on the authority of Augustine. In article 4 of question 60 of the *Summa,* he is represented both as thinking that sensible things are the least of things "without which humans are able
to live well," and also that sacraments involve a physical element and the coming of the divine Word. These are, both of them, genuine statements of Augustine, difficult to reconcile.[35] Thus the matter turns, rather, on the question
of human nature. If humans have intellectual intuition, then they do not need
sensible signs to lead them to the holy. On this aspect of anthropology, Augustine and his followers are, at best, ambiguous. As heirs of one tradition of
Neoplatonism, they seem to allow for an intellectual intuition independent
of sensation. Dionysius is Aquinas's source for another tradition of Neoplatonism affecting Western medieval theology, a tradition cohering with what
Aquinas will learn from Aristotle. For it we humans cannot come to the divine
except through the sensible. And so, signs which would lead us must be sensible, not because signs are, by nature, sensible but rather because what God
would use to make us holy must be adapted to our condition. By this route we
come back to affirm the genuine text of Augustine, the *De doctrina Christiana*
text which appeared in the first objection of the first article in this question:

And hence what are principally called signs are what are offered to the senses, as Augustine says in the second book of *De doctrina Christiana,* "a sign is something which, over

---

34. Aquinas, *Super Evangelium S. Ioannis Lectura,* ed. R. Cai (Turin/Rome: Marietti, 1951), cap.
3, lect. 4, no. 443: "Propter humanam cognitionem: nam, sicut Dionysius dicit, divina sapientia ita
omnia ordinat ut unicuique provideat secundum modum suae conditionis. Homo autem est naturaliter cognoscitivus; oportet ergo eo modo dona spiritualia hominibus conferri, ut ea cognoscant; 1
Cor. 2:12: ut sciamus quae a Deo donata sunt nobis. Naturalis autem modus huius cognitionis est ut
spiritualia per sensibilia cognoscat, cum omnis nostra cognitio a sensu incipiat. Oportuit ergo ad hoc
quod intelligamus id quod spirituale est in hac regeneratione, quod esset in ea aliquid sensibile et materiale, scilicet aqua: per quod intelligamus quod sicut aqua lavat et purgat corporaliter exterius, ita et
per Baptismum homo lavatur et purgatur interius spiritualiter."

35. *ST* III, q. 60, a. 4, obj. 3: "'Res sensibiles sunt minima bona sine quibus homo recte vivere potest,'" and ibid., s.c.: "Augustinus dicit super Ioan: 'Accedit verbum ad elementum, et fit sacramentum.'"

and above the specific form which it impresses upon the senses, causes some further object to enter our cognition." Intelligible effects, however, do not have the essential reason of signs unless they are made known through some sign.[36]

Because the invisible body is not itself sensible, it could then only be called a sacrament "insofar as it is signified through something sensible" *(quodammodo sacramenta inquantum sunt significata per aliqua sensibilia).* Augustine's definition is saved from its reversal by Lanfranc through an Aristotelian and Dionysian philosophical theology.

In sum, the pseudo-Augustinian *Sentences of Prosper* are not rejected as such, but their teaching is not able to overcome, for Aquinas, Augustine's genuine definitions of sign and of sacrament as visible sign. By an Iamblichan-Dionysian Neoplatonic anthropology Aquinas freed himself from the confused condition of the Augustinian textual tradition. The theology of the sacraments is determined by Aquinas's fundamental understanding of God and the human. The theological anthropology which provides a place for Augustine's definitions is very different from that of Augustine himself; indeed it is the historically actual alternative in the Middle Ages and, perhaps, the only philosophically possible alternative.[37]

---

36. *ST* III, q. 60, a. 4, ad 1: "Effectus autem sensibilis per se habet quod ducat in cognitionem alterius, quasi primo et per se homini innotescens, quia omnis nostra cognitio a sensu oritur. Effectus autem intelligibiles non habent quod possint ducere in cognitionem alterius nisi inquantum sunt per aliud manifestati, idest per aliqua sensibilia. Et inde est quod primo et principaliter dicuntur signa quae sensibus offeruntur: sicut Augustinus dicit in II De doctrina Christiana, ubi dicit quod 'signum est enim res praeter speciem, quam ingerit sensibus, facit aliquid aliud in cognitionem venire.' Effectus autem intelligibiles non habent rationem signi nisi secundum quod sunt manifestati per aliqua signa. Et per hunc etiam modum quaedam quae non sunt sensibilia, dicuntur quodammodo sacramenta, inquantum sunt significata per aliqua sensibilia."

37. On these alternatives in the Middle Ages, see the selections from M.-D. Chenu, *La théologie au douzième siècle,* translated as *Nature, Man, and Society in the Twelfth Century,* trans. Jerome Taylor and Lester K. Little (Chicago/London: University of Chicago Press, 1968), 20–26, 60–64, 119–28; my "The Place of the Proof for God's Existence in the *Summa theologiae* of St. Thomas Aquinas," *Thomist* 46 (1982): 380–93; and Richard Schenk, "From Providence to Grace: Thomas Aquinas and the Platonisms of the Mid-Thirteenth Century," *Nova et Vetera* 3:2 (Spring 2005): 307–20, parts 3 and 4.

Wisdom Eschatology in Augustine and Aquinas

Matthew L. Lamb

The theme "Aquinas the Augustinian" provides an occasion to overcome some contemporary stereotypes that pit a Platonic St. Augustine against an Aristotelian St. Thomas Aquinas. Augustine, in this scenario, is a world-despising rigorist wrapped up in a subject-centered, self-communicative approach to questions, whereas Aquinas is identified with a world-affirming, object-centered metaphysical approach.[1] There are differences between the two theological giants. But the differences are far more complementary than contradictory. The erection of contradictory contrasts has occasioned misreadings by contemporary writers unaware of the Cartesian or Kantian lenses through which they project onto the ancient texts typically modern and postmodern dualisms of subject and object.[2]

1. A recent example of a stereotype of Augustine is in James O'Donnell, *Augustine: A New Biography* (New York: Harper & Row, 2005). This work illustrates that a study of classical languages must be complemented by serious philosophical and theological study that knows the realities being expressed in the verbal signs; otherwise the interpreter reads back into the ancient texts his own prejudices. The use of such a stereotypical contrast between Augustine and Aquinas can also be seen to underline the popularized caricature of Pope Benedict XVI's theological vision in Joseph Komonchak, "The Church in Crisis: Pope Benedict's Theological Vision," *Commonweal* 132 (2005): 11–14.

2. On reading too much of Descartes back into Augustine, cf. Stephen Menn, *Descartes and Augustine* (Cambridge: Cambridge University Press, 1998); and Charles Taylor, *The Sources of the Self: The Making of Modern Identity* (Cambridge, MA: Harvard University Press, 1989), 127–58. Paul Ricoeur in his *Time and Narrative*, trans. K. McLaughlin and D. Pellauer (Chicago: University of Chicago Press, 1984–1988), vol. 1, 5–30, vol. 3, 12–22, contrasts Augustine and Aristotle, while giving a neo-Kantian reading of Augustine in which the dialectic of interiority and exteriority is lost in favor of "enigmas within enigmas within paradox." What for Augustine is the fullness of life becomes for Ricoeur a

These supposed dualisms and oppositions fade away in the reflections of Augustine and Aquinas on eschatology. Augustine is very interested both in the joys of the beatific communion with God and to show that faith in the resurrected bodies of the damned and the blessed is not irrational. Against Platonists, Porphyry, and others, Augustine discourses at length, giving numerous examples from Pliny, Tacitus, Virgil, Varro, and others of unexplained physical and bodily events—all with the purpose of indicating how his contemporaries believed all sorts of wonders. So why would they think it impossible for resurrected human bodies to enjoy the bliss of heaven or the pains of hell in eternity? Aquinas shares in these questions, addressing them with a far more developed set of metaphysical categories than Augustine.

Because eschatology depends upon a faith-illumined knowledge and wisdom about the *telos* or end of the whole of redeemed creation, the first section deals with what I term their wisdom eschatology. The second half will sketch their reflections on the resurrection of the body and last judgment.

Augustine's Graced Ascent to Wisdom

Augustine narrates in books 5 through 7 of his *Confessions* the fundamental importance in his own life of the intellectual conversion in which he came to conceive spiritual substances as real. Reality is not confined to material or corporal things. Yet this intellectual conversion had not yet transformed his living and his mind. Precisely because the Platonic books called for such a *"conversio,"* a turning toward intelligence and reason, his life could be true to that conversion only when he discovered it, not as unreachable goal—for Augustine might know the good but still could not live it—but, as he writes:

I should have become responsive to You [oh God] through your Books with my wounds healed by the care of your fingers, I might be able to discern the difference between presumption and confession, between those who see what the goal is but do not see the way, and the Way [Christ] which leads to that blessed fatherland wherein we are meant not only to discern but to dwell.[3]

"limit idea" which is replete with "ontological negativity" (vol. 1, 25–26). Indeed, Ricoeur terms Augustine's notion of God's eternity as *"totum esse praesens,"* "the highest form of negativity." But for Augustine this notion of eternity is creative, not negative. On the tendency to put Aquinas in a "scholasticism" that includes Descartes and Kant, see a study done with John Dewey's assistance by Joseph L. Perrier, *The Revival of Scholastic Philosophy in the Nineteenth Century* (New York: Columbia University Press, 1909).

3. *Confessions*, 7, 20.

Only when his intellectual conversion was taken up into the grace of his conversion to Christ Jesus did the infinite spiritual reality of the Word Incarnate enable him to overcome the disordered desires that darkened and distracted his mind. Only then did the Triune Divine Presence infuse Augustine's life; love of the absolute good God enabled Augustine to live morally. God as infinite, divine *esse, nosse, et amare,* as the creator of all things, is the Presence creating, sustaining, and redeeming them. The Triune Divine Presence is both utterly transcendent and immanent—more intimate to Augustine and all human beings than he or they are to themselves.[4] The truth of faith enabled Augustine through the gift of the Holy Spirit to love God with God's own love. It is the Divine Presence—Truth Itself—that is the touchstone for the reality and truth in all of existence, including all of Augustine's thoughts and actions, his life both here and hereafter.

The *Confessions* of Father, Son, and Spirit situate Augustine's sins of pride and presumption in a narration of humility and forgiveness with an intimacy opened into the very life and love of the Triune God. Personal identity is experienced as communion in a most profound conversation between Augustine and God and all that God has created and redeemed. The movement of Augustine's soul from *exteriora* to *interiora* never leaves the *exteriora* behind, just as the move from *interiora* to *superiora* never leaves the *interiora* behind.[5] In each movement of the soul what is higher takes up the lower into its wiser context. History, both Augustine's personal history as well as all of human history, is constituted by this threefold movement toward conscious conversation and communion with the Triune God.

History is most fully realized in the eschatological new heavens and new earth of the City of God in mutual communion and presence with all that is. Narrating his descent into disordered desire and pride, Augustine illustrates how sin cuts one off from genuine friendship and communion. He does not give the names of his friends and lovers, for he realized that he did not love them as they truly are in God, but that they were only objects of his disordered egoistic presumption. Only in his graced ascent to God does he realize how he cannot know who he is without knowing and loving others in communion with the divine *"spiritalis substantia"* creating man in his own image

4. *Confessions,* 3, 6; *Enarrationes in Psalmos* Ps. 118, sermo 22.

5. *De Trinitate,* 14, 3; *De duabus animabus,* 19; *Enarrationes in Psalmos* Ps. 145, sermo 5; *Epistulae* 55, 34, 2; 40, 44, 2; *Confessions,* 7, 17; 10, 6; 11, 6.

and likeness as a substantial unity of body and soul. It is the unity-identity-whole of each human being who is called to an eternal destiny.

Augustine reflects on the eschatological fulfillment of creation in which the blessed will enjoy the supreme *interiora* of the Triune God. "No evil will be there, and no good thing lacking." Nor is the *exteriora* abandoned, for the risen will enjoy the vision of God, the epiphanic radiance of the Triune God. "Wherever we turn the spiritual eyes of our bodies we shall discern, by means of our bodies, the incorporeal God directing the whole universe"—the whole of creation will be iconic of the Triune God. True eternal glory and justice and goodness radiant with the holiness of Father, Son, and Spirit will suffuse the whole of the new heavens and the new earth.[6]

A Clarification by Contrast

To clarify this wisdom perspective of Augustine by way of contrast, Pierre Manent indicates how the notion of substantial unity, derived from the Greeks and so central in Catholicism, was precisely what the moderns such as Descartes, Hobbes, Spinoza, Locke, and Rousseau would "implacably destroy."[7] Nature as created by God is abolished only to be handed over to be constructed by man who, in his presumption, assumes the throne and lordship of history. Manent pointedly writes:

In the beginning, the world was without form and void, without laws, arts, or sciences, and the spirit of man moved over the darkness. Such, in brief, are the first words man speaks to himself when, rejecting alike both Christian law and pagan nature, he decides to receive his humanity only from himself and undertakes to be the author of his own genesis. Hobbes, Locke, and Rousseau give us three synoptic versions of this genesis that all proclaim the same good news.[8]

Rousseau's own *Confession* illustrates this presumption of self-creation whereby his own ego proclaims its uniqueness with a distant nature providing only the stage, the places, and dates of his egophany, as Voegelin aptly terms it.[9] Gone is the conversion to and conversation with God as the touchstone

6. *De civitate Dei,* XXII, 29–30.

7. Pierre Manent, *The City of Man,* trans. Marc LePain (Princeton, NJ: Princeton University Press, 1998), 111–55.

8. Ibid., 183.

9. Jean-Jacques Rousseau, *Confessions,* trans. J. M. Cohen (New York: Penguin, 1985), 17, 606: "My purpose is to display to my kind a portrait in every way true to nature, and the man I shall por-

of reality. Instead Rousseau's touchstone is his own solitary ego *(res cogitans)* and the dates and places *(res extensa)*. Rousseau's own identity is his own creation—nature only provides the mold—his book is the proclamation of who *he* is, not his friends, certainly not his mistresses and the offspring he quickly dispatched to orphanages. So he concludes his *Confessions* with the egophanic assertion that if anyone disagrees that he is an honorable man, that person ought to be "stifled." Reality is sensed as dated and placed. His conscious self-presence is contracted into the walls of his own monadic consciousness as he acts out his historical self-creation on the stage of a sensate world of dates and places whose significance he seeks to define by his own will.

Wisdom is being eclipsed by this presumption. Rousseau's self-presence is caught up in ever more elaborate rationalizations for his "l'amour-propre" that can never be satisfied.[10] If, for Augustine, the whole of creation and history is fulfilled in the communion of the blessed in eternal life, Rousseau rejects this sapiential view for a historicism truncated to his own ego presumption. Historical reality is left to externally observable dates and places, *res extensa*, and his egophanic self-absorption, *res cogitans*.

If Rousseau tended to explore the presumption of the *res cogitans*, Spinoza found a way of reducing the meaning of the Bible to a textual *res extensa*. His *Theological Political Treatise* laid foundations for historical-critical methods of biblical exegesis by doing to the Bible what was being done to nature: "I may sum up the matter by saying that the method of interpreting Scripture does not widely differ from the method of interpreting nature—in fact, it is almost the same."[11] Such an interpretative study of the Scripture restricts itself to the texts alone. No appeal can be made to faith, for that is private and personal, sharply separated from reason. Faith plays no role in the interpretation of Scripture.

Spinoza deconstructs the sapiential approach to Scripture in two decisive

---

tray will be myself. Simply myself . . . I am made unlike anyone I have ever met; I will even venture to say that I am like no one in the whole world. I may be no better, but at least I am different. Whether Nature did well or ill in breaking the mold in which she formed me, is a question that can only be resolved after the reading of my book." On egophany, cf. Eric Voegelin, *Anamnesis,* ed. and trans. Gerhart Niemeyer (Notre Dame, IN: University of Notre Dame Press, 1978), 97–118. On Rousseau's distortions of Augustine, cf. Paul J. Archambault, "Rousseau's Tactical (Mis)Reading of Augustine," *Symposium* 41 (1987): 6–14.

10. Jean-Jacques Rousseau, "L'amour de soi, qui ne regarde qu'à nous, est content quand nos vrais besoins sont satisfaits; mais l'amour-propre, qui se compare, n'est jamais content et ne saurait l'être, parce que ce sentiment, en nous préférant aux autres, exige aussi que les autres nous préfèrent à eux, ce qui est impossible."

11. *Theological Political Treatise* (New York: Dover), 99.

steps: 1) Do not treat the Bible as a whole; do not treat books of the Bible as wholes; break up the text into discrete parts. One text is to find its meaning only by relation to other texts. A universal rule is to accept as meanings of the texts only what anyone can perceive from studying the text as a *res extensa.* 2) The truth question is explicitly excluded from interpretations of the Bible. The texts are not to be taken as true when they are referring to any realities not perceptible by the human senses. Spinoza makes clear that biblical interpretation does not concern itself with the truth of the texts, but only with perceptible meanings.[12] So the meaning of an eschatological or apocalyptic verse can only be answered by reference to another text, and any truth questions must be resolutely stifled.

Challenge to Recover Augustine's Wisdom Eschatology

Recovering an eclipsed wisdom is no easy task. The acquisition of metaphysical wisdom must face the daunting tasks of properly ordering the sciences to manifest the integral heuristic and open relations among them. Theological wisdom depends upon such a metaphysical wisdom, as Pope John Paul II indicates in *Fides et ratio,* yet it also requires a wisdom this world and all human effort cannot attain, the absolutely supernatural gift of wisdom and its revelation in the visible and invisible missions of the Word Incarnate and Holy Spirit carried forward in the sacramental sanctifying, doctrinal teaching, and apostolic governing of the Church.[13] As Augustine himself wrote in *De quantitate animae:*

What is divinely and singularly handed on in the Catholic Church . . . is that only the divine Creator is to be worshiped from Whom, through Whom and in Whom all things exist. The unchangeable principle, unchangeable wisdom, unchangeable charity is the one true and perfect God Who never was not, never will not be, and never will be other than He is. Nothing is more hidden [*secretius*] and nothing more present [*praesentius*].[14]

12. The Bible and nature are cut up into parts; there is no given whole, only fragments to compare with other fragments. Any grouping of fragments or parts is arbitrary. As Newton's mechanics sought only three-dimensional perceptible motions, so Spinoza's canons of interpretation recognize only those perceptible textual meanings found in the Scriptures as a perceptible book. *Theological Political Treatise,* 101: "We are to work not on the truth of passages, but solely on their meaning. We must take special care, when we are in search of the meaning of a text, not to be led away by our reason insofar as it is founded on principles of natural knowledge (to say nothing of prejudices): in order not to confound the meaning of a passage with its truth, we must examine it solely by means of the signification of the words, or by a reason acknowledging no foundation but the Scriptures themselves."

13. John Paul II, *Fides et ratio,* no. 83, etc.

14. Augustine, *De quantitate animae,* 34, no. 77.

Within this context, I shall spell out some elements in what I call the sapiential eschatology of Augustine and, in the next subsection, that of Aquinas.

Augustine sees the *"exteriora, interiora, et superiora"* held together in the eternal creating, sustaining, and redeeming presence of the Triune God. To understand Augustine's notion of divine presence—and the human presence *(interiora)* that is the analogue—it is necessary to undergo the process of intellectual, moral, and religious conversion that he narrates. There is needed, therefore, a dialectical discernment whereby Augustine's achievement is not simply reduced to textual comparisons. A major criterion for the intellectual aspect of Augustine's ongoing conversion is his overcoming the limitations of materialism and naive realism. It would be a mistake, in my judgment, to reduce, as Peter Brown does, the way of life his intellectual conversion demanded to a career change "which everyone could understand."[15]

By adverting to the nature of intelligently knowing the truth, Augustine understood that the eternal divine presence creates and sustains the totality of time in all its concrete particularity and universality. Eternity does not denigrate time, but creates it. Augustine presents God as *"totum esse praesens,"* the fullness of Being as Presence freely creating, sustaining, and redeeming the universe and all of human history in the Triune Presence. All extensions and durations, all past, present, and future events, are present in the immutable and eternal understanding, knowing, and loving who are Father, Word, and Spirit. The eternal God creates the universe in the totality of its spatio-temporal reality. There is no before or after in God's eternal presence.[16]

Wisdom Eschatology of Aquinas

The greatest contribution of Aquinas to eschatology is his profound analysis of beatitude as the fulfillment of the deepest desires of intelligent crea-

15. This is the approach in Peter Brown, *Augustine of Hippo: A Biography* (Berkeley: University of California Press, 1967), 101–14. Brown writes on p. 101: "Augustine's reading of the Platonic books had done one thing which everyone could understand: they had brought Augustine to a final and definitive 'conversion' from a literary career to a life 'in Philosophy.'" This tends to reduce intellectual conversion to no more than a career change. It is unfortunate that so influential a biography could miss the depths of what was so central to Augustine's life. Only those who similarly undergo an intellectual conversion can understand what it means. Note Ernest Fortin's similar criticism of the biography in *The Birth of Philosophic Christianity* (Lanham, MD: Rowman & Littlefield Publishers, 1996), 307–9.

16. Cf. Augustine, *Confessions*, 11, 10–13; also Frederick Crowe, "Rethinking Eternal Life: Philosophical Notions from Lonergan," *Science et Esprit* 45 (1993): 25–39, and 45 (1993): 145–59.

tures and the whole of creation. Aquinas spelled out in careful cognitive and metaphysical terms the full implications of St. Augustine's narration of the soul's movement from *exteriora* to *interiora* to *superiora*.[17] Eternal beatitude in the beatific vision contextualizes Aquinas's eschatology within the orders of wisdom so fundamental to his entire speculative theology. Because he could unite the *exteriora* and *interiora* to the *superiora* Aquinas was able to show the intelligibility of the resurrection of the body and the *telos* of the whole material universe in the whole Christ, Head and members.

Aquinas offers a speculative precision to Augustine's more meditative reflections by calling attention to the "order of wisdom." Divine Being is Infinite Act and Infinite Wisdom, so that "in God his operation is his substance; thus, as his substance is eternal, so is his action. But it does not follow that an operational effect is eternal, but that the effect is according to the order of wisdom, which is the principle of [divine] operation."[18] Divine Wisdom can be known by intelligent creatures in ever fuller ways according to how they participate in the Divine Wisdom or Divine Light. Indeed, the Divine Wisdom is the Triune God knowing and loving Himself as Father, Son, and Holy Spirit, and knowing and loving all else into being as finite participations of the divine Trinitarian being.

A sapiential eschatology overcomes tendencies toward instrumentalizing both nature and divine revelation. Neither Augustine nor Aquinas succumbed to dualisms of soul and body as two natures with a subjectivist mind *(res cogitans)* and an objectivist matter *(res extensa)* that underpin instrumental rationality and so derail modern efforts at understanding eschatology.[19] This dualism is rooted in the modern failure to appreciate, as Aquinas's sapiential eschatology does, how the revelation of eschatology in Holy Scripture supernaturally fulfills the finality of the created universe rather than simply destroying and negating it in a final conflagration, as if that were all. The trials of the end time are not the final act in the drama of human history but the birth pangs to the

---

17. St. Augustine, *Confessions,* 1, 1. See also Jean-Pierre Torrell, *Saint Thomas d'Aquin: maître spiritual* (Fribourg: Éditions Universitaires de Fribourg, 1996), 456–69.

18. *In I Sententiis,* 8, 3, 1, ad 4: "In Deo autem operatio sua est sua substantia: unde sicut substantia est aeterna, ita et operatio. Sed non sequitur operationem operatum ab aeterno, sed secundum ordinem sapientiae, quae est principium operandi." See also ibid., 35, 1, 5, ad 3; *De veritate,* 23, 2; *De potentia,* 1, 1, ad 8.

19. See Rudolf Bultmann, *History and Eschatology* (New York: Harper & Row, 1962), who presents the problem of eschatology as a doctrine of the destruction of the world, only to turn eschatological passages into a subjectivist existential "now time" of the believer.

eternal consummation of the universe and history in the kingdom of God.[20]

The blessed know the divine wisdom that redeems us through the Word Incarnate and why this wisdom chose not to remove evil through power, but to transform evil into good through the mysterious life, death, and resurrection of Jesus Christ. This beatific wisdom will completely fulfill the most profound desires of our minds and hearts. The specific desire of human nature is to know truth and love the good. We desire to understand everything, knowing both individual things and all things. There is no opposition between the universal and the particular, the individual person and the human race. The light of reason is elevated and healed by the light of charity-informed faith; this in turn is elevated by the light of glory. All are ever-higher created participations in the Divine Eternal Light.[21]

One of the great joys of the beatific vision will be finally to understand the beauty and wisdom of each and every thing that has occurred in one's life, in the lives of loved ones, and indeed in the whole of human history. The blessed will understand why God allowed evil and sin with all the histories of human suffering and how God's wisdom and Christ's redemptive mission transform that evil and suffering into the glory of eternal bliss. This understanding will be such that even the most insignificant event will be finally intelligible within the beauty of the whole of creation. All of the most painful questions and "whys" that spring from the countless histories of suffering, all will be answered in the joy of the beatific vision. As the risen Christ's glorified body had the wounds of his passion, so the blessed will understand that God's wisdom triumphs over sin and suffering. This wisdom will also manifest the mercy and justice of any damned in hell.[22] The special gifts and auras of each of the blessed will show forth the harmony and beauty of the whole of creation in the symphonic glory of the entire created universe.[23]

The Resurrection of the Whole Body of Christ

Aquinas was known for his profound analysis of the knowledge of the blessed, bringing out the *interiora* of Augustine. But Augustine was also con-

---

20. Contemporary scholarship is indicating how apocalyptic eschatology involves transformative symbols of the transcendent; see Brian Daley, *The Hope of the Early Church* (Peabody, MA: Hendrickson Publishers, 2003); and Bernard McGinn, *Visions of the End* (New York: Crossroad, 1979).

21. See *De veritate*, 18, 1, ad 1; *ST* I, 84, 5; *De Trinitate*, 1, 3, ad 1.

22. See *ST*, suppl., qq. 93, 94.

23. See *ST*, suppl., qq. 95, 96.

cerned, much against the Platonists and Manicheans, to show the reasonableness of faith in the resurrection of the body. Aquinas also insisted on this important doctrine of divine and Catholic faith. The *exteriora* would, together with the *interiora*, be transformed in the "new heavens and the new earth" of the kingdom of God, the *superiora*.

During his earthly life Jesus Christ in his human knowledge knew by the light of glory what faithful Christians believe because of his teachings.[24] The more we love someone, the more we suffer in his or her sufferings. The more we love someone, the more our hearts are broken when they offend us. Divine Wisdom chose to redeem us, not by removing evil through power, but by transforming evil into good through suffering. So the Word became incarnate. He whose infinite love creates all things, loving them into existence, becomes man to redeem sinful humans through his passion, death, and resurrection.

It is in this context that Augustine first mentions the resurrection in his *De moribus ecclesia catholicae* where, having cited Ephesians 3:14–19 and 1 Corinthians 15:22, he goes on to write of the triumph of the martyrs' love:

> knowing that by using it [the body] well and wisely, its resurrection and reformation will, by the divine help and decree, be without any trouble made subject to its [the soul's] authority. But when the soul turns to God wholly in this love, it knows these things and so will not only disregard death, but will even desire it. Then there is the great struggle with pain. But there is nothing, though of iron hardness, which the fire of love cannot subdue. And when the mind is carried up to God in this love, it will soar above all torture free and glorious, with wings beauteous and unhurt, on which chaste love rises to the embrace of God.[25]

The use of *"reformatio"* with resurrection anticipates his later reflections on how the martyrs' faith and love for Christ unite their sufferings to those of Christ on the Cross.[26] The wise power of God is such that He can trans- or reform body and soul into an eternal kingdom of justice and love as He raised up Christ Jesus.[27] Augustine's wisdom eschatology tends to move from the concrete histories of the sufferings of the faithful to their glorification, which involves the resurrection of the re-formed body.[28] As he states in *Sermon 361*:

---

24. See *ST* III, q. 9, a. 2. See also Guy Mansini, "Understanding St. Thomas on Christ's Immediate Knowledge of God," *Thomist* 59 (1995): 91–124.

25. *De moribus ecclesiae catholicae,* I, 34–35; I, 40–41.

26. *De civitate Dei,* XXII, 7.

27. Ibid., XXII, 8, the longest chapter in the entire *De civitate Dei,* with discussions of miracles witnessed by many, especially at the reception of the relics of St. Stephen, the first martyr.

28. See Brian Daley, "Resurrection," in *Augustine through the Ages,* ed. Allan D. Fitzgerald (Grand Rapids, MI: William B. Eerdmans Publishing Company, 1999), 722–23.

"If faith in the resurrection of the dead is taken away, all Christian teaching perishes. . . . If the dead do not rise, we have no hope of a future life; but if the dead do rise, there will be a future life."[29] And in this future life we shall see the infinitely perfect wisdom and justice of God.[30]

Aquinas provides a theology of the passion, death, and resurrection of Christ that indicates how the *"interiora"* of the passion of Christ and his resurrection embraces the whole of creation in his redemptive knowledge and love. In Aquinas's view Jesus Christ, in his human consciousness, had not the light of faith, as we do, but the light of glory, in no way dulling his pain, suffering, and sorrow. Since he was not yet glorified in his humanity, the light of glory did the opposite. The higher the created consciousness, the greater will be the suffering. As a weak analogy might put it, someone with a finely tuned ear for music will suffer more intensely when someone sings off key. Knowing and loving the Triune God both divinely and humanly, only Christ's human nature united hypostatically to the Word could take up into his human mind and heart each and every human being with all his and her sins and sufferings. Jesus Christ, the divine Person of the Word Incarnate suffered more than all the sufferings of human beings throughout history put together.

As the Word Incarnate, Christ holds every human being in his human mind and heart, as the beloved is present in the lover, the known present in the knower. The concrete universality of all the uniquely individual and most painful histories of suffering are present in Christ's love for each and every one of us on the Cross.[31] So it is that we are baptized into Christ's death. And so it is that we fill up in our own lives what is wanting in the sufferings of Christ, for as disciples of Christ the Church carries forward the visible mission of the Word Incarnate in her rendering present Christ in his Paschal mystery.[32]

As in the New Testament, the sapiential eschatology of Aquinas situates the bodily resurrection within the context of the Paschal mystery.[33] In the

---

29. *Sermones*, 361, 2.

30. *De civitate Dei*, XX–XXII.

31. See *ST* III, q. 10, a. 2; q. 46, aa. 5–8. Note the importance of the highest Christology possible, as it is defined by the great Councils, if one is going to take the concrete histories of suffering seriously. Only God incarnate can redeem a human history, each page of which is stained with so much suffering and blood.

32. See *ST* III, q. 66, a. 2.

33. See Matthew Levering, *Christ's Fulfillment of Torah and Temple: Salvation According to Thomas Aquinas* (Notre Dame, IN: University of Notre Dame Press, 2002), 130–40; also his *Scripture and Metaphysics: Aquinas and the Renewal of Trinitarian Theology* (Oxford: Blackwell Publishing, 2004), 110–43.

Summa contra gentiles, Aquinas introduces the resurrection of the body after discussing the sacrament of marriage as embodying the love of Christ for
his Church.[34] Since the first man brought sin into the world, and through
sin death (Rom 5:12), so Christ redeems us from both sin and, at the end of
the world, death. The resurrection of the body is caused by the resurrection
of Christ.[35] Aquinas indicates how faith in the resurrection of the body in no
way contradicts what we know of human nature by reason. Reading his reflections more than seven centuries later, it is remarkable how the metaphysical principles validly illuminate the issues involved.[36]

A wisdom approach emphasizes the *intelligibility* of the cosmos and of
all that God creates and redeems. Any miraculous character of events does
not mean their "unintelligibility," as if God were doing something irrational. Rather, there are events which we cannot understand by the light of reason, but their intelligibility will be understood by the light of glory. What we
know by faith as miraculous we shall understand by the light of glory—hence
the efforts of the Fathers and Aquinas to offer natural analogues to provide
a fruitful but imperfect understanding, at least insofar as what is affirmed in
faith does not contradict the truths of reason. They take up a series of possible
objections to the resurrection of the body, responding to them in turn.[37]

Aquinas's metaphysics demands the kind of intellectual conversion re-
counted by Augustine in order to understand how the intelligibility of the
human soul causes the corporality of the human person. Thus he is able to
dispatch the concerns of those who point to the obliteration, disintegration,
or disappearance of corpses. As he writes:

None of any human's essential principles yields entirely to nothingness in death, for the
rational soul which is man's form remains after death, . . . the matter, also, which was subject to such a form remains in the same dimensions which made it able to be the individual matter. Therefore, by conjunction to a soul numerically the same, a human being will
be restored to matter numerically the same.[38]

34. See *SCG* IV, 78–79.
35. See *ST,* suppl., q. 76, a. 1.
36. See, for example, Bernard Lonergan, *Insight: A Study of Human Understanding* (Toronto: University of Toronto Press, 1992), 410–617; Benedict Ashley, *Theologies of the Body: Humanist and Christian* (Braintree, MA: Pope John Center, 1995), 565–645; John Wippel, *The Metaphysical Thought of
Thomas Aquinas: From Finite Being to Uncreated Being* (Washington, DC: The Catholic University of
America Press, 2000).
37. See St. Augustine, *De civitate Dei,* XXII; and Aquinas, *ST,* suppl., qq. 75–86; *SCG* IV, 81–90.
38. *SCG* IV, 81, 7. For the dualism of Descartes's notion of human beings as a composite of "two
natures," one corporeal and the other intellectual, see Rene Descartes, *Discourse on Method and Medi-*

Nominalism and a pervasive Cartesian dualism lead moderns and postmoderns to imagine that body and soul are two different "things." Soul and body are not, however, two distinct things but components of one reality, a human being. Aquinas states that an immortal soul without bodily resurrection would satisfy neither the promises of the Gospel nor the deepest desires of the human heart. Aquinas argues that human beings cannot attain perfect happiness, beatitude, and justice in this life, and therefore the resurrection is needed if human beings are to realize their natural and supernatural end willed by God.[39]

In answering the objections to bodily resurrection, Aquinas maintains the God-given dignity of individual persons. God's knowledge and love create the totality of all things and the singularity and uniqueness of each and every thing.[40] The resurrection guarantees that the unique singularity of each human being, in the fullness of their individual personhood, will be rewarded or punished according to their own unique responses to God's loving gifts to them. Human beatitude requires a specifically human and personally individual resurrection, not some vague or abstract perpetuation of the species:

Wherefore *humanity* signifies nothing else besides the essential principles of the species; so that its signification is only partial. On the other hand *man* signifies the essential principles of the species, without excluding the principles of individuality from its signification: since man signifies one having humanity, and this does not exclude his having other things: wherefore its signification is complete, because it signifies the essential principles of the species actually and the individualizing principles potentially. But *Socrates* signifies both actually, even as the genus includes the difference potentially, whereas the species includes it actually. From this it follows that both the very same man and the very same humanity rise again, by reason of the survival of the rational soul and the unity of matter.[41]

The mystery of the resurrection, while natural insofar as "it is natural for the soul to be united to the body," is not natural in its efficient cause since divine power alone can bring it about.[42]

---

tations on First Philosophy, trans. Donald A. Cress (Indianapolis: Hackett Publishing, 1985), 17–42; and his *Treatise on Man,* in *The Philosophical Writings of Decartes,* vol. 1, trans. J. Cottingham, R. Stoothoff, and D. Murdoch (Cambridge: Cambridge University Press, 1985), 99–108. It is ironic that moderns tend to project their own dualism back onto the ancients and medievals, when the latter would never say that humans had two natures.

39. See *ST,* suppl., q. 75, aa. 1–3.   40. See *ST* I, q. 14, a. 11.
41. *SCG* IV, 81, 10.   42. *SCG* IV, 81, 14.

The unique singularity of each of the billions of human beings in all the details of their lives and actions are present in the creating and redeeming Triune God. Aquinas sees the resurrection of the body as the clear testimony to the profound interpersonal character of all the Triune God does for us. As he remarks, if God intended the immortality of the human race only as a species, generation would suffice for that.

But the resurrection is not ordered to the perpetuity of the species, for this could be safeguarded by generation. It must, then, be ordered to the perpetuity of the individual: but not to the soul alone, for the soul already had perpetuity before the resurrection. Therefore it regards the perpetuity of the composite. Man rising, therefore, will live forever.[43]

The interpersonal intimacy is such that the risen glorified bodies are totally transformed to be fully iconic of the holiness and love of the Triune God and the Risen Jesus. Intussusceptive and reproductive functions are no longer present in the immortal and transformed human persons in the ecstasy of ever fuller understanding and love of the Triune God. The iconic beauty of each and every embodied human person will take up all the bodily aspects in the glory of the new heavens and new earth. The bodies of the blessed will be totally transparent in the joy and ecstasy of communion in the Body of Christ.[44]

Aquinas's sapiential eschatology attends to the whole as creating and sustaining and redeeming individuals in all their singular existence. Only an Infinitely Wise and Loving Father could know and love through the Holy Spirit so many countless human persons into existence as members of the Mystical Body of his own Son, the Word Incarnate. They are not "countless" or an "abstraction" to God's Infinite Intelligence and Love; each and every one is known and loved as only God knows and loves them.[45] The ultimate dignity of the human person is his or her eschatological communion with all the blessed in the new heavens and new earth of the eternal Kingdom of God:

Accordingly, just as the soul that enjoys the vision of God will be filled with spiritual brightness, so by a kind of overflow from the soul to the body, the latter will be, in its own way, clothed with the brightness of glory. Hence the Apostle says (1 Cor 15:18): "It is sown," namely the body, "in dishonor, it shall rise in glory": because now this body of ours is opaque, whereas then it will be translucent, according to Matthew 13:43: "Then shall the just shine like the sun in the kingdom of their Father."[46]

43. *SCG* IV, 82, 6.   44. See *SCG* IV, 83–85.

45. See *ST* I, q. 20, a. 2.   46. *SCG* IV, 86, 2.

Nor will corporeal creatures *(exteriora)* simply disappear:

> Since then the corporeal creation is disposed of finally in a manner that is in keeping
> with man's state, and since men themselves will be not only delivered from corruption,
> but also clothed in glory, as we have stated, it follows that even the material creation will
> acquire a certain glory of brightness befitting its capacity. Wherefore it is said in Revela-
> tions 21:1: "I saw a new heaven and a new earth": and in Isaiah (65:17–18): "I create new
> heavens, and a new earth, and the former things shall not be in remembrance, and they
> shall not come upon the heart. But you shall be glad and rejoice for ever." AMEN[47]

For Aquinas there is anticipated what would later be termed the "concrete
universality" of all things in Christ.[48] Jesus Christ knows and loves each and
every human being far better than any of us know ourselves. This concrete
universality of Jesus Christ's knowledge and love of us is the theological reality of his judgment of each of us at our death and all of us in the last judgment:

> When it is asked whether Christ knows all things in the Word, "all things" may be tak-
> en ... properly to mean that "all things" include whatsoever is, will be, or was done, said,
> or thought, by whomsoever and at any time. And in this way it must be said that the soul
> of Christ knows all things in the Word. . . . Now everything belongs to Christ and to
> his dignity, inasmuch as "all things are subject to Him" (1 Cor 15:27). Moreover, He has
> been appointed Judge of all by God, "because He is the Son of Man," as is stated in John
> 5:27; and therefore the soul of Christ knows in the Word all things existing in whatev-
> er time, and the thoughts of men, of which He is the Judge, so that what is said of Him
> (Jn 2:25), "For He knew what was in man," can be understood not merely of the divine
> knowledge, but also of his soul's knowledge, which it had in the Word.[49]

The judgment of Christ manifests both the justice and mercy of God insofar
as he who judges us is the one who suffered for us on the Cross.[50]

---

47. *SCG* IV, 97

48. See Henri de Lubac, *Catholicism: Christ and the Common Destiny of Man,* trans. Lancelot C.
Sheppard and Sr. Elizabeth Englund, O.C.D. (San Francisco: Ignatius Press, 1988), 48–81, 326–50;
Hans Urs von Balthasar, *A Theology of History* (San Francisco: Ignatius Press, 1963), 92.

49. *ST* III, q. 10, a. 2.

50. *ST* III, q. 14, a. 2; q. 59, aa. 2 and 3; suppl., q. 90, a. 1; *In Heb.* 2:14–18 [136–54]. Both justice and mercy are present in Christ's freeing mankind of sin; see *ST* III, q. 46, a. 1, ad 3: "That man
should be delivered by Christ's Passion was in keeping with both his mercy and his justice. With his
justice, because by his Passion Christ made satisfaction for the sin of the human race; and so man was
set free by Christ's justice: and with his mercy, for since man of himself could not satisfy for the sin
of the whole of human nature, as was said above (q. 1, a. 2), God gave him his Son to satisfy for man,
according to Rom 3:24: 'Being now justified by his grace as a gift, through the redemption that is in
Christ Jesus, whom God put forward as a sacrifice of atonement, through faith in his blood.' And this

Wisdom attends to the whole of the creation as divinely ordered and re-deemed, so Aquinas indicates that the judgment of Christ reveals that no amount of evil agents and actions can thwart God's wisdom. Those intelligent agents who willfully turn a created good away from the divinely ordered wis-dom—which is always a violent removal of the particular good from its or-der—suffer the just punishments due such acts. The evil of such punishments are indeed willed by God's all good wisdom, where the evil of sin is not so willed by God. For in sinning intelligent agents do violence to their own be-ing and nature. Again, it is only in the perspective of Aquinas's sapiential es-chatology that we can understand the mystery of divine justice and mercy.

The contexts of nominalism and voluntarism distorted predestination and damnation as exercises of an inscrutable divine power. In the wisdom per-spective that places the intelligibility of all of reality as present in the Divine Infinite Intelligence and Love of God, one can appreciate how it is precise-ly because of the Divine Intelligence, Love, Justice, and Mercy that God re-spects the free decisions of intelligent creatures. Aquinas's analysis of the pun-ishments of the damned indicates that God respects the choices they have made in turning away from the Divine Goodness. They violently frustrated the natural orientation of their natures toward the good, and therefore seek to disrupt the goodness of the created order.[51]

Central in sapiential eschatology is the intelligence and reason operative in the order of the universe. Could intelligent creatures frustrate the order of creation by their prideful self-assertion to disrupt that order through violently removing some particular good from its orientation toward God? If so, then a consequence would be the possibility of a radical depersonalization of the universe by evil. The Triune God would not be God! Thus it is for the good of the wise order of the whole universe that evil angels and humans suffer the punishments of hell:

It must be granted that God inflicts punishments, not for his own sake, as though He took pleasure in them, but for the sake of something else: namely on account of the or-der that must be imposed on creatures, in which order the good of the universe consists. Now, the order of things demands that all things be dispensed by God proportionally; for which reason it is said (Wis 11:21) that God does all things in *weight, number, and*

---

came of more copious mercy than if He had forgiven sins without satisfaction. Hence it is said (Eph 2:4): 'God, who is rich in mercy, out of the great charity wherewith He loved us, even when we were dead in sins, made us alive together in Christ.'"

51. See *ST,* suppl., q. 98, aa. 1–5.

measure. And, as rewards correspond proportionally to acts of virtue, so do punishments to sins: and to some sins eternal punishment is proportionate, as we have proved. Therefore for certain sins God inflicts eternal punishment that in things there may be maintained the right order which shows forth his wisdom.[52]

This wisdom of divine justice is well illustrated in Dante's *Divine Comedy,* where no one in hell or in purgatory ever complains that they should not be suffering the punishments they are; indeed, their state of punishment is precisely what their own evil actions have brought about.[53] They are the causes of their own damnation by their rejection of the orientation of their own beings toward the goodness of God. So Aquinas concludes that it would be unreasonable to expect that they could ever enjoy the beatific vision given the obstinacy of their opposition to the divine goodness.[54] So also, their resurrected bodies do not share in the translucent beauty of ordered goodness, but rather in the dark suffering of their opposition to the light and beauty of the Triune God shining through the transformed new heavens and new earth.[55]

The sapiential eschatology of Aquinas, building upon patristic eschatologies, understands the eschatological and apocalyptic passages in Scripture as revealing the transformation of the whole of creation so that it fully manifests the divine wisdom, beauty, and goodness. This contrasts with those who view these passages as involving or portending widespread devastation or ultimate doom.[56] A wisdom approach indicates clearly how what is catastrophic from the viewpoint of this world is only the purification needed for transition to the Kingdom of God.[57] Because the whole material universe is created for human beings to give glory to God, it too will share in their glorious beatitude. Where sin and evil turn the universe into idolatrous darkness and disorder, grace and glory will render the universe fully iconic of the divine wisdom.

Enjoying beatific communion with the Father in the Son with the Holy Spirit, the blessed will see how God has disposed all things with divine wis-

---

52. *SCG* III, 144, 10.

53. See *ST* I, q. 47, a. 3; q. 48, aa. 3, 5, and 6; q. 49, a. 2. See also Robert Royal, *Dante Alighieri: Divine Comedy, Divine Spirituality* (New York: Crossroad, 1999); and Anthony Cassell, *Dante's Fearful Art of Justice* (Toronto: University of Toronto Press, 1984).

54. See *ST,* suppl., q. 99, a. 3; and *SCG* IV, 93–94.

55. See *ST,* suppl., 86; and *SCG* IV, 89–90.

56. Various dictionary definitions of "apocalyptic" as "involving widespread devastation or ultimate doom" contrast with the use of the term in Augustine or Aquinas. "Ultimate doom" can only occur in a mind that is not illumined by faith in Christ Jesus.

57. See *SCG* IV, 97, 4–6.

dom, how He brought good out of all the evil and suffering endured by all the blessed when they lived on earth. The final state of the whole of creation finds its glorious consummation in the ecstatic union of all the blessed with the Triune God, so that they will understand how their lives here on earth were conformed to the wisdom of Christ Jesus who redeemed us, not by removing evil through power, but by transforming evil into good through his passion, death, and resurrection. The whole cosmos will be transfigured in the glorious presence of the whole Christ in whom each and every one of the blessed will be enraptured in communion with each other in the infinite understanding and love of the Triune God.

We have much to learn from the wisdom eschatologies of St. Augustine and St. Thomas Aquinas. All of theology is, after all, subaltern to the knowledge of the Triune God and the blessed in heaven.

Contributors

MICHAEL DAUPHINAIS is associate dean of faculty and assistant professor of theology at Ave Maria University. With Matthew Levering, he has written *Knowing the Love of Christ: An Introduction to the Theology of St. Thomas Aquinas* and *Holy People, Holy Land: A Theological Introduction to the Bible,* and has co-edited *Reading John with St. Thomas Aquinas.* He is the co-editor of the English edition of *Nova et Vetera.*

BARRY DAVID is associate professor of philosophy at Ave Maria University. He previously taught at St. Anselm College and Franciscan University of Steubenville. His specialty lies in the areas of Augustinian studies, metaphysics, and ethics. He has written numerous articles on philosophy. He holds the Ph.D. from the University of Toronto.

GILLES EMERY, O.P., is professor of dogmatic theology at the University of Fribourg and a member of the International Theological Commission. He has written *La Trinité créatrice, Thomas d'Aquin, Traités: Les raisons de la foi, les articles de la foi,* and *Trinity in Aquinas.* He has co-edited, with Pierre Gisel, *Le Christianisme est-il un monothéisme?* and *Postlibéralisme? La théologie de George Lindbeck et sa réception.* He is a member of the editorial board of the *Revue Thomiste.*

HARM GORIS earned his Ph.D. at the Catholic Theological University in Utrecht, the Netherlands, with a dissertation on God's foreknowledge and providence in Aquinas. He teaches systematic theology at the Faculty of Catholic Theology of Tilburg University, the Netherlands. He is a member of the Thomas Institute at Utrecht.

WAYNE J. HANKEY is Carnegie Professor of Classics at Dalhousie University and King's College. Since 1997 he has served as editor of *Dionysius.* In addition to numerous scholarly articles, he has written *God in Himself, Aquinas' Doctrine of God as Expounded in the Summa Theologiae, Pantokrator, the Cosmic Christ: A Theology of Nature,* and *One Hundred Years of Neoplatonism in France: A Brief Philosophical History.* He has co-edited *Deconstructing Radical Orthodoxy: Postmodern Theology, Rhetoric and Truth.*

MARK JOHNSON, associate professor of theology at Marquette University, is the author of more than twenty-five articles. He is writing a monograph, *Nature, Grace, Sin, and Glory: The Moral Universe of St. Thomas Aquinas,* which presents Aquinas's moral teaching from a medievalist's perspective. He is also working on a critical edition of the early Dominican Paul of Hungary's *Summa de penitentia.*

MATTHEW L. LAMB is professor of theology at Ave Maria University. Previously he taught at Boston College and Marquette University. He has published more than 125 articles and essays in a variety of journals and has written *History, Method, and Theology* and *Solidarity with Victims.* He is the translator of St. Thomas Aquinas's *Commentary on St. Paul's Letter to the Ephesians.* He is currently preparing a monograph entitled *Eternity, Time, and the Life of Wisdom.*

MATTHEW LEVERING is associate professor of theology at Ave Maria University. He is the author of *Sacrifice and Community: Jewish Offering and Christian Eucharist, Christ's Fulfillment of Torah and Temple: Salvation According to St. Thomas Aquinas,* and *Scripture and Metaphysics: Aquinas and the Renewal of Trinitarian Theology.* With Michael Dauphinais he has co-edited *Reading John with St. Thomas Aquinas.* He serves on the editorial board of CUA Press's Thomas Aquinas in Translation series, and is co-editor of the English edition of *Nova et Vetera.*

GUY MANSINI, O.S.B., is associate professor of systematic theology at Saint Meinrad School of Theology, and has served as a visiting professor at the Pontifical Gregorian University. In addition to numerous scholarly articles, he is the author of *The Meaning and Truth of Dogma in Edouard Le Roy and His Scholastic Opponents* and *Promising and the Good.* He has co-edited *Ethics and Theological Disclosures: The Thought of Robert Sokolowski.*

BRUCE D. MARSHALL is professor of historical theology at the Perkins School of Theology, Southern Methodist University. In addition to his ecumenical work and numerous articles on a wide range of topics, he is the author of *Trinity and Truth* and *Christology in Conflict* and of several articles on Aquinas and Trinitarian theology.

JOHN P. O'CALLAGHAN is associate professor of philosophy at the University of Notre Dame. He has written *Thomistic Realism and the Linguistic Turn: Toward a More Perfect Form of Existence,* and has co-edited, with Thomas Hibbs, *Recovering Nature: Essays in Honor of Ralph McInerny.* The author of numerous articles, he recently published "Creation, Human Dignity, and the Virtues of Acknowledged Dependence" in *Nova et Vetera.*

JOHN M. RIST is professor emeritus at the University of Toronto. He was formerly Regius Professor at the University of Aberdeen and has served as a visiting fellow at the University of Cambridge and the Hebrew University of Jerusalem. In addition to around ninety scholarly articles, he has written thirteen books, including *The Mind of Aristotle, Augustine: Ancient Thought Baptized, On Inoculating Moral Philosophy against God,* and *Real Ethics: Rethinking the Foundations of Morality.*

MICHAEL S. SHERWIN, O.P., is associate professor of moral theology at the University of Fribourg, Switzerland. He has also taught at the Dominican School of Philosophy and Theology. He has translated *Morality: A Catholic View* from the French edition by Servais Pinckaers, O.P. In addition to numerous scholarly articles, he is the author of *By Knowledge and by Love: Charity and Knowledge in the Moral Theology of St. Thomas Aquinas,* which won the 2006 Charles Cardinal Journet Prize.

Index

act/potency, xix, 111, 119, 120

action, human, xxi, 98, 148, 149, moral 88, 90, 158

Adam, xx, 90, 92, 139, 141, 149, 150, 151, 152, 153, 154, 155, 156, 157n35, 158, 166

Aertsen, Jan70n20

Against Two Letters of the Pelagians (Augustine),160, 164–66, 169n34

agape, xxi, 183n7

agent, moral 93, 198, 199, 273

Albert the Great, xiv, 146n4, 158n38, 173n53, 200n90

al-Ghazzali, 80

Altissiodorensis, Guillelmus 146n4

Ambrose, xii, 22

angels, 19n117, 35, 106, 108, 115, 120, 124, 124n59, 129, 130, 138–43, 190, 192, 198, 273; mind of, 70, 120, 138–39

animals, 16, 35, 103, 104, 105, 106, 109, 114, 117, 119, 120, 122–25, 134, 135, 140, 142, 144, 148, 197

Anselm, xiii, xiiin14, xxiii, 52n21, 146n4, 153, 181n1, 185n17, 187n28, 187n29, 249n17

Answer to Julian (Augustine), 162, 166n28

Answer to the Pelagians (Augustine), 166n26, 166n28

anthropology, 256–57

Apollinarianism, 219, 239

Apollos, 177

Apostles, xxi, 152, 175, 176, 178, 216, 219–20, 232, 235, 240

Appetite. *See* power

Aquinas, Thomas. *See* individual works

Archambault, Paul J., 262n9

Arianism, 9, 10, 19, 25, 102, 104, 111, 118, 124–25, 127, 132, 141, 143

Aristotle, xi, xii, xiin6, xiii, xiv, xvi, xviii, xix, xxiii, 63, 69, 71, 74–75, 77–78, 80, 82–83, 87–89, 93, 96, 98–99, 127n64, 135, 167n31, 190, 197–98, 201, 204, 233, 240, 243, 244–45, 255–56, 258n2

Aristotle: *Categories,* 84; *De generatione animalium,* 94, 97; *Liber de causis,* 245; *Metaphysics,* 91, 122n54; *Nicomachean Ethics,* 97, 156, 190n45, 200; *Politics,* 94; *Posterior Analytics,* 109, 123; *Topics,* 26,

Ashley, Benedict, 269n36

Athanasius, 234

Augustine, authority of, 43, 58, 61, 64, 146–47, 167, 246, 254–56; word of the heart, 63. *See also* individual works

Auriol, Peter, 60n42

authority, 172, 228, 231–34, 235, 244, 255, 267

Averroes, 80, 82–83, 87–88, 243

Avicenna, 79, 80, 82–83, 85n10, 87–88

Baladier, Charles, 182n5

baptism, 150–51, 158n38, 177, 197, 248n14, 249, 256n34

Barnes, Michel René, 44n6, 145n1

Bartholomew of Capua, 167n29

Batillon, Louis J., 167n30

beatific vision, 24, 34, 39, 40, 148, 265, 266, 274

beatitude, xiin3, xiv, 148, 174, 183, 184n9, 190, 192, 195, 201–3, 225–26, 264–65, 270, 274. *See also* blessedness, happiness

Beiting, Christopher, 158n38

Benedict XVI, Pope, xxi, 175, 258n1

Aquinas the Augustinian was designed and typeset in Garamond by Kachergis Book Design of Pittsboro, North Carolina. It was printed on 60-pound Natural Offset and bound by McNaughton & Gunn of Saline, Michigan.